OWL

D1381564

MINORITY NATIONALISM AND THE CHANGING INTERNATIONAL ORDER

MINORITY NATIONALISM AND THE CHANGING INTERNATIONAL ORDER

Edited by
MICHAEL KEATING
and
JOHN McGARRY

OXFORD
UNIVERSITY PRESS

OXFORD

UNIVERSITY PRESS

Great Clarendon Street, Oxford OX2 6DP

Oxford University Press is a department of the University of Oxford.
It furthers the University's objective of excellence in research, scholarship,
and education by publishing worldwide in

Oxford New York

Athens Auckland Bangkok Bogotá Buenos Aires Cape Town
Chennai Dar es Salaam Delhi Florence Hong Kong Istanbul Karachi
Kolkata Kuala Lumpur Madrid Melbourne Mexico City Mumbai Nairobi
Paris São Paulo Shanghai Singapore Taipei Tokyo Toronto Warsaw

and associated companies in Berlin Ibadan

Oxford is a registered trade mark of Oxford University Press
in the UK and in certain other countries

Published in the United States
by Oxford University Press Inc., New York

British Library Cataloguing in Publication Data
Data available

Library of Congress Cataloging in Publication Data
ISBN 0–19–924214–3 ✓

1 3 5 7 9 10 8 6 4 2

Typeset by Hope Services (Abingdon) Ltd.
Printed in Great Britain
on acid-free paper by
T.J. International Ltd.,
Padstow, Cornwall

ACKNOWLEDGEMENTS

The editors would like to thank the Social Sciences and Humanities Research Council of Canada, the Council on European Studies, and the European Science Foundation for providing funding for the conferences at which the draft chapters were discussed. John McGarry also received financial help from the United States Institute of Peace. Kristine Holder and Patti Lenard provided invaluable research assistance, helping, among other things, to ensure that the editors were always working with the correct drafts and that the papers were presented to the press in a reasonably tidy and uniform fashion. Finally, our thanks goes to Dominic Byatt and Amanda Watkins at Oxford University Press for their encouragement and patience.

M.K.
J.McG.

CONTENTS

I: Comparative and Philosophical Perspectives

II: Case-Studies

FIGURES

TABLES

ABBREVIATIONS

AKEL	Progressive Party of the Working People (Cyprus)
BSE	bovine spongiform encephalopathy, 'mad cow disease'
CIS	Commonwealth of Independent States
CiU	(Catalan) Convergència i Unió
CTP	Republican Turkish Party (Cyprus)
CVP	Christelijke Volkspartij (Christian People's Party) (Belgium)
DUP	Democratic Unionist Party (Northern Ireland)
EC	European Community
EFA	European Free Alliance
EU	European Union
IRA	Irish Republican Army
MEP	Member of the European Parliament
Mercosur	Southern American Free Trade Area
MP	Member of Parliament
NAFTA	North American Free Trade Agreement
NATO	North Atlantic Treaty Organization
NUTS	nomenclature of territorial units for statistics
OSCE	Organization for Security and Cooperation in Europe
PR	proportional representation
RLP	Republican Labour Party (Northern Ireland)
SDLP	Social Democratic and Labour Party (Northern Ireland)
SMP	single-member plurality (electoral system)
SNP	Scottish National Party
STV	single transferable vote
TKP	(Turkish Cypriot) Communal Liberation Party
TRNC	Turkish Republic of Northern Cyprus
Unficyp	United Nations Peacekeeping Force in Cyprus
UUP	Ulster Unionist Party (Northern Ireland)
VNP	Vlaams-Nationale Partij (Flemish National Party)
VVP	Vlaamse Volkspartij (Flemish People's Party)

LIST OF CONTRIBUTORS

Tozun Bahcheli, *King's College, University of Western Ontario*
Julie Bernier, *University of Toronto*
Michael Cavanagh, *University of Strathclyde*
Walker Connor, *Trinity College, Hartford, Connecticut*
Mireya Folch-Serra, *University of Western Ontario*
Katherine E. Graney, *Skidmore College*
Michael Keating, *University of Aberdeen and European University Institute*
Will Kymlicka, *Queen's University, Ontario*
Janet Laible, *Lehigh University, Bethlehem, Pennsylvania*
David D. Laitin, *University of Chicago*
Daniel Latouche, *Institut National de Recherche Scientifique, Montreal*
John McGarry, *University of Waterloo, Ontario*
James Mitchell, *University of Strathclyde*
Margaret Moore, *University of Waterloo, Ontario*
Joan Nogue-Font, *University of Girona*
Jürg Steiner, *University of North Carolina at Chapel Hill and University of Berne*
Mitja Žagar, *Institute for Ethnic Studies, Ljubljana*

CHAPTER 1

Introduction

MICHAEL KEATING AND JOHN MCGARRY

Nation and State

There is a long tradition in politics and the social sciences of equating the concepts of nation and state. Relations between states are routinely described as international relations, competitions between the sports teams of different states are international events, and the global institution in which state authorities meet is the United Nations. Hobsbawm writes that the nation 'is a social entity only insofar as it relates to a certain kind of modern territorial state, the nation-state, and it is pointless to discuss nation and state except insofar as both relate to it'.[1] In the French language the association is so strong that the terms are often used interchangeably. In English the compound noun 'nation-state' denotes a singular entity, usually seen as the fundamental building-block of the international order.

The tendency to conflate 'nation' and 'state' flows from a traditional view that sees nation-states as the product of historical evolution, either through the consolidation of territories and their forging into unities, or through the break-up of multinational empires, to produce 'sovereign governments which have no critical regional or community cleavages'.[2] Generally, the consolidation model is said to characterize the building of the nation-state in western Europe and the fragmentation model that of central and eastern Europe, although there are exceptions, such as Ireland and Norway. In either case, nationalist conflict is seen as the product of an incomplete evolution that will disappear in due course.

This model of the nation-state originated in Europe but has subsequently been exported to the rest of the world. It has been backed up by modernist social science from the nineteenth century onward, with its strong normative assumptions and its teleological tendencies and bias against anything that might appear pre-modern. Marxism, drawing heavily on Darwinian and other nineteenth-century ideas of progress, saw little future for historyless peoples. For the liberals, John Stuart Mill famously remarked: 'Nobody can suppose that it is not more beneficial for a Breton or a Basque of French Navarre to be a member of the French nationality than to sulk on his own rocks, the half-savage relic of past times. The same remark applies to the Welshman or the Scottish highlander.'[3] Durkheim wrote that 'we can almost say that a people is as much advanced as territorial divisions are more superficial'.[4] The idea gained further substance from the behaviourist social science coming from the United States after the Second World War. Seymour Martin Lipset could see minority nationalism as part of the 'revolt against modernity'.[5]

Modernists have argued, then, not only that national minorities will disappear, but that this is normatively desirable. Both the process of modernization and the universalist values of the Enlightenment are identified with the consolidated nation-state. So Ralph Dahrendorf, writing at a time when the nation-state appears in danger, argues that we need nation-states in the modern world in order to secure social solidarity and other collective benefits, but then insists that these can not be based on supposedly 'ethnic' units like Catalonia or Wales, but only on large consolidated states like Germany.[6] Such normative views have important public-policy ramifications. States should seek to assimilate minorities, and they should refrain from institutional accommodations that would hinder the elimination of differences. Steps such as minority self-government or group-based representation in the central government are normally ruled out in favour of centralized government and protections for individual (but not group) rights.

The limits of these forms of modernism have been sharply exposed by the recent evolution of the state system, which is being transformed from above by the emergence of a new transnational order and from below by the assertion of territorial and cultural identities. With the apparent reversal of the tendency to national integration and the re-emergence of ethnic and nationalist politics, history itself is being revised and the old teleological accounts of the evolution of the European state system called into question. Recent scholarship shows the evolution of the state system as problematic, conflictual, and contingent.[7] Rather than a unidirectional process, it is seen as something that can be reversed or take off in different directions. Maintaining the cohesion of complex states is a constant task of statecraft and not a once-and-for-all achievement.[8] In a longer historical perspective, the consolidated nation-state, as it emerged from the nineteenth century, is perhaps the exception in a world characterized by complexity and multiple layers of identity and authority.

Globalization and the Nation-State

The nation-state system is now experiencing a number of important changes. The most commonly used term for this new order is 'globalization', a complex and often confusing term which, like so many social science concepts before it, has been stretched beyond the limits of its usefulness. There are several dimensions of globalization that are relevant to our collection. First, there is a process of global economic integration, with increased mobility of capital, goods, and services, and, to a lesser extent, labour, and the rise of the transnational corporation. This has eroded the state framework for economic activity and made it difficult for states to manage their insertion into the international trading order. It has also made it harder for states to manage their internal territorial economies through tariffs, taxes, and subsidies, and has helped shift the balance between political power and the market in favour of the latter.

Second, globalization has a cultural dimension. Facilitated by new communications technology and increased travel, the use of English as a lingua franca has expanded. Various types of global culture have emerged, although most of this is really a product of the national culture of the United States. There has also been a significant increase in migration, both within and between states, creating new multicultural challenges.

Third, there is the rise of new understandings of human rights at a global level, with transgressions seen as justifying violations of the principle of state sovereignty. This has been accompanied by the proliferation of international non-governmental organizations (NGOs), such as Amnesty International and Human Rights Watch, and the construction of new forms of international jurisprudence, including the International Criminal Court and the war crimes tribunals for Rwanda and the former Yugoslavia. There is even an increased preparedness, as Kosovo makes clear, to justify armed intervention to uphold minority rights, although it remains to be seen how widespread this practice will become.

Fourth, new institutions are being built with transnational reach, some global, such as the World Trade Organization, but the most powerful being regional in scope, notably the European Union (EU).

The connection between these regional institutions and globalization is not always clear. For some, they represent globalization plus, a deepening at the continental level of the same processes at work on a world scale. For others, they are globalization minus, a way of limiting the impact of global change by pooling the powers of sovereign states. One important difference between the two is that regional integration, especially in Europe, involves institution-building and is a way of bringing back politics and potentially limiting the subordination of territories to market forces.

One reaction to globalization understood in these ways has been the re-emergence of arguments that bear a resemblance to the modernization theories of the past. Neo-liberal political economists insist that markets will break down particularist and pre-modern forms of identity. Other liberals express confidence that the post-war spread of universal human rights will overcome divisions within states. Academics like Dahrendorf and Miller have defended the old nation-state model and reaffirmed the need for state and nation to coincide.[9] In their view, this is necessary to maintain the solidarities needed to maintain redistributive practices and to withstand the disintegrative effects of global capitalism.

Globalization, however, has also helped to produce post-national thinking. From this perspective, the hegemony of national identities is being eroded, and being replaced by more complex multiple identities. Individuals, it is believed, are now forming non-territorial allegiances, along lines of function, gender, or sexual orientation, and multiple territorial allegiances, to city, region, state, and beyond.[10] In some accounts, allegiances to nation-states are being transcended by allegiances to larger communities, such as Europe or even the world. Writing at the end of the 1980s, Eric Hobsbawm claimed confidently that it was not only national minorities that were being absorbed by the new supranational restructuring of the globe but all nations and nation-states: 'the very fact that historians are at last beginning to make some progress in the study and analysis of nations and nationalism suggests that, as so often, the phenomenon is past its peak. The owl of Minerva which brings wisdom, said Hegel, flies out at dusk. It is a good sign that it is now circling round nations and nationalism.'[11]

A major difficulty with these modernist and post-modernist perspectives is that they run counter to observed reality: rather than eroding minority nationalisms, globalization has occurred alongside their emergence or re-emergence. This has been the case not only in the developing world, where it could be argued that the processes associated with globalization are not yet far advanced, but also in the developed West. A strong nationalist movement has emerged in Quebec since the 1960s, and in 1995 came within a percentage point of winning a referendum on sovereignty. In Great Britain, which metropolitan political scientists portrayed forty years ago as a homogeneous nation-state, there are now significant nationalist movements in Scotland and Wales. The possibility that Britain will break up no longer seems unthinkable. Belgium has recently been decentralized, and there is now a strong Flemish nationalist movement. In Spain significant nationalist movements have emerged in the Basque Country, Catalonia, and Galicia. Even the unity of Switzerland seems threatened by ethno-regional divisions. The national divisions in Northern Ireland also seem to have been unaffected by several decades of globalization and continental integration.

Explaining Minority Nationalism

There have been differing explanations of this apparent paradox of globalization and disintegration. Ohmae follows a strictly functionalist logic, arguing on the basis of new theories of regional development that it is sub-state regions that form the basic building-blocks of the new global economy. From this he jumps directly to politics, equating the rise of regional economies with the decline of the nation-state.[12] Others observers adopt what we might call the 'simmering cauldron' theory, that the powerful state and the international order of the cold war suppressed ancient ethnic sentiments and hatreds that erupted as soon as the lid was taken off.[13] A third set of theories favours instrumentalist explanations: that ethnic and national identities are said to be fabricated by political elites in order to take advantage of changing international conditions.[14]

We have problems with all of these accounts, our preference being for more complex and contextual forms of analysis that take account of the interplay between historical, economic, cultural, and political factors. While we accept the argument that global economic restructuring has altered the political economy of regionalism and minority nationalism in important ways,[15] the functional argument is not a satisfactory explanation of the emergence of various nationalisms. The emergence of Quebec nationalism, to take one case, is importantly related, not only to functional changes, but to the cultural threat posed by the spread of English in North America (exacerbated by a declining francophone birth rate), the spread of universalist norms in English Canada which erect obstacles to the accommodation of

Quebec group rights, and to the way in which politicians in Quebec and the rest of Canada have reacted to these developments.

Simmering cauldron or primordialist explanations of the emergence or re-emergence of nationalism ultimately posit a non-explanation by arguing that things have always been this way. It is true that the new nationalisms have emerged where there are existing fault lines or raw materials for the construction of identity. However, the identities often undergo important changes in conditions of modernity. Thus, the (ethnic) identity of French Canadians (Canadiens), largely Catholic, conservative, and non-nationalist, has been transformed by changes in the post-war period into a strong secular nationalism, its proponents demanding greater self-government and even independence. Flemish ethnic identity is similarly being converted into a national identity. Although Basque nationalism emerged originally in the late nineteenth century in response to an earlier period of globalization, it is now being importantly readapted in the 1990s in response to a new version. While there has been a powerful Scottish identity for some time, it has existed alongside a strong British identity. Only since the 1970s has the former made inroads at the expense of the latter, with a significant nationalist movement emerging in Scotland. Many of the re-emerging nationalisms are 'civic' rather than ethnically particularist (Latouche, Chapter 9), and are responses to the need to reconstitute a public space in the new state order. There is no doubt that the new conditions of world society give greater legitimacy to nationalisms based on civic rather than ethnic principles. Simmering-cauldron theories cannot explain such changes.

Instrumentalist explanations, on the other hand, place too much importance on the role of nationalist elites, and are often a way of denying the authenticity and deep-rootedness of national sentiment. They fail to explain why some elites in some circumstances are able to foment nationalism, while others are not, or why nationalist elites are more successful in mobilizing people than their socialist or supranationalist counterparts. The case of the Northern League in Italy is instructive here, an elite-driven movement largely sparked by the failure of the Italian state in the context of globalization and European integration, which has had a measurable but strictly limited success in convincing its constituents.[16]

Contrary to Hobsbawm and others, we believe that the processes associated with globalization, rather than undermining minority nationalism, help explain its strength. The lowering of international tariffs and the construction of regional economic associations, particularly the European Union but also the North American Free Trade

Agreement (NAFTA), have helped to reduce the risks associated with independence and have heightened the popularity of nationalism in places such as Scotland and Quebec. Even small countries now have easier access to global markets. The growth of multilateral defence alliances, such as the North Atlantic Treaty Organization (NATO), has also lowered the costs of statehood.

The spread of global culture, the state's weakening ability to redistribute resources, and the easier movement of capital and labour have played an important part in producing nationalist responses. In several cases, national minorities fear the results of these changes, whether it is economic decline, threats to language and culture, or the swamping of their homeland by migrants (Kymlicka, Chapter 4; Laible, Chapter 11). This is why minority nationalists often seek control over policy instruments in the fields of culture, economics, and immigration, instruments that would allow them to withstand or adapt to the effects of globalization. Paradoxically, however, the same technological developments that bring global culture have equipped national minorities with their own vernacular media, which they can then use to mobilize nationalist defences (Folch-Serra and Nogue-Font, Chapter 8).

Arguably, the spread of universal human rights has facilitated minority nationalism rather than eroded it. Minority nations everywhere have seized on the right of self-determination in particular, a freedom that originally attached to individuals, but now is inextricably linked to peoples and nations. The resurgence of Irish nationalism in Northern Ireland during the 1960s began as a campaign for human rights, and was heavily influenced by the American civil rights movement.[17] While it was the state's denial of rights that promoted Irish nationalism, in Canada it was the state's embrace of individual rights that brought a minority nationalist response. Since the adoption of the Charter of Rights and Freedoms in 1982, the dominant view in English Canada has been that the country is made up of equal individuals and that no groups should have special rights. This is at odds with the view of Quebeckers, and also of aboriginal first nations, that Canada is a multinational partnership rather than a single nation of undifferentiated citizens. The reluctance of English Canada to accept a compromise that marries both individual and group rights explains much of Canada's current constitutional difficulties.

More generally, by giving rise to a plethora of international organizations that have challenged the authority of states over their citizens, globalization may have encouraged minority claims. In Europe the European Commission has established some links with regions of states to incorporate them into the policy process. International NGOs, such as Amnesty International and Human Rights Watch, and international tribunals such as the European Court of Human Rights, increasingly intervene on behalf of minorities against states. Multi-government organizations, such as NATO and the Organization for Security and Co-operation in Europe (OSCE), seem more prepared to infringe state sovereignty to protect minorities, including in Iraq and Yugoslavia. There is an increasingly permissive external environment for minority assertiveness.

While it is clear that the modernist–post-modernist view that globalization is eroding differences is seriously flawed, there is also a problem with the normative belief that minority nationalisms should be eroded. First, these norms are largely a result of bias, with their liberal, leftist, and Marxist exponents usually coming from large majority nations. Second, they are the result of a failure to be sensitive to content and context. Minority nationalisms can give rise to dangerous passions and conflict, as the Serb campaign in Croatia in 1991 or the IRA campaign in Northern Ireland demonstrates. They can also, however, be a necessary mechanism for social cooperation and solidarity, a framework for self-government and democracy, and a source of cultural richness and diversity. They are not inherently different from majority nationalisms in these respects.[18] Third, conflict and divisiveness is more obviously a result of how a minority nation is managed than of its mere existence. Given the resilience of national identity, once mobilized, we believe that efforts to accommodate it are more likely to promote its benign aspects than attempts to eliminate it.

International Change and the Accommodation of Minority Nationalism

The changes we have described have helped to encourage minority nationalism. They may also have created an environment that is more favourable to its accommodation, though this should not be exaggerated and is largely restricted to those parts of the world where the changes are most advanced. First, while it is still clearly in its infancy, there is a growing international regime that places human and minority rights ahead of state sovereignty. There is an increasing number of international treaties that uphold human and minority rights, and an array of international tribunals, such as the European Court of Human Rights, whose job it is to enforce these rights. There is also a proliferation of NGOs, such as Amnesty International and Human

Rights Watch, who have made it more likely that transgressions will be publicized. In extreme cases, as we have pointed out, NATO and the United Nations have been prepared to condone armed intervention in sovereign states on behalf of minorities. One effect of this may be to make minorities more assertive, but it also creates incentives for state authorities to accommodate rather than repress.

Second, the benign treatment of minorities has become one of the costs of entry into attractive economic and military alliances like the EU and NATO. The incentive of membership in the EU helped stabilize democracy in Spain, and an important element in this was accommodation of the minority nations. Similar inducements are currently having a positive effect in would-be member states such as Estonia, Poland, Bulgaria, and Slovakia. On the other hand, Turkey has continued its repression of Kurds despite the damage this does to its prospects for EU membership, and Turkish Cypriots seem unwilling to forgo their unilateral declaration of independence in return for joining Greek Cyprus in the EU (Bahcheli, Chapter 10). Both cases show clearly that the economic benefits of entry into regional economic associations are not enough to produce moderation if vital national interests are considered to be at stake.

Third, the EU is working in a number of complex ways that are making state authorities more accommodating and moderating minority demands. Ceding some form of autonomy to national minorities seems to be more thinkable today as a result of the weakening of the concept of sovereignty. European states that have pooled their sovereignty in Brussels have been more inclined to decentralize power than in the earlier era of unitary sovereign states. Within the past twenty-five years Spain, Belgium, and the United Kingdom have all decentralized to minority groups. Even France, the home of Jacobinism, has given the Corsicans their own regional assembly, although the idea of ratifying the European Convention on Minority Languages is too much for many leading politicians on both right and left. The United Kingdom has engaged in an embryonic shared-sovereignty arrangement with another state, the Republic of Ireland, over a part of its territory, Northern Ireland. The weakening of traditional notions of sovereignty has also affected minorities, with many of them seeking arrangements that fall short of independence. Thus, nationalists in Wales and in Catalonia have explicitly renounced statehood as a goal in favour of nation-building in a new form. The Flemish nationalists of the Volksunie seem content to allow Belgium to continue as long as the region of Flanders is also strengthened (Laible, Chapter 11). While other nationalists want their own states, such as those in the Scottish

National Party and the Flemish Vlaams Blok, they are careful to place their demands in the context of the EU.

The EU also provides opportunities for stateless nations to project their identities within a wider political space. There are a range of specific opportunities to influence policy and operate within the international arena without becoming states. Regions of states have been allowed to cooperate across state frontiers, and to establish multiple channels of access to Brussels. Their presence has been officially recognized through the Committee of the Regions. Should these measures of accommodation fail, the EU may even provide an insurance mechanism to ensure that secession is peaceful and carries minimum economic costs, as long as the successor states are all contained within the Union.

Whether these circumstances can be repeated outside the EU is a more difficult question, and depends on the presence of several conditions. One is an acceptance of the limitations of the doctrine of sovereignty in modern conditions. While several minority nationalist movements outside Europe have effectively abandoned the quest for a separate state, recognizing that other forms of power and autonomy are vital, this is far from the rule. Partly in consequence, there is a profound reluctance on the part of states to offer autonomy lest this lead to secession. A second condition for moderation is international security. It is no coincidence that the scramble for statehood on the part of minorities in Europe came in the early twentieth century, a time of international tension culminating in the First World War. It is quite striking that in the debates about nationalism in Scotland, Catalonia, and Flanders the issue of security hardly arises, so solid is the acceptance that security in Europe must be collective and not a matter for individual states. This condition also applies to Quebec, but not to central and eastern Europe or beyond. A third condition is free trade and continued market access so that new forms of autonomy will not impose new economic barriers and costs. A fourth condition is the existence of an overarching regime of human rights, applicable both to individuals and to cultural minorities, ensuring that autonomy for one group will not lead to oppression of its internal minorities. The final condition is an institutional set of mechanisms that gives a reality to these features and provides a common political space within which conflicts can be resolved.

The Chapters

The contributors to this book have been asked to address two hypotheses; that the changing international order and transformation of the state is serving to encourage the emergence or re-emergence of minority nationalisms; and that they also provide new opportunities for its accommodation and management. The first chapters are general and theoretical. Michael Keating (Chapter 2) looks at the changing state order and the way in which nationalist demands have been refocused, then at the ways in which sovereignty can be unpacked to allow expression to multiple identities. Margaret Moore (Chapter 3) addresses the issue of cosmopolitanism and identities, arguing that large states do not have a monopoly of universal values and that minority nationalisms can equally well be the carriers of modernity. Will Kymlicka (Chapter 4) addresses an issue that arises directly from globalization, that of immigration, specifically looking at the assimilation of immigrants into minority nationalist communities. While some observers, dismissing minority nationalism as a form of tribalism, assume that minorities will be intolerant of immigrants, Kymlicka shows that this is another of the metropolitan prejudices we referred to earlier and that minorities should be subject to the same tests of tolerance as majorities. On this test, they seem to fare well.

The region where the conditions outlined above are most advanced is Europe, hence the focus in the case-study chapters is on that continent. Europe has a dense web of institutions for organizing political, economic, social, and security space. Economically, there is a set of concentric circles, with the eleven countries of the single currency, surrounded by the EU, the European Economic Area, and then the web of association and pre-accession agreements taking in most of the continent. There is an emerging human rights regime focused on the Council of Europe and its charter, together with guarantees for minority rights through the work of the OSCE.[19] Security in western Europe has been collectivized since the 1940s under NATO and, while the future security system is not clear, we do know that it will be a collective one. Finally, there is an overarching political order, providing forms of supranational authority and a range of opportunities for stateless nations to intervene in policy matters. It is not surprising, then, that there is a strong relationship between European supranational integration and the assertion of minority nationalism, as several of our chapters show.

Walker Connor (Chapter 6) takes issue with various forms of economic determinism, which have reappeared in the debate on Europe. He notes that minority nationalism cannot be explained purely by

erence to economic grievance and that economic remedies will not
cessarily make it go away. He also shows how national identities of
various forms continue to mould the European project and how far we
are from a Europe in which national identities disappear. Jurg Steiner
(Chapter 7) argues that, even though Switzerland is not a member of
the EU, European integration is a centrifugal force within the country,
deepening existing lines of cleavage as the different communities react
differently to the European challenge. While this might be of concern
to a Swiss nationalist, Steiner argues that there is nothing to fear here.
On the contrary, it may be a liberating process, allowing Swiss citizens
to adopt multiple identities and roles.

David Laitin (Chapter 5) looks at the question of language in the
European context. While European integration has often been seen as
a form of state-building analogous to the nation-state-building of the
last century, Laitin argues that this is an anachronistic view. Europe is
being built in conditions of late modernity and hence does not have
the same requirements for identity formation and socialization as the
classic nation-state. Drawing a parallel with India, he argues that
Europe is likely to develop a multiple-language regime in which the
maintenance of traditional languages is compatible with the commitment to global communication. Mireya Folch-Serra and Joan Nogue-
Font (Chapter 8) also look at language, examining the vernacular press
in Catalonia. They find that, within this highly Europeanized region,
there is ample space at the local level for a vibrant vernacular culture
not dependent on government subsidy, a finding which reinforces
Laitin's claims. This local press in turn helps to sustain and restructure
national identities in Catalonia. Their chapter is evidence that local
culture networks can survive and even thrive, given new communications technologies, despite the spread of global culture.

If observers in the past tended to see a contradiction between
minority nationalism and European integration, there may be a tendency nowadays to see them as natural and eternal allies. Reality is more
complicated, as the following chapters show. James Mitchell and
Michael Cavanagh (Chapter 12) show how minority nationalists in the
United Kingdom have used European integration strategically and
tactically to advance their claims, tracing the differences between
them. Janet Laible's study of Flanders (Chapter 11), on the other hand,
cautions against too facile an equation of European integration and
minority nationalism. As she argues, while Flemish nationalists,
including those in the radical Vlaams Blok, see opportunities in
European integration, they also regard it as a serious threat to Flemish
autonomy and culture.

John McGarry (Chapter 14) explores the effects of continental integration and international change on Northern Ireland, the site of western Europe's most violent conflict. He argues that these developments have not produced an erosion of identities or support for political integration, despite predictions that they would. On the other hand, they have had a number of benign effects on the conflict, and have helped to provide a new context for its management and new opportunities for imaginative thinking. Tozun Bahcheli's chapter on Cyprus (Chapter 10) is less optimistic. Like McGarry, Bahcheli shows there has been no erosion of identities in the face of globalization or European integration. However, he also argues that European integration has not provided new opportunities for conflict management.

Outside the EU, the opportunities are fewer, as our non-EU cases show. The post-Soviet space has created a series of power vacuums and opportunities for nation-builders to construct new forms of autonomy. Julie Bernier (Chapter 16) discusses the 'nationalizing' impulses of post-independence Latvia and Estonia. Her chapter explains that a number of international organizations—the OSCE, the Council of Europe, and the EU—have intervened in these states on behalf of minorities. The interventions, according to Bernier, have had some success, causing authorities to relax discriminatory measures and erecting obstacles to the introduction of such measures in the future. Katherine Graney's study of Tatarstan (Chapter 13) shows how this region of Russia has formulated a form of stateless nationalism which, like that of Catalonia, seeks to avoid a head-on confrontation with the state, while building effective autonomy. It has consciously chosen the European model even to the point of joining European organizations.

The case of Quebec (Latouche, Chapter 9) is more difficult, since there is nothing corresponding to the European array of overarching institutions. So Quebec nationalists are divided into several groups. The softest nationalists seek special status within Canada, retaining the state framework while repatriating most of the domestic functions of government. A slightly more radical group favour sovereignty together with a new partnership with Canada to manage common problems, the formula put to the voters in the referendums of 1980 and 1995. Others, like former premier Jacques Parizeau, think that Quebec could become independent without a bilateral agreement with Canada, given the existence of NAFTA, which would secure market access, and the ability to free-ride by using the Canadian currency. Nationalists of almost all colours are agreed that security is not an issue, since Quebec would remain tied into the North Atlantic defence community. Daniel Latouche traces the evolution of Quebec nationalism and its uneasy relationship with a changing Canadian nationalism. Like us, he notes that the death of nationalism has often been prematurely announced but that it remains a vital principle in contemporary politics. Like some of the other authors, he is sceptical about the idea that globalization and regional economic integration provide a painless middle way between provincial autonomy and national independence. He argues that the conditions of globalization and the construction of a civic community may require the establishment of a Quebec state.

In central and south-eastern Europe nationalist conflict has experienced a dramatic revival since the end of the cold war. Yet experience is more varied than some of the exponents of simmering-cauldron theories would have us believe. There have been violent conflicts in Bosnia, Croatia, and Serbia, but Slovenia seceded from Yugoslavia after only a short conflict and established a stable democracy. Czechoslovakia broke up, but peacefully, and both successor states are seeking entrance to the EU. The experience of the Hungarian minorities outside Hungary has been varied. There is a widespread agreement that nationality issues in this region cannot be resolved by establishing classical nation-states, given the lack of agreement about boundaries and group identities. Instead, a new overarching regime is needed, to replace the imperial (Habsburg, Ottoman, Russian, and Soviet) systems of the past. Mitja Žagar (Chapter 15) examines south-eastern Europe and the ways in which the international community, particularly the EU, might act to moderate nationalist demands and provide new mechanisms for their expression and accommodation.

NOTES

1. E. Hobsbawm, *Nations and Nationalism since 1780* (Cambridge: Cambridge University Press, 1990).
2. K. Deutsch, *Nationalism and Social Communication: An Inquiry into the Foundations of Nationality* (Cambridge, Mass.: MIT Press, 1966).
3. J. S. Mill, *Utilitarianism, On Liberty and Considerations on Representative Government* (London: Dent, 1972), 395.
4. É. Durkheim, *The Division of Labour in Society* (New York: Free Press, 1964), 187.
5. S. M. Lipset, 'The Revolt against Modernity', in Lipset, *Consensus and Conflict: Essays in Political Sociology* (New Brunswick: Transaction, 1985).
6. R. Dahrendorf, 'Preserving Prosperity', *New Statesman and Society*, 13/29 (Dec. 1995), 36–40. This was all the more remarkable since at that time Germany's citizenship law was based on strict blood descent, while the Catalans and Quebecois were falling over themselves to insist that anyone could join their nation, merely by an act of will.

7. C. Tilly, *Coercion, Capital and European States* AD *990–1990* (Oxford: Blackwell, 1990); C. Tilly, 'Entanglements of European Cities and States', in C. Tilly and W. P. Blockmans (eds.), *Cities and the Rise of States in Europe,* AD *1000 to 1800* (Boulder, Colo.: Westview Press, 1994); H. Spruyt, *The Sovereign State and its Competitors* (Princeton: Princeton University Press, 1994); A. Osiander, *The States System of Europe, 1640–1990: Peacemaking and the Conditions of International Stability* (Oxford: Clarendon Press, 1994).

8. M. Keating, *State and Regional Nationalism: Territorial Politics and the European State* (London: Harvester Wheatsheaf, 1988); M. Keating, *The New Regionalism in Western Europe: Territorial Restructuring and Political Change* (Aldershot: Edward Elgar, 1998).

9. Dahrendorf, 'Preserving Prosperity'; D. Miller, *On Nationality* (Oxford: Oxford University Press, 1995).

10. R. Kearney, *Postnationalist Ireland: Politics, Culture, Philosophy* (London: Routledge, 1997).

11. Hobsbawm, *Nations and Nationalism*, 183.

12. K. Ohmae, *The End of the Nation-State: The Rise of Regional Economies* (New York: Free Press, 1995).

13. D. P. Moynahan, *Pandaemonium: Ethnicity in International Politics* (Oxford: Oxford University Press, 1993).

14. P. Brass, 'Elite Competition and the Origins of Ethnic Nationalism', in J. G. Beramendi, R. Maíz, and X. M. Núñez (eds.), *Nationalism in Europe: Past and Present* (Santiago de Compostela: University of Santiago de Compostela, 1994).

15. M. Keating, *Nations against the State: The New Politics of Nationalism in Quebec, Catalonia and Scotland* (London: Macmillan, 1996 and 2001); Keating, *The New Regionalism*.

16. R. Biorcio, *La Padania promessa: La storia, le idee e la logica d'azione della Lega Nord* (Milan: Il Saggiatore, 1997).

17. B. Dooley, *Black and Green: The Fight for Civil Rights in Northern Ireland and Black America* (London: Pluto Press, 1998).

18. W. Kymlicka, 'Misunderstanding Nationalism', *Dissent* (Winter 1995), 130–7; Keating, *Nations against the State*; Moore, Ch 3 in this volume.

19. J. Jackson Preece, *National Minorities and the European Nation-States System* (Oxford: Oxford University Press, 1998).

PART I

COMPARATIVE AND PHILOSOPHICAL PERSPECTIVES

CHAPTER 2

———

Nations without States: The Accommodation of Nationalism in the New State Order

MICHAEL KEATING

Introduction

Nationalism has historically been associated with the state and state-building. Yet in a world in which the state is in many respects weakened, penetrated by transnational and sectoral interests, nationalism appears to be resurgent. It is the argument of this chapter that the transformation of the state has in fact encouraged the re-emergence of nationalisms within states, but at the same time provides opportunities for the non-violent resolution of nationalist conflict. This requires a break with the state-centred tradition of much historical and political science research, an appreciation of the importance of other frameworks of identity and collective action, and a search for opportunities for accommodating nationalist demands within the emerging international regimes. Not all types of nationalist movement can be accommodated in this way, however, and we still lack a new model of the state that provides a formula for the recognition of nationality and self-government in diverse forms.

Nationalism and the State

There is one school of thought that associates nationalism by definition with the nation-state. Hobsbawm writes that a nation 'is a social entity only insofar as it is related to a certain kind of modern ritorial state, the "nation-state" and it is pointless to discuss nation and nationality except insofar as they relate to it.'[1] Anthony Smith also includes the desire to establish a state as one of the defining features of nationalism,[2] though this does not feature in his later writing, where it is recognized that a state is only one possible outcome of nationalist success. In the French language the association of state and nation is so entrenched that the term 'nation-state' is considered a redundancy.[3] This identity of state and nation is tenable only if, like Hobsbawm, we confine both to the period c.1760–1990, seeing nationalism as the doctrine born of German thinkers of the eighteenth century and crystallized first as a result of the French Revolution, which linked political power to popular sovereignty, and demanded a definition which encompassed both. A broader definition of nationalism, however, focusing on self-determination and self-government irrespective of the constitutional form which these takes, allows us to trace it further back and to project it into the present and the future. The Scottish Declaration of Arbroath (1320) can be seen as a form of nationalist assertion, albeit linked to a contractual and feudal order rather than modern mass society.[4] Similarly, the non-separatist nationalism of the Catalan Convergència i Unió (CiU) coalition in the present era represents an authentic expression of nationalism. Certainly, nationalism in the age of the nation-state represents a particular form, with its own distinct characteristics, but it is not the only one.

State-centred social science has a continual tendency to distort analysis by forcing all political phenomena into the procrustean bed of the state, but if we can detach nationalism conceptually from it, then we open up a new vista of opportunities for the accommodation of nationalist demands in a world in which the state is, if not disappearing, then transformed in important ways. This approach also enables us to address the apparent paradox that, in a world of globalization and weakened states, nationalism seems to be on the rise. The transformation of the nation-state and the 'end of sovereignty'[5] has spawned a considerable literature, with diverging views on whether or not the state is in retreat. What is clear is that it has been transformed under pressures from three sides. From above it is affected by the globalization of economic exchanges, the rise of global culture (whether or not this is really a form of American cultural hegemony), and the establishment of international regimes in trade (such as the World Trade Organization, WTO or the North American Free Trade Agreement, NAFTA), in defence (notably the North Atlantic Treaty Organization, NATO) and in politics (with the European Union, EU). From below, it is affected by the rise of new social and political movements in its constituent territories and by the institutional decentralization that has been a feature of most contemporary democracies. Laterally, the state is affected by the trend to deregulation and the rise of neo-liberal ideology, and by the advance of civil society in formerly state-bound countries.

The effects of these changes are extremely complex, but one general tendency is to the disarticulation and even disintegration of public space. In its heyday the state represented the coincidence in territory of a number of systems.[6] There was a recognizable national economy, albeit part of wider trading systems. 'National' culture and identity were generally fostered by the state and in turn legitimized the state by constituting it as a nation. The common sense of identity in turn legitimized policies of social solidarity and redistribution and, together with a state apparatus, made possible the trade-offs between economic efficiency and equity that maintain social stability. Citizenship was defined by membership of a state, and rights (and, in European constitutions, obligations) were generally attached to this citizenship. The state sustained institutions, which determined public policies, and provided mechanisms for representation and accountability in this process. Categories of analysis were rather rigid, and nationalist movements, especially after the beginning of the First World War, faced a stark choice between statehood and limited regional self-government. In the modern era these functions and processes no longer coincide to the extent to which they did in the past. Economic change is understood as a global process, often mediated by local territorial factors, with the nation-state playing a smaller role. Culture and identity have both globalized and localized, while identities have become plural and multiple, determined not merely by who people are but by the context in which they find themselves. Civil rights have become increasingly detached from the state and are expressed in a universal idiom or, in Europe, through the European Convention on Human Rights. Policy-making has often disappeared into complex networks spanning the public and private sectors, and the state and international system, escaping from national institutions and thus from democratic accountability. Yet along with these tendencies to complexity and differentiation, there are elements of an emerging transnational economic and political order. The global free-trade regime of the WTO regulates matters previously managed unilaterally or bilaterally by states. Regional free-trade regimes in North and South America and in Europe are even more specific. Human rights in Europe are regulated by the Council of Europe, with its European Court of Human Rights. The International War Crimes Tribunal goes further, in providing the means for punishing transgressors. These emerging regimes may provide new mechanisms and institutions for conflict management and resolution.[7]

This transformation has affected different states in very different ways. In France, with its strong statist tradition, there has been a pro-state reaction and an attempt to maintain the state model in the face of European integration and global change, while professing support for the European project. In states with existing territorial fault lines, such as Canada, the United Kingdom, Spain, and Belgium, one effect has been to deepen these lines, reinvigorating territorial and nationalist movements which state policies had at one time been able to contain. In particular, the territorial exchange underpinning state management policies, under which territories would give loyalty to the state or support to the government in office, in exchange for protection from the global market, resources, and favourable policies, is undermined. As territories find themselves dependent less on the state and more on the global market or transnational regime, their loyalty to the state is weakened. The weakening of the 'nation-state' as a focus of identity may also lead to a search for a new sense of belonging, and for new bases for solidarity in the face of the disintegrative pressures of the market. It is not just pre-existing divisions that are mobilized here. New cleavages can be opened or old materials used to construct new forms of collective identity. More widely, there is a search for new principles of collective action and the re-establishment of a public space. The new dispensation also presents strategic opportunities for elites and political entrepreneurs to build new bases of support and power systems.[8]

The New Nationalisms

The new social and political movements, loosely subsumed under the term 'nationalist', or 'ethnic', vary considerably both in their support base and in their claims. The two key elements in the support base are identity and territory, which may or may not coincide. At one extreme are non-territorial ethnic minorities, like European Jews, Gypsies, or the various ethnic groups of the United States. At the other extreme are purely territorial movements seeking to build territorial systems of action in the face of the global market. Some of these have little cultural or historical basis, and are conventionally classified as 'regional' rather than 'national'. In between are movements that combine identity and territory in three ways. In some cases, the territorial and the cultural–identity bases coincide, as in Scotland; here we have a territorially integrated nationalism. In others, a single territory is contested by two groups; these are the divided societies. In a third type, a single group spills over state or administrative boundaries; these are transstate nationalisms, which may be irredentist, as in Ireland, or stateless, as in the Basque Country. It is the relationship between felt identity or 'ethnicity' and territory that creates the issue of nationalism,[9] with sometimes one being stronger, sometimes the other. There are movements based on identity or culture, notably in central and eastern Europe, where historically, strong states did not arise to frame overarching national identities. Instead, the break-up of empires from the nineteenth century was linked to the rise of ethnic politics and the search for ethnically based states. In other cases, territory is prior, and national identity is forged within it, as happened in Scotland, Poland, and more recently in Flanders.[10]

TABLE 2.1. *Support bases of territorial or ethnic movements*

Non-territorial	Territorially-integrated	Divided societies	Trans-state nations	Purely territorial
One group No territory	One territory/ One identity	Two identities/ One territory	Two territories One identity group	No group identity

All this gives rise to great terminological confusion. One can talk of nationalism in Scotland, Wales, or Quebec, since these places are widely recognized as nations, the population see themselves as such, and they have established nationalist movements with defined agendas. In the case of Flanders,[11] the term is more controversial.[12] In Spain the constitution makes a distinction between the Spanish 'nation' and the 'nationalities and regions' that compose it. At one time it was understood that the reference to nationalities covered only Catalonia, the Basque Country, and Galicia, but in 1996 the Spanish conservative government, inspired no doubt by the desire to dilute the meaning of the term, agreed to incorporate it in the autonomy statutes of Aragon and Valencia. The Italian Lega Lombarda and the broader Lega Nord have sought, in moving from federalism to separatism, to conjure up a nation of Padania[13] together with an imaginative history as 'the oldest community of Europe'.[14] Their imagined nation of Padania is not taken seriously outside their own ranks. Bavarian politicians often make claims about the special status of their region, invoking its past as an independent kingdom,[15] but only intermittently, as after the First World War and very briefly after the Second World War, has this been seen by a few actors as non-German. Other *Länder* have established territorial systems of action and a sense of political identity, but without raising nationalist issues. Sicily has its own distinct history, its language, a strong sense of identity, and an autonomous government, yet it is rarely referred to as a nation.[16] Brittany is usually seen as a region, and Breton groups normally describe themselves as regionalist, but sometimes nationalist themes are aired. So in some cases we have nations, because there is general agreement on this, while elsewhere nationhood is claimed on one side and denied on the other.

While establishing a descriptive distinction between nationalism and mere ethnic politics on one side, or mere regionalism on the other, may be almost impossible, there is a normative difference. The crucial distinction between their claims appears to lie in the area of legitimacy; in the claim to self-determination; and in the framework in which these claims are advanced. Asserting nationhood implies that the nation, however defined, is the primary social grouping to which allegiance is due, the basis for social organization, and that it possesses the right to self-determination.[17] National claims situate the territory or group as a subject of the international order more easily than regions, which are usually mere divisions of state territory. This right might be accepted by others or it might not. It does not entail that the nation must exercise this right in order to establish its own state; indeed it would be a contradiction in terms to say that a nation has a right to self-determination and then insist that this must take only one political form. It is perfectly consistent for a nation to assert the right of self-determination, but then use this to negotiate its position in a broader political order, recognizing the strengths and weaknesses of its position. Saying that nations differ from other groups in the right to self-determination, of course, does not provide an external standard for determining which territorial or identity groups are nations and which are not. Such a search is probably futile, given the value-laden and political nature of the subject. This very difficulty provides a further reason for detaching the nation from the state, since if the existence of nationhood implied statehood it would become very important to be able to determine who had it and who did not. A 'fuzzy' definition of nationhood opens up a range of intermediate solutions, including the sort of semantic juggling that features in the Spanish constitution. The normative distinction cannot, however, be so easily dismissed. Once states recognize their component parts as nations with the right, however constrained, to self-determination, they are logically obliged to negotiate their accommodation within the state, rather than treating them as mere divisions of the national territory, to be organized according to their convenience.[18]

The intersection of identity and territory gives two dimensions to the resulting nationalist conflicts: the external dimension, or whether the territory should secede or change its constitutional status; and the internal dimension, that is the relationship among the groups within it. This distinction is important but should not be pushed too far. What has distinguished nationalist from other ethnic conflicts has been precisely the question of which state the territory should belong to, and even in non-divided societies secessionist demands may open up internal cleavages. The demands emanating from the new nationalisms are also diverse. It is common to distinguish among cultural, economic, and political dimensions of nationalism. Cultural demands are often focused on language, where this is seen as threatened with extinction or relegation to low-status uses. Economic demands focus on unfavourable treatment by the state or on opportunities for betterment in the international market or transnational trading areas. On the political dimension, there are state-seeking nationalisms, autonomist nationalisms, which seek more self-government within the state, and movements that want to transform the state order, getting away from the classic, sovereign state formula altogether.

Managing Diversity

Accommodation and management strategies in the past focused largely on the state, although some conflicts were internationalized. Often states sought to disaggregate minority demands, satisfying some without having to concede others. Provision can be made for teaching and using minority languages, without altering the structure of political power, as has happened in Wales. Religious schools are a concession to cultural minorities used in states without a prohibition on non-secular public instruction. Multiculturalism is a strategy of accommodating diverse cultural elements without changing the constitution of the state, although this is seen by some nationalists, for example in Quebec, as a strategy to dilute their demands by banalizing the idea of difference and reducing them to a mere cultural minority. Territorial concessions can be on policy or on political autonomy. Regional policies can be used to divert resources to specific places, and government spending can be targeted both to regions and to non-territorially concentrated groups. Political responses include devolution or regional government, federalism, and special self-government provisions for specific territories. Another strategy is to establish channels of access for the minorities concerned into the central state. So Scotland since 1885 and Wales since 1965 have secretaries of state in the central government, whose role of governing the nations on behalf of the state (at least until 1999) is complemented by that of representing territorial interests at the centre.[19] Consociationalism involves co-opting elites in the minorities, giving them a share of central power and distributing resources proportionally.[20]

Many of these devices for accommodating minorities are undermined by changes in the state, the market, and society. Economic response mechanisms are more difficult in an era of globalization and free trade in which the state is losing control over its own spatial economy. Differentiated policy responses are challenged by the rise of individual rights and demands for equity. Consociationalism is made more difficult by the erosion of the integrated subcultures or pillars that supported strong leadership and permitted deals to be made and bargains to be kept.[21] Globalization and continental integration have also eroded the distinction between domestic and foreign affairs, and encouraged national minorities to seek redress for their grievances, as well as resources and opportunities, in the international arena.

Reterritorialization of Politics

This has coincided with a tendency towards the reterritorialization of politics, and of minority nationalist politics in particular, which further undercuts centralizing strategies such as consociationalism and makes it more difficult to unpack demands functionally. There are three impulses to the reterritorialization of politics: functional, political, and normative. In some respects, it is true that territory has lost its functional significance. Globalization of production and exchange, together with technology, have weakened the links between natural-resource endowments and location of production and permitted capital to move around in search of the most profitable site. Mass communication, again helped by new technologies, has eroded local cultures and aided the emergence of a global cultural and entertainment market. Yet, in other respects, the functional importance of territory has increased. Economic restructuring is increasingly appreciated as a territorially-specific phenomenon, as the characteristics of particular places determine their ability to compete in the global economy.[22]

Territory has proved to be the best foundation for culture and language policies. Since territorial proximity is still the basis for most communication, the instruments available, television apart, tend to be territorially based and focused, and language rights are most conveniently allocated territorially. Territory is the site of interconnections among functional spheres, and so of the capacity to engage in public-policy interventions. The construction and maintenance of specific identities depend on these interconnections. So cultural protection and development require an economic base, while cultural identity in turn may provide the basis for collective action to underpin the new models of economic development.[23] Shared identity can sustain social solidarity, which in turn can encourage collective action and an integrated model of development in the face of the disintegrating effects of global markets. So in a modern society control of territory becomes more and not less important for functional autonomy.

Politically, territory is important as the basis for governing institutions since there are almost no examples of non-territorial government, either within or across states. Social movements also tend to operate and mobilize territorially, either because, like the environmental movement, their interests are essentially tied to the use of space, or because territory is the most effective basis for organization. Reactions to the effects of the global market are often territorial, as the disjuncture between the global rationality of the multinational corporation and the spatial rationality of the local community is felt. So what may be a rational market strategy of plant closure from the overall perspective of the firm is felt locally as a loss of jobs and income not only for the affected workers but for the entire community. Hence the prevalence of local struggles against plant closures, with class and sectoral conflicts assuming a territorial form. More generally, social solidarity may be assuming a territorial form with the decline of class attachments and the institutions that sustained them. This has encouraged some convergence of the new nationalisms with other social movements.

Normatively, the territorial principle allows for the emergence of a form of particularism that is non-exclusive, new forms of civic nationalism that reject ethnic criteria for membership.[24] The extent to which this happens in practice is highly variable, with some manifestations of territorial politics being highly inclusive and tolerant, while others represent a claim by one ethnic group for exclusive control over a territory shared with another. Territory is also the most effective basis for the building of democratic and representative institutions, and underpins the establishment of a deliberative democracy, which requires a shared public space.[25] While in theory this public space could be non-territorial, with citizens connected electronically, this raises a series of questions concerning who would control the technology and who would be admitted to its use. Finally, the territorial principle for making autonomy claims, because it is non-exclusive and modelled on the state itself, carries greater external legitimacy. It is noteworthy that nearly all minority nationalist movements in western Europe, as well as in Quebec, have moved from a doctrine of ethnic particularism to a civic discourse based on territorial nationalism, explicitly including all citizens resident within the territory as members of the nation.[26]

So politics and public life, in a global age, are reterritorializing, and minorities are increasingly tending to make territorial claims. Systems providing for non-territorial accommodation and consociationalism are giving way to territorial nationalism,[27] for example in Quebec and Flanders, where nation-building projects are underway, or in the Basque Country, where a complex series of provincialist, foral, and linguistic demands has been subsumed in a movement to construct a territorial nationalism. The old distinctions among types of movement are also being eroded. In divided societies competition for control of the territory is accentuated as non-territorial mechanisms become more difficult to practise. The distinction between regionalist and nationalist movements is also eroding, especially in Europe. Regionalism is no longer exclusively framed by the nation-state but is also projected within the broader European political space in the 'new regionalism'.[28] Nationalist movements, for their part, have in many cases moderated their demands and sought to join forces with the Europe of the Regions movement.

Accommodating Nationalism

State restructuring and global change thus encourage the re-emergence of nationalisms within established states. This is not a paradox but represents two sides of the same phenomenon. Some of these new and re-emergent nationalisms are state-seeking movements in the traditional sense, wanting to substitute new states for the old. In territorially integrated societies like Scotland,[29] or Norway in 1905, the principle at stake is relatively straightforward. In divided societies, or trans-state societies, territorial secession may raise as many problems as it solves. The legitimacy of secession is almost always contested by some people within the seceding territory, raising questions about the size of majorities required to achieve it and the rights of minorities, who may themselves demand the right to secede, or to remain within the host state. The drawing of boundaries and whether to use existing jurisdictional lines laid down for other purposes, ethnic boundaries, or determination by referendum, raise further issues. This poses intractable problems in a place like the Basque Country, where there is dispute over whether self-determination would be for all seven provinces together; for the ones in Spain only; for each individually; for the three provinces forming the present Basque Autonomous Community; for these three plus Navarre; or for them and Navarre separately. Even should minorities within the seceding territory not make secessionist claims of their own, the question of the individual and collective rights that they might claim is raised. There are also substantial economic costs associated with the process of secession and the maintenance of a state.

It is possible, however, that the new state order might provide mechanisms for managing nationalist conflict short of secession. Once again, this applies differently in the varying contexts of territorially integrated societies, divided societies, and trans-state societies. For territorially integrated societies the question is whether new forms of self-government falling short of classical statehood are possible. In divided societies the question is whether the new global and continental order can provide ways in which both identities can receive recognition, while not giving either monopoly control of the territory. In trans-state societies the main question is whether new expressions of common identity are possible, and borders can be made more permeable, without provoking the conflict implied in two simultaneous secessions. These external and internal dimensions are closely connected. An attenuated form of independence will present less of a provocation to minorities within the territory, while reducing the significance of borders can facilitate common action between members of the same linguistic or identity group in two states. Complex systems of authority, at sub-state, state, and supra-state level can also facilitate the emergence of, and legitimize, multiple identities and allow citizens and groups to operate in multiple spheres, giving expression to their identities and policy preferences. On the other hand, over-complex systems merely bring us back to the public-choice problem, that deliberative democracy is discouraged, government becomes incomprehensible, and power flows into the hands of political entrepreneurs willing and able to invest the time and resources required to work the system and operate in multiple spheres.[30] So we do still need political institutions and public fora in which debate can take place and decisions be made.

Independence in . . .

One possibility is provided by the existence of continental and international regimes, which externalize many of the contentious policy issues, provide an external support system for the independence of small nations, and reduce the costs of self-determination. This is not a new idea. Before the First World War many of the national movements in the Habsburg empire aimed for self-government within the imperial framework rather than separation. Scottish nationalism before the 1930s was almost always articulated within the framework of empire, seeking dominion status like that of Canada or Australia. The present era opens up new opportunities. For example, within the NATO area there is generally no external security threat,[31] while security for the area as a whole has been collectivized. It is therefore possible for Quebec sovereigntists to argue that the defence posture of an independent Quebec would be no different from its present one as part of Canada. It is notable, indeed, that in all the debates on independence in Quebec and Scotland in recent years defence and security issues have hardly featured. International regimes might also lessen fears for the rights of minorities within seceding territories. The Council of Europe, custodian of the European Convention for the Protection of Human Rights, has made respect for the rights of ethnic minorities a condition for accession for the new democracies of central and eastern Europe, and the incorporation of the convention into the law of individual states provides an external basis for individual rights.

Most discussion has focused on the effects of trading regimes on the viability of independence. Kenichi Ohmae[32] argues that the existence of global free-trade regimes and the imperatives of global competition are eroding large nation-states and permitting the emergence of the 'regional state', a form of territorial trading company. The argument is based on a strict economic determinism and a neo-liberal ideology that wants to see the state fade away, taking with it social solidarity and deliberative democracy. Most of the new nationalists would deny such a vision, and insist that they are seeking to create new forms of solidarity and a capacity to confront the global economy rather than be dominated by it. So political attention has focused on the emergence of continental free-trading regimes, especially NAFTA and the EU, and the opportunities they provide for new forms of territorial autonomy within them. These potentially reduce the cost of independence both to the seceding territory and to the host state, preserving market access and factor mobility. They may enable small states to externalize costly items, such as negotiating common standards or support for declining sectors, or maintaining a national currency. In so far as the free trade regimes are institutionalized, they provide an external support system, common policies, and structured opportunities for small states to influence the policies of bigger states and the system as a whole, rather than being policy-takers, forced to adopt the policies of their larger trading partners. This logic already works in Europe, where the EU has permitted small states to maintain their viability and avoid domination by Germany. One reason for proceeding to a single currency, indeed, is that this will provide more influence for smaller countries than they would have as part of a Deutschmark zone.

So a policy of independence within the free-trade zone has been adopted by a number of nationalist parties, most explicitly the Parti Québécois and the Scottish National Party. The Flemish Volksunie has this as a long-term aim, while the Flemish Christian Democrats and the Basque Nationalist Party are a little more ambivalent about their long-term goals, although certainly sympathizing with the idea. The Esquerra Republicana de Catalunya came out for independence in the 1990s, and placed this in the context of Europe, albeit a future 'Europe of the peoples' rather than the actual EU. Other nationalist parties, such as the Welsh Plaid Cymru, evoke Europe more vaguely as the framework for a post-state order, while the Catalan governing coalition CiU plays a very active role in the European arena, using it as a platform for nationalist projection, while discounting talk of independence. A language of calculated ambivalence permits it to exploit opportunities where they occur, gradually assuming more of the reality of self-government.

While both NAFTA and the EU are invoked as external support systems for independence, they provide very different opportunities. The EU provides a ready-made institutional system, in which states are represented, with votes in the Council of Ministers allocated by population to give small states a disproportionate voice. NAFTA provides no such institutions, but is managed by intergovernmental negotiations in which power is determined largely by economic weight. Adhering to the EU in the event of secession would also be much easier than in the case of NAFTA. The EU possesses a body of law which is common to the entire area, and states merely have to agree to accept the *acquis communautaire*, that is the existing corpus of law and policy. Pro-European nationalist movements have generally declared themselves quite happy to accept this, although the Scottish National Party (SNP) makes an exception for the Common Fisheries Policy. NAFTA, on the other hand, is a complex bundle of trilateral, bilateral, and sectoral agreements, with a great deal less common content, so that there is no *acquis communautaire* to which to adhere. Nor does NAFTA provide for a common currency, or free movement of persons, so that Quebec sovereigntists have had to propose that it be supplemented by a bilateral agreement with Canada. Another difference concerns the degree of protection from the market provided by each regime. NAFTA rules on subsidies apply directly only to the signatory states, so that Quebec's distinct economic model is not threatened. As a member of NAFTA, however, Quebec would be subject to the full rigour of trading rules and the impact of the continental market. The EU differs from this in two respects. Rules on subsidies and government involvement in the economy apply equally to states and sub-state governments, so that secession would not increase the degree of market exposure. On the other hand, the EU itself maintains provision for protection against the full rigour of the market, in the form of the Social Chapter, setting out minimal labour rights, and the structural funds, which provide compensation for regions and sectors adversely affected by market restructuring. All of this makes independence within the EU a great deal less risky than independence in NAFTA. As the EU extends its competences, the risk diminishes, allowing a progressive move to effective independence. The country that has travelled furthest down this road, with simultaneous decentralization to the regions and insertion into the inner core of Europe, is Belgium, so that many people in Flanders now predict that the move to the single currency will provide the occasion for the effective dissolution of the Belgian state. Similarly, the European currency has been presented as an occasion for secession by the Lega Nord, allowing it to detach itself from the lira, which it proposes that southern Italy should retain.

Independence within free-trade areas may reduce the costs of independence, but it does not eliminate them. Transition costs may be high, transaction costs of various sorts may be raised by independence, and institutions may have to be reinvented.[33] Another problem is the transition. While it is easy to envisage a post-independence regime in which both sides, through rational self-interest, agree to maintain or establish relationships of cooperation and exchange, it is less easy to see how one could get there. The very idea of secession raises strong passions on both sides, reducing the likelihood of cooperation. Given the risks and uncertainties involved, voters in the seceding territory will need a strong motive to vote for secession, and this is most easily provided by appeals to ethnic particularism and hostility to the old state and its people. So secessions are not generally followed by relationships of close cooperation and partnership. The case of Ireland is sometimes cited as a precedent for secession while retaining links. Yet the links in that case, including common citizenship and the free-travel area, were retained at the insistence of the British government, which refused to accept Ireland's claim to full independence by treating it as a foreign state, even after the declaration of the Republic in 1949.[34] A currency union was retained until the 1970s, but free trade ceased in the 1930s and was not resumed until the European Free Trade Association agreements of the 1960s. Common arrangements, including the shared currency, soon fell apart after the break-up of Czechoslovakia,[35] showing that the process of separation, once started, is difficult to control. On the other hand, accession to the European Community in 1973 certainly helped Ireland to become more independent of the United Kingdom.

There has been a lot of discussion as to whether Quebec would be allowed into NAFTA or Scotland into the EU after secession. There seems no reason to believe that they would not be allowed in, since this would imply their expulsion from existing arrangements. On the other hand, there would certainly be opposition from other member states to secessionist nations seeking independent representation in EU institutions. No Spanish government would relish the precedent of Scottish independent membership and the example it would give to Catalans and Basques.[36]

Independence within transnational regimes would be easier in territorially integrated societies, where the territorial and identity bases for nationalism coincide. It could also address the issue of divided societies, by reassuring minorities within seceding nations, by reducing the stakes in independence, and by providing guarantees for civil rights and against economic discrimination. On the other hand, it is clear that neither anglophones nor native peoples would be greatly mollified by the assurance that Quebec would remain in NAFTA. Proposals for an independent Northern Ireland within the EU similarly fail to address the issue of control within the new state. In the case of Northern Ireland, where the issue is to which state the province should belong, independence would satisfy neither group. Nor is Europe necessarily seen as a neutral or benign influence. It is supported by moderate Catholics in Northern Ireland as an external source of support, but opposed both by Protestants and by extreme nationalists. In the Basque Country, too, Europe is favoured by moderate nationalists but opposed by the extreme element, as it conflicts with their fundamentalist vision of the nation and independence.

Unpacking Sovereignty

One way of taking advantage of the new transnational regimes without raising divisive issues of secession or independence is to unpack the idea of sovereignty both functionally and territorially. This is the recognition and extension of part of current reality, namely that states are not sovereign as they were in the past, and that authority is pooled and shared. So functions and responses to specific types of demand can be divided and distributed among the three levels or minority nation, state, and transnational regime. For more complex and divided societies, more complex arrangements can be devised. One scenario is a neo-medievalism of overlapping spheres of authority in government, the market, and civil society. Functional autonomy could be distributed in various ways, and identity expressed in different forms. So an individual could be a member of the broad Basque nation for some purposes, a citizen of the smaller Basque Autonomous Community for others, a citizen of Spain, and a European. A Northern Ireland Catholic could be Irish for some purposes, a member of an Ulster community for others. Another variant of this, where there is no agreement on common identity, is effectively to privatize the issue, in the way Western countries have privatized religion by severing its links with the state while allowing it an important role in civil society.[37] To suggest that nationalism can be detached from politics altogether, however, would be to miss an important feature of it, the link between identity, culture, and politics.[38] Unpacking might be primarily non-territorial, aiming to break the link between identity and control of territory; or it may be territorial, seeking new relationships among territorial societies. Given the links between territory, identity, and politics that we have already noted, nationalism is increasingly likely to take a territorial form.

The most elaborate system for accommodation in Europe is in Belgium, where successive constitutional reforms have provided for devolution of powers both to three territorial regions (Flanders, Wallonia, and Brussels Capital) and to three linguistic communities (the Flemish, the French, and the German). At the same time competences have been transferred upwards to Europe. In this way, a system of national consociationalism, in which policies were bargained at the centre, has given way to territorial and community devolution and federalism, in which groups autonomously make their own policies. Regions are responsible for hard services and territorially based services, while the linguistic communities are responsible for cultural matters, education, and 'personalizable' services, such as health and social services. This is not really a combination of territorial and non-territorial devolution, as sometimes thought, since the language communities have defined and immovable boundaries. The dual system was adopted in order to deal with the problem of Brussels, a predominantly francophone (but formerly Flemish-speaking) city within the territory of Flanders, and in practice, the territorial governments have emerged as the dominant players. The Flanders region and Flemish language community have effectively merged, while the French language community organizes much of its activity through the regional administrations of Wallonia and Brussels. The German language community is a very minor player. Regions and communities have full external powers in matters of their own competence, and use the provision of the Maastricht Treaty allowing sub-state governments to represent the state in the European Council of Ministers when regional or community matters are on the agenda. These arrangements appear to work better in Flanders, where the institutions are merged,[39] illustrating the importance of territorial cohesion to effective modern government. Despite the effort to separate out competences, there is still a need for cooperation, especially on the Walloon side and in Brussels, and in relation to European matters, where the consent of the various actors is required before Belgium can take a position in the Council of Ministers. Veto points have thus remained, bringing back in the old consociational principle. In Flanders there is a widespread view that the present arrangement is, like the others before it, transitional, and will eventually give way to an independent state of Flanders, the only obstacle being the status of Brussels.[40]

Another example of unpacking sovereignty is the series of British and Irish agreements on Northern Ireland, notably the Anglo-Irish Agreement of 1985, the Downing Street Declaration of 1995, and the Belfast Agreement of 1998. These provided an 'Irish dimension', allowing Northern Ireland Catholics to express their Irish identity, while giving the government of the Irish Republic a voice in the government of Northern Ireland. Both governments have effectively disclaimed absolute rights of sovereignty over Northern Ireland, the British government by declaring that it had no selfish political, economic, or strategic motive for remaining there and the Irish government by repealing the clause in its constitution asserting actual sovereignty over the North. In this way, it is hoped that the substantive and symbolic concerns of both communities can be addressed, while power-sharing arrangements are built to deal with the territorial government of the province. Of course, if the conflict is about control of territory and in which state this control will be located, then none of this addresses the problem, but the changing global and European context provides powerful reasons for not thinking of it in these terms. A particularly interesting innovation is the British–Irish Council (Council of the Isles), which brings together a variety of sovereign and non-sovereign bodies including the UK government, the Republic of Ireland, the Scottish Parliament, the Welsh and Northern Ireland Assemblies, the Channel Islands, and the Isle of Man. Europe has affected thinking on the Catholic side more than among Protestant politicians, who tend to be strongly opposed to it, but has also provided a new context for cooperation between the British and Irish governments, enabling the overall framework to be put in place. This case is discussed more fully by John McGarry (Chapter 14).

The idea of unpacking sovereignty is also present in cross-border cooperation agreements, which now exist across every frontier in western Europe. Most of these have economic objectives, or concern functional cooperation in matters like infrastructure or environmental policy, but a number of the accords affects disputed borders, or borders that run through historic nations or linguistic groups. Examples would be the border between Northern Ireland and the Republic of Ireland; the border between France and Spain, which cuts the Basque and Catalan territories in two; the Austrian–Italian border in the Tyrol; the Danish–German border; and the French–Belgian border. In all these cases, programmes are in effect with the support of the European Commission to encourage cross-border cooperation and exchange. Europe does not in these cases serve to erase the border by making it functionally irrelevant, as might be thought. On the contrary, where the border is open to challenge, states and local interests opposed to integration will seek to reinforce it and discourage cross-border activity. So programmes for cooperation across the Irish border have not changed attitudes among unionists[41] and there have been demonstrations in Denmark against cross-border cooperation with Germany. The contribution of the new European order is not to abolish the border but, first, to make it secure and recognized; and then, on this basis, to make it more penetrable. So there is a series of agreements across the French–Spanish border in the Basque Country, allowing the emergence of certain types of cultural exchange and collaboration. Mutual recognition of the Italian–Austrian border has facilitated cross-border cooperation in the Tyrol.

Forms of unpacked sovereignty already exist across Europe in the form of historic rights and special arrangements for parts of states.[42] Rokkan and Urwin[43] identify the 'union state' as one in which territories have been incorporated by treaty or accord, preserving their historic rights which are immune to the sovereignty claims of the state, an idea pursued by other writers more recently. A similar idea is Jellinek's idea of 'fragments of state'.[44] These rights were at one time common across Europe, for example in pre-revolutionary France,[45] and in the Basque provinces of Spain they survived until the middle of the nineteenth century. Even then, they were replaced by the *concierto económico*, a special fiscal arrangement allowing the three Basque provinces and Navarre to raise their own taxes and pass an agreed sum over to the state.[46] The Anglo-Scottish Union of 1707 took the form of a treaty in which specific features of Scottish society, notably the law, the burghs, and the church, were preserved and secured.[47] Since then a series of special measures has been passed for the government of Scotland, in recognition of its special status. Quebec's special position within Canada has been recognized in many respects through history, despite the difficulties which many Canadians have in coming to terms with the idea. These doctrines of historic territorial rights, at one time thought of as archaic or redundant, have now come back into play as historic territories have sought to renegotiate their place in the new state and continental order. What they bring is a recognition that asymmetry is a long-standing element in the territorial state, and that these historic territories should be able to negotiate their position within the state, rather than being treated as an undifferentiated part of the state territory. They are also based upon a notion of authority that is both ancient and very modern, that of shared and limited sovereignty.[48]

If we put this in the context of continental integration, the possibilities are extended further. It may be possible for a territory to function as a semi-detached state, somewhere between the state and the continental regime. This idea of an intermediate status or 'third way' receives wide support from public opinion in places like Quebec, Catalonia, and Scotland. There are many historic examples, such as the territories of the Austro-Hungarian empire, which was a dual monarchy, the Hungarian part of which functioned as a centralized state, while the other part (which did not even have an official name) was a looser conglomeration of territories. Other dual monarchies were Norway–Sweden between 1815 and 1905 and England–Scotland between 1603 and 1707. On Europe's Atlantic periphery, contemporary examples of semi-detached territories exist (the Faroes, the Isle of Man, Greenland), as do regions with special status (Canaries, Azores, Madeira). The micro-states of Andorra, San Marino, Monaco, and Vatican City are technically sovereign, but hardly count as states in the usual sense. West Berlin had an ill-defined relationship with the

Federal Republic of Germany between 1949 and 1990, and Danzig and Trieste were 'free cities' between the wars. In the former Soviet Union there are formally independent states with a high degree of dependence (Belarus and some of the central Asian republics) and non-independent territories with effective independence (see Graney, Chapter 13). NAFTA and the EU might in some ways facilitate the creation of such semi-independent places, since they would relieve them of many of the burdens of statehood and allow a degree of free-riding. Special-status territories could certainly survive more easily within the new transnational regimes than under the weak aegis of the League of Nations. Drèze[49] proposes the status of 'regions of Europe' for difficult territories, allowing them to accede directly to the EU, but without either the burdens or the rights of statehood. While there are many historic territories that defy the usual norms of statehood in Europe, however, there is no provision for creating new ones, either in the EU or in any of its member states. In some respects, indeed, both the EU and NAFTA make such indeterminate status rather more difficult, since only states are represented in their institutions. In order to have a say in the new Europe or in NAFTA, you need to have a state, and this factor is itself a force against disintegration.

Stateless Nation-Building

Another way in which the new global order can be used to manage nationalist conflict is more pragmatic, and focused less on constitutional matters than on functional autonomy. In this strategy, leaders of stateless nations will concentrate on the conditions for maintaining and developing their culture, on building institutions and the capacity for self-government in civil society, and on developing an economic model that permits a degree of autonomy in the global trading order. Territorial integration within the minority nation and policy effectiveness become more important than constitutional matters. There is an emphasis on nationalism and symbolism, but issues of sovereignty are put aside, and fights with the central state staged only on negotiable issues. There is a strong emphasis on external action, but this is distinguished from classical diplomacy by focusing on economic and cultural issues, rather than security matters, and by a close association between government and private actors. This strategy would be associated with successive non-nationalist governments in Quebec, with recent governments in Flanders, and with the Catalan CiU government. The idea is that the state system is now so penetrable, and the opportunities within continental regimes and the global trading order so great, that nation-building can proceed without the necessity to declare formal independence. In the case of Catalonia, this strategy is given historical legitimization by harking back to its past as a medieval trading nation, part of a complex confederal system within the kingdoms of Aragon and Spain, and operating in the local arena, the Spanish arena, the imperial arena (under Charles V), the Mediterranean, and, from the eighteenth century, the Americas. Flanders has also sought some historical legitimization for its initiatives, while pursuing its own concept for Europe, the Europe of the Cultures, in which a specific place will be found in European institutions for regions with their own cultures (meaning in effect minority nations).

This strategy is more likely to work in territorially integrated than in divided societies since it does not in itself resolve the internal problem. Yet it might also make a contribution here in two respects. These movements, by focusing on nation-building, are concerned to increase the extent of territorial integration; while, by reducing the stakes in the nationalist movement, they are able to build a broader coalition of support. This attenuation of the content of nationalism is not accepted by all movements, even in territorially integrated societies. The SNP is little attracted by the Europe of the Regions vision, clinging to the old distinctions, drawing inspiration in this from Scotland's historic experience as an independent state. The Flemish Volksunie plays both games, pressing for a stronger regional presence in Europe, while insisting that in the long term Flanders will be playing among the states; the Flemish Christian Democrats at one time appeared to be moving in the same direction. These stateless nation-building strategies are, further, driven by opportunities and the search for spaces in the state and continental order, in which the territory can be inserted. They are dependent on strong leadership, the capacity to mobilize resources, a favourable position in the continental trading order, and good connections across the political and business world. They are therefore more likely to be found in the prosperous and central regions than in the periphery, and do not provide a universal solution to the issue of nationalist accommodation.

So the new state order does provide new opportunities to accommodate nationalist conflict. It blurs the issue of sovereignty, allowing the re-emergence of forms of qualified and negotiated sovereignty which were lost with the rise of the 'nation-state' with its monopolistic claims on sovereignty. It lowers the stakes in the distribution of powers between states and their component territories, since many powers are now located outwith the state altogether. It provides opportunities for multiple identities to develop and receive expression. In some cases, it may ease the transition to independence, when accommodation within the state proves impossible. Perhaps most importantly, it provides opportunities for nation-building within the state and civil society, focusing on opportunities and openings rather than formal constitutional matters. On the other hand, many people within the respective 'national majorities' refuse to accept the legitimacy of minority identities; and we still do not have a model of the state that can accommodate the complex and asymmetrical realities of the contemporary world.

NOTES

This paper was written while I was visiting scholar at the Rockefeller Foundation Center at Bellagio, Italy, in Aug. 1997. I am grateful to Tony Hepburn for comments on an early draft.

1. E. Hobsbawm, *Nations and Nationalism since 1780* (Cambridge: Cambridge University Press, 1990), 9–10.
2. A. D. Smith, *Theories of Nationalism* (London: Duckworth, 1970), 21.
3. In the draft French translation of my book *Nations against the State* (*Nations against the State: The New Politics of Nationalism in Quebec, Catalonia and Scotland* (London: Macmillan, 1996; French trans. Montreal: Presses de L'Université de Montréal, 1997).), the terms *état* and *nation* were used interchangeably to translate nation and state and, even when I had corrected the text, the publisher insisted on a change of title to avoid what seemed a contradiction in terms.
4. This was drafted by the monks of Arbroath following the repulsion of attempts by the Angevin kings of England to conquer Scotland and the ascension of Robert the Bruce. In it the Scottish aristocracy and Highland chiefs declared: 'We are bound to him [Robert] for the maintaining of our freedom both by his right and his merits . . . Yet if he should give up what he has begun, seeking to make us or our kingdom subject to the king of England or the English, we should strive at once to drive him out as our enemy and a subverter of his own right and ours . . . for as long as one hundred of us remain alive, we will never on any conditions be subject to the lordship of the English.'
5. J. Camilleri and J. Falk, *The End of Sovereignty? The Politics of a Shrinking and Fragmenting World* (Aldershot: Edward Elgar, 1991).
6. Its heyday would be the period *c.*1870–1970. The nation-state is not, *pace* most international relations scholars, the product of the Peace of Westphalia. The only European state that has the same boundaries now as in 1648 is Portugal. The interventionist nation-state is largely the product of late 19th-century nation-building.
7. On the other hand, they may represent a weakening of political authority in the face of the market. Economic regimes such as NAFTA and the EU may, if not accompanied by political institution-building, represent a further retreat of power out of representative institutions. The Maastricht provisions, laying down

inflexible monetary and fiscal targets for states and providing for the transfer of important economic powers to an unelected and unaccountable European Central Bank, further accentuate these tendencies.

8. I am accepting here that both accounts of ethnic and nationalist mobilization—that it represents mass bottom-up pressure, and that it is a strategic tool of elites—can be true under various circumstances.

9. I am carefully avoiding using ethnicity as a causal or explanatory concept. Ethnicity, like nationalism, is a social construction, the result of mobilization, not the cause. No one has ever succeeded in defining it independently of its constituent parts. As a social category, however, ethnicity may be used to refer to groups that mobilize on the basis of shared, usually ascriptive, characteristics. To the degree that this mobilization succeeds, the group constitutes itself as an ethnic group and this then becomes part of the social reality facing its members.

10. B. Kerremans, 'The Flemish Identity: Nascent or Existent?', *Res Publica*, 2 (1997), 303–14. It is sometimes argued that these territorially based nationalisms are such only because the societies in question are 'ethnically homogeneous'. Again, this begs the question of how the various groups across the old Polish–Lithuanian confederation were forged into territorial nations, especially given the fact that the original national distinctions were vertical and not horizontal; or how the Angles, Saxons, Gaels, Irish, Norse, and Normans cohered into a Scottish nation.

11. Flemish national or 'ethnic' identity is even more recent and is a compound of the territorial identity of one part of the present region (historic Flanders) and a language shared with a neighbouring state (the Netherlands).

12. Kerremans, 'The Flemish Identity'.

13. R. Biorcio, *La Padania promessa: La storia, le idee e la logica d'azione della Lega Nord* (Milan: Il Saggiatore, 1997).

14. G. Onesto, *L'invenzione della Padania: La rinascita della comunitá piú antica d'Europa* (Ceresola: Foedus, 1997).

15. Although Bavaria as we know it was a creation of the Napoleonic era. See A. Mintzel, 'Political and Socio-Economic Developments in the Postwar Era: The Case of Bavaria, 1945–1989', in K. Rohe (ed.), *Elections, Parties and Political Traditions: Social Foundations of German Parties and Party Systems* (New York: Berg, 1990).

16. Ganci is an exception. See M. Ganci, *La nazione siciliana* (Naples: Storia di Napoli e della Sicilia, 1978).

17. British unionist intellectuals have often recognized this, using it as an argument against home rule for the smaller nations. Thus A. V. Dicey and C. Wilson argued that Ireland and Scotland respectively should not have their own parliaments because they would inevitably become the focus of sovereignty claims. (A. V. Dicey, *A Leap in the Dark: A Criticism of the Principles of Home Rule as Illustrated by the Bill of 1893*, 3rd edn. (London: John Murray, 1912); C. Wilson, 'A Note of Dissent', in *Scotland's Government*, Report of the Scottish Constitutional Committee (Edinburgh: Scottish Constitutional Committee, 1970).

18. This factor appears totally to have escaped the understanding of the last British government. Having declared in an official document, *Scotland and the Union*, that 'no nation can be kept in a union against its will', John Major proceeded to deny the legitimacy of Scottish claims to negotiate their place within the union, insisting that the sovereign parliament could act unilaterally 'Foreword by the Prime Minister', in Secretary of State for Scotland, *Scotland and the Union* (Edinburgh: HMSO, 1992). Similarly, the Labour Party accepted in the Scottish Constitutional Convention in 1988 that the Scottish people had the sovereign

right to negotiate their own form of government, then insisted that nothing would alter the sovereignty of Parliament. In Canada there is a dispute between the majority of Quebeckers and the majority of Canadians outside Quebec over whether Quebec is one province among ten, or one nation of two (or three with the native peoples).

A further complication is that not all territories with inherent historical rights are nations. The Basque provinces individually are the repository of the foral rights, and the original Basque agitation of the 19th century was based on provincialism, but now the Basque movement is recognized as a modern nationalism.

19. Since 1972 Northern Ireland has a secretary of state, but this role is more of a proconsular one and has never been performed by a locally elected politician.

20. Recent interpretations of consociationalism discount its use as a mechanism of social conflict management. After all, if the groups are *ex hypothesi* in conflict, why should they agree to cooperate? Instead, they see it as a means by which leaders of traditional social groups faced with integration seek to preserve their power by strengthening communal barriers and establishing their own monopoly of contact with the political system. H. Kriesi, *Le Système politique suisse* (Paris: Economica, 1995).

21. This is true even on the revisionist accounts of consociationalism, although there the emphasis is on the changed opportunities and resources available to leaders.

22. M. Storper, 'The Resurgence of Regional Economies, Ten Years Later', *European Urban and Regional Studies*, 2/3 (1995), 191–221.

23. M. Keating, 'The Political Economy of Regionalism', in M. Keating and J. Louhglin (eds.), *The Political Economy of Regionalism* (London: Frank Cass, 1996).

24. Keating, *Nations against the State*.

25. The failure to appreciate the importance of deliberation in democracy is the principal theoretical weakness of public-choice approaches, which advocate allowing people to form whatever partial associations they wish to perform specific collective functions.

26. This does not, of course, mean that all the citizens themselves recognize this identity. Some of these societies remain divided.

27. Again, this is true whether consociationalism is seen as a mechanism for containing community conflict or as a strategy for sustaining community leadership. In Flanders the movement for territorial federalism responds to elite strategy and has little public support, while in the other cases it is driven from below.

28. R. Balme (ed.), *Les Politiques du néorégionalisme: Action collective régionale et globalisation* (Paris: Economica, 1996); S. Pintarits, *Macht. Democratie und Regionen in Europa. Analysen und Szenarien der Integration und Desintegration* (Marburg: Metropolis, 1996); M. Keating, *The New Regionalism in Western Europe: Territorial Restructuring and Political Change* (Aldershot: Edward Elgar, 1998).

29. Here the only dispute is over the maritime boundary and, since this determines ownership of the offshore oil reserves, it is a critical one economically, but without implications for control of population.

30. This might include political leaders, business firms, multilinguals, diasporas, or cosmopolitan intellectuals.

31. The Greek–Turkish hostility would provide an exception to this.

32. K. Ohmae, *The End of the Nation-State: The Rise of Regional Economies* (New York: Free Press, 1995)

33. R. Young, *The Secession of Quebec and the Future of Canada* (Montreal: McGill–Queen's University Press, 1995); Groupe Coudenberg, *Cost of Non-Belgium: La valeur ajoutée de la Belgique fédérale* (Zellik: Rowlarta, 1996).

34. Irish citizens were free to vote in British elections because the British refused to regard them as foreign, but British citizens gained the right to vote in Ireland only after the Anglo-Irish Agreement in the 1980s.
35. Young, *The Secession of Quebec.*
36. One suspects that French politicians and commentators, who have little appreciation of the issue, would probably see it as a devious plot by *les anglo-saxons* to get themselves an extra set of votes!
37. J. P. Derriennic, *Nationalisme et démocratie: Réflexion sur les illusions des indépendantistes québécois* (Montreal: Boréal, 1995).
38. A. D. Smith, *Nations and Nationalism in a Global Era* (Cambridge: Polity Press, 1995).
39. S. De Rynck, 'Culture civique et rendement institutionnel: Les régions belges', in P. Le Galès and C. Lequesne (eds.), *Les Paradoxes des régions en Europe* (Paris: La Découverte, 1996).
40. This is a very big obstacle. The most diehard and ethnically-minded Flemish nationalists might give it up and fall back on a rural and inward-looking Flemish identity. For most Flemish politicians, however, abandoning a city that is within the territory of Flanders and is the political and economic capital of Flanders as well as the European capital would be unthinkable.
41. E. Tannam, 'EU Regional Policy and the Irish/Northern Irish Cross-Border Administrative Relationship', *Regional and Federal Studies*, 5/1 (1995), 67–93.
42. M. Herrero de Miñón, *Derechos históricos y constitución* (Madrid: Taurus, 1998).
43. S. Rokkan and D. Urwin, *Economy, Territory, Identity: Politics of West European Peripheries* (London: Sage, 1983). J. Mitchell, *Strategies for Self Government: The Campaigns for a Scottish Parliament* (Edinburgh: Polygon, 1996); L. Brockliss, D. Eastwood, and M. John, 'From Dynastic Union to Unitary State: The European Experience', in L. Brockliss and D. Eastwood (eds.), *A Union of Multiple Identities: The British Isles, c.1750–1859* (Manchester: Manchester University Press, 1997).
44. G. Jellinek, *Fragmentos de Estado*, trans. M. Foster, M. Herrero de Miñón, and J. Esteban (Madrid: Civitas, 1981).
45. F. Braudel, *L'Identité de la France: Espace et histoire* (Paris: Arthaud-Flammarion, 1986).
46. J.-L. de La Granja, *El nacionalismo vasco: Un siglo de historia* (Madrid: Tecnos, 1995).
47. This feature of the Union as fundamental law has never been accepted by the British Parliament, which insisted on assuming the English tradition of parliamentary sovereignty. In 1953 Lord Justice Cooper in *McCormick* v. *Lord Advocate* ruled that the doctrine of parliamentary sovereignty did not apply in Scotland and could not be used to overturn provisions of the Union, but added that, if it did so, there was effectively no remedy.
48. It is notable that of four territories in which nationalist movements are seeking new forms of autonomy, Scotland, Catalonia, Flanders, and Quebec, all have histories as parts of imperial systems in which authority was negotiated, pactism and inherited rights played an important role, and absolute sovereignty claims on the part of the state were never accepted.
49. J. Drèze, 'Regions of Europe', *Economic Policy*, 17 (1993), 265–307.

CHAPTER 3

Globalization, Cosmopolitanism, and Minority Nationalism

MARGARET MOORE

The theme of this volume is how minority nations are affected by globalization. By 'globalization', I refer to increased global economic trade, the liberalization of economic markets, the advance of the multinational corporation to many corners of the globe, and capital mobility.

The ideal of a cosmopolitan culture is, some argue, possible in this new context of interdependency. The dream of a cosmopolitan global culture was shared by both Marx and eighteenth- and nineteenth-century Enlightenment thinkers, and their contemporary counterparts. Marx, for example, conceived of nations as playing an important role in supporting a capitalist economy with a large population base, a large territory, and a viable bureaucratic structure. He also assumed that the forces of the capitalist economy would lead to the demise of many minority nations and the consolidation of a common cosmopolitan culture.[1] Enlightenment theorists, from Condorcet to Descartes, Voltaire to d'Alembert, also shared this vision of a cosmopolitan (global) culture. Condorcet, for example, argued that the emancipation of the individual from fixed social roles would lead to the gradual decline of cultural definitions of identity, the emergence of a universal language, and a single global society.[2]

The contemporary heirs to this tradition have argued that the current context of global economic restructuring has reduced the natural barriers between national and ethnic groups and at last made the realization of the 'dream' of a cosmopolitan culture possible. In the closing passage of his book *Nations and Nationalism since 1780* Hobsbawm argues, for example, that the age of nationalism is past.

Hobsbawm welcomes this development, viewing nationalism as a backward and atavistic romanticization of the past, which may 'die' a prolonged and difficult death as its adherents resist the inevitable change that accompanies global capitalism, but that is doomed to the 'dustbin' of history.

There are, I think, three distinct, but related misconceptions or problems inherent in this view, which I discuss in the three sections of this chapter. The first misconception involves the relationship of nationalism to the economic 'base' of society. Many proponents of cosmopolitanism have assumed that nations are modernist constructions, functional at a certain stage in industrialization, but that, as the world economy becomes more interrelated, the nation will be transcended by supranational institutions. Minority nationalism, with its celebration of particular national and cultural identities, is a doomed romantic or conservative reaction to the economic forces in favour of increased political cooperation at the supranational level and increasingly standardized cultural forms across the globe.

The second misconception is that acculturation—that is, increasingly common standardized cultural forms—will necessarily or automatically translate into the assimilation of minority nations. I argue that even if globalization leads to increased acculturation, it does not necessarily lead to the demise of minority nationalism, or national forms of identity.

The third misconception or problem with this conception involves the underlying ideal of a truly global, cosmopolitan culture. In the section dealing with this misconception I put forward three arguments designed to question whether the ideal of a 'cosmopolitan culture' should be regarded as an 'ideal'. I argue that this ideal has several problems: it is not genuinely global and neutral; it involves the false identification of minority nationalism with exclusivist ethnic isolation; and it fails to meet the requirement of minimal realism. All these concerns should lead us to adopt a new view of minority nationalism, in which minority nationalism is viewed as consistent with an enlightened cosmopolitanism and with managed globalization of the economy.

Misconception 1: Nations are Obsolete in the New Order of Interdependency and Internationalism

Many proponents of cosmopolitanism, and critics of minority nationalism, have argued that minority nations are a romantic and conservative reaction or resistance to global economic forces, which make no sense in the global economy. What is needed, it is suggested, is increased international cooperation to cope with the global reality of the economy, not the proliferation of smaller and smaller units, claiming sovereignty over smaller and smaller pieces of territory.

This view frequently draws on the work of historians of nationalism, such as Hobsbawm, who have pointed out that the nation-state is a modern construction, serving important functions in the nineteenth century, with the modernization of the economy, and the bureaucratization of the state. Nationalism, or the modern nation-state, it is suggested, no longer makes sense. Supranational political institutions are necessary to cope with the interdependent nature of the global economy. Minority nationalism, by which is meant the assertion of small nationalities within larger states, is an attempt to copy the nation-state model, which is itself outdated, and so should be dismissed as a doomed romanticism.

There is some truth to this claim. It is true that absolute sovereignty on the Westphalian model makes less and less sense in the global economic era. Practice has, to some extent, overtaken theory, and in two ways. First, there is some evidence of the erosion of Westphalian sovereignty, in favour of international action in defence of certain norms or a certain conception of state legitimacy. Secondly, the move toward regional economic associations has involved limitations on state sovereignty, for states are increasingly acting in cooperation with others, and in this interdependent world, are increasingly dependent on the actions and cooperation of others. In this section I will argue that, while this is true, it does not mean that the nation is an obsolete category of no relevance to the (post-)modern world, but only that the nation and its context are being transformed. Moreover, I shall argue that these transformations tend to strengthen minority nationalism, rather than suggesting its obsolescence.

First, state sovereignty has been eroded by the notion that the international community has obligations towards individual members of other states. Action on this idea of political legitimacy runs counter to the notion of the territorial integrity of states and the absolute sovereignty of states over their internal affairs. It is difficult to pinpoint the origins of this view, or even to claim that it is now the dominant one, for it is certainly not consistently applied or universally accepted, but, beginning in the 1970s, there was a sense that *legitimate* states had to meet minimal standards of human rights towards their (individual) members. This was the basic insight behind the anti-apartheid movement, which sought to isolate South Africa from the rest of the international community, and also underlay the 1975 Helsinki Accords, and the Copenhagen Agreement of 1990, which superseded the earlier Helsinki Accords.[3]

More recently, since the end of the cold war, there have been several cases of international intervention in the 'domestic affairs' of states—in the Kurdish region of Iraq, and in Somalia, Rwanda, Bosnia, Kosovo, and Cambodia. Not all were completely successful, but they were not simply an exercise for extending their backers' range of influence or securing their own (self-)interest, narrowly defined.[4] In each case United Nations involvement, which was authorized by the Security Council, was provoked by a humanitarian disaster or an injustice, and the stated aims of intervention were either to end the conflict or to deliver relief. This intervention also suggests that the era of the individual nation-state is being transformed; and that any nation that is seeking national independence or national sovereignty in the traditional sense is probably revering an ideal whose time is passing.

Secondly, the traditional nation-state model, developed in the nineteenth century, viewed the economic sphere in national terms, as subject to national regulations and controls. Historically, states were instrumental in breaking down the barriers erected by the medieval charters of towns and corporations, as well as in instituting a common currency and a common system of weights and measures.[5] Central to eighteenth- and nineteenth-century nation-building policies was the promotion of national economic policy. This frequently involved various forms of protectionism, in addition to internal liberalization and the development of infrastructure to facilitate capitalist development.

This traditional nation-state model is challenged by the globalization of the economy, and especially the mobility of capital markets. These have reduced the ability of the state to pursue national economic policies. States have had to respond to this new situation by restructuring the economy, with various forms of regional mobilizations, such as the North American Free Trade Agreement (NAFTA), the Association of South East Asian Nations, the European Union (EU), and Mercosur. These have further limited the sovereignty of individual member states by constraining them to abide by the rules and procedures (and, in the case of the EU, the law) of the association.

In this context, the idea of absolute sovereignty and autarkic economic policies for small nations make very little sense. In fact, it made very little sense prior to this erosion of state sovereignty. For example, in 1945 Alfred Cobban, in his book *National Self-Determination*, criticized President Woodrow Wilson's principle of national self-determination on the grounds that economic autarky on the part of smaller states would not work, that these minority nations could not be viable states in the sense of pursuing their own independent national economic policy.[6] In the era in which he wrote, when the international state system presupposed national economies, Cobban was right.

However, many contemporary minority nations, operating in the context of regional economic associations and the erosion of absolute sovereignty, do not aspire to this form of control over their economy. Most minority nationalists do not seek to resurrect the traditional sovereign nation-state on an even smaller scale, with complete national control over their economy. Many minority nationalists in Quebec and western Europe (Catalonia, Flanders, Scotland) are liberal democrats: they support access to a global economy and favour the regional associations that make this possible, as well as traditional liberal and democratic rights and the rule of law. They have supported increased liberalization of the economy, though with a concern that this is consistent with the reproduction of their culture and identity.

It is wrong, therefore, to associate minority nationalism with a backward-looking quest to realize the Westphalian sovereignty system. This is to saddle minority nationalists with the charge of being anachronistic and romantic, in the pejorative sense, which is quite against the evidence. Rather, minority nationalism can convincingly be seen as a particular response to the global restructuring of the economy. In some cases, nations which could not be viable under the traditional nation-state model, described by Cobban, have a role to play in the context of regional economic associations and military defence pacts. The context has changed the criteria of viability: after all, in what sense is Luxembourg 'viable'?

While critics have argued that the new context has affected the sovereignty and independence of states, and so made the very idea of state sovereignty questionable, one could claim, on the contrary, that the new context has opened up a new political space in which minority nations can operate. Minority nations are no longer as dependent on their host (multinational or binational) state, and are more dependent on international and continental regimes, like NAFTA or the EU, and the International Monetary Fund. Sovereignty is, indeed, being transformed into something quite different, but this does not mean the demise of minority nationalism. Rather, these developments have redefined national autonomy as a space in which nations, and especially small nations, can play off their various forms of dependency against one another.[7]

Moreover, there is a plausible case, mainly associated with Michael Keating's book *Nations against the State*, that smaller units like nations have advantages over larger nation-states.[8] This is partly because they have a higher degree of interaction and mutual trust, and this social consensus is necessary to manage change. Even more importantly, small nations, in part because of this high degree of social interaction, can adapt more quickly to changes in their environment, and are better positioned to promote local skills and resources, which is crucial to adapting to changes in the global environment.

In short, we may be moving beyond the traditional Wesphalian nation-state. International and continental regimes have replaced some of the functions of the traditional sovereign state. But this does not mean that minority nationalism is harking back to an ideal whose time has passed. Rather, this new context has opened up opportunities for political space that may permit new nationalism to flourish. Globalization has helped to give rise to a new context of both (*a*) international regimes and international cooperation in a global economy, and (*b*) local and regional forms of social solidarity to cope with these changes.

Misconception 2: Cultural Homogeneity will Solve the 'Problem' of Minority Nationalism

In this section I argue that the view that globalization will lead to a common cosmopolitan culture and the demise of minority nationalism is based on a misunderstanding of the relationship between national identity and 'objective' characteristics such as culture and language. The argument that globalization will lead to increased cultural homogeneity and that this will eventually erase the desire for institutions to protect and promote these distinct cultures assumes a 'snooker ball' view of nationality, according to which different nationalities have distinct cultures and languages.

The desire to base nationality on objective cultural characteristics is understandable, but it is almost certainly false. Indeed, it is often remarked by anthropologists, sociologists, and political scientists who study national conflicts that national (and ethnic) identities require some 'cultural marker', some mechanism for mutual recognition of members (and so implicitly a method for recognizing outsiders), but that these do not necessarily correlate with sharp linguistic or cultural differences.[9] Of course, in some cases, national identities do correspond to cultural differences, but, even then, it is not clear that the identities are *based* on the different cultures. Rather, the political or institutional structures that correspond to national identities, or the various mechanisms of boundary maintenance that groups employ, can be used to *reinforce* cultural homogeneity and so increase the extent to which the members of the group are different from outsiders. Whatever the precise relationship, the important point is that linguistic and cultural differences are not central to national identities because national identities can be mobilized along other lines.

This insight, while initially counter-intuitive, at least for people who like to ground distinct identities, and especially conflicts about identities, in some 'deeper', more objective characteristic, is confirmed when we think about some of the most violent conflicts between competing national (or ethnic) groups. If we compare Northern Ireland, Burundi, Rwanda, and the former Yugoslavia with Canada, Switzerland, Belgium, what is important about the first group is that here (*a*) the level of violence involved in the conflicts tends to be greater, and (*b*) the members of the antagonistic communities speak the same language and have broadly similar cultural values; whereas, in the latter group (*a*) relations between the communities are generally peaceful, and (*b*) the members of the communities speak different languages and exhibit deeper cultural differences. In other words, cultural differences do not correspond with the violence or intensity of the conflict.

This cultural similarity is often recognized by the groups themselves. For example, in Northern Ireland, where there are two distinct and mutually antagonistic national communities on the same territory, the conflict between the two groups is not about some objective cultural difference. Despite a common misconception, it is not religious in nature. The groups are not arguing over the details of doctrinal interpretation. Religious leaders—priests, nuns, ministers—are not targets for violence, as they were in the Reformation period, when conflict was genuinely religious.[10] Interestingly, anthropological studies reveal that the conflict is not perceived by the people as about cultural difference. A 1968 survey of cultural similarity in Northern Ireland revealed that 67 per cent of Protestants thought the Northern Irish of the opposite religion were the 'same as themselves', while only 29 per cent thought the same about the English. Similarly, 81 per cent of Catholics regarded Ulster Protestants as 'the same as themselves', but only 44 per cent thought this about southern Catholics.[11] Similar results have been found by Rosemary Harris, an anthropologist studying a rural community in Northern Ireland, who argued that, despite social segregation, there was a 'considerable area within which Catholics and Protestants shared a common culture'.[12]

Analysts of the conflicts in the former Yugoslavia, especially those who adhere to the elite-manipulation school of conflict analysis, almost universally emphasize the cultural similarities between the different groups.[13] Analysts begin the puzzle of explaining what happened in the former Yugoslavia by noting that, prior to the conflict, Serbs, Croats, and Muslims shared a common life, language, physical appearance, and a lot of history. The Muslims were among the most secularized Muslims anywhere in the world. One of the primary divisions was between urban and rural communities, which meant, in effect, that an urban Serb would have more in common with her urban Croat neighbour than with rural Serbs. In short, the groups themselves were culturally very similar; and cultural variation was as great *across* groups as within them.

There is a wonderful (for my purposes) dialogue between Michael Ignatieff and a Serb gunner in Croatia in 1995, which Ignatieff recounts. Ignatieff tells the gunner that he can't tell Serbs and Croats apart. At first, the gunner tells him that Croats and Serbs have nothing in common. Everything about them is different. Then, a few minutes later, he says: 'Look, here's how it is. Those Croats, they think they're better than us. Think they're fancy Europeans and everything. I'll tell you something. We're all just Balkan rubbish.'[14] Ignatieff uses the example to illustrate how the gunner's personal knowledge of these people as friends and neighbours ('we're just the same'), prior to the outbreak of the violence, conflicts with the political and ideological message of Serb leaders that Serbs and Croats are culturally distinct, antagonistic communities.

I don't wish to deny Ignatieff's point that the political leadership attempted to escalate the violence and divisions between the two communities for their own ends. Nevertheless, I think Ignatieff makes an additional point that warrants greater consideration, for it bears on the relationship between cultural differences and national identity. He points out that national divisions are not necessarily based on, and do not correspond to, deep cultural differences. If it is the case that national divisions are not necessarily based on different cultures, then it is wrong to infer from the cultural similarity of the groups that the national divisions are not genuine. And if national divisions are not based on cultural differences, then eroding cultural differences—making the groups more culturally similar—may not have any effect on the intensity of national divisions or national conflict.

The preceding discussion draws an implicit distinction between national identity and cultural difference. This also makes better sense of some of the examples discussed in this chapter. Buchanan offers an example of a native member of an unviable indigenous culture who is reluctant to adopt a more viable, western, capitalist culture. I would argue that the best way to understand this case is not in terms of culture, but in terms of identity. Many do seek to appropriate elements from other cultures in order to modernize, but what they don't want to give up is their identity as native. In the case of the person on the sinking lifeboat, one can imagine that it would be particularly problematic (dislocating) to be required to adopt the *identity* of the group that rammed and stole your boat in the first place, thus causing it to sink. Analogously, in the case of Northern Ireland, it would be particularly problematic to adopt the identity of the group that oppressed members of your group, and dispossessed your forefathers of their land; or, in the case of the former Yugoslavia, to adopt the identity of the group that engaged in large-scale slaughter against your people. None of this means that you blame the current people; but only that this identity is one that would be difficult for you to adopt, because your own identity is at least partly developed in relation to it.

I think Kymlicka was groping for something like the distinction that I am making here, between cultures and identities, in *Multicultural Citizenship*, but his own culturalist argument did not permit him to develop it adequately. Kymlicka argues, quite rightly, that during the Quiet Revolution French Quebec changed dramatically from a religious and rural society to a secular and urban one. He is at pains to emphasize that his argument does not involve a static and fossilized conception of culture: rather, it is natural for cultures to change as a result of the choices of their members. We must, therefore, 'distinguish the existence of a culture from its "character" at any given moment'.[15] However, the distinction between the existence of a culture and its character is not very clear or helpful. A much more useful distinction, which I think captures the relationship between a shared sense of nationality and changing culture, is that between a specific culture and the subjective sense of *identity*. The identity of people as Québécois (or Canadian) may not change, even while cultures do and can change, even quite dramatically. In the Quebec case, the identity did change, as more and more French Canadians living in Quebec have identified themselves as Québécois (rather than Canadian). This is not predicted by the direction of cultural change, for polling results have suggested that, at the same time, people living in Quebec are becoming more similar to other Canadians in terms of their norms and values.[16]

National identities, in contrast to cultures, are relatively intractable since they can remain the same even while cultures are changing, and perhaps becoming increasingly similar. This is why, as Walker Connor noted, and I cited earlier, assimilation is quite rare. Acculturation can and does occur, perhaps even frequently, but what is much rarer is assimilation in the sense that the identity of the group (as a distinct group) is given up and absorbed into the identity of a different group. This also means that the connection that proponents of globalization make—between (*a*) globalization and the attendant greater cultural homogeneity, and (*b*) the demise of minority nationalism—is quite tenuous. With globalization, there may indeed be greater cultural homogeneity, but this does not necessarily lead to a reduction in minority nationalism. All that is required for a national identity to persist is some marker to tell the groups apart (and this might be such a small thing that it comes down to the person's last name). To achieve the complete eradication of all signs of a distinct identity is extremely difficult, especially for a group that is living on its own territory and has the demographic strength to survive as a distinct community. Globalization may make the groups appear, to the outsider, more alike; but it will probably not have any bearing on the group identities that people have.

Misconception 3: The Ideal of a Cosmopolitan Culture

In this section I examine and critique the presupposed normative ideal which I call 'the ideal of a cosmopolitan culture'. This ideal has been articulated in some recent work in normative political philosophy, particularly by Jeremy Waldron and Allen Buchanan.[17] Their work suggests a cosmopolitan ideal which, they contend, is more attractive and philosophically defensible than nationalism. I argue that this ideal underlies a line of criticism of minority nationalism. I suggest in this section three reasons why this ideal should be questioned.

While this ideal is often referred to as 'cosmopolitanism' in the literature, it is only distantly related to the *political* ideal of a unified world government, or *cosmopolis*. In this context, the term 'cosmopolitanism' refers to a global culture, which is similar across the globe, and which transcends local and particularist forms of identity.

Jeremy Waldron contrasts the nationalist vision of the individual, as situated within a particular culture, sharing a heritage of custom and ritual, sharing a (real or imagined) history and sense of homeland, with that of a freewheeling cosmopolitan life, lived in a kaleidoscope of culture. He invokes several images of the cosmopolitan—migrants, frequent flyers, perpetual refugees (like Rousseau)—but, Waldron says, the distinctive characteristic of a cosmopolitan is 'his refusal to be defined by his location or his ancestry or his citizenship or his language'.[18] Waldron elaborates: 'Though he may live in San Francisco and be of Irish ancestry, he does not take his identity to be compromised when he learns Spanish, eats Chinese, wears clothing made in Korea, listens to arias by Verdi sung by a Maori princess on Japanese equipment, follows Ukrainian politics, and practices Buddhist meditation techniques.'[19] In Waldron's view, the existence of a cosmopolitan lifestyle demonstrates the falsity of the Herderian argument that humans *need* a secure cultural framework. 'It can no longer be said that all people *need* their rootedness in the particular culture in which they and their ancestors were reared in the way that they need food, clothing and shelter.'[20] While cultural fragments are necessary to the cosmopolitan lifestyle, there is no need for a *particular* culture to be politically protected. Thus, Waldron questions the liberal-nationalist view that the state can legitimately express a particular national identity, and the nationalist argument with respect to self-determination.

Buchanan makes the same point about human needs for particular cultures, although in the context of an indigenous culture faced with a modern technological culture. He notes the possibility that members of an unviable, traditional culture 'can leave the sinking ship of one culture and board another, more seaworthy vessel'.[21] He suggests that those people who seek to try to preserve their culture by demanding political self-government or political rights within a state are 'like people who refuse to be rescued from their sinking lifeboat because it is *their* craft and because any other vessel seems alien and untrustworthy to them. Indeed, they demand that we provide them with timbers and pumps (special group rights, greater autonomy, and/or other resources) to shore up what we have every reason to believe is a doomed vessel.'[22] In this passage Buchanan ignores the fact that in many cases the reason people demand timbers and pumps is in part because they have had their boats smashed and stolen.[23] He also suggests, like Waldron, that, while some cultural structure is necessary as a context to make choices, as a good from which people choose, no particular cultural structure is necessary, and certainly no homogeneous cultural structure is necessary. Using the state to defend a particular culture that is not viable in the cultural marketplace of ideas is therefore irrational and indefensible. By contrast, cosmopolitanism, conceived here as a *mélange* of cultural elements, is more compatible with liberalism, because it is consistent with the liberal ideal that governments should be neutral with respect to individuals. Cosmopolitanism is attractive, in part, because it suggests a way in which it is possible to be neutral on issues of culture: specifically, government neutrality is possible when the public sphere is comprised of a *mélange* of cultural fragments, but no particular culture is supported.

There are three normative problems with this ideal, which I will discuss in turn. The first issue concerns whether the cosmopolitan culture is simply Americanism writ large. This is part of the case that Benjamin Barber has made in his book *Jihad v. McWorld*.[24] There he claims that what passes for global culture is really the ethos of consumerism, which is fuelled by the expansionist imperatives of large American corporations. This objection to cosmopolitanism presses on the genuine cosmopolitan (and neutral) character of the global culture. It identifies the so-called 'global culture' with the powerful engine of international capitalism. Cosmopolitan culture, on this argument, is merely a 'mask' for the predominance of American (or, at the least Western, individualistic) culture, and not truly a *mélange* of different traditions.

Now, it is clear that the crude version of this argument cannot be right. There is obviously much fruitful cultural interchange, and a global culture may involve much intermixing in artistic styles and food preferences and music from different parts of the globe. Our present cosmopolitan culture, to the extent that we have one, does not simply involve the proliferation of McDonalds and Burger Kings, but can also lead to Thai restaurants becoming fashionable and Indian curry houses displacing the traditional British fare of fish and chips in the United Kingdom.

This does not mean, however, that the marketplace of cultural ideas and norms and practices is operated on a level playing-field. Global capitalism tends to favour those cultures that operate in technologically advanced economies; and some languages and cultural narratives and practices will be disadvantaged in relation to other cultures. Thai restaurants may proliferate globally as well as McDonalds, but it will be hard for Thai movies to compete with Disney, given the tight hold that some companies have on the global distribution of films.[25] Because the various cultures of the world do not compete on a level playing-field, state action in support of minority cultures can be justified in terms of an appeal to equality or fairness. Indeed, this appeal is at the heart of most arguments for state action in defence of minority nations.[26]

Secondly, this argument works by presupposing the very limiting, and almost certainly false, assumption that cultures are based on ethnic descent.[27] Waldron, for example, thinks that an Irish American who eats Chinese food and listens to Italian opera is 'living in a kaleidoscope of cultures', when in fact it is clear that the person is merely utilizing the diverse opportunities afforded to her in her own culture. Most minority nations, especially those with strong liberal-democratic traditions, such as Quebec, Catalonia, and Scotland, do not try to use the state to 'purify' their culture from all 'external' influences. At most, they simply attempt to protect certain elements of their culture, such as their language, or certain industries that are central to the reproduction of culture (such as literature and film), from overwhelming foreign domination. They seek a democratic mandate to gain greater control over the shape of their society, the very conditions in which they exist, and to use this to negotiate the terms on which they engage with global forces. This is quite different from the caricature drawn by Waldron and Buchanan, in which nationalism is identified with a kind of ethnic purist isolationism. This caricature ignores the extent to which minority nations embrace the basic tenets of liberalism and democracy and the rules of the global marketplace. They merely intend to do so in a way that protects, at the same time, the reproduction of their identity as Scots or Québécois or Catalans.

This brings us to the third problem with this kind of argument. This is the terms of the debate in which cosmopolitanism is conceived. Both Buchanan and Waldron focus on the fact that a cosmopolitan identity is possible. They may indeed be right that this is possible. But there are two distinct questions here. One is the issue of existential identity and whether nationalism is an attractive way of life. This is part of the case that Waldron makes, and the vision he paints of a freewheeling, jet-setting, culturally eclectic way of life does have its attractions (particularly to an academic audience). The other issue, and the one that most liberal-nationalists are dealing with, is not that of which way of life is existentially attractive, as a way of life, but rather what is the appropriate response to the fact that many people do have national identities and attachments. This second question takes it as an empirical given that national identity is important for most people, in conditions of modernity. Cosmopolitanism is a possibility, but most liberal nationalists will claim that it is of limited sociological significance. What is more common, of course, is the case of someone who has lived in two cultures or two societies and feels allegiances and identities to both, such as the person who feels both Polish and American, speaks Polish and English, occasionally returns to Poland for a visit (or longs to, depending on financial considerations) but has made her home in America, and also feels American. This is not the same as the rootless cosmopolitan who has no national identity and no national attachments whatsoever.

Once we distinguish between these two types of questions it becomes clear that the real issue is not whether having a particular national identity is rational or defensible or justifiable, but whether it is rational, justifiable, defensible to expect people to *give up* their national identity. Indeed, it may be the case that once one has a particular national identity, associated with a particular culture or language or way of life, it is not rational to give it up. Ernest Gellner makes this point well, arguing that, in conditions of modernity—where the imperatives of industrialization lead to increased standardization and homogenization, the introduction of mass elementary schooling, and standard modes of interaction—cultural definitions of identity, such as the language one speaks, one's education and modes of interaction, and other cultural attributes, assume a new importance.[28] To compare the person who refuses to give up her culture because it is hers with the person who refuses to board another life-raft is to underestimate seriously the importance and value of national and cultural identity to most people. It suggests that people consider their interests apart from their national identity, when in fact their sense of nationhood is an important constitutive part of their identity, and what counts as an *interest* crucially depends on their conception of who they are (their identity).[29]

Conclusion

Thus far I have identified three problems with the normative ideal of a cosmopolitan culture, which I think justify us in viewing its normative underpinnings as based on a misconception. I have argued, first, that the ideal of cosmopolitan culture is not genuinely global and neutral; secondly, that proponents of cosmopolitanism falsely identify minority nationalism with exclusivist ethnic isolation; and thirdly, that this ideal fails to meet the requirement of minimal realism, in treating the important question of what we do with the national allegiances and identities that people have. I think these three concerns together should raise doubts about the cosmopolitan ideal, at least as it is put forward by its contemporary proponents in normative theory.

In this chapter, I have argued against a dominant critical view of minority nationalism. On this view, globalization is making possible the realization of the ideal of a 'cosmopolitan culture'. Minority nationalism is compared unfavourably with cosmopolitanism: it is viewed as anachronistic and less attractive than the cosmopolitan ideal.

This line of argument involves three interrelated arguments: first, that nationalism is anachronistic in the context of global capitalism; secondly, that acculturation will lead to the demise of minority nationalism; and thirdly, that national forms of identification are less ideal than the promotion of a global cosmopolitan culture.

Each of these arguments is seriously flawed. First, I argue that there is strong evidence that minority nationalism is even more relevant in the global economic era, for it opens up more political space for smaller nations and these are adaptable to changes in the global economic environment. Secondly, even if globalization does lead to increased cultural homogeneity, I argue that this does not necessarily mean that minority nationalism will be eroded. The second line of criticism is based, I argue, on a false 'snooker ball' view of nationality, according to which different nationalities have distinct cultures and languages. Finally, I question the normative ideal of a cosmopolitan global culture. I argue that it is not genuinely global and neutral, and involves a false and unrealistic view of minority nationalism.

This critique of the view that the demise of minority nationalism is inevitable, either because of globalization or because of an increasingly standardized culture, has implications for how we should regard nationalism. If nationalism, and national forms of identity, are not likely to wither away (as I have argued) and if coercive assimilation is normatively unacceptable as well as unproductive (as I have argued), then it follows that we must learn to live with national identities, to recognize them and accommodate them.

I have also tried to suggest that this accommodation should not be regarded simply as a realistic assessment of the limitations of state-building and the stubbornness of human particularist attachments. Rather, national forms of identity can coexist with universal ideals such as liberalism and democracy. While I have not argued for that position directly, I have tried to clear away some of the misunderstandings that attach to minority nationalism and the caricature of minority nationalists as ethnic purist isolationists. Minority nations, like many majority nations, often embrace the basic tenets of liberalism and democracy and the rules of the global marketplace. Nationalism (at least of the liberal-democratic variety) is consistent with, indeed functional to, the global economic environment. It is also an important basis from which individuals can be cosmopolitans at least in the sense of appreciating and experimenting with other modes of living (without necessarily changing their identities) and availing themselves of at least some of the opportunities afforded by the global economy.

I have not discussed here the kind of recognition or accommodation that is required, or the extent to which the new world order might facilitate more imaginative institutional arrangements, especially in cases where two national groups are co-mingled on the same territory. There is a range of factors that should be taken into account, on a case-by-case basis, in deciding what kind of recognition is appropriate. These include: the nature of the minority; the nature of their identity (for example, whether nested or not); and whether or not they are territorially concentrated. These are important in order to judge the form that recognition should take—whether secession, or devolved power in a federation, or other forms of non-territorial autonomy for national minorities are desired and appropriate. Recognition may, of course, be withheld, but, if the arguments of this chapter are valid, we should not expect that national identities will then simply wither away, or that minority nations will voluntary assimilate into the majority group.

NOTES

I would like to thank Michael Keating, John McGarry, and the participants at the Conference on Minority Nationalism and the State, University of Western Ontario, Nov. 1997, for their helpful comments on the ideas contained in this chapter. I am also grateful to the Social Sciences and Humanities Research Council of Canada for research funding and Patti Lenard for research help.

1. This interpretation of Marx's thought is found in W. Connor, *The National Question in Marxist–Leninist Theory and Strategy* (Princeton: Princeton University Press, 1984), 7–8. For a different interpretation, see E. Benner, *Really Existing Nationalisms: A Post-Communist View from Marx and Engels* (Oxford: Clarendon Press, 1995).
2. See T. Schereth, *The Cosmopolitan Ideal in Enlightenment Thought* (Notre Dame, Ind.: University of Notre Dame Press, 1977).
3. Allen Buchanan also makes the link between political legitimacy and the anti-apartheid movement. See A. Buchanan, 'Democracy and Secession', in M. Moore (ed.), *National Self-Determination and Secession* (Oxford: Oxford University Press, 1998). See also T. M. Franck, 'The Emerging Right to Democratic Governance', *American Journal of International Law*, 86 (1992), 46–91.
4. A. C. Arend and R. Beck, *International Law and the Use of Force: Beyond the U.N. Charter* (New York: Routledge, 1993); D. Philpott, 'Self-Determination in Practice', in Moore (ed.), *National Self-Determination and Secession*.
5. M. Keating, *Nations against the State: The New Politics of Nationalism in Quebec, Catalonia and Scotland* (London: MacMillan, 1996), 30–3; E. Weber, *Peasants into Frenchmen: The Modernisation of Rural France, 1870–1914* (London: Routledge & Kegan Paul, 1979).
6. A. Cobban, *National Self-Determination* (Oxford: Oxford University Press, 1945), 157–66.
7. Keating, *Nations against the State*, 62–4.
8. Ibid., 52–8.
9. W. Connor, *Ethnonationalism: The Quest for Understanding* (Princeton: Princeton University Press, 1994), 32–6; T. H. Eriksen, *Ethnicity and Nationalism: Anthropological Perspectives* (London: Pluto Press, 1993), 38–46; D. Horowitz, *Ethnic Groups in Conflict* (Berkeley: University of California Press, 1985), 36–54.
10. J. McGarry and B. O'Leary, *Explaining Northern Ireland* (Oxford: Blackwell, 1995), 171–213.

11. R. Rose, *Governing without Consensus: An Irish Perspective* (London: Faber, 1971), 218.
12. R. Harris, *Prejudice and Tolerance in Ulster* (Manchester: Manchester University Press, 1972), 131.
13. M. Ignatieff, 'Nationalism and the Narcissism of Minor Differences', *Queen's Quarterly*, 102/1 (1995), 13; P. Mojzes, *Yugoslavian Inferno* (New York: Continuum Press, 1995), xvi; N. Malcolm, *Bosnia: A Short History* (New York: New York University Press, 1994), 282; C. Bennett, *Yugoslavia's Bloody Collapse: Causes, Course and Consequences* (New York: New York University Press, 1995), 247.
14. Ignatieff, 'Nationalism and the Narcissism of Minor Differences', 13–14.
15. W. Kymlicka, *Multicultural Citizenship* (Oxford: Oxford University Press, 1995), 104.
16. W. Norman, 'The Ideology of Shared Values', in J. Carens (ed.), *Is Quebec Nationalism Just?* (Montreal: McGill–Queen's University Press, 1995).
17. J. Waldron, 'The Cosmopolitan Alternative', and A. Buchanan, 'The Morality of Secession', both in W. Kymlicka (ed.), *The Rights of Minority Cultures* (Oxford: Oxford University Press, 1995).
18. Waldron, 'The Cosmopolitan Alternative', 95.
19. Ibid.
20. Ibid., 100.
21. Buchanan, 'The Morality of Secession', 357.
22. Ibid., 357–8.
23. I am grateful to Brendan O'Leary for pointing this out to me.
24. B. Barber, *Jihad vs. McWorld* (New York: Ballantyne, 1995). Barber is not an exponent of either cosmopolitanism or minority nationalism. His basic argument is that there is an important dialectic between globalization and what he calls 'tribalism'. The argument for this relationship is 'supported' mainly by recounting how the forces of tribalism (e.g. Serb gunners) are frequently clad in Adidas running-shoes and Nike shirts and know all about Michael Jordan. These connections are not rigorously argued for. He does, however, provide a good argument for the American, consumerist bias of much of what is termed globalization.
25. See Barber, *Jihad vs. McWorld*, 137–51.
26. An appeal to equality is implicit in Will Kymlicka's argument for minority rights in *Liberalism, Community and Culture* (Oxford: Clarendon Press, 1989) and *Multicultural Citizenship*.
27. I owe this point to Kymlicka, *Multicultural Citizenship*, 85.
28. E. Gellner's basic argument about the role and significance of culture under conditions of modernity is elaborated in *Nations and Nationalism* (Ithaca, NY: Cornell University Press, 1983) and *Plough, Sword, Book: The Structure of Human History* (London: Collins Harvill, 1988).
29. See C. Calhoun, 'The Problem of Identity in Collective Action', in J. Huber (ed.), *Macro–Micro Linkages in Sociology* (Newbury Park, Calif.: Sage, 1991).

CHAPTER 4

Immigrant Integration and Minority Nationalism

Will Kymlicka

Virtually every recent discussion of minority nationalism has begun by emphasizing that its survival and resurgence was not predicted by theorists of modernization and globalization. Globalization was supposed to extinguish minority national identities, to be replaced either by a supranational cosmopolitan identity, or by a post-national civic or constitutional identity. This prediction has been proven clearly wrong. Most minority nationalisms are as strong now as ever before, and show no sign of losing steam. Indeed, minority nationalism is today a truly global phenomenon, found in every corner of the globe. As Walker Connor puts it, powerful minority nationalisms can be found:

in Africa (for example, Ethiopia), Asia (Sri Lanka), Eastern Europe (Romania), Western Europe (France), North America (Guatemala), South America (Guyana), and Oceania (New Zealand). The list includes countries that are old (United Kingdom) as well as new (Bangladesh), large (Indonesia) as well as small (Fiji), rich (Canada) as well as poor (Pakistan), authoritarian (Sudan) as well as democratic (Belgium), Marxist–Leninist (China) as well as militantly anti-Marxist (Turkey). The list also includes countries which are Buddhist (Burma), Christian (Spain), Moslem (Iran), Hindu (India), and Judaic (Israel).[1]

There are still those who deny that minority nationalism is compatible with modernity, and who view these manifestations of minority nationalism as the last gasp of pre-modern values, fighting a defensive rearguard action against the inevitable forces of globalization. But it is increasingly realized, I think, that minority nationalism has survived and thrived because it has proven able to adapt itself to modernity, and to accommodate and satisfy modern needs and aspirations. Indeed, minority nationalism has proven to be an effective vehicle by which national groups can modernize their societies, and participate more actively in the global economy and in the increasingly dense networks of international law and civil society.

To be sure, globalization does raise many new challenges for minority nationalism, and my chapter will focus on one of these: the impact of immigration. Discussions of globalization typically focus on the dramatic increase in the global movement of goods and capital, and perhaps also on the global circulation of ideas. But a less noted aspect of globalization is the movement of people, particularly the significant increase in the numbers of economic migrants. This has indeed been called the 'age of migration', as people from poorer countries, or from rural areas within a country, migrate to the burgeoning cities in the West which are the nexus of the global economy.[2] And some of these cities are located in the heartland of national minorities: Montreal (Quebec), Barcelona (Catalonia), Bilbao (Basque Country), Glasgow (Scotland), Brussels (Flanders), Geneva (French-speaking Switzerland). Some of these cities have been magnets for immigrants for decades; others are only recently seeing significant numbers of immigrants. But immigration is becoming an increasingly important reality of the major cities within the territory of national minorities.

How does the presence of these immigrants affect minority nationalist movements? Surprisingly, there has been relatively little written on this topic. There has been a great deal of discussion of both minority nationalism and immigration in recent years. However, these two topics have generally been discussed in isolation from each other; the interaction between them has received much less attention.

Since both minority nationalism and immigration challenge the traditional model of a culturally homogeneous 'nation-state', they are often treated as complementary but separate processes of deconstructing the nation-state. In reality, however, they are often intimately connected, and not always in complementary ways.

Consider typical cases of minority nationalism in the West: Catalans, Basques, Puerto Ricans, Scots, Québécois, Flemish. Each of these groups sees itself as a distinct and self-governing nation within a larger state, and has mobilized along nationalist lines to demand greater regional self-government and national recognition. However, the movement of significant numbers of immigrants into the minority's region is affecting the sort of national identity, and nationalist mobilization, that is feasible and/or desirable. Many minority nationalists have seen these changes as regrettable, and have viewed immigrants as a threat, rather than potential benefit, to the national minority.

Immigration, therefore, is not only a challenge to traditional models of the nation-state; it is also a challenge to the self-conceptions and political aspirations of those groups which see themselves as distinct and self-governing nations within a larger state. Indeed, some commentators insist that all forms of minority nationalism are by definition 'ethnic' or exclusionary, and hence inherently antagonistic to immigrants.

My chapter will offer a more nuanced view of the relationship between immigration and minority nationalism. I will attempt to outline some of the issues which arise when immigrants settle in areas of a country dominated by a national minority. When are the claims of immigrants in conflict with the aspirations of national minorities, and when are they compatible or even mutually reinforcing? Since my background is in political theory, my main interest is in exploring the normative issues raised by this coexistence of immigration and minority nationalism. That is, I am interested not only in how the claims of immigrants and national minorities relate to each other, but also in how they relate to the underlying principles of liberal democracy, such as individual freedom, social equality, and democracy. Which sorts of accommodations or settlements amongst immigrants and national minorities are most consistent with liberal-democratic norms of justice and freedom, and which settlements would be unjust and in violation of liberal-democratic norms?

I will begin by outlining some recent work by liberal political theorists on the importance of accommodating ethnocultural diversity. A growing number of liberal theorists defend both the claims of national minorities to self-government, and the claims of immigrant groups for greater accommodation of their ethnocultural identities and practices. However, as I noted, relatively little has been written discussing the potential conflict between these two sorts of claim. Yet these claims can and often do come into conflict: indeed, immigration of any sort has typically been seen as a threat to minority nationalism. Some commentators argue that this conflict is inherent and intractable, since minority nationalisms are by definition forms of 'ethnic nationalism' that are ethnically exclusive. I will argue that this view is empirically inaccurate regarding many minority nationalisms within the West, and rests on a misunderstanding of the nature of minority nationalism. Many minority nationalisms today welcome immigrants, and allow them to maintain and express their ethnic identity, while simultaneously encouraging their integration into the minority nation. Some

minority nationalisms, in short, are as 'civic' or 'post-ethnic' as majority nationalisms. However, the likelihood that a national minority will
adopt such a post-ethnic model of minority nationalism seems to
depend on a number of factors. In particular, it may require a range of
policies (e.g. regarding language, education, and employment) that
give the minority some control over the process of immigrant integration, and that establish or protect the pre-eminence of the minority's
language on its historic territory. And this creates a potential dilemma,
for these linguistic and educational policies may be quite illiberal. The
very policies which make a post-ethnic form of minority nationalism
possible may themselves be inconsistent with liberal norms and values.
If so, is it permissible to adopt illiberal policies in order to create the
conditions under which civic forms of minority nationalism can
emerge? I conclude with some tentative reflections on this question,
but do not offer any definitive answers.

Liberal Culturalism: An Emerging Consensus?

The philosophical debate on the accommodation of ethnocultural
diversity is relatively new. Indeed, for most of this century issues of
ethnicity have been seen as marginal by political theorists. Much the
same can be said of other academic disciplines, from sociology to
geography to history. Today, however, after decades of relative neglect,
the question of rights of ethnocultural minorities has moved to the
forefront of political theory. For example, the last few years have wit-
nessed the first philosophical books in English on the normative issues
involved in secession, nationalism, immigration, multiculturalism, and
indigenous rights.[3]

While this debate is relatively new, I think we can already detect an
emerging consensus in the literature. First, there seems to be growing
acceptance of the principle that national minorities are entitled to
some form of distinctive political status, including territorial self-
government where that is feasible. Territorially concentrated groups
that were involuntarily incorporated into the state should not be
forced to adopt the majority's national identity, but should have the
rights and powers needed to sustain themselves as distinct national
societies within the larger state. If groups like the Québécois, Catalans,
Flemish, or Scots see themselves as distinct nations within the larger
state, then their national distinctiveness should be recognized in public life and public symbols, through such things as official-language
status, self-government rights, and recognition of their distinct legal

traditions. In accepting the legitimacy of these minority nationalisms, liberal nationalists reject the goal of a world of homogeneous nation-states, and accept the necessity and legitimacy of 'multi-nation' states within which two or more self-governing nations are able to coexist.

This is part of a broader movement that seeks to reconcile liberalism and nationalism. According to defenders of liberal nationalism, it is a legitimate function of the state to protect and promote the national cultures and languages of the nations within its borders: both the majority nation and the minority nations. This can be done by creating public institutions that operate in these national languages; using national symbols in public life (e.g. flags, anthems, public holidays); and allowing self-government for national groups on issues that are crucial to the reproduction of their language and culture (e.g. schemes of federalism or constitutionalism to enable national minorities to exercise self-government).[4]

In addition to these nations, there are also many types of non-national cultural groups that seek recognition and accommodation, such as immigrant and refugee groups, religious minorities, or even non-ethnic cultural groups like gays or the disabled. Unlike nations, these groups do not typically seek to form separate and self-governing societies, but rather seek greater accommodation within the mainstream society. And this leads us to a second area of possible convergence in the recent literature—namely, on ideas of liberal multiculturalism.[5] Liberal multiculturalism accepts that such groups have a valid claim, not only to tolerance and non-discrimination, but also to explicit accommodation, recognition, and representation within the institutions of the larger society. Multiculturalism may take the form of revising the educational curriculum to include the history and culture of minority groups; creating advisory boards to consult with the members of minority groups; recognizing the holy days of minority religious groups; teaching police officers, social workers, and health care professionals to be sensitive to cultural differences in their work; developing regulations to ensure that minority groups are not ignored or stereotyped in the media; and so on.

In order to qualify as *liberal* forms of nationalism or multiculturalism, certain conditions must be met: membership of ethnocultural groups must not be imposed by the state, but rather should be a matter of self-identity; individual members must be free to question and reject any inherited or previously adopted ethnocultural identity, if they so choose, and have an effective right of exit from any identity group; these groups must not violate the basic civil or political rights of their members; and accommodations for national minorities and immigrant groups must seek to reduce inequalities in power between groups, rather than allowing one group to exercise dominance over other groups.

We can describe both liberal nationalism and liberal multiculturalism as forms of 'liberal culturalism'. Liberal culturalism is the view that liberal-democratic states should not only uphold the familiar set of common civil and political rights of citizenship that are protected in all liberal democracies; they must also adopt various group-specific rights or policies that are intended to recognize and accommodate the distinctive identities and needs of ethnocultural groups. Such policies range from multicultural education policies to language rights to guarantees of political representation to constitutional protections of treaties with indigenous peoples.[6] For liberal culturalists, these various forms of group-specific measures are often required for ethnocultural justice, although to be consistent with liberal culturalism they must meet a number of conditions, like those listed above.[7]

Liberal culturalism has arguably become the dominant position in the political theory literature today, and most debates are about how to develop and refine the liberal-culturalist position, rather than whether to accept it in the first place.

The Conflict between Immigrant Multiculturalism and Minority Nationalism

So both minority nationalism and immigrant multiculturalism can be seen as part of a larger movement towards liberal culturalism. And because both challenge the traditional model of a culturally homogeneous 'nation-state', they are often seen as allies, at least at the level of theory. They are both participants in the new politics of identity, both fighting to expand the room within which citizens can express their identities and diversities, and so share a commitment to principles of pluralism and the recognition of difference.

However, on the ground, the relation between the two is much more complicated. As I noted earlier, the forces of globalization have meant that many multi-nation states have experienced significant levels of immigration into the homeland of a national minority (e.g. Quebec, Flanders, Catalonia, Basque Country, Scotland). This has raised the question of whether minority nationalisms can accommodate immigrant multiculturalism. Are national minorities capable of including immigrants in their self-conception, and thereby becoming themselves 'multicultural'?

At first glance, the answer seems to be 'no'. The relation between national minorities and immigrants has historically been fraught with tension. Large-scale immigration has typically been seen as a threat to national minorities. For one thing, there is a strong temptation for immigrants to integrate into the dominant culture (which usually offers greater mobility and economic opportunities). Many immigrants to Quebec, for example, would opt to learn English rather than French, if given the choice. (This was certainly the historical pattern, until the Quebec government made it more difficult for immigrants to choose English.) And if immigrants in a multi-nation state integrate into the majority group, the national minority will become increasingly outnumbered and so increasingly powerless in political life. Moreover, states have often deliberately encouraged immigrants (or migrants from other parts of the country) to settle in lands traditionally held by national minorities, as a way of swamping and disempowering them, reducing them to a minority even within their historic territory. (Consider the fate of Indian tribes and Chicanos in the American south-west.)

Moreover, the fact that immigrants seem able and willing to integrate into the dominant society is often used as grounds for insisting that national minorities also integrate. If immigrants can successfully integrate, the majority often asks, why not national minorities? If immigrants are satisfied with modest forms of multicultural accommodations within the larger society, rather than seeking self-government in order to maintain themselves as separate and distinct societies, why not national minorities?

In addition, immigrants are unlikely to understand or share the mentality of *la survivance* which national minorities typically have developed in their many years (or centuries) of struggle to maintain their distinct language, culture, and political autonomy. So even if immigrants do learn the minority's language and integrate into the minority's society, they are still unlikely to support nationalist mobilizations. They may join the minority nation, but they are unlikely to become minority nationalists.[8]

For these and other reasons, there has been a pronounced tendency for national minorities to adopt a defensive and exclusionary attitude towards immigrants. As a result, minority nationalisms have often taken the form of 'ethnic' nationalisms that privilege bonds of blood and descent, that are deeply xenophobic and often racist, and that seek to exclude immigrants.

Given this history, the idea that minority nationalism and immigrant multiculturalism are allies in the pursuit of a more pluralist or tolerant form of cultural politics seems odd. Rather than challenging or decentring pretensions of national homogeneity, minority nationalism seems, if anything, to be a reversion to a pre-modern, illiberal form of nationalism, even less tolerant of diversity than the sort of nationalism and national identity promoted by Western states.

This connection between minority nationalism and ethnic nationalism is so strong that many commentators view minority nationalism as *inherently* based on ethnic exclusiveness, and as inherently opposed to 'civic' nationalisms based on shared political principles. For example, Thomas Franck argues that minority nationalisms are forms of 'romantic tribal nationalism', which he describes as a kind of virus or 'craze' which has infected national minorities in many parts of the world. He sharply distinguishes this romantic tribal nationalism from an earlier form of nationalism, typified by American and French revolutionary nationalism, that was based, not on common blood or culture, but on political principles, particularly principles of freedom and equality. Whereas romantic tribal nationalism is an illiberal, exclusive, and defensive reaction to modernity, the American–French form of nationalism is liberal, inclusive, and forward-looking.[9]

Similarly, David Hollinger distinguishes two kinds of multiculturalism: an illiberal 'pluralist' model, typified by minority nationalisms, that assigns people to groups on the basis of blood or descent, and which treats groups as permanent and enduring, and as the subject of group rights; and a liberal 'cosmopolitan' or 'post-ethnic' model, typified by multiculturalism in the United States, that accepts shifting group boundaries, multiple and hybrid identities, and which is based on voluntary affiliations and individual rights. He describes Québécois nationalism and other 'ethnic nationalisms' as the extreme form of 'pluralist' multiculturalism, which he says is based on the same logic as racial segregation.[10]

To take one more example, consider Michael Ignatieff's discussion of the distinction between 'ethnic' and 'civic' nationalism. According to Ignatieff, 'ethnic' nations, like Germany, define membership in terms of shared descent, so that people of a different racial or ethnic group (e.g. Turkish guest-workers in Germany) cannot acquire citizenship no matter how long they live in the country. 'Civic' nations, like the United States, are based, not on descent or culture, but on allegiance to certain political principles of democracy and freedom, and are in principle open to anyone who lives in the territory. Ignatieff argues that only civic nationalism is compatible with liberalism, democracy, and peace.[11]

This civic–ethnic distinction is a familiar one, of course, and there is a well-established debate about whether German nationalism is civic or ethnic. What is striking, however, is that Ignatieff, like Franck and Hollinger, automatically assumes that minority nationalisms are 'ethnic' nationalisms: that is, based on blood and descent. They differ about which majority nationalisms fall into the civic or ethnic category, but they all agree that minority nationalisms fall into the ethnic–racialist category.

For all of these authors, then, minority nationalism is an obstacle, not an ally, in the quest for a more tolerant and inclusive form of political community. It is not a partner with immigrants in the building of new forms of post-ethnic or post-national democracy, but rather is fighting a rearguard action to maintain an outdated form of ethnic nationhood.

Can they be Reconciled?

This equation of minority nationalism and ethnic nationalism is understandable given the historical tensions mentioned earlier. But the assumption that minority nationalisms are inherently ethnic nationalisms is, I think, mistaken, and increasingly inadequate as an account of minority nationalisms in the West.

Consider Quebec. According to Franck, contemporary minority nationalisms exhibit a xenophobic desire to exclude those who are different. In reality, Quebec has a very proactive immigration policy: its per capita immigration is roughly the same as that of the United States. Control over immigration is one of the powers Quebec nationalists have sought and gained, and the province administers its own immigration programme, actively recruiting immigrants, most of whom are non-white. It seeks immigrants from all over the world as a way of building what it calls its 'distinct society'. Quebec knows that, due to declining birth rates and an ageing population, it needs immigrants in order to succeed as a modern society. The Quebec government encourages immigrants to learn French, of course, just as the American government encourages immigrants to learn English. If they do learn French, they are seen as full members of Quebec society.[12]

To be sure, the issue of whether or how to integrate immigrants was a contentious one in Quebec for many years. But the approach it has developed since the 1970s—known as 'interculturalism'—is similar to the multiculturalism policy in many Western states: it seeks to affirm and accommodate ethnocultural identities and practices within common institutions, subject to three important principles:

- recognition of French as the language of public life;

- respect for liberal democratic values, including civil and political rights and equality of opportunity; and
- respect for pluralism, including openness to and tolerance of others' differences.

These three principles form the bedrock of the 'moral contract' between Quebec and immigrants that specify the terms of integration.[13] These principles are virtually identical to the principles underlying the Australian multiculturalism policy, which is widely (and rightly) seen as one of the most successful models of immigrant multiculturalism in the world.[14]

Under this approach, immigrants are not only granted citizenship under relatively easy terms, but are encouraged by Quebec's own 'interculturalism' policy to interact with the members of other ethnic groups, to share their cultural heritage, and to participate in common public institutions. The result is just the sort of fluid 'cosmopolitan' multiculturalism within Quebec that Hollinger endorses. (Indeed, the level of acceptance of interracial marriage is considerably higher in Quebec than in the United States.) Far from trying to preserve some sort of racial purity, Quebec nationalists are actively seeking people of other races and faiths to come and join them, integrate with them, inter-marry with them, and jointly help build a modern, pluralistic, distinct society in Quebec.

Quebec is not unique in this. Consider Catalonia. It has had a very high in-migration rate, mainly from other regions in Spain. These immigrants have been welcomed and accepted as members of the Catalan society, and are seen as a vital part of the project of Catalan *renaixença*. It is too early to tell how well the more recent immigrants from North Africa, who (unlike migrants from the rest of Spain) are neither European nor Catholic, will integrate. But it is certainly the official policy of the Catalan government to promote the integration of all residents, whatever their religion or skin colour, and this non-racialist conception of nationhood is backed by popular opinion.[15]

Or consider Scotland. It has not had the same level of in-migration as Quebec or Catalonia, but here too a non-racialist conception of nationhood is firmly entrenched both in the platform of the main nationalist party (the Scottish National Party) and in popular opinion. Migrants from elsewhere in Britain have integrated well, and it is accepted that the more recent immigrants from Asia and Africa must also be accepted as 'Scots'.

Or consider Puerto Rico. It has had relatively few immigrants in the past, but now receives an increasing number of people from the Caribbean. For most of these immigrants, Puerto Rico is initially seen as a stepping-stone to the continental United States, but some stay and integrate into Puerto Rican society. The idea of a non-racialist nation is, in this case, quite natural, since Puerto Rican society (unlike mainland United States) has always been a self-consciously mestizo society with high levels of inter-marriage between white settlers, blacks, and Indians.[16]

All of these minority nationalisms are firmly post-ethnic in Hollinger's sense. To be sure, not all minority nationalisms are post-ethnic: racialism remains a stronger force in both Basque and Flemish nationalism. In these cases, there is an ongoing struggle between a liberal–inclusive conception of nationhood and the racialist–exclusive conception, and this struggle is reflected both within the nationalist political parties and in popular opinion. The liberal–inclusive conception, though a strong force in both Flemish and Basque nationalism, is not yet hegemonic, the way it has become in Quebec, Catalonia, and Scotland. We can find similar struggles between liberal–inclusive and racialist–exclusive conceptions in many cases of nationalist mobilization amongst indigenous peoples.[17] In short, the extent to which a particular form of minority nationalism is ethnic–racialist or post-ethnic–civic can only be determined by examining the facts, not by conceptual fiat or armchair speculation. And the clear trend throughout most Western democracies is towards a more open and non-racial definition of minority nationalism. In the case of Quebec, for example, the overwhelming majority of Quebeckers forty years ago believed that to be a true 'Québécois' one had to be descended from the original French settlers; today, fewer than 20 per cent accept this view.[18]

This is a dramatic change in the nature of Québécois identity, which has indeed incorporated immigrants into its self-conception, and turned itself into a post-ethnic, multicultural nation. And this openness is recognized by immigrants, who are now much more inclined to integrate into Québécois society. For example, whereas the overwhelming majority of second-generation immigrants in Quebec used to become anglophones, now most think of themselves as 'Québécois', and speak French at home. Unfortunately, this change has not yet been recognized by most theorists of nationalism: indeed, it has been rendered invisible by the assumption that minority nationalisms are inherently ethnic nationalisms.

Why has this shift towards a post-ethnic form of minority nationalism occurred? For essentially the same reasons it has occurred within majority nations. Like majority nations, national minorities often need immigrants to fill economic niches, or to counter-balance negative demographic trends (that is, an ageing population and declining birth rate). Moreover, it has become clear that migration is difficult if not impossible to control fully, and that a certain level of in-migration is certain to continue. Hence there is increasing interest among national minorities in the question of how to integrate immigrants into their 'nation'. This of course is the same question majority nations have had to face—such as, how to integrate immigrants into the Dutch, Spanish, or Italian nation. And the answer that national minorities increasingly come up with is very similar to the approach adopted by majority nations. Both majority and minority nations are moving towards a conception of national identity which is post-ethnic and multicultural; both emphasize the linguistic and institutional integration of immigrants, while simultaneously accepting and accommodating the expression of immigrant ethnicity.

Rethinking the Terms of the Debate

The fact that minority nationalisms can be, and increasingly are, post-ethnic nationalisms that are open to immigrants raises a number of important policy questions, which I will discuss in the next section. But it also suggests that we need to rethink dramatically the way we think and talk about minority nationalism. We do not yet have the sort of conceptual framework we need to make sense of these new forms of post-ethnic minority nationalisms: too often we continue to rely instead on outdated myths and misconceptions.

For example, there is a tendency in the literature to assume that the conflicts raised by minority nationalisms within Western democracies are conflicts between a civic (post-ethnic) nationalism promoted by the state, and an ethnic (racialist) nationalism promoted by the national minority. In reality, however, in most Western democracies these conflicts are between two competing forms of civic–post-ethnic nationalism. Both state nationalism and minority nationalism are defined in post-ethnic, non-racialist terms.[19] And in so far as these conflicts are between two forms of post-ethnic nationalism, I can see no reason why liberals should automatically privilege majority or state nationalism over minority nationalism.

Secondly, there is a tendency to assume that if the majority nation is not defined in ethnic terms, but rather is a nation open to all regardless of ethnic descent, then minority nationalisms become inherently unnecessary and pointless, except for those groups obsessed with racial purity. For example, Rogers Brubaker claims that it is difficult to assert a status as national minority in states such as the United States that do not have clear dominant ethnocultural nations. If the nation that legitimates the state as a whole is not clearly an ethnocultural nation but a political nation, open, in principle, to all, then the background condition against which the claim of national minority status makes sense is missing.[20]

The example of Puerto Rico in the United States—or of Quebec in Canada, Scotland in Britain, Corsica in France—shows that this analysis is deeply flawed. National minorities do not seek to maintain themselves as distinct societies because they are excluded on ethnic grounds from membership in the dominant nation. Rather, they mobilize as nations because they cherish their own national identity and national institutions, and wish to maintain them into the indefinite future. National minorities organize to defend their distinct society and culture whether or not they are eligible for inclusion in the dominant nation.

We cannot make any headway in understanding minority nationalism within Western democracies unless we understand that it is not necessarily, or even typically, adopted as a compensation for exclusion from the majority nation. Rather, it is adopted because of an intrinsic commitment to the maintenance of the minority's own national identity, culture, and institutions. Hence, the fact that the majority nation is post-ethnic does nothing, in and of itself, to resolve or eliminate the claims of national minorities.

Thirdly, there is a tendency to assume that minority nationalism is the extreme form of what Hollinger calls 'pluralist' multiculturalism (i.e. based on a static, descent-based, and exclusive conception of group identity and membership), and hence diametrically opposed to what he calls 'cosmopolitan' or 'post-ethnic' multiculturalism (where group identities and membership are fluid, hybridic, and multiple). In reality, however, minority nationalism and cosmopolitan multiculturalism operate at different levels. Nationalism is a doctrine about the boundaries of political community, and about who possesses rights of self-government. Minority nationalists assert that, as 'nations within', they have the same rights of self-government as the majority, and form their own self-governing political community. It is perfectly consistent with that view to insist that all nations—minority and majority—should be post-ethnic nations. This indeed is one way to understand the idea of *liberal* nationalism: liberal nationalism is the view that nations have rights of self-government, but that all nations, majority or minority, should be post-ethnic.

Minority nationalism need not, therefore, be the opposite of cosmopolitan multiculturalism. In so far as it is guided by a liberal conception of nationhood, minority nationalism does not reject cosmopolitan multiculturalism: rather it is a doctrine about the unit within which cosmopolitan multiculturalism should operate. Should cosmopolitan multiculturalism operate within Canada as a whole, or Quebec? Within Spain as a whole, or Catalonia? Within Britain as a whole, or Scotland? Within the United States as a whole, or Puerto Rico? In none of these cases is the debate about the merits of post-ethnic multiculturalism; nor is it a debate between 'civic' and 'ethnic' nationalism. All of these nations, majority and minority, share a post-ethnic model in Hollinger's sense. The debate is whether there is just one post-ethnic nation within the state, or more.

Fourthly, there is a tendency in the literature to conflate two separate claims. The first claim is that in order to be legitimate, nationalisms must be post-ethnic. I agree with this claim, and have defended it myself. It is one of the defining features of a liberal nationalism. The second claim, however, is that a post-ethnic model of civic nationalism is inherently incompatible with the recognition of minority nationalism. This second claim is, I think, mistaken (and indeed inconsistent with the practice of most Western democracies, including the United States).

Finally, we need to rethink the cliché that minority nationalisms are defensive protests against globalization and modernization. I have already noted that this cliché cannot account for the way some national minorities actively seek immigrants. But consider economic policy. Nationalist regions are often firm proponents of economic liberalization and free trade. Support for the North American Free Trade Agreement was higher in Quebec than in the rest of Canada. Similarly, support for the European Union (and for the Maastricht Treaty) is higher in Catalonia than elsewhere in Spain, and higher in Scotland than in the rest of Britain. These minority groups see free trade and globalization as a crucial part of the modern society they wish to build.[21] So these movements cannot plausibly be seen as defensive reactions against modernity. They are open societies—open to immigration and free trade, and to interacting with others more generally. In some cases, they are more cosmopolitan than majority groups.

In short, the inherited view that minority nationalisms represent an illiberal, exclusive, and defensive reaction to modernity is multiply mistaken, at least in the context of Western democracies. Some minority nationalisms represent a liberal, inclusive, and forward-looking embrace of modernity and globalization, and are potentially just as 'civic'–post-ethnic and cosmopolitan as majority nationalisms. And, as I noted earlier, liberal-democratic theory, as of yet, provides us with no clear guidelines for assessing or resolving conflicts between competing civic nationalisms within a state.

Unresolved Tensions

To say that many minority nationalisms are now post-ethnic is not to say that there aren't particular difficulties concerning the integration of immigrants into a minority nation. Indeed, it may be that rather special circumstances need to be in place for such a post-ethnic multicultural form of minority nationalism to arise. First, it requires that the national minority exercise some control over the *volume* of immigration, to ensure that the numbers of immigrants are not so great as to overwhelm the ability of the society to integrate them.

This is particularly important because, as I noted earlier, states have often encouraged immigrants (or migrants from other parts of the country) to move into the historical territory of the national minority. Such large-scale settlement policies are often deliberately used as a weapon against the national minority, both to break open access to their territory's natural resources, and to disempower them politically, by turning them into a minority even within their own traditional territory.[22]

This process is occurring around the world, in Bangladesh, Israel, Tibet, Indonesia, Brazil, etc.[23] It happened in Canada: recall Sir John A. MacDonald's comment about the Métis: 'these impulsive halfbreeds ... must be kept down by a strong hand until they are swamped by the influx of settlers'.[24] And the same process occurred in the American south-west, where immigration was used to disempower the indigenous peoples and Chicano populations who were living on that territory when it was incorporated into the United States in 1848.

This is not only a source of grave injustice, but is also the most common source of violent conflict in the world. Indigenous peoples and other homeland minorities typically resist such massive settlement policies, even with force, if necessary.[25] And to protect against these unjust settlement policies, national minorities need and demand some control over the numbers of immigrants.

Secondly, it requires that the national minority exercise some control over the *terms of integration*. As I noted earlier, immigrants have obvious incentives to integrate into the majority society, if given the choice, and in many countries have historically tended to do so. This means that special policies may be needed to encourage or pressure immigrants to integrate into the minority's culture. For example, national minorities may demand that immigrants send their children to schools in the minority's language, rather than having the choice of majority or minority language schooling. Similarly, the courts and public services may be conducted in the local language. These measures are intended to ensure that immigrants or migrants who settle in the region are willing to integrate into the local culture.

The measures to encourage integration may go even further. In Quebec, for example, a law was passed banning the use of languages other than French on outdoor commercial signs. This was intended to give Quebec a particular *visage linguistique*, in order to make clear to immigrants that French was indeed the language of public life. (This law was subsequently relaxed so that other languages in addition to French are allowed, but the law still requires that French be included on all commercial signs.)

These policies are sometimes criticized as illiberal. And perhaps they are. But here we reach a genuine dilemma. For such illiberal policies may be required if national minorities are to integrate immigrants successfully. Studies suggest that immigrants will only learn the minority language if it is seen as a 'prestige' language, as the language of economic success, political advancement, or high culture. Immigrants will not learn a minority language if it is seen as the language of the working class or of the countryside, as French was in Quebec prior to the 1960s. (Although anglophones were a minority in Quebec, they formed the business and media elite until the 1960s.) Immigrants will only integrate into a minority language group if they see that the minority language is the language of business, politics, law, and high culture.

The Quebec government has therefore systematically gone about increasing the 'prestige' of the French language. This has been done in part by subsidizing French language services, education, and media; but also by stronger forms of pressure and coercion, including laws restricting access to English language schooling; laws requiring the use of French on commercial signs; and laws giving employees the right to speak French in the workplace. The provincial government has set about creating a francophone elite in business, law, education, culture, and politics, precisely so as to make it attractive for immigrants to integrate into the francophone rather than anglophone societies.

These policies have often been interpreted as evidence of ethnic nationalism, as an attempt to create an ethnic hierarchy in which the descendants of the original French colonists stand above all other ethnic groups. But that is quite misleading. In reality, these policies have been adopted, at least in part, precisely in order to shift Québécois nationalism from an ethnic to a post-ethnic form of nationalism. The nationalist leaders wanted to attack the older ethnic model of nationhood, and wanted Quebeckers to accept the necessity and desirability of attracting immigrants, and of becoming a post-ethnic, multicultural society. These leaders reasoned, correctly I believe, that the shift from an ethnic to a post-ethnic definition of Québécois nationhood could only occur if Quebeckers were persuaded that immigrants would contribute to Québécois society, rather than integrate into the anglophone society, and that immigrants would not dramatically change the balance of power between English and French in Canada. And this required establishing a range of incentives and pressures to ensure that the majority of immigrants would indeed become part of the francophone society in Quebec.

This was a bold strategy. And, as I noted earlier, the evidence suggests that it has worked. The overwhelming majority of Quebeckers now adopt a post-ethnic definition of Québécois nationalism; and the majority of immigrants to Quebec now seek to integrate into the francophone society. One could argue, then, that these policies were not the expression of ethnic nationalism, but rather were the last nails in the coffin of ethnic nationalism in Quebec. I think we can see the same situation in Catalonia. Here too the willingness to adopt a post-ethnic conception of minority nationalism has depended on the existence of a range of policies that enhances the prestige of the minority language and that pressures immigrants to integrate into the minority society.

By contrast, the residual strength of an ethnic conception of Basque and Flemish nationalism may be due, in part, to the fact that Basque and Flemish have not achieved the same prestige status in the eyes of immigrants.[26]

This suggests an interesting dilemma. Many commentators commend Quebec nationalism for abandoning an ethnic definition of nationhood, but criticize it for its illiberal policies on education and commercial signs. If I am right, however, we cannot separate these aspects of Quebec nationalism. The illiberal policies on schools and signs are precisely what has made it possible for Quebeckers to shift from an ethnic to a post-ethnic definition of nationhood. And if so, then we face a hard choice. Should we insist on a rigorous adherence to liberal norms of individual choice, knowing that this will stop and perhaps reverse the shift from an ethnic to a post-ethnic definition of Québécois nationalism, or should we accept some limited deviation from liberal norms in order to consolidate and extend the shift to a civic form of minority nationalism?[27]

I have no definite answer to this question. It surely depends on how great the violation of liberal norms would be. Restricting the language of commercial signs is one thing; restricting the language of newspapers, churches, or private schooling (as sometimes happens in eastern Europe) is another. However, I would offer a qualified defence of the permissibility of using some illiberal policies in order to overcome ethnic nationalism, for two reasons: (*a*) the majority of immigrants themselves seems to think that this is an acceptable trade-off. Many immigrants in Quebec have not in fact objected to the principle that schools are publicly funded only in the minority language, in part because they see how this principle is connected to a broader strategy for making Quebec a more inclusive society. They see these policies, not as a rejection of their participation and inclusion in Québécois society, but rather as clarifying the terms of integration; (*b*) ethnic nationalism is such a dangerous phenomenon, capable of such great violence and hatred, that I am inclined to look favourably on any policies that would help to dislodge and dispel it, even if they are mildly illiberal. Some commentators view the sign law in Quebec as the first step on a slippery slope towards much greater interference in freedom of speech. My concern is different. I have no fear that Quebeckers will relinquish their basic commitment to free speech. I am, however, concerned about the potential contained within all forms of ethnic nationalism for racism, xenophobia, and ethnic cleansing. And if the potential for these evils is increasingly remote in Quebec, it is in part because of mildly illiberal policies that have created the conditions under which a post-ethnic, multicultural form of Québécois identity could emerge and gradually displace the older ethnic definition of nationhood.

Conclusion

I have tried in this chapter to raise some questions about the challenge that immigration raises for minority nationalism in an era of globalization. Is it acceptable for a national minority to impose more stringent integration requirements for immigrants than a majority does? Is it acceptable for a national minority to expect or require immigrants to come to share their nationalist identity and goals? More generally, what is a morally legitimate and defensible attitude for national minorities to take towards immigrants? To what extent is it morally required that national minorities become 'multicultural'? To what extent can immigrants be expected, or required, to identify with the nationalist project? I have not tried to provide a definitive answer to any of these questions. I am not myself sure how the claims of minority nationalism and immigrant multiculturalism should be reconciled, or what a morally permissible balance between the goals of *la survivance* and accommodation of immigrant ethnicity would be.

However, I am persuaded that we need to rethink these issues, and that, in order to do so, we need to set aside many of the prejudices and myths that have informed the debate so far. Minority nationalisms are not inherently illiberal, pre-modern, or xenophobic. Some are; some are not. We need to look at each case of minority nationalism on its own terms, and examine the nature of its self-understandings and aspirations. We may find that the conflict between minority nationalism and immigrant multiculturalism is not as serious as it looks at first glance.

However, there will almost certainly be some conflict, even under the best of circumstances. Given that national minorities feel vulnerable to the majority, and may view immigrants as likely to defect to the majority, it will be more difficult for them to adopt multiculturalism policies that accommodate the identities of immigrants. Immigrant multiculturalism and minority nationalism are not necessarily enemies, but nor are they easy allies. The sorts of policy required to achieve a successful form of multicultural integration may be more complicated, and in some ways less liberal, than those which the majority can adopt. And this raises difficult questions that political theorists are only beginning to address.

NOTES

1. W. Connor, 'National Self-Determination and Tomorrow's Political Map', in A. Cairns et. al. (eds.), *Citizenship, Diversity and Pluralism: Canadian and Comparative Perspectives* (Montreal: McGill–Queen's University Press, 1999).
2. S. Castles and M. Miller, *The Age of Migration: International Population Movements in the Modern Age* (London: Macmillan, 1993).
3. See R. Baubock, *Transnational Citizenship: Membership and Rights in Transnational Migration* (Aldershot: Edward Elgar, 1994); A. Buchanan, *Secession: The Legitimacy of Political Divorce* (Boulder, Colo.: Westview Press, 1991); W. Kymlicka, *Multicultural Citizenship: A Liberal Theory of Minority Rights* (Oxford: Oxford University Press, 1995); D. Miller, *On Nationality* (Oxford: Oxford University Press, 1995); J. Spinner, *The Boundaries of Citizenship: Race, Ethnicity and Nationality in the Liberal State* (Baltimore: Johns Hopkins University Press, 1994); Y. Tamir, *Liberal Nationalism* (Princeton: Princeton University Press, 1993); C. Taylor, 'The Politics of Recognition', in A. Gutmann (ed.), *Multiculturalism and the 'Politics of*

Recognition' (Princeton: Princeton University Press, 1992); M. Galenkamp, *Individualism and Collectivism: The Concept of Collective Rights* (Rotterdam: Rotterdamse Filosofische Studies, 1993); J. Tully, *Strange Multiplicity: Constitutionalism in an Age of Diversity* (Cambridge: Cambridge University Press, 1995); I. M. Young, *Justice and the Politics of Difference* (Princeton: Princeton University Press, 1990); A. Phillips, *The Politics of Presence: Issues in Democracy and Group Representation* (Oxford: Oxford University Press, 1995); M. Walzer, *On Toleration* (New Haven: Yale University Press, 1997). I am not aware of full-length books written by philosophers in English on any of these topics pre-dating 1990. For collections of recent philosophical articles on these issues, see: P. Lehning (ed.), *Theories of Secession* (London: Routledge, 1998); J. McMahan and R. McKim (eds.), *The Morality of Nationalism* (New York: Oxford University Press, 1997); W. Kymlicka (ed.), *The Rights of Minority Cultures* (Oxford: Oxford University Press, 1995); M. McDonald (ed.), *Collective Rights, Canadian Journal of Law and Jurisprudence*, special issue, 4/2 (1991), 217–419; J. Baker (ed.), *Group Rights* (Toronto: University of Toronto Press, 1994); J. Raikka (ed.), *Do we Need Minority Rights?* (Dordrecht: Kluwer, 1996); T. van Willigenburg, R. Heeger, and Wibren van den Burg (eds.), *Nation, State and the Coexistence of Different Communities* (Kampen: Kok Pharos, 1995); I. Shapiro and W. Kymlicka (eds.), *Ethnicity and Group Rights* (New York: New York University Press, 1997); J. Couture, K. Nielsen, and M. Seymour (eds.), *Rethinking Nationalism* (Calgary: University of Calgary Press, 1998); M. Moore (ed.), *National Self-Determination and Secession* (Oxford: Oxford University Press, 1998); R. Beiner (ed.), *Theorizing Nationalism* (Albany: State University of New York Press, 1999); W. Schwartz (ed.), *Justice in Immigration* (Cambridge: Cambridge University Press, 1995).

4. For recent (qualified) defences of nationalism from a liberal perspective, see Tamir, *Liberal Nationalism*; A. Margalit and J. Raz, 'National Self-Determination', *Journal of Philosophy*, 87/9 (1990), 439–61; Miller, *On Nationality*; M. Canovan, *Nationhood and Political Theory* (Cheltenham: Edward Elgar, 1996); Taylor, 'The Politics of Recognition'; C. Taylor, 'Nationalism and Modernity', in McMahan and McKim (eds.), *The Morality of Nationalism*; Walzer, *On Toleration*; Spinner, *The Boundaries of Citizenship*; W. Kymlicka, *States, Nations and Cultures: Spinoza Lectures* (Amsterdam: Van Gorcum, 1997).

5. For defenders of liberal multiculturalism, see Kymlicka, *States, Nations and Cultures: Spinoza Lectures*; Spinner, *The Boundaries of Citizenship*; Taylor, 'The Politics of Recognition'; Baubock, *Transnational Citizenship*; J. Raz, 'Multiculturalism: A Liberal Perspective', *Dissent* (Winter 1994), 67–79; Phillips, *The Politics of Presence*; Young, *Justice and the Politics of Difference*.

6. For a helpful typology, see J. Levy, 'Classifying Cultural Rights', in Shapiro and Kymlicka (eds.), *Ethnicity and Group Rights*.

7. Elsewhere I have explained these constraints in terms of two categories: external protections and internal restrictions. Liberal culturalism rejects the idea that groups can rightfully restrict the basic civil or political rights of their own members, including their right of exit. Such 'internal restrictions' are deeply problematic from a liberal point of view. However, a liberal conception of multiculturalism can accord groups various rights against the larger society, in order to reduce the group's vulnerability to the economic or political power of the majority. Such 'external protections' are consistent with liberal principles. However, they become illegitimate if, rather than reducing a minority's vulnerability to the economic or political power of the larger society, they instead enable

a minority to exercise economic or political dominance over some other group. To oversimplify, we can say that group-specific measures are consistent with liberal culturalism if (*a*) they protect the freedom of individuals within the group; and (*b*) they promote relations of equality (non-dominance) between groups. See Kymlicka, *Multicultural Citizenship*, chs. 3, 8.

8. This is the situation in Quebec today. As a result of the policies described later in the chapter, Quebec has been quite successful in integrating immigrants into the French-speaking society. Moreover, many of these immigrants have come to think of themselves as 'Québécois', and feel a stronger sense of identification with Quebec than with Canada. But even these immigrants who identify as Québécois are extremely unlikely to support independence, and indeed in the 1995 referendum voted overwhelmingly against secession.

9. See T. Franck, 'Tribe, Nation, World: Self-Identification in the Evolving International System', *Ethics and International Affairs*, 11 (1997), 151–69, and my reply in W. Kymlicka, 'Modernity and Minority Nationalism: Commentary on Thomas Franck', *Ethics and International Affairs*, 11 (1997), 171–6.

10. See D. Hollinger, *Postethnic America: Beyond Multiculturalism* (New York: Basic Books, 1995), 131, 134. These explicit references to minority nationalism are relatively peripheral to Hollinger's argument, and so perhaps not too much weight should be placed on them. However, his hostility to minority nationalism is implicit throughout his book. For example, he argues that the liberal cosmopolitan model rejects 'the notion of legally protected territorial enclaves for nationality groups' (p. 91); and refuses to 'endow with privilege particular groups, especially the communities that are well-established at whatever time the ideal of pluralism is invoked' (p. 85). These passages implicitly reject the essence of minority nationalism. After all, national minorities typically claim legally recognized rights of self-government over their traditional territories, and the justification for these claims is precisely that these societies were 'well-established' prior to being incorporated into a larger state. Hollinger's theory implicitly seems to rule such minority nationalist claims out of court.

11. M. Ignatieff, *Blood and Belonging: Journeys into the New Nationalism* (New York: Farrar, Straus & Giroux, 1993).

12. For a careful evaluation of Quebec's immigration policy, see J. Carens, 'Immigration, Political Community, and the Transformation of Identity: Quebec's Immigration Policies in Critical Perspective', in J. Carens (ed.), *Is Quebec Nationalism Just?* (Montreal: McGill–Queen's University Press, 1995). He argues that Quebec's immigration policy 'is morally legitimate and fully compatible with liberal democratic principles'. Indeed, he concludes by saying that it may 'provide a model for other liberal democratic societies, particularly in Europe, of a way to combine a strong sense of national identity with a deep commitment to liberal democratic values' (p. 74).

13. For a clear statement of these three principles, and the moral contract more generally, see Government of Quebec, *Let's Build Quebec Together. Vision: A Policy Statement on Immigration and Integration* (Quebec City: Government of Quebec, 1990).

14. Except of course that the Australian policy specifies English as the language of public institutions. See Office of Multicultural Affairs, *What is Multiculturalism?* (Canberra: Office of Multicultural Affairs, Department of the Prime Minister, Apr. 1995). For a more detailed discussion of the relationship between Quebec's 'interculturalism' policy and the multiculturalism adopted by Australia or the Canadian federal government, see W. Kymlicka, *Finding our Way: Rethinking Ethnocultural Relations in Canada* (Toronto: Oxford University Press, 1998), ch. 4.

15. For a discussion of attitudes to immigrants in Catalonia, see J. D. Medrano, *Divided Nations: Class, Politics and Nationalism in the Basque Country and Catalonia* (Ithaca, NY: Cornell University Press, 1995), 158–61.

16. See M. N. Portillo, 'Puerto Rico: Surviving Colonialism and Nationalism', in F. Negron-Muntaner and R. Grossfoguel (eds.), *Puerto Rican Jam: Essays on Culture and Politics* (Minneapolis: University of Minnesota Press, 1997).

Of course, the nature of the immigration differs in Flanders. Flanders has few migrants from other parts of Belgium (unlike Catalonia or Scotland), or indeed from elsewhere in Europe. Since most of the migrants to Flanders are from North Africa, they differ in their language, religion, and race from the native-born Flemish. By contrast, most migrants to Catalonia came from elsewhere in Spain, and so shared the same Catholic religion as the native-born Catalans, and were fellow (white) 'Europeans', differing primarily in their language. And in Scotland most migrants came from England or Wales, so they shared a Protestant religion and English language with the Scots, as well as being seen as fellow Europeans. The integration process is easier when one or more of race, religion, and language is shared between the immigrants and the national minority. In this sense, the Flemish had the most difficult task of these various national minorities.

17. See W. Kymlicka, 'American Multiculturalism and the "Nations Within"', in D. Ivison, W. Sanders, and P. Patterson (eds.), *Political Theory and the Rights of Indigenous Peoples* (Cambridge: Cambridge University Press, forthcoming) for a more detailed discussion of how indigenous conceptions of nationalism and nationhood relate to other forms of minority nationalism.

18. See J. Crête and J. Zylberberg 'Une problématique floue: L'Autoreprésentation du citoyen au Québec', in D. Colas, C. Emeri, and J. Zylberberg (eds.), *Citoyenneté et Nationalité: Perspectives en France et au Québec* (Paris: Presses Universitaires de France, 1991).

19. In many countries of eastern Europe, by contrast, both sides to the conflict are forms of ethnic nationalism: state nationalism and minority nationalism are both defined in terms of ethnic descent. It is relatively rare to find a civic nationalism opposed to an ethnic nationalism: what we find are either civic versus civic conflicts, or ethnic versus ethnic conflicts.

20. R. Brubaker, *Nationalism Reframed: Nationhood and the National Question in the New Europe* (Cambridge: Cambridge University Press, 1996), 60 n. 6.

21. For a survey of the attitudes of minority nationalists–secessionists towards free trade, see B. Davis, 'Global Paradox: Growth of Trade Binds Nations, but it also Can Spur Separatism', *Wall Street Journal*, 30 June 1994, A1.

22. J. McGarry, 'Demographic Engineering: The State-Directed Movements of Ethnic Groups as a Technique of Conflict Resolution', *Ethnic and Racial Studies*, 21/4 (1998), 613–38.

23. See P. Penz, 'Development Refugees and Distributive Justice: Indigenous Peoples, Land and the Developmentalist State', *Public Affairs Quarterly*, 6/1 (1992), 105–31; P. Penz, 'Colonization of Tribal Lands in Bangladesh and Indonesia: State Rationales, Rights to Land, and Environmental Justice', in M. Howard (ed.), *Asia's Environmental Crisis* (Boulder, Colo.: Westview Press, 1993).

24. Quoted in F. G. Stanley, *The Birth of Western Canada: A History of the Riel Rebellions* (Toronto: University of Toronto Press, 1961), 95.

25. T. Gurr, *Minorities at Risk: A Global View of Ethnopolitical Conflict* (Washington, DC: Institute of Peace Press, 1993).

26. Shafir argues that part of the explanation for the Catalans' greater openness to immigrants, compared to the Basques, is the greater prestige of the Catalan

language. See G. Shafir, *Immigrants and Nationalists: Ethnic Conflict and Accommodation in Catalonia, the Basque Country, Latvia and Estonia* (Albany: State University of New York Press, 1995).

27. Parenthetically, I think that this is what Charles Taylor should have argued in his influential 'The Politics of Recognition' paper. Taylor defended Quebec's sign law on the grounds that it involved only a minor deviation from liberal norms in order to enable Quebeckers to pursue their distinctively communitarian vision of the common good. In reality, Quebeckers are no more communitarian than other Canadians, and do not share a conception of the common good. I would defend minor deviations from liberal norms, not in order to make room for communitarianism, but rather to make it possible to shift from an ethnic to post-ethnic nationalism.

CHAPTER 5

National Identities in the Emerging European State

David D. Laitin

Globalization has facilitated both the breaking down of boundaries that once separated the populations of nation-states and the creation of new boundaries that challenge the national pretensions of nation-states. This contradictory dialectic is currently being played out in Europe, where the boundaries of nation-states are inexorably being eroded by the statelike incursions of the European Union (EU), and where the pretensions of nation-states are being challenged by regional movements claiming to represent unrepresented nations. To a considerable extent, therefore, globalization has facilitated the construction of both a vast European proto-state and numerous local quasi-states. The relationship of today's nation-state minorities claiming autonomy for their quasi-states to an emerging European project remains obscure. This chapter attempts to clarify that relationship by historicizing the emerging European state, and suggesting that this new state form will encompass a nation that is much more a cultural configuration (one which promotes continental, national, and local cultures) than a standardized national culture. Here I will be looking only at one realm of culture: language. I shall show that there is emerging an institutionalized 'constellation' of languages that will be a unique European constellation, reflecting a unique European identity.[1] The languages in the constellation will not all be unique to Europe, but the specific constellation of them will be the core of a layered European linguistic identity. The specification of Europe's new language constellation will be taken as a prototype of the combined forms of pan-European and subnational identities that are characteristic in our era of globalization.

An implication of my argument, consistent with the leitmotif of this volume, is that the political relationship between cultural minorities living within the boundaries of historic states and the dominant cultural groups who identify with the putative national culture is in the process of change, in at least two ways. For one, a new institutional outcome becomes not only possible, but acceptable to minority nationalists (from what Kymlicka calls 'societal cultures'[2]) and state bureaucrats. This is an outcome where a culturally distinct region within a historic state gets some autonomy from its former political centre and recognition in an extra-state organization (here the EU) that is more or less equal to the recognition accorded to its state. Secondly, the leaders of nationalizing states who have looked askance at such notions as layered or multiple identities will face a strong counter-force in the form of an interest for layered national identities.[3] These two points do not imply that cultural wars will become less conflictual or less violent; rather, the implication here is that the arenas of conflict and the imagined settlements of those conflicts are changing. In the conclusion I shall elaborate a bit on these themes. Future research ought to develop them further.

Contradictory Trends in Contemporary Europe

Among the observers of European integration there has long been a divide between the tortoises and the hares.[4] While some saw a European state emerging out of elite bureaucratic processes, others focused their attention on the slow processes in which ordinary people change their national identities. Sophisticated syntheses modelled the contradictory processes in a more dialectical form. Once a dialectical process is accepted, the force of nationalism becomes ambiguous. On the one hand, nationalism breaks the wave towards a new Europe; on the other hand, the idea of Europe pushes (often those same people) towards new shores.

On the power of nationalism, the analyst of European affairs can show how the national idea crushed the capitalist prudentialism of the Bundesbank that tried to slow down the process of German reunification; how it set Czech and Slovak intellectuals, formally united in anti-communism, against each other; and how it unleashed independence movements in Slovenia, Georgia, Armenia, the Baltics, Uzbekistan, and elsewhere in a collapsing Soviet 'union'. Eric Hobsbawm's stunning exegesis, written just before the nationalist uprisings in the Soviet Union and eastern Europe, confidently asserts

that the national quest is, by the late twentieth century, a spent historical force. Brilliant he was; but wrong. The national idea seems to be as
powerful and as inexplicable today as it was to Lenin at the outbreak
of the Great War in 1914.[5]

However, the movement for a united Europe proceeds apace.
Crucial elements of cultural distinction now give way to continental
standards. Germans might well have to live with speed limits on their
Autobahns; Spaniards feel pressured to work with only a single hour
for lunch. And the role of national languages in west European education is becoming somewhat more restricted. In a study of eight leading business schools in Europe by *L'Expansion*, reported by the *New
York Times*, all relied on English as a medium of instruction, and in
four of them English was the sole medium of instruction.[6] The
brouhaha in France over the issue of English as the medium of scientific exchange in the journal of the Louis Pasteur institute seems
arcane today. Even in the sensitive area of movies, French Césars
(equivalents of the US Oscars) in all categories save 'best film' can go
to films produced in any language, as long as there is significant French
involvement.[7] National culture, nearly all elites in France now agree,
must give way to the realities of globalization. Even in the stridently
nationalizing states of the former Soviet Union and of the former
Warsaw Pact, nationalist parties quickly lost appeal, and gave way to
parties that promised more secure futures in a global economic environment.

Nationalism versus globalization—these counter-pressures are seen
most starkly over issues concerning language. The status of English in
western Europe, Russian in the former Soviet Union, and English and
French in the states that received independence since 1945, all raise
sensitive political issues. On the one hand, globalization makes these
languages tools for international communication. People don't want
to be left behind on the train of history, and will equip themselves with
language repertoires that meet current needs. On the other hand, the
pressures for national identity are most keenly felt in the domain of
language. People want to keep their mother tongues alive, even if those
languages are left behind in the world of technology and interdependence. Will globalization in language outpace the national idea? If so,
how is it that the national idea can mobilize people to risk their lives
and property for independence, yet allow people to give up perhaps
the most visible aspect of their national identity to the demands of
globalization? Observers of nationalism are indeed both awed by its
power and dumfounded by its weakness. These contradictory trends
must be kept in mind when one assesses the future of the European

project. Highlighting the overlapping language repertoires constituting a continental constellation, as I do in this chapter, gives due weight to both the power and weakness of nationalism.

Language, to be sure, is but one cultural component of national identities. Religion, family structure, dress, the arts, the media, and sport form other components, helping to constitute an 'imagined community' of people who have mostly never met.[8] Yet, as Tocqueville observed, 'the tie of language is perhaps the strongest and most durable that can unite mankind'. He felt that religious diversity would strengthen America, yet linguistic sharing was the key to a common identity.[9] Many theorists of the nation-state, from the nineteenth-century Romantics, through Soviet communists exemplified by Stalin, to twentieth-century modernization theorists such as Deutsch and Gellner, focus primarily on language as the core cultural component of national identities.[10] The fact of great linguistic diversity in Europe has often been cited as the highest barrier preventing the emergence of a genuine European nation.[11] My argument here is that in twentieth-century state-building a shared language constellation, rather than a particular language, is the marker of a successful national project. Europe, I shall show, is on that road towards a coherent language constellation.

Looking Backward: Language and Early State Construction

Rationalization in general, and in language as well, has been a characteristic process in the construction of the modern state. Max Weber used the term 'rationalization' to refer to the process of efficient and orderly rule.[12] The development of a professional civil service, with a well-specified division of labour, was for Weber the essence of rationalization in the modern state. The establishment of sharp territorial boundaries, the standardization of the calendar, and of weights and measures, and the issuance of a common currency are other important examples of state rationalization.

Weber did not systematically explore language rationalization.[13] Yet the use of state power, through administrative regulation and public education, to standardize language within the boundaries of the state is precisely what he had in mind with his concept of rationalization. Legal uniformity is easier to assure when court decisions are delivered and recorded in a common language. Tax can be collected more efficiently and monitored more effectively if merchants all keep their books in the same language. State regulations can more efficiently be disseminated if translations are not necessary for compliance to take place. And territorial boundaries are easier to patrol if the population at the boundary speaks the language of its political centre, one that is distinct from the language of the population on the other side of the boundary. Given these considerations, it is not surprising that rulers of states have sought to transform their multilingual societies into nation-states through policies that can be called 'language rationalization'.

Language rationalization policies usually entail the specification of a domain of language use (e.g. appeals court cases, or church sermons) and a requirement that the language chosen by the ruler be employed within that domain. When rulers have established power over a territorially distinct speech community, they are easily able to induce some of its members to become bilingual, so as to translate documents from the language of the speech community to the language of the ruler. To the extent that political rule is stable, more and more members of the newly incorporated speech community will find it useful to learn the language of the ruling elites. Language rationalization is successful when there are a sufficient number of bilinguals among linguistically distinct communities so that the business of rule can be transacted in a single language.

Language rationalization strategies were employed so successfully in France, Japan, and Spain that these countries began to be considered in the nineteenth century (not by all people, and certainly not by people who considered themselves part of minority language groups) as 'natural' nations. The image of a rationalized nation-state was a powerful one, enough to impel political movements in Italy, Germany, Serbia, and Tamil Nadu seeking to construct new states based upon linguistic boundaries.

To give a sense of the process of language rationalization, consider the case of Spain. Spain was a multilingual empire when the Catholic monarchs, Ferdinand and Isabella presided over the final reconquest of the peninsula from Muslim rule. Castilian, Catalan, Basque, and Galician were the major languages of Spain. The Habsburg kings, following the treaties of Ferdinand and Isabella, respected regional differences in language and in law. Spain's wealth from overseas conquest, however, attracted artists and writers from all over Europe, and Castilian became a language of prestige throughout the peninsula. The literary florescence of the Golden Century (mid-sixteenth to mid-seventeenth century) induced well-to-do families throughout the kingdom to educate their children in Castilian.

It was not until 1716 and the Decree of the Nueva Planta, under Spain's first Bourbon king, Philip V, that Castilian became Spain's language for official business. A series of decrees in 1768–71 required all primary and secondary education to be in Castilian, and in 1772 all commercial establishments were required to keep their accounts in Castilian. Despite these laws, multilingualism persisted in Spain, though virtually all citizens became fluent Castilian speakers and all educated Spaniards became literate in Castilian. Spain's status as a 'nation-state' was often questioned by Basque and Catalan nationalists; but the Spanish state through the regime of Francisco Franco (1936–75) relied exclusively on Spanish to conduct its business.

The construction of the modern state, then, has long been considered synonymous with the construction of a 'nation-state', a political unit in which there would be greater cultural homogeneity within its boundaries than across them.[14] To be sure, the historical record provides anomalies such as Switzerland, where societal multilingualism coincides with strong feelings of national solidarity. What is interesting about the Swiss case, however, is the rigidity of cantonal language rationalization that has brought greater levels of language homogenization within cantons than within most nation-states. Despite historical anomalies and the far-sighted analysis of the Austro-Marxists, who indeed saw the multilingual state as normal, the idea that real states have unique national languages became the conventional wisdom by the turn of the twentieth century for people as diverse as Lenin and Woodrow Wilson.

Looking Forward: Language and the Post-Colonial State

State construction for many countries that achieved independence from colonial rule in the twentieth century has not followed the pattern of early developers. To explain this difference, analysts of post-colonial state construction at first misread the historical evidence and equated the naturalization of language homogeneity in the modern European state with the supposed naturalness of European boundaries. In this regard, colonial boundaries were considered deficient, or arbitrary. Tanzania's founding president, Julius Nyerere, once noted that Africa's boundaries are so absurd that political prudence required sanctifying them. His ironic observation implicitly assumed that boundaries in Europe were natural.

Once the historical record is clarified, one might surmise that the post-colonial states may well remain linguistically heterogenous for centuries (as did their European counterparts in similar stages of state construction), but that eventually unique national cultures (with a single official language) would be fashioned. This surmise is based on the assumption that state construction follows standard patterns no matter what the world historical time in which the process began.[15]

State development, however, needs to be historicized. Consider India. India is a post-colonial multilingual state that is not moving towards rationalization or linguistic uniformity. During its independence struggle the Congress Party leaders assumed that, upon achieving independence, some form of Hindi should be India's official language. But the Indian Administrative Service and other bureaucratic agencies operated entirely in English, the language of colonial rule. Officials in these agencies had a strong interest in preserving English as the language of administration. Although the Indian constitution called for the imposition of Hindi as the All-Union language fifteen years after independence, opposition from bureaucrats and from citizens in non-Hindi speaking areas indefinitely delayed the change. Consequently, there are now two All-Union languages, each of which can be used for official dealings within the Indian state.

Meanwhile, during the 1950s, citizen pressures at the regional levels compelled the government to redraw federal boundaries consistent with language zones. Each state has an official language today, and the governments of most of them are zealously pursuing language rationalization policies within their states. By one official measure, as of 1980, only 2.7 per cent of the Indian population has as its primary language a language different from the official language of their state.[16] The Indian constitution, however, assures all minorities the right to an education in their own language.

India thus has a multilingual state in which citizens who wish to have a broad range of mobility opportunities must learn 3+1 languages. English and Hindi are necessary languages for communicating with the central state. It is necessary as well to speak the language of the state in which you live. This makes for a 3-language outcome. A citizen of Tamil Nadu must learn English, Hindi, and Tamil to be able to communicate successfully in a wide range of contexts within India. Those citizens who live in states where Hindi or English is the official language need learn only 3−1 or 2 languages. Citizens who are language minorities in some states (for example, Marathi speakers in Karnataka) must learn 3+1 languages: Hindi, English, Marathi, and Kannada (the state language of Karnataka). Thus there is a range from 2 to 4 (that is 3+1) languages that citizens must know. The resulting language constellation, unique to India, is in equilibrium in that no individuals or groups have an interest in subverting it. It is therefore probable that India will remain a multilingual state.

What explains the inexorable move towards rationalization in early state-building experiences and the stable 3 + 1 outcome in India? A first difference has to do with changes in the nature of the business of rule. By the twentieth century virtually all states were engaged in activities in which the language used had noticeable effects on the general population. As states were in competition with one another for centuries, successful innovations in one state became a point of reference for others. Those states that provided compulsory education to the young, drafted 'citizens' into a national army, and employed large numbers of literates in a rationalized bureaucracy became very powerful, and were consequently attractive models for less prominent states. For the initial cases of state consolidation, the expansion in functions occurred after state rationalization of language had been successfully completed. In France, for example, there was sufficient knowledge of French (although not widespread) in the mid-nineteenth century so that a teaching corps and an officer corps could run a school system and army in French.[17]

With twentieth-century state-building, rulers have felt it necessary for their states to perform all evolutionarily acquired state functions. This phenomenon can be partly explained by the competitive model of state functions, and to the 'modular' (that is, easy to copy in outline) aspect of nationalist ideology.[18] The ideology of necessary state function comes out clearly in the words of the Kher Commission examining the question of a national language for India:

Modern Governments [it reasoned] concern themselves so intimately and so extensively with all aspects of social and even individual existence that inevitably in a modern community the question of the linguistic medium becomes an important matter of concern to the country's governmental organization. In the conduct of legislative bodies, in the day-to-day dealings with citizens by administrative agencies, in the dispensation of justice, in the system of education, in industry, trade and commerce; practically in all fields in which it has to interest itself in modern times, the State encounters and has to tackle the problem of the linguistic medium.[19]

In the 1950s no serious politician in India suggested that, as a new country, India should perform only those functions performed by European states in their early periods of rationalization.

This historical change implies that rulers of the new states have needed to be far more sensitive to the linguistic repertoires of their citizens than were rulers that consolidated states in earlier centuries. Imposing a specific language as the sole language for rule on a population that does not speak it will more likely mobilize the population when the state is already providing public education and local health services than when it was not involved in such activities. The data from India show that people from non-Hindi-speaking zones are often quite willing to learn Hindi (to watch movies, and television docudramas of Hindu sagas), but become rebellious if the use of Hindi is enforced in schools, or is used (at the expense of local languages) in state hospitals. Standard policies of language rationalization similar to the Nueva Planta in Spain cannot be legislated in India at low political cost.

A second historical factor that distinguishes the Indian case from the European ones concerns the effect of modern colonialism on political–bureaucratic relations. In the post-colonial state there is a conflict of linguistic interest between national politicians and senior bureaucrats, one in which the latter group has a strategic advantage. State-builders of early modern Europe had an administrative service loyal to them. Max Weber, in his classic study of bureaucracy, notes that modern states are distinctive in that they employ officials who earn a salary that is paid irrespective of their loyalty to the ruler. The burden of contemporary state-builders is that they were handed modern bureaucracies in order to accomplish tasks best performed by loyal knights and retainers.

Civil servants in post-colonial states regularly deviated from Weberian bureaucratic norms.[20] But while these bureaucrats quickly gave in to practices that are corrupt and therefore subverted the norms of a neutral civil service, they never abjured the perquisites of office (regular salary payments, health benefits) enjoyed by their European predecessors. An expensive and entrenched bureaucracy with high status presented a challenge to political leadership in the new states that earlier monarchs never had to face.

This problem also applies to the issue of language rationalization. The party elites who fought for independence in India had different interests from the administrative elite that remained on salary during the period of transition from colonialism to independence.[21] The bureaucrats had a vested interest in the perpetuation of the colonial language as the official language of state, while the politicians had a mixed interest. They wanted to give official status to indigenous languages, for this would draw them closer to the people. But they were also interested in getting compliance and support from the bureaucracy, which would be charged with carrying out their social and economic programmes. Because the politicians were willing to relinquish their goal of a unique national language in order to get compliance from the bureaucracy for the administration of an economic development programme, the language rationalization project was abandoned.

The 3+1 language outcome in India was therefore the unintended outcome of an intense political process that involved Congress politicians, bureaucrats, state-level politicians, and the mobilized public. Central politicians were willing to live with English as the *de facto* language of central rule just so long as Hindi was sufficiently promoted (as a legal language of inter-state communication; as a required language for secondary-school graduation) as to assure its hegemony among indigenous languages. Central bureaucrats were occasionally bothered by dealing with Hindi language requirements, but they were clear winners in assuring the dominance of English in their domain. State-level politicians were able to assure their autonomy by running their state business in state languages. Appointments to government positions within the states were thereby practically reserved for sons of the soil. Finally, citizens could hardly mobilize against the 3+1 outcome. Practically no citizen was denied the right to education in his/her mother tongue or mobility opportunities in having access to the state language, Hindi or English.

To support the claim that the 3+1 outcome is stable, one might examine the 1977 election of the Janata government, which was brought to power in the wake of Prime Minister Indira Gandhi's ill-fated state of emergency, in which civil liberties were suspended. In the post-emergency government, 221 out of 299 elected representatives of Janata came from Hindi-speaking areas. This represented a government clearly committed to a Hindi vision of India. Once in government, however, the Janata immediately stood behind Nehru's language concessions, promising that Hindi would never be centrally imposed.[22] In light of this experience, the 3+1 language policy appears now to be in equilibrium, in the sense that the costs for change, for any party, outweigh the benefits of the status quo.[23]

Part of what is meant by a multiple-language equilibrium is an institutionalized set of norms governing which language is to be used for which social domains. Thus, the Indian multilingual equilibrium does not mean that all languages can be used for all purposes. Rather, the domains for languages are functionally specific, and clear social norms give guidance on which language is proper for which type of interaction. Nor does the multilingual equilibrium imply that the languages are on a strict hierarchy, with English for 'high' functions and state languages for 'low', a situation closely related to the phenomenon known as 'diglossia'.[24] Jobs and other opportunities are associated with fluency in Hindi and the state languages, so they will not be marginalized to live only in the world of nursing mothers. The languages are not of equal prestige, to be sure; but Hindi and the state languages continue to have considerable élan in a range of important social, political, and economic domains. The number of languages, then, and their functionally specific domains of use help constitute India's 3 + 1 equilibrium.

The dynamic leading to a 3 + 1 outcome can be portrayed in a simple model, one that applies to other post-colonial states.[25] Consider a game in which the ruler of the central state can choose as official either the colonial language or the dominant indigenous lingua franca. Should the ruler choose the latter, the bureaucrats (who got their jobs based on facility in the colonial language) get to choose whether to accept the new language regime or to subvert it (by continuing to operate in the language of colonial rule). Once the bureaucrats choose, regional leaders (representing distinct language groups) can decide whether to promote the local vernaculars in a serious way, or to promote them merely a symbol of local identity.

If nationalist fervour pushes the ruling political elites to choose a national language as the official one for state business, the bureaucrats will reject this solution, and defy the centre. With a *de facto* situation of a divided centre, regional elites are not under great pressure to conform, and have some leeway in promoting local vernaculars for education, and for jobs in the local administration, which would give their groups (as opposed to migrant communities) virtual monopoly control over a set of state resources. In reaction to this cacophony, the centre can punish neither the bureaucrats (whom they need for basic administration) nor the local leaders (who could defy the centre through an alliance with the central bureaucrats). All the centre can do is make an alliance with minorities in the states, assuring them that their languages won't be ignored in the school systems where they are minorities. This model demonstrates the logic of the 3 + 1 outcome in India, and it has implications elsewhere in the post-colonial world.

Indeed, many other post-colonial countries, including Nigeria, Congo (Kinshasa), Kenya, and the Philippines, may follow India's track, with a colonial and an indigenous language sharing central stage in the business of rule. In others, such as Algeria and Zimbabwe, the colonial language will remain as a lingua franca, but not at the expense of the continued official reliance on indigenous languages, at least on the regional level. To be sure, some post-colonial states, such as Indonesia, Cambodia, Malaysia, Tanzania, and Somalia (despite the civil war), are on the road towards rationalization. But given the changed international environment of state-building in the twentieth

century, the 'normal' path seems to be towards some form of institutionalized multilingualism.

Multiple Identities and the New European State, or, the Emergence of a 2 + 1 Standard Language Repertoire

'Europe', to the extent that it is consolidating as a state form, will more
likely follow twentieth-century patterns than patterns consistent with
sixteenth- to eighteenth-century state-building. To expect otherwise
would be to de-historicize state-building processes. To be sure, the
analogy with India is not perfect. Europe does not have a popularly
based national movement supporting a nation-building strategy. Nor
can Europe's states be usefully compared with India's, as the latter
states did not experience centuries of sovereign rule. Yet there are
some striking trends on the road towards European integration, quite
similar to those in Indian state-building, with similar implications for
language repertoires.

The initial trend worth noting is the true Europeanization of
English as the lingua franca of the new European state. The second
trend is the tenacity of the state languages in the educational systems
of the present member states. The final trend is the successful incur-
sion of regional languages into regional educational systems and
bureaucracies. These trends have parallels to what has taken place in
India, and they provide a basis for predicting the language repertoires
of future European citizens. This constellation appears to be a 2+1
formula where the state language and English are universal elements of
individual repertoires. People who live in linguistically distinct
regions will command a third (2+1) language. English speakers in
England need be fluent in only one (2−1). Thus a unique language
constellation will emerge.

English as Europe's Lingua Franca

Almost any accounting procedure will show that English has come to
dominate French and German, and indeed all languages of Europe, as
the language of international communication. Eurobarometer surveys show that 51 per cent of European Community (EC) citizens
report knowing English, dominating French (42 per cent) and
German (33 per cent).[26] In a quantitative study of the European language 'constellation', De Swaan distinguishes between the pay-offs

for learning a language that would enable direct communication (that is, with native speakers of that language) and indirect communication (that is, with people who speak it as an auxiliary language). The power of English, he found, is in the latter category. His conclusion is that, in the constellation after United Kingdom's entry into the EC:

English now was the most attractive single language for outsiders, and what is more, the speakers of all other languages in the constellation preferred English as an additional language over any other. Since any speaker could therefore expect all other language learners in the constellation to prefer English, they had every incentive also to choose English. Only the English had an incentive to learn German or French as their first foreign language, but they might refrain from learning any languages at all, confidently waiting until the rest of the constellation had joined them.[27]

With the collapse of the Berlin wall, and the possible inclusion of many east Europeans into the EC language constellation, the number of native German speakers is greater than those of English. However, since so many of these new entrants into the constellation speak English as a second language, English remains in first place. In a study supported by the European Commission, it was found that 83 per cent of secondary-school pupils in the EU were learning English as a foreign language, compared with 32 per cent learning French and just 16 per cent German.[28] Even in a country such as Estonia, which had a German ruling class for nearly a millennium and continued business interchanges, independence from Soviet control has induced a cascade towards English as the language of international communication. In a 1993 survey of 1,454 Estonian respondents to the question of which language is most important for foreign business contacts 90 per cent said English, and only 7.9 per cent said German.[29] Even on the German side of the European periphery, then, English has become the dominant second language. Perhaps more important, the new relative prominence of German in eastern Europe seriously weakens French's role in the wider European constellation.

Perhaps the best indicator of the tide towards English is the fact that people throughout Europe (and the world) are willing to pay privately for its acquisition. English as a Foreign Language is a global industry, and the UK earns about 6 billion pounds annually on language exports. Meanwhile, according to Coulmas, Germany spends about 450 million Deutschmarks to promote German culture overseas, with some significant part for language, and France expends as much as 1.5 per cent of its gross national product on the defence of French.[30]

People are willing to pay high personal costs to learn English; they have to be bribed to learn French or German. The microeconomic handwriting is on the wall.

French, to be sure, still plays an important role in EC affairs. It was the sole official language of the Coal and Steel Community, the precursor of the EC. In Brussels, Strasbourg, and Luxembourg, three core Eurocratic centres, French is a dominant language. And French remains the principal language of a significant percentage of Eurocrats to this day. There is no doubt that French political and bureaucratic pressure can stem the tide of English for a considerable time; but the failure of French to prosper on its own terms in the current constellation of languages cannot be denied.

Germany is a more interesting case, in that its currency is unbeatable while its language is marginal. Despite the high relative number of native German speakers in the EC, German has an official role in only eight countries in the world (as opposed to sixty-three for English), and because of the issue of guilt in Second World War, German plays no role in the United Nations. Even in Germany, scientists publish more original research results in English than in German (Springer-Verlag, a leading scientific publisher, has 80 per cent of its list in English).[31] Germany would, more so than France, be able to challenge English's hegemonic language role; but it has much less of an incentive to do so, inasmuch as most elite Germans already operate in English in international forums.

Because the issue of language is so sensitive, the Commission has tried to avoid even recognizing the trends. In 1988 it urged in a policy statement that 'Member States should be encouraged to ensure that all official Community languages are on offer within their educational system, even if there is an increasing trend towards certain languages.'[32] It has even been suggested that perhaps some 'antitrust' legislation should be enacted against English.[33] In 1996 the unveiling of the future Euro-currency had no recognizable words in any known language. But the logic of the market is clear: English has become the virtual lingua franca of the EC. For political reasons, however, this social fact has not been officially acknowledged. State languages maintain their functions.

Whatever the trends towards a lingua franca, there is no evidence of any trend away from the state languages within state boundaries.[34] In all EC countries children learn their national languages first, and go to school where these languages remain the principal media of instruction. Newspapers, television, leisure-time reading, advertising, and official local and state services all continue to operate in the state languages. The rise of English in Europe has not displaced the state languages on any of the avenues of daily life.

In fact, the EC, comprised of member 'states', has been assiduous in protecting state languages. A well-funded programme called Lingua promotes state languages in other countries, so that a French parent working in, say, Italy, will be able to get a French-medium education for her children.[35] More politically, the Commission has not questioned the member states' prerogative in subsidizing publications in the state languages. Such activities would normally be seen as an unfair trade practice, but if a language (as opposed to a wine) is to be protected, the EC has been reluctant to intervene.[36] To be sure, the European Court of Justice declared against a Netherlandic law that prohibited Dutch-language advertisements on foreign channels. This was a strange law anyway, and it was meant to protect Dutch products, not the Dutch language. But the EC has permitted governments to require a certain percentage of broadcasts within a country to be in a specified language, and this restraint of trade is overlooked due to the sensitive matter that is at stake.[37] Whatever the rise of English, then, the state languages have a firm social footing in the realities of everyday life in Europe, and in the corridors of state power. There may well be a 'hollowing-out' of the nation-state, as some post-Fordist commentators have argued, but it is not happening in the realm of language.[38]

New Institutional Support for Regional Languages

The rise of one language (English) hasn't even meant the fall of regional languages. In fact, the European language constellation in the past generation has been more favourable to regional languages (minority languages within established states) than have the states themselves. In 1981 the Arfé Resolution was adopted in the European Parliament, which called for a charter for regional languages. As a result, a European Bureau for Lesser Used Languages was established in Dublin. By 1983 policies protecting language minorities became a recurrent item in the European budget.[39]

Regional language groups, politically dead for centuries, have become mobilized and mobilizable. In Italy significant Albanian, Catalan, Provençal, Friulian, German, Slovene, Occitan, and Sardinian minority language groups have been identified, with the German and Slovene communities already politically mobilized.[40] In France German, Occitan, Breton, Catalan, Flemish, and Corsican all have over 100,000 speakers. In Germany there is a large and growing

Polish-speaking community. In the United Kingdom Irish, Scottish Gaelic, and Welsh are the principal regional languages. Their official recognition is dubious. But the referendums in 1997 paved the way for a Scottish Parliament and a Welsh Assembly, with an assumption that home rule would lead to greater official support for regional languages. In Belgium, with two official languages, there is also a moderately sized German language community, which, since the Accords of Saint-Michel of 1992, has an elected German Assembly.[41] The Belgian regions have their own delegated official with the official Belgian permanent representative to the EU. Denmark, too, has a significant German-speaking community. And Holland's Frisian-speaking community already has political support from the EC, to the chagrin of Dutch authorities.[42] The recognition of these language communities by the EC, like the *korenizatsiia* policies of the early Soviet state, gives a legitimacy and a political agenda for mobilized elites from these groups to press new language demands further on the European political stage. The semi-official recognition of Catalan as a Community language is the first elevation of a regional language into a Community-wide function.[43] While it is true that state languages get stronger and more regular subsidies than the regional languages,[44] and while it is also true that member states have the right to define which languages spoken within their borders are official minority languages,[45] the footing and resources of these regional languages have been strengthened by EC intervention.

Indeed the constraints against the development of the regional languages in most of Europe seem high. Simons reports on the *oc* revival movement in southern France. Despite the missionary zeal in which these languages are promoted, she also notes the habits and practices of using French that go back for generations, and also the minimal resources available to the revivalists. The effort appears quixotic.[46] One therefore gets the impression that regional languages may be more of a luxury consumption item for the few than a serious revival movement that will coercively demand language competence in the regional language for all who live within the regional boundaries. Local educational authorities might require a year or two of study of the regional language in primary schools. Urban professionals living outside the region may enrol their children in summer courses, or give a contribution to the local language activists, or even take a course themselves to reconnect with their roots. However, these symbolic acts can have longer-term consequences. Once funded, language activists, allied with politicians and businessmen seeking higher levels of autonomy from the central state, can set a coercive language regime far beyond the expectations of those who began to support it as a leisure activity.

'Europe' as the Ideological Foundation for 2 + 1 Repertoires

In this section I shall suggest an ideological mechanism, coming from outside the core of the EC, that is pushing towards the institutionalization of the 2+1 language equilibrium. First I will look at the use of the concept of Europe in Catalanist ideology; I will then look at the meaning of 'Europe' in Estonia, one of the states that is seeking to join the EC.

The Role of 'Europe' in Catalan Discourse

The concept of Europe will play an important role as a mechanism institutionalizing these trends inducing individuals to adopt stable multicultural identities. This point can be illustrated by examining 1980s rhetoric in Catalonia. Catalonia has for millennia been a cosmopolitan centre for trade and culture; yet for the past century it has also been the centre of a language and cultural revival movement that is apparently provincial. Catalonia's split image was ambiguously represented during the 1992 Olympic Games, where Barcelona's internationalist art, cuisine, and intellectual currents were juxtaposed to its political programme of proclaiming Catalonia as a country separate from Spain.

In a content analysis of the Catalan language press in 1984–5, Laitin and Rodríguez found that in editorial discourse the two leading Barcelona newspapers used the word 'Europe' the most, and this was followed by 'Catalonia'.[47] These two powerful images reinforced each other in the overarching ideological theme that was evident in both the newspaper of the left and that of the centre right.

This discourse strategy serves an array of ideological purposes. First, Catalan nationalists do not wish to be accused of provincialism in their self-distancing from Madrid. They are often accused of this when they appeal to local language and regional customs. To be part of Europe is bigger, more international, than being part of Spain. During the civil war (1936–9) many Catalans found freedom and had an encounter with 'modernity' or with a 'progressive world' by travelling back and forth between Catalonia and France; it was Franco, Catalanists claim, who was the provincial, who never travelled outside Spain in his four decades of rule. To counter the French epithet that

Africa begins at the Pyrenees, which was reinforced by Franco in his claim that 'Spain is different', Catalans have sought to promote themselves as more international, more cosmopolitan, than 'Spaniards'. Catalans, then, identify with Europe because they see themselves as more European than Spanish, and they have often talked about post-Franco democratization as part of a *vocació europea* ('European commitment'), that will allow the Generalitat (the Catalan administration) to 'make explicit what is the reality [of the Spanish state] which the Constitution imposes'. The reality of Spain as a compound of autonomies will be fulfilled, *Avui* (the centre-right Catalan language paper) argues, due to the 'European and progressive commitment which characterizes the Catalan people'.[48] Therefore, those who have framed Catalan discourse connect themselves to a wider political entity that is democratic and modern, in large part to prove that they themselves, in their promotion of a regional language, are not narrow, autocratic, or provincial.

The second ideological purpose that Europe serves in Catalanist ideology is analogic. Europe is a political category that is growing in authority yet is not a 'state'. Catalans want their government, which is also not a 'state', to grow in authority as well. These Catalanist claims for political recognition, by stating an explicit relationship between Catalonia and the supranational entity l'Europa ampliada ('expanded Europe'), are expressed by *Avui* when its editors write:

President Pujol [of the Catalan autonomous government] had clearly enunciated the philosophy which underlies his government's project. It is a philosophy that attempts to make the Europe of the States compatible with the Europe of the regions—or of the nations. This is because it is only realistic to recognize that at this time it is easier to build the Europe of the 12 than the Europe of the 110. At this point, the Generalitat should deepen its understanding of the president's political philosophy in order to make it more consistent, and even more important, to enrich it with specific propositions that could help to upgrade the role of the regions.

Europe, for *Avui*, is therefore a model of non-state authority in the modern world that has relevance for Catalonia's claims.[49]

Thirdly, Europe is relevant within a Catalan nationalist discourse because to conceive of Europe as a compound of *regions i nacions sense Estat* ('regions and nations without a state'), or to write about Europe as constituted by *autonomias* (autonomous communities) and *pobles* (peoples), as the Catalan language newspapers do, implies that all states are multinational. This is why the editorial refers to Spain as *l'Estat espanyol*. *Avui* here positions itself as an outsider to that state and uses this language to emphasize that states are far more internally diverse than their self-image of 'nation-states' implies, and that they must all confront the *realitat plural* ('pluralist reality') within their boundaries. We can see this argument in the following discussion:

[The construction of the EC's] Council of Regions . . . was . . . a first important step in the pursuit of new bonds among the diverse peoples of the European Community. . . a Europe which is much more diverse than the Europe of the 12 and which represents in a much more correct manner the various peculiarities of the European peoples. The re-creation and the institutionalization of the Europe of the regions is not at all easy. The internal organizations of each one of the member states are sufficiently different and they don't have tight relations. On the other hand, that which we can call the historical inertia of the States weighs like a gravestone on the construction of this new way of understanding what Europe is all about.[50]

In a democratic European Community, the Catalanist argument goes, the peoples of Europe (the Catalans, the Flemish, the Alsatians, the Corsicans, the Bavarians, the Scots) will not be deterred by the vagaries of ancient history. They will have an equal claim to representation in Europe as do the states.

 Diari (the left-leaning Catalan language journal that Laitin and Rodríguez analysed) refers to Europe in a tone similar to that of *Avui*. For the editors of *Diari*, Catalanist claims for regional autonomy are reinforced by the idea of a Europe that overcomes sociopolitical configurations along the lines of statehood. *Diari* relies upon expressions such as 'Europa sense fronteres' ('Europe without borders'), 'Comunitat Europea' ('European Community'), 'Europa unida' ('united Europe'), or 'Comunitat Econòmica Europea' ('European Economic Community') to reify a notion of an already existing European entity. In an editorial called 'L'Europa del 92: Un punt de partida' ('Europe of 1992: A Point of Departure'), *Diari* only once refers to Europe in terms of states, but in a vague manner: 'l'Europa dels Sis' ('the Europe of the Six'). For the remainder of the editorial we read about nationalities, but not about states. Consider this fragment: 'In dislodging the economic issue, the Greeks on the one hand, and the Spaniards and French on the other, will have the task in the next 18 months of carrying out the Germans' policy [when their representative was the EC president] and to close the social and political dossiers which are necessary for the Act of Union.'[51] Lexically, *Diari* writes as if it is the *pobles* of Europe rather than their states who are engaged in the key negotiations. This is because *Diari* uses pluralized nouns to refer to the social agents—*els grecs*, *els espanyols*, and *els francesos* rather than their 'nation-state' terms—for example, Greece, Spain, France. *Diari* thus, like *Avui*, legitimizes European nations at the expense of its states. In Catalanist political discourse, then, it is the mythical homogeneous nation-state that is defunct—the rise of a multinational Europe and a non-state Catalonia will simultaneously erode the legitimacy of contemporary state boundaries.

The model of European state-building from a Catalanist perspective is not one that would erase cultural difference; rather it is one in which putative state-builders would be politically compelled to acknowledge and promote national-cultural difference. While the rhetorical use of 'Europe' has helped serve Catalan political interests, an important consequence of this rhetorical practice is to normalize the idea of 'one region, many identities' in a way that the ideal of 'one language, one state' pervaded European political discourse throughout the nineteenth century.

'One region, many identities' as an ideology is consistent with strategies to promote Catalan (as the regional language), Spanish (as the state language), and English (as the European language) as the standard repertoire for well-educated Catalans in the next century. Linz's data on the multiple identities of Catalans, who feel both Spanish and Catalan at the same time, lend support to this trend towards stable multilingualism.[52] To my great surprise, however, while participating in a conference of a Catalan scientific organization in Girona in April 1994, I met a few graduate students who were in effect monolingual in Catalan. If these incidents are a signal of a broader trend towards a kind of regional tribalism, the thesis in this chapter will be undermined. The incentives, nonetheless, remain for Catalans to develop full facility in three languages.

The Role of 'Europe' in Post-Soviet Nationalism

With the collapse of the Soviet bloc, Europe is in the process of expansion, and the ideological mechanism described in the section above could well be strengthened with the expansion of the Community. In Estonia (and in other multinational post-Soviet states) the discourse of 'Europe' has parallel implications for language repertoires as did the discourse of 'Europe' in Catalonia.

But first a bit of background. Since the Russian conquest of today's Estonia in 1710 a slow but significant immigration (first officials, then merchants, and finally nobles who received manors as grants from the tsar) of Russians began to take place. After the completion of the St Petersburg to Tallinn railway in 1870, a more significant wave of workers, seeking work in the newly-built factories, settled in Estonian towns.[53] After the Second World War a massive wave of immigration (and the forced displacement of the Estonian population) 'Russianized' the north-eastern region of Estonia. In the border city of Narva, for example, by the 1989 census nearly 95 per cent of the population identified itself as Russian-speaking. Although there were many Ukrainians, Belarusians, and Jews in this wave, today's rhetoric classifies them all as part of a 'Russian-speaking population'.[54]

The Estonian independence movement in the wake of the Soviet collapse could not ignore the monolingual Russian-speaking population. Although many Estonian leaders worked to induce the Russian speakers to migrate back to their 'homeland', most of these people considered Estonia to be that homeland, and had no intention (nor any place) to 'return'. The diverse Estonian political factions eventually accepted the reality of the Russian presence but agreed among themselves that fluency in Estonian would become a sine qua non for Estonian citizenship. Russian speakers would need to pass an examination in the Estonian language (a language that is not of the Indo-European family, and quite difficult for Slavic speakers to learn) to become citizens, or to work in a whole range of white-collar jobs.

While this reads like a standard battle over cultural hegemony within a single state, 'Europe' plays a key role in its development. The Estonian Parliament was considering a 'law on foreigners' (read 'Russians') in the summer of 1993, which stipulated the documents that non-citizens would need to procure in order to maintain their rights as working residents of Estonia. Leaders of the Russian-speaking population were outraged (more by the language of the law's title than its contents), and appealed to international standards of human rights to block its passage. Sergei Sovetnikov, a former parliamentarian, wrote an open letter to President Lennart Meri in which he pointed out that Estonia's recent entry into the Council of Europe was premissed on the acceptance of international standards of rights. The proposed law, he wrote, 'means that no sooner have we entered into the European home, than we are taking our first step to leave it'.[55] The law was passed by Parliament, but the constitution required the president to sign it. In an unprecedented step he asked for and received advice from a committee of jurists from the Council of Europe, which recommended certain changes to better assure the rights of non-citizens. Meri outraged his prime minister by refusing to sign the law, and went on state television to justify his unusual step. 'Estonia is constructing a European precedent,' he said, 'and this will give impulse to European integration. Estonia is answering to Europe; and Europe will answer to Estonia.'[56]

In terms of language, I have already mentioned the strong incentives for Estonians to learn English, replacing Russian as their language of international communication. Most Estonians see only Estonian and English as absolutely necessary to establish themselves as Estonians and Europeans. Although many speak Finnish, Swedish, German, and Russian (which will decrease significantly within a generation) the 2-language repertoire (Estonian and English) will be the standard minimum for Estonians. 'Europe' for the Russian-speaking population also means learning English, and many of them feel desperately behind the Estonians in this quest. But being part of Europe requires them (as they see Russia falling into a chaos that they identify as non-European) to learn the state language of Estonia. Middle-class professionals therefore spend their evenings and free time at state language centres learning Estonian in order to qualify for their jobs and citizenship. They complain in no uncertain terms to the state authorities not of the near impossibility of their burden, but of the insufficiency of Estonian instruction for their children. To be sure, learning English and Estonian is not at all seen as a substitute for Russian. The Russian-speaking leaders have demanded and the Estonian state is committed to provide schools where the medium of instruction will remain Russian. Maybe not in this generation, but by the next, the Russian-speaking population of Estonia will have a standard 3-language repertoire (Russian, Estonian, and English), which will signal their nationality, their citizenship in Estonia, and their simultaneous membership in 'Europe'.

'Europe' is important to the Estonians and Russian Estonians, just as it is to Catalans. It cleans nationalism of its ugly connotations, and sets up a model of human rights in which minorities (and minority languages) receive protection from higher authorities. It is a potential coalition of minorities and small nationalities, all locked into standard multicultural (and multilingual) identities, that seeks to build a European reality. Even supposing that post-Soviet states successfully nationalize—with a single official language, that of the titular nationality—there is reason to believe that their entry into Europe (something for which there is already a strong societal consensus) will give added support to the 2+1 European language constellation.

The Political Calculus of the 2 + 1 Outcome

There is, then, a rhetorical–ideological basis for a multilingual European state. Is there a comparable political basis? Many Euro-ideologues have speculated on a multicultural theme in order to gain support for the European idea. Lepsius writes of a 'nationalities state' to elide the problem of what the European 'nation' would look like.[57] Du Granrut seeks to paint a 'utopian' picture of a twenty-first-century state (a Europe of the Regions) in which people will remain closely aligned with their historical regions, and be protected in this by membership in Europe.[58] But such Euro-visions, as Michael Keating argues, are incautious. 'The nation-state', he reminds us, 'never monopolized political action in Europe in the past; and in the present it remains a powerful actor.' Furthermore, he and Sylvia Pintarits point out that to count on the European Commission to undermine state power is a fantasy, as 'the commission needs the states, and is more interested in policy effectiveness and efficient delivery than in broad issues of political restructuring'.[59]

It is beyond the scope of this chapter to analyse the political (as opposed to the ideological) mechanisms that might foster the 2+1 language equilibrium described above. But a few observations are in order to suggest the political conditions that could fulfil this ideological vision. It should be noted at the outset that a prediction of a multilingual language equilibrium does not require a utopian vision of the EC. Many of the features that I have presented—like the consolidation of English as the lingua franca—are robust equilibria already occurring. And for the prediction to be borne out, there is no requirement for a weakened nation-state. Yet for the trends outlined here to occur requires a political jump-start for the regions.[60] Is there any evidence for this? The answer here can only be a weak affirmative, and is based upon the political interests of the Commission.

The major impetus for an EC language policy, from the point of view of the Commission, is budgetary. With each new official language, the cost of translation increases significantly, as translators are needed for every dyadic language communication. Already about 14 per cent of the Commission's 11,000 staff work in translation and interpretation services, and this constitutes 40 per cent of the administrative budget. The annual cost of language issues is approaching 1 billion ecus per year.[61]

The principal administrative justification for these costs is that since each EC law automatically becomes a law for the member states, all regulations must be in all state languages. But this is hardly a convincing explanation, inasmuch as most of the reports and memoranda produced by the community are not laws, yet are translated. Furthermore, sophisticated work on 'language risk insurance' would permit the use of lingua franca contracts and regulations in which signatories would be protected if they broke the law due to language failure.[62] Insurance for misunderstanding would be far cheaper than the titanic load of translation. The opposition to a single official language is political, rather than legal or technical.[63]

Rationalization of administration in English is only the tip of the iceberg for the Commission in regard to the regions. Already the EC is facing a nightmare in its regional policies given that there is no consistent territorial definition of a region, and they come in all sizes and shapes. The Nomenclature of Territorial Units for Statistics (NUTS) system is complicated beyond belief, making the administration of regional policy quite difficult.[64] The political process that works to rationalize the collection of regional statistical data could easily spill over into a rationalization of criteria for recognition of regional languages, for those regions that have distinct languages.

Rationalizing NUTS is no trivial matter, as regional policy is beginning to dominate Commission attention. The Preamble of the Maastricht Treaty assures that 'decisions are taken at greatest proximity to the people'. This statement helped the Commission, along with a coalition of regionalists, to foster the Committee of the Regions. It is really made up of a patchwork of representatives, from German *Länder*, regional autonomies of Belgium, Italy, and Spain, the French regions, and English counties, and then mayors of small communities, of big cities, and presidents of French departments. Yet in 1996 it attained a status equal to the EU's Economic and Social Committee, which is institutionally weak, but much greater than the previous situation of the Consultative Council. Very propitious for this alliance is that it has been propelled by the actions of the German *Länder*, seeking to halt the EC from intervening in their competencies. In conjunction with this, the structural funds distributed by the EU in its regional policy have grown from 64 billion ecu in 1989–93 to 141 billion ecu for 1994–9, and now is a third of the EU budget. These funds since 1988 have been disbursed according to Commission-set criteria rather than member state agreements, and the technical criteria involve funding projects based upon 'Community initiatives', which has worked to the advantage of regional applicants, especially the *Länder*. The national governments have not pushed this trend; rather the force is with the European Commission with its regionalist allies.[65] To the extent that the *Länder* push for greater power for the Committee of the Regions (for purposes of their autonomy, and to procure development funds), they may be perfectly happy to support the linguistic demands of their allies on the committee as part of a wider bargain. This would be far more powerful than if only the regions with linguistic programmes fought for themselves.[66]

If regions are strengthened through the new structural funds being funnelled through the Committee of the Regions, their leaders will have the resources to make greater economic, political, and cultural demands on their states and on the EC. And it is those regions with potential language demands that will be able to exert the most influence. In a recent analysis of 125 regions of Europe it was reported that fifty-one of them had distinct languages. Of those fifty-one, twenty had an effective regional party recognizing its interests in the national parliament, while only one of the seventy-four regions without a distinct language had such a party.[67] Although regions with a distinct language are a minority of all subsidized regions, that minority will have a stronger organizational presence in European politics to influence policy. Thus the linguistically distinct regions can give political support to the EC rationalizers, and for a coalition that would find a 2+1 language outcome quite satisfactory, without antagonizing basic state interests.

This political dynamic leading to a stable European language constellation is somewhat distinct from the model portrayed for post-colonial states. In Europe English has become the *de facto* lingua franca (as Hindi had become in at least north India). As Eurocrats seeking efficiency seek to ride this trend—promoting English at all opportunities—they face subversion especially from the bureaucrats of the national states that constitute Europe. Eurocrats must agree to protect state bureaucracies and languages in order to survive. In this situation of the division of linguistic authority, the regional leaders who have new resources coming through European institutions have a historic opportunity. By promoting local vernaculars, they get the unexpected support of the Eurocrats, who see in a 2+1 language outcome one that allows for a single European language for inter-state and all-Union business. This outcome would have the same equilibrium qualities as does the 3+1 outcome in India.

Conclusion

It would be historically inaccurate to argue that, because there is little cultural rationalization going on in Europe, there isn't any evidence of a new European state. This view neglects that states constructed in the twentieth century have different cultural configurations from those that were constructed in the sixteenth to eighteenth centuries. The argument of this chapter is that there is a process of state-building in Europe going on today, except that it looks more like India's experience since 1947 than France's since 1516.

This thesis has several implications. First, the future European citizen will have multiple languages and multiple cultural identities. She or he will be European (probably expressed through gutless English), a citizen of a core European state (the official members of the EC), and possibly as well, a member of a protected minority (or regional) language community. Some citizens will need to learn only one language (English speakers in England); most will require two (German, French, Dutch speakers in Germany, France, the Netherlands). Many others will be fluent in three, such as Catalans living in Spain (English, Spanish, and Catalan), Frisians living in the Netherlands (Frisian, Dutch, and English), and Slovenians living in Italy (Slovene, Italian, and English). Individual multilingualism within an institutionalized constellation of language repertoires and multiple identities will become normal, as it has in India. Thus linguistic diversity within Europe is not a sign of state failure; rather it is a sign that Europe is emerging as a twentieth-century state.

Another implication of the new institutional outcome for the centre and periphery at the state level is that with the European proto-state involved in the politics of autonomy, relations between the state and region will be less zero-sum, and more fluid. And so, with Catalonia and Spain having representation in Brussels, and with both the Catalan and Spanish languages (albeit at different levels) having official status, Catalonian autonomy politics is no longer solely directed at getting ever higher levels of autonomy from Spain. At least part of its effort is in getting more or less equal representation in Brussels as does Spain. Not only does this change the institutional locus of autonomy politics, but it offers a new equilibrium—one in which Catalonia accepts its position as an autonomous community within Spain as long as Spain accepts Catalonia's status as an institutionalized member of the European proto-state. Should Estonia become a member of the EC, one would expect the Russian speakers of Estonia to seek the kind of representation achieved by the Catalans in Brussels. Their political focus, divided between Tallinn and Brussels, would make the cultural conflicts within Estonia more fluid, with a wider range of potential solutions.

A third implication is that many Europeans will resent political pressures to declare their national identities in the way that Stalin compelled Soviet citizens to do on their internal passports. This does not mean that there will not be—as we all have gruesomely observed in post-Yugoslav Bosnia, Croatia, and Serbia—political entrepreneurs seeking to establish their own power by drawing sharp cultural boundaries around the groups they hope to represent. In fact, I have argued that these cultural strategies remain a major potential cause of ethnic violence.⁶⁸ Rather, it means that the new institutional configuration described in this chapter will help to create a powerful counter-force to such entrepreneurs, with an interest in making the world safe for multiple and layered national identities.

How generalizable are these conclusions that new institutional outcomes for centre–periphery conflicts are becoming available in the context of more global political institutions, and that there is a new interest in the protection of multiple and layered national identities? To a considerable extent, the EU is unique in the world today. Nowhere else in the world is there a proto-state made up of sovereign political units. In this sense, the lessons of this chapter are not robust across the world's regions, despite the trans-regional forces of globalization. However, I think it useful to think of globalization not as pressing for an alternative to the nation-state, but rather as opening up a new arena in which national and identity politics will be contested. The new multilingual equilibria and the considerably empowered interest in layered identities, both afforded by globalization, are worthy of sustained political analysis.

NOTES

This chapter is a revision to and an updating of 'The Cultural Identities of a European State', published in *Politics and Society*, 25/3 (Sept. 1997), 277–302. It also adds new material to address concerns of this volume. Sources of funding and borrowings from other articles are acknowledged there. The author would, however, like to thank again Peter Katzenstein, Rogers Brubaker, and James Fernandez for comments on earlier drafts of this chapter, and Michael Keating for helping me in the revision for this volume.

1. A. De Swaan, 'The Evolving European Language System: A Theory of Communication Potential and Language Competition', *International Political Science Review*, 14/3 (1993), 241–55.
2. W. Kymlicka, *Multicultural Citizenship* (Oxford: Clarendon Press, 1995).
3. For a sensitive definition of what a 'nationalizing state' means in practice, see R. Brubaker, 'National Minorities, Nationalizing States, and External National Homelands in the New Europe', *Daedalus*, 124/2 (Spring 1995), 107–32.
4. P. Katzenstein, 'Hare and Tortoise: The Race towards Integration', *International Organization*, 25/2 (1971), 290–5; E. Haas, *The Uniting of Europe* (Stanford, Calif.: Stanford University Press, 1958); K. Deutsch *et al.*, *Political Community and the North Atlantic Area* (Princeton: Princeton University Press, 1957); J. Ruggie, 'Collective Goods and Future International Collaboration', *American Political Science Review*, 66/3 (1972), 874–93.
5. E. Hobsbawm, *Nations and Nationalism since 1780* (Cambridge: Cambridge University Press, 1990).
6. *New York Times*, 29 May 1991.

7. Ibid., 18 Jan. 1993.
8. B. Anderson, *Imagined Communities: Reflections on the Origin and Spread of Nationalism* (London: Verso, 1983).
9. A. de Tocqueville, *Democracy in America* (New York: Schocken Books, 1961), 14.
10. On the German Romantics, see W. Von Humboldt, *Linguistic Variability and Intellectual Development* (Philadelphia: University of Pennsylvania Press, 1971), ch. 1; J. Stalin, *Marxism and the National Question* (New York: International Publishers, 1942); E. Gellner, *Nations and Nationalism* (Ithaca, NY: Cornell University Press, 1983), esp. ch. 6; K. Deutsch, *Nationalism and Social Communication* (Cambridge, Mass.: MIT Press, 1953).
11. For a typical discussion on the problem of language for European unity, see the chapters in G. Braga and E. Monti Civelli (eds.), *Linguistic Problems and European Unity* (Milan: Franco Angeli, 1982).
12. M. Weber, *Economy and Society* (Berkeley: University of California Press, 1968), 71 (economic rationalization); 1108 (educational rationalization); 655, 809–38 (legal rationalization).
13. See the discussion of language, the nation, and the state in M. Weber, 'The Nation', in H. H. Gerth and C. W. Mills (eds.), *From Max Weber* (New York: Oxford University Press, 1958), 177–9.
14. The classic statement of this position is that of Deutsch in *Nationalism and Social Communication*. For a powerful empirical demonstration of this point, see S. Watkins, *From Provinces into Nations* (Princeton: Princeton University Press, 1991).
15. This position is consistent with Deutsch's theories in *Nationalism and Social Communication*. See C. Black, *The Dynamics of Modernization* (New York: Harper & Row, 1966).
16. J. E. Schwartzberg, 'Factors in the Linguistic Reorganization of Indian States', in P. Wallace (ed.), *Region and Nation in India* (New Delhi: Oxford University Press, 1985).
17. E. Weber, *Peasants into Frenchmen: The Modernisation of Rural France, 1870–1914* (Stanford, Calif.: Stanford University Press, 1976).
18. Anderson, *Imagined Communities*, ch. 5.
19. B. G. Kher, *Report of the Official Language Commission* (New Delhi: Government of India Press, 1956), 11.
20. R. Price, *Society and Bureaucracy in Contemporary Ghana* (Berkeley: University of California Press, 1975).
21. Politicians and bureaucrats can well be the same people, or from the same family. Nehru, for example, had three close relatives in the Indian Civil Service. See D. Potter, *India's Political Administration* (Oxford: Clarendon Press, 1986), 129. When this occurs, we can say the individual or family is cross-pressured, as the theory here is positing 'roles' rather than individuals.
22. K. L. Gandhi, *The Problem of Official Language in India* (New Delhi: Arya Book Depot, 1984), ch. 3.
23. Game theorists would be reluctant to call the outcome described as an equilibrium. Through backward induction, they could point out, the Congress leaders should have known they would have lost to the bureaucrats, and sought to rationalize English rather than Hindi. The reason that all parties are satisfied lies in the phenomenon of 'sour grapes'. See J. Elster, *Sour Grapes* (Cambridge: Cambridge University Press, 1983). Indian politicians now glorify the 3+1 outcome as if it were their original goal, and consistent with India's historical diversity.
24. C. Ferguson, 'Diglossia', *Word*, 15 (1959), 325–40.

25. This model is specified more fully in D. Laitin, 'Language Policy and Political Strategy in India', *Policy Sciences*, 23/24 (1989), 428–30.
26. Commission of the European Communities, *Eurobarometer*, no. 28 (Dec. 1987), 78.
27. De Swaan, 'The Evolving European Language System', 248–9. Although de Swaan does not address this issue, clearly the economic, military, political, and cultural dominance of the United States—and not the mere entry of the United Kingdom into the EC—explains the power of English as the continental lingua franca.
28. *The Economist*, 14 Jan. 1995, 45.
29. These data are from a survey run by Jerry Hough and David Laitin, under a National Science Foundation Grant SES9212568, 'Nationality and Politics: The Dismemberment of the Soviet Union'. Data from that project are deposited in the Inter-University Consortium for Political and Social Research Archive, University of Michigan.
30. F. Coulmas (ed.), *A Language Policy for the European Community: Prospects and Quandaries* (Berlin: Mouton de Gruyter, 1991), 24–5.
31. U. Ammon, 'The Status of German and Other Languages in the European Community', in Coulmas (ed.), *A Language Policy*.
32. Coulmas (ed.), *A Language Policy*, 13.
33. Ibid. 26–7.
34. See M. Simons, 'A Reborn Provençal Heralds Revival of Regional Tongues', *New York Times*, national edn., 3 May 1993. In her entertaining report, she correctly points to the energetically administered programmes within the regions of France compelling students to learn 'their' language. But when she writes that 'the [central] government has concluded that France's regional languages enrich the national heritage rather than pose a threat to the country's identity', she under-emphasizes the continuing state interest in the promotion of French.
35. B. De Witte, 'The Impact of European Community Rules on Linguistic Policies of the Member States', in Coulmas (ed.), *A Language Policy*, 174–5.
36. Ibid. 173.
37. Ibid. 167.
38. B. Jessop, 'Post-Fordism and the State', in A. Ash (ed.), *Post-Fordism: A Reader* (London: Blackwell, 1994).
39. Coulmas (ed.), *A Language Policy*, 14–16.
40. E. Zuanelli, 'Italian in the European Community: An Educational Perspective on the National Language and New Language Minorities', in Coulmas (ed.), *A Language Policy*, 293.
41. Du Granrut, *Europe*, le temps des regions (Paris: LGDJ, 1994), 59.
42. Some data for this paragraph are from the Commission of the European Communities, *Linguistic Minorities in Countries Belonging to the European Community* (Luxembourg: Office for Official Publications of the European Communities, 1986). The data do not cover Spain, Portugal, and Greece.
43. See the resolution of the European Parliament, 'On Languages in the Community and the Situation of Catalan', A3-0169/90. The Catalans hardly got what they asked for in this resolution, but the call for *inter alia* 'the publication in Catalan of the Community's treaties and basic texts' was considered by Catalans as a foot in the door.
44. H. Koch, 'Legal Aspects of a Language policy for the European Communities: Language Risks, Equal Opportunities, and Legislating a Language', in Coulmas (ed.), *A Language Policy*, 174–5.
45. A. Tabouret-Keller, 'Factors of Constraints and Freedom in Setting a Language Policy for the European Community: A Sociolinguistic Approach', in Coulmas (ed.), *A Language Policy*, 47.

46. Simons, 'A Reborn Provençal'.
47. D. Laitin and G. Rodríguez, 'Language, Ideology and the Press in Catalonia', *American Anthropologist*, 94/1 (1992), 9–30. See M. Folch-Serra and J. Nogue-Font, Ch. 8 in this volume, for the suggestion that the regional newspapers in Catalan, published in Barcelona, do not reflect popular discourse, but rather a top-down discourse from government to people. Further research is needed to see whether the local press that they highlight provides a different view of Europe than did Laitin and Rodríguez's content analysis of *Avui* and *Diari*.
48. *Avui*, 14 June 1985.
49. *Avui*, 6 June 1985.
50. *Avui*, 19 June 1985.
51. *Avui*, 30 June 1988.
52. J. J. Linz and A. Stepan, 'Political Identities and Electoral Sequences: Spain, the Soviet Union and Yugoslavia', *Daedalus*, 121 (1992), 128.
53. A. Loit, 'Nation-Building in the Baltic Countries, 1850–1918', in J. G. Beramendi, R. Máiz, and X. M. Núñez (eds.), *Nationalism in Europe: Past and Present* (Santiago de Compostela: University of Santiago de Compostela, 1994).
54. D. Laitin, *Identity in Formation: The Russian-Speaking Populations in the Near Abroad* (Ithaca, NY: Cornell University Press, 1998).
55. *Narvskaia Gazeta*, 29 May 1993.
56. *Narvskaia Gazeta*, 13 July 1993.
57. Cited in R. Wildenmann, *Staatswerdung Europas? Optionen für eine Europäische Union* (Baden-Baden: Nomos, 1991), 19–41.
58. Du Granrut, *Europe*, 198–200.
59. M. Keating, 'The Invention of Regions: Political Restructuring and Territorial Government in Western Europe', *Environment and Planning*, 15 (1997), 383; M. Keating and S. Pintarits, 'Europe and the Regions: Past, Present, and Future', *Comparative Social Research*, 17 (1998), 41.
60. Grin presents an interesting, but unconvincing, economic logic to the success for some of Europe's regional languages, having to do with trends in intra-European trade. F. Grin, 'European Economic Integration and the Fate of Lesser-Used Languages', *Language Problems and Language Planning*, 17/2 (1993), 107.
61. Coulmas (ed.), *A Language Policy*, 22–6.
62. Koch, 'Legal Aspects of a Language Policy', 147ff.
63. See the parliamentary admonitions demanding equality of all languages in parliamentary affairs, in Coulmas (ed.), *A Language Policy*, 7.
64. See L. Hooghe and M. Keating, 'The Politics of EU Regional Policy', *Journal of European Public Policy*, 1 (1994), 368–93.
65. C. Ansell, K. Darden, and C. Parsons, 'Dual Networks in the European Union', MS, Berkeley, Calif.; Du Granrut, *Europe*, 185–6.
66. Another unexpected outcome of EC support for regions is the incentive for states to create regions where they did not exist before. In Ireland this has already occurred. See M. Keating, 'The Invention of Regions', 388.
67. J. D. Fearon and P. van Houten, 'The Politicization of Cultural and Economic Difference: A Return to the Theory of Regional Autonomy Movements', Paper presented to the Annual Meeting of the American Political Science Association, Boston, 3–6 Sept. 1998, 22.
68. Laitin, *Identity in Formation*, ch. 12.

CHAPTER 6

From a Theory of Relative Economic Deprivation towards a Theory of Relative Political Deprivation

WALKER CONNOR

The first part of this chapter attempts to criticize the very common tendency to exaggerate the impact that economic factors exert upon ethno-national conflict. When commenting on cases of such conflict, spokespeople for at least one of the groups, journalists, and scholars have all tended to emphasize the economic dimension of the struggle. Data concerned with intergroup differences in income, occupation, and general living standards are customarily given great prominence in such case-studies, and the implicit or explicit message is that the conflict would tend to evaporate if these economic discrepancies were reduced or eradicated. The frequency of such analyses both reflects and reinforces a more generalized theory of group relations (usually called 'the theory of relative economic deprivation') that maintains that ethno-nationalism is at bottom economic in impulse.[1]

It is quite understandable that analysts should lean towards economic explanations because it must be acknowledged that economic discrepancies between ethnic groups are a near-universal. Given the distribution pattern of ethno-national groups plus what might be termed the 'law' of uneven, regional development, this is hardly surprising.

As illustrated in ethnographic atlases, most of the populated land mass of the world is divided into ethnic homelands—territories whose names reflect a particular people. Catalonia, Croatia, Finland, Iboland, Kurdistan (literally 'land of the Kurds'), Lithuania, Mongolia,

Nagaland, Pakhtunistan, Poland, Scotland, Somaliland, Swaziland, Sweden, Tibet, Uzbekistan, and Zululand constitute but a small sampling. Non-homeland, immigrant societies, such as the United States, represent the exception. A few states—such as Japan—are uni-homeland. Most states are multi-homeland.

As noted, this geographic distribution of ethno-national groups into distinctive homelands is sufficient in itself to assure the existence of economic discrepancies among groups because of uneven, regional economic development. Though the unevenness is apparent when we contrast huge areas such as continents, most, if not all, states also reflect economic differentials between regions. This is true of ethnically homogeneous and heterogeneous states alike. Among the contributing factors are regional variations in such categories as topography (ease of transportation), climate, soils, availability of natural resources and raw materials, population density, the current technological capabilities of the local populace, distance from potential markets, the comparative advantage of local industry with regard to age of plant and equipment and margin of profit, and the enduring effect of earlier decisions regarding investments and locating of support industries and facilities (the infrastructure).[2]

As a result, then, of the geographic distribution of ethno-nations and the uneven development of regions, defining ethno-national conflicts in terms of economic inequality is a bit like defining them in terms of oxygen: where you find the one, you can be reasonably certain of finding the other. Yet while no analyst, to my knowledge, has blamed the presence of oxygen for ethnic conflict, several have been prepared to blame economic discrepancies between groups.

One of the great dangers of economic statistics when applied to ethno-national groups is that the figures are apt to convey far more than they warrant. Spokespeople for ethno-national movements can be expected to point to economic disparities as prima-facie evidence of discrimination. 'The figures speak for themselves!' is a well-worn saw. Armed with firm statistical evidence of economic disparities and supported by the protestations of disadvantaged groups, observers of ethno-national problems have therefore been partial to socio-economic explanations and to solutions aimed at a closing of economic gaps between groups.

An intriguing aspect of charges of economic discrimination is that they are usually based upon a comparison between two groups within the same state. The statistical discrepancy between Scots and Swedes, for example, is far greater than that between Scots and the English. But it is only between themselves and the English that

Scottish national leaders find the explanation for the economic gap in discrimination.

The quite evident reason for the greater propensity to charge discrimination in an *intra*-state than in an *inter*-state situation is that economies are generally construed to be primarily state-wide enterprises. Thus, we speak of the American, British, or Russian economy. Whether such a compartmentalized view of economics is valid, particularly in an age of growing trading blocs and so-called 'multinational corporations', is beside the point. Today people perceive the government as the chief regulator of the economy and take umbrage if they feel that their group is not getting its fair share of their country's total pie. But even if one accepts this view of the government as the essentially unfettered judge of how resources are to be distributed within a state's borders, why does it follow that disparities among ethno-nations must be due to purposeful discrimination? If true, why do even greater disparities characterize the much less controlled global economy?

The possibility that ethno-national discrimination is at work within a given state is, of course, quite strong. Discrimination within Northern Ireland, for example, is a major element in the poorer economic and occupational status of the Irish as contrasted with the non-Irish.[3] But as a last bit of evidence that discrimination need not be present to produce economic discrepancies between ethno-nations, consider the relative economic positions of the Castilians, Hindus, and Malays. As just noted, government is usually considered the not-too-invisible hand behind the allocation of economic resources. Yet, although each of these groups is the politically dominant nation within its respective state (Spain, India, and Malaysia), Basques and Catalans enjoy higher living standards than Castilians, Sikhs higher than Hindus, and Chinese (within Malaysia) higher than Malays. Similarly, in the former Soviet Union, Armenians, Estonians, Georgians, Latvians, and Lithuanians enjoyed higher living standards than the politically dominant Russians. And prior to the dismemberment of Yugoslavia, Croats and Slovenes were economically well ahead of the dominant Serbs.

It is evident, then, that discrimination cannot be deduced simply from economic statistics. At this point, however, it is good to remind ourselves of that first rule of human behaviour: it is not *what is* but *what people perceive as is* that has behavioural consequences. And viewed through an ethnic prism, a disadvantageous economic imbalance is very apt to be seen as the product of discrimination. But this suggests that it is ethnicity that can impregnate economic data with the power to incite rather than vice versa. In situations where no ethno-national division is present, regionally defined groups will accept unfavourable economic disparities between themselves and others in the state which, had they coincided with ethno-national groups, would bring charges of discrimination and rumblings of political separatism. Consider the case of two adjoining regions of Canada and the United States, Quebec and Maine. As Table 6.1 indicates, median family income in real terms for the two regions is quite comparable. And, so far as their relative situation within their respective state is concerned, Quebeckers occupy a more favourable position in the economic structure than do Mainers. Nevertheless, the Parti Québécois makes much of the economic discrepancies between Quebec and Ontario as evidence of discrimination and of the fact that Quebec would be better off to go it alone. Mainers are also quite well aware that the economic plight of their state is unfavourable when contrasted with the rest of the Union as a whole, and politicians are regularly elected there on the promise of bringing more industry and higher living standards to Maine. But Mainers see no conspiratorial discrimination in their situation, and acknowledge that geography (location at the end of the railhead) is much more to blame. Demands for autonomy or separatism have not been heard.

TABLE 6.1. *Comparison of family incomes*

State	Median family income unit ($)[a]	Standing relative to all comparable units	As percentage of country-wide median figure	As percentage of wealthiest comparable unit	As percentage of poorest comparable unit[b]
Quebec	18,592	4/10	94.3	87.1	136.9
Maine	16,208	48/50	81.4	57.3	112.9

[a] Figures take into account the US inflation rate, as well as the offsetting exchange rate. The median income for Quebec families remained higher than that for Maine families. Prince Edward Island and Arkansas.

[b] British Columbia and Alaska.

Sources: US Bureau of the Census *Statistical Abstract of the United States*, 1982–1983 (Washington, DC: US Government Printing Office, 1982); *Canada Yearbook*, 1980–1989 (Ottawa: Minister of Supply and Service, 1981).

The Quebec–Maine illustration is not unusual. Most states, as noted, reflect sharp regional variations in income. But autonomist and separatist movements, which have truly deserved being described as regionalist rather than as nationalist, have been scarce indeed. On the

other hand, approximately 50 per cent of all states have been confronted by ethno-national movements in recent years, and many of the
afflicted states have been simultaneously facing several such movements.[4]

Another interesting sidelight on this issue of the homogeneous versus the heterogeneous situation is that regional economic variations
within a single state are very unlikely to have precipitous edges. In the
absence of state borders, economic regions are set off from one
another by twilight zones rather than by sharp demarcations.[5] So far
as ethnic homelands are concerned, this means that any economic discrepancy between peoples immediately on either side of an ethno-
national border is apt to be infinitesimal. Thus, the general economic
plight of the peoples living on either side of, and in proximity to, the
English–Scottish border is comparable, and, if economics determined
social consciousness, both these adjacent peoples should respond
as one. But the English and Scots view the same facts quite
differently. It is the sharp separation between membership and nonmembership in an ethno-national group and not the far more subtle
economic shading between regions that takes precedence in determining viewpoint.

The theory of relative economic deprivation also fails to explain
alienation from the state on the part of relatively economically advantaged peoples. There are numerous national groups who are extremely
dissatisfied with their group's status in relation to another group
within the state, even though the second group—the target of their
resentment—is not as economically advantaged. Basques and Catalans
manifest resentment towards the poorer Castilians, Sikhs towards the
Hindus, Ibos and Yorubas towards the Hausas, and Chinese (within
Malaysia) towards the Malays. Of the fourteen non-Russian peoples
who possessed their own republic within the former Soviet Union, the
five who were traditionally the most nationalistic—the Armenians,
Estonians, Georgians, Latvians, and Lithuanians—were those who, as
a group, were economically advantaged relative to the Russians. The
same held true of the Croats and Slovenes towards the less prosperous
Serbs of the former Yugoslavia.

If an economic gap between groups was the cause of ethnic tension, then a closing of the gap should result in a lessening of tensions.
But such is not the case. For example, commencing in the 1950s and
1960s, Slovakia received a disproportionately large share of Czechoslovak investment, and the gap between Slovaks and Czechs narrowed. Yet, Slovak unhappiness with the Czechoslovak state
continued to rise.[6]

Nor does a complete reversal in the economic status of two groups necessarily lead to similar alterations in attitudes. Thus, dissatisfaction grew among the Flemings during an age when the economic situation within Belgium heavily favoured the Walloons. But as the gap closed and then again widened—this time in favour of the Flemings— Flemish disenchantment with sharing a unitary political system with the Walloons continued to grow. Per capita income in Flanders first surpassed that in Wallonia in 1955. By 1974 per capita income in Flanders was 13.7 per cent higher than it was in Wallonia. Yet in a poll conducted in 1978 a remarkable 44.1 per cent of Flemings indicated that Flanders should separate from Belgium; by comparison, separatist sentiment among Walloons was only 22 per cent.[7] This poll occurred while Belgium was facing an economic crisis, but in another 1978 poll 46.7 per cent of the people of Wallonia perceived the crisis as extremely grave as compared to only 36.3 per cent in Flanders.[8] That is to say, the relationship between either 'relative economic depriva- tion' or popular perception of an immediate economic threat, on the one hand, and, on the other, dissatisfaction with sharing a political union with the other national group was an inverse one.

There are also numerous cases where a people have followed a course of nationalistic behaviour, although aware that their actions would probably adversely affect them economically. Thus, during the late 1960s and 1970s the separatist-oriented Parti Québécois substan- tially increased its share of the vote despite broadly held, well- grounded fears that such a vote would cause capital flight and a lowering of living standards within Quebec.[9] Similarly, for some years the people and the Communist Party leadership of the Baltic soviet socialist republics resisted, rather than sought, new investment capital from Soviet planners, because experience had shown that greater industrialization brought with it an influx of Russians and other non- indigenous compatriots, a *price* deemed too high to pay for increased living standards.[10] Still other examples of ethno-national groups acting contrary to their best economic interests might include the popular movement throughout west European states to expel the *Gastarbeiter*, even though these workers perform the most undesir- able jobs and expulsion would lead to a lowering of living standards for the indigenous population. As far back as 1964, when the *Gastarbeiter* phenomenon was still in its infancy, a poll of West Germans indicated that nearly two-thirds (64 per cent) of the respon- dents were prepared to work an extra hour per week, *without finan- cial remuneration*, 'if this would make the employment of foreigners unnecessary'.[11] And by 1982 a German newspaper would acknowledge: 'When one speaks of policies on foreign workers one is no longer referring to opportunities to help them but to the search for ways of sending them home.'[12] With physical expulsion ruled out in post-Nazi Germany, the government currently encourages Turks and other foreigners to leave through such devices as offering each adult the equivalent of $6,000 to return home and an additional bonus of $1,000 for each child that returns with them.[13] Meanwhile, resentment against the guestworkers, manifested in the election successes of anti-immigrant parties (such as Jean-Marie Le Pen's National Front in France), in public opinion polls, and in physical assaults,[14] has been at least as flagrant within Belgium, France, Italy, Sweden, Switzerland, and the United Kingdom. Indeed, a survey conducted throughout the fifteen member states of the European Union (EU) in late 1997 uncovered a remarkable level of anti-immigrant sentiment. One third of all those questioned admitted to being 'very' or 'quite' anti-immigrant, while an additional third acknowledged harbouring some anti-immigrant sentiment. (Given that most people do not wish to acknowledge prejudices publicly, a much higher figure can be presumed.) Western Europe had been suffering an economic slump at the time, but economic concerns did not appear to exert great influence on attitudes. Even among those describing themselves as 'very' anti-foreigner, 10 per cent agreed that their countries have benefited from immigration.[15] The inability of economic factors to explain the anti-immigrant sentiment was further highlighted during the 1998 elections within Denmark, where, despite the lowest percentage of foreigners within any west European country and despite a booming economy, anti-immigration sentiment heavily influenced the results.[16]

Germany offers yet another remarkable illustration of a people behaving contrary to their 'best interests'. Even while encouraging the *Gastarbeiter* to leave and despite recognition that reunion with East Germany would entail great economic sacrifices over the coming years, West Germans overwhelmingly supported that reunion. One poll, conducted in February 1990, indicated the support of 81 per cent of the West Germans, only 6 per cent less than the figure for East Germans.

Despite such evidence that economic concerns may not be primary causes, governments, when faced with ethnically inspired unrest, customarily respond with promises of greater economic investment—a larger piece of the country's economic pie. The dismal record of this stratagem as a means of sating ethno-national aspirations again suggests that economic concerns are seldom the fundamental issue. Indeed, as we have seen, in some cases a national group desires less—not more—economic development.

What all of this indicates, then, is that economic causation offers an unsatisfactory explanation for ethno-national dissension. This is not to deny that economic considerations can play a role in one or another situation. Claims of economic injustice (real or imaginary) can act as a catalyst or exacerbator, and are often to be found in ethno-national propaganda. But this acknowledgement of a catalytic role for economic forces is quite removed from a perception of economic deprivation as a necessary precondition of ethno-national tensions. Economic differentials are but one of several possible catalysts. A mass influx of outsiders into an ethnic homeland, for example, is a far more potent one. Desecration of a temple or mosque is sufficient to trigger mayhem between Arab and Jew in Israel. In Belgium it is enough that a city mayor of a French-speaking community within Flanders refused to speak the Flemish language.[17] In still other circumstances, any catalyst may be difficult to discern, as noted in the following excerpt from a commentary on an outbreak of mass violence between Sikhs and Hindus:

The speculation has concentrated on political, social, and religious causes. . . . No doubt there is at least some truth in all such speculation. Political, social, and religious tinder is ever present in Indian society, and it takes but a spark to ignite it. . . . Yet the more the violence is explained, the more incomprehensible it seems. One moment, there is no mob; Hindus and Sikhs are living side by side along a back lane, sharing a single water tap, buying from and selling to each other, sometimes arranging marriages between their children. The next moment, the same Hindus are killing their Sikh neighbors and setting fire to the Sikhs' homes and shops. The mob often seems to function more like a natural phenomenon, like a hurricane or a volcano, than like a human phenomenon—people weighing risks and rewards, for instance. It lashes and disappears, it erupts and subsides, without saying what it wants, what it needs, how those needs can be satisfied or anticipated, how the aroused passions can be checked.[18]

Although the catalyst for this or that outbreak might be difficult to discern, the recurring incidence of ethno-nationally inspired dissonance within multinational states establishes the inherent instability of multinational polities. And a sense of relative political deprivation offers a better explanation for this inherent instability than does relative economic deprivation. Nationally-conscious peoples who are ensconced in an ethnic homeland resent being ruled by non-members of the group.[19] And, as noted earlier, most peoples of the world live within an ethnic homeland that is emotionally and inextricably associated with the evolution and the destiny of their group. Consonant with what was once popularly termed 'the principle of nationality' and, more recently 'the right of national self-determination', nationally-conscious homeland peoples tend to feel that they have a natural right to self-rule over the homeland and its inhabitants. The slogan of the Quebec movement, 'Maîtres chez nous' ('Masters of our home'), succinctly captures the animus of most ethno-national movements. The destiny of the nation must be in the hands of the members of the nation.

The enunciated goals of an ethno-national movement can be and usually are quite varied. In addition to those demanding political autonomy or independence, some may feel that cultural matters (control of education, language use, or religion) are most important; others may stress control over the environment, including control over industrial investment; still others may feel that control over immigration and emigration is the primary concern; and yet others may feel that having the police and security forces composed of members of the nation is the most vital issue. But all of these are ultimately a matter of political control. Kwame Nkrumah's famous paraphrase of the biblical injunction contained a great truth: 'Seek ye first the political kingdom and all these things will be given unto you.' Protection of the nation's culture, the homeland's resources, the ethnic purity of the homeland, the physical safety of the nation, and the like all rest upon political power.

The desire that the destiny of the nation be in the hands of members of the nation should not be simply equated with separatism. The essence of the national self-determination imperative is choice, not result. It holds that a national group has the right to secede and form its own state *if it so desires*. But electoral data and opinion polls in a number of modern, democratic, first-world states indicate that a majority—usually a substantial majority—are often prepared to settle for something less than independence. I earlier noted a 44 per cent preference for separatism among Flemings and a 22 per cent preference among Walloons. By contrast, data on the Basques indicate that the percentage of those strongly committed to separatism probably peaked in the late 1970s at about 36 per cent.[20] A survey conducted within Scotland in 1992 indicated that 24 per cent favoured independence.[21] In the case of the Québécois, the data suggest that proseparatists never surpassed 20 per cent of the Franco-Canadian community prior to 1990.[22]

While separatists were a minority in these cases, a preponderant percentage of those same groups did favour major alterations in their country's power structure—that is to say, they desired a much greater measure of meaningful autonomy. In a 1968 poll of Franco-Canadian youth (17 to 19 years of age), for example, while only 13 per cent favoured separatism, 68 per cent favoured greater autonomy for Quebec, and only 8 per cent preferred no change in Quebec's status.[23] Similarly, while in the above-mentioned 1992 poll in Scotland 24 per cent preferred separatism, 52 per cent desired greater autonomy and only 24 per cent preferred the status quo. Similarly, in a 1990 poll only 8 per cent of Slovaks favoured total independence, but 71 per cent desired a major decentralization of political power, while only 16 per cent favoured no major changes.[24]

There are numerous reasons why most members of a national group may be prepared to settle for autonomy rather than independence. A major consideration is that some form of autonomy may be all that can realistically be considered to be achievable. Such an assessment is most apt to be made in an authoritarian milieu. But the issue of feasibility can also exert a restraining influence within a traditionally democratic setting. In the case of the aforementioned poll in which only 13 per cent of the Franco-Canadians opted for independence, an additional 43 per cent desired it but did not believe it feasible either immediately (37 per cent) or ever (6 per cent).[25]

Another factor accounting for a willingness to settle for something less than total independence—at least in the democratic states of western Europe and Canada—is that the state enjoys a reservoir of good will. Members of national groups, even groups who are not dominant in the state, do not necessarily perceive loyalty to national group and loyalty to country as incompatible. Thus, while the Québécois express a greater affinity towards Quebec than towards Canada, they nonetheless express a powerful sense of affection towards Canada.[26] Similarly, although the Basques have good reasons historically (most recently their experiences during the Franco regime) to distrust the Spanish state, some 10 per cent of respondents to a poll chose to identify themselves as 'more Basque than Spanish' in preference to the more limited category of 'Basque'.[27] At least to this 10 per cent 'Basque', while being considered the more important identity, was not perceived as excluding a significant measure of affinity for the Spanish state. In like manner, in a 1992 poll only 19 per cent of Scots elected to describe themselves as 'Scottish not British', while 40 per cent selected 'more Scottish than British' and 33 per cent selected 'equally Scottish and British'.[28] That the state should enjoy a significant measure of affection is not surprising. The state has powerful means for politically socializing (programming) its citizens, not the least of which is control of education (and especially control of the manner in which history is interpreted and taught). Even if the state is viewed with only marginal sympathy, it is not incongruous that most members of a national minority are prepared to settle for autonomy. Autonomy has the potential for satisfying the principal aspirations of the group. Devolution—the decentralization of political decision-making—has the potential for elevating a national group to the status of masters in their own home. And this may be quite enough. Ethno-national aspirations, by their very nature, are more obsessed by the dream of *freedom from* domination by outsiders than by *freedom to* conduct relations with states. Ethnocracy need not presume independence, but it must presume *meaningful* autonomy at the minimum.

Switzerland, while certainly not immune to ethnically inspired dissension, demonstrates that a multinational democracy can survive if the political system is sufficiently decentralized.[29] The confederal, cantonal structure of the country, combined with its ethnic map, minimizes the possibility of domination by the numerically predominant Germanic element. In the case of the one canton within which a sizeable French-speaking minority was dominated by the Germanic element, a successful secession movement was waged by the francophones during the 1970s. But, most instructively, the secessionists aspired to secede only from the German-dominated canton of Berne, not from Switzerland. Given their own ethnocracy (canton), they considered their right to national self-determination fulfilled. Following, if somewhat haltingly, this same path, a number of Western democracies, most notably Belgium, Italy, Spain, and the United Kingdom, have at least partially assuaged ethno-national aspirations through devolutionary steps. Thus, Basque support for separatism fell dramatically from 36 per cent to 12 per cent following the granting of an autonomy statute.[30]

But why do we say these countries have assuaged rather than satisfied national aspirations? It was earlier noted that most members of a national minority are prepared to settle for *meaningful* autonomy. Autonomy is an amorphous concept, meaning quite different things to different people. It may refer to very limited devolution or to regional control over everything other than foreign policy, which is to say, it can depict any situation on the continuum between total subordination to the centre and total independence.

The multifaceted meanings of autonomy account for the dismal record of attempts to implement it. Typically, there will be those associated with the centre who will tend to view even minimal devolution as tantamount to secession and will pressure the government to concede in practice as little as possible. On the other side, those who hold a maximalist view of autonomy will perceive any manifestation of the centre's presence in the homeland as violating the spirit of autonomy. More moderate national leaders will be under pressure from the maximalists, to say nothing of the separatists, to squeeze more concessions from the centre if they desire to maintain their following. In this atmosphere mutual recriminations and charges of bad faith abound. This is how Robert Clark has described the Basque experience with autonomy as of the mid-1980s: 'The combination of two years of euphoric gains (1979 and 1980) followed by five years of disappointment and failure has produced in the Basque population feelings of betrayal and frustration with sharply negative consequences for both the Basque political system and for the desegregation of power in Spain generally.'[31]

Simply agreeing to introduce autonomy is therefore no guarantee of peaceful accommodation. The search for adjustments in the system sufficiently acceptable to both sides so as to render their respective extremists isolated and ineffectual may fail. A formula for power-sharing will be difficult to achieve and, if achieved, will be subject to periodic demands for alterations.

Recent events in Canada dramatize well the dangers. As noted, separatist sentiment among the Québécois has traditionally infected less than 20 per cent of the population. But when some of the provinces rejected a constitutional change that would have recognized Quebec as a 'distinct society', those in favour of political separation surpassed the 50 per cent mark.

The price of peacefully accommodating ethnic heterogeneity is therefore probably continuous negotiation. However, attitudinal polls, the history of Switzerland, developments in such democracies as Belgium, Canada, Italy, Spain, and the United Kingdom indicate that successful accommodation need not be delusory. A starting-point is to acknowledge that the problems posed by ethno-national heterogeneity are fundamentally political, not economic, in nature.

The case for the paramountcy of a theory of political deprivation as against a theory of economic deprivation may appear to some as refuted by the movement towards the integration of western Europe. Has not the lure of economic reward caused nations willingly to surrender substantial political authority to the EU? A reply requires that we again differentiate between the attitudes of national groups that are clearly dominant within a state—for example, the Castilians, English, French—and minority nations such as the Basques, Welsh, or Alsatians. By contrast with the attitudes of the dominant group, there are at least three reasons why minorities within western Europe are apt to contemplate the diminution of state sovereignty with a greater measure of enthusiasm. One involves a degree of political alienation: since the state in which they find themselves is not perceived as the state of their particular nation, the state's survival is not as emotional a cause as it is for the dominant nation. Secondly, many of the minorities are either dissected by a political border or at least separated by one from a culturally akin people. Any development which tends to eradicate the barrier functions of the border thereby tends to unite the nation. Creation of the European Economic Communtiy (EEC) permitted closer ties between the French-speaking people on either side of the border between France and Italy's Val d'Aosta and between the Alsatians and Germans. Similarly, the co-entry of the United Kingdom and the Republic of Ireland into the EEC held out the promise of closer ties between the people of the Republic and the Irish minority within Northern Ireland. This same motive was behind the drive of the Basques and Catalans in promoting membership for Spain and why the German-speaking South Tyroleans within Italy desired full membership for Austria. Thirdly, there are many separatist factions who hold out the prospect of full membership in the EU for their nation in order to encourage greater support for independence.[32] Thus, membership in the EU becomes associated with greater, not less, political self-reliance for the group.

So much for the minorities: so far as the dominant nations are concerned, it is essential to differentiate their attitudes towards political integration, on the one hand, and military and economic integration, on the other. As I noted more than two decades ago:

Military and economic cooperation are not inconsistent with national consciousness, when the results of such cooperation are perceived as beneficial to the national interest. Thus, de Gaulle's nationalism did not blind him to the economic and prestige-related advantages that might accrue to *la grande nation* from membership in the EEC. It did, on the other hand, cause him to shy from political integration and to demand a *Europe des états*.[33] This formula of a Europe of states serves well the national interest of those nations, such as the English, French, and German, who are clearly dominant in a large state, a factor which explains London's willingness to enter the EEC only after becoming persuaded that the general drift of events was in accord with the de Gaulle formula. Already in a position to make the major decisions affecting the fate of their nation, these *staat volk* have not perceived so great a need for a more radical restructuring of the political system as have the minorities.[34]

The fact is that the campaign for political, in contradistinction to economic and military, integration has been elite-driven and has not aroused strong grass-roots support among those nations dominant in their states.

The Maastricht Treaty of 1992, which was sculpted to be a great leap in political integration, has never been popularly endorsed. Of the twelve member states at the time of the treaty's passage, only three permitted a referendum on the issue. The Danes, by a slender majority, rejected it in June 1992, and the reasons for this bear directly upon the issue of the relative power of economic versus political concerns.

A closer look at the milieu surrounding the vote is therefore warranted. The Danish elites all heavily supported the treaty: labour and management organizations, nearly all of the news media, and the trans-party political establishment. Moreover, it could not be claimed that the electorate was not well informed. The campaign lasted a month, more than half a million copies of the treaty's full text were distributed without charge, and the issues were well covered by the media. As Alastair Thomas concludes, most Danes 'had a clear grasp of the issues.' Thomas further notes that whereas in earlier referenda on the European Community (1972 and 1986) the matter 'was presented in economic terms, and the Danes voted hard-headedly for their economic advantage', and although those elites favouring Maastricht attempted once again to emphasize economic considerations, 'the issue was clearly that of closer political union, [a prospect that] alarmed many opponents, who felt they had joined an economic community and were highly skeptical about political union'.[35]

Not too much significance should be given to the closeness of the negative-vote victory. The Danes had been permitted to vote on a special watered-down version of the treaty that excluded a common currency and a joint defence system.[36] Moreover, many who voted for ratification did so for national security reasons: a major plank in the campaign promoted by the yes vote was that any affirmative vote would be an essential guarantee against the spectre of a militarily resuscitated and unreined Germany.

The fear-of-an-unbridled-Germany card was played with much greater abandon during the campaign leading up to the French referendum. This campaign produced a narrow victory for the treaty, 51 to 49 per cent. But 21 per cent of those voting for the treaty acknowledged that fear of German domination in Europe had been a factor in their decision. In short, absent the fear of Germany, the treaty would have rather handily been rejected. The point, then, is that, as in the case of the Danish vote, the issue was not simply nationalism versus political integration. Nationalism was on both sides of the issue. If you fear Germans and desire to deny them freedom of action, vote 'yes'. If you do not desire to place the destiny of our nation in the hands of others, vote 'no'.

Elsewhere, with the exception of Ireland, no referendum was

permitted, despite a series of polls indicating a strong majority in favour of such an option. A number of attitudinal polls, however, have indicated displeasure with the Maastricht Treaty. Thus, in a poll conducted immediately before the Danes were to vote a second time on the Maastricht Treaty, two-thirds of the Germans polled stated that they hoped the Danes would again reject the treaty, even though acknowledging that such a vote would scrap plans for a federal Europe.[37] British polls have consistently echoed this sentiment. Typical was a Gallup poll of December 1996, documenting that while only 15 per cent of the United Kingdom respondents wished to be part of a federal western Europe, 54 per cent would like to see western Europe return to the pre-Maastricht status of a common market.

Admittedly, any type of economic integration requires a surrendering of a measure of political decision-making. But the data suggest that most west Europeans desire to minimize the authority granted to the repeatedly castigated 'Brussels bureaucrats' and the European Parliament. Integrationists had long argued that popular disrespect for the European Parliament, as manifested in low turnouts for elections to that body, was due to the Parliament's lack of significant power. Invest it with important functions it was argued, and Europe's citizens would warmly embrace it. The parliamentary elections scheduled for June 1999 were therefore seen as auspicious, because the Parliament, under the terms of the Amsterdam Treaty of 1997, had been empowered to amend or block acts of the two non-elected EU bodies (the Council and the Commission). Moreover, shortly before the election great publicity had been focused on the Parliament due to its central role in causing the entire Commission to resign over a major financial scandal. Despite all this (plus the long-awaited introduction of the euro in January of the same year), a majority of the eligible electorate did not vote. In Britain turnout was only 23 per cent, in Finland, 27 per cent; and in France the 47 per cent who did vote represented the smallest percentage to do so in the history of country-wide elections.[38] Moreover, in many cases those who voted did so to express anti-integrationist sentiment. This was most notable within the United Kingdom, where the Conservative Party, which had been humiliated in the last election for the House of Commons, staged a truly remarkable victory on an anti-euro platform. In other cases, particularly in Germany, where the incumbent Social Democrats fared badly against the Christian Democrats, those who voted were more concerned with expressing their views on domestic politics than on Europe. In any event, the elections were seen as evidence of the failure of the EU idea to transcend national identities and loyalties.

One post-Maastricht manifestation of let-the-people-decide occurred in 1994, when Austria, Finland, Sweden, and Norway held popular referendums on joining the EU. Norway voted 'no'. A majority in the first three countries voted in favour, but subsequent changes in attitude raise the very significant question of a right of political divorce. Two recent polls indicate that only 20 or 27 per cent of Swedes would vote affirmatively today. In Austria, which was the most favourably disposed to joining, support plummeted from 66.4 to 40 per cent in less than two years. Moreover, that a vote for membership in the EU cannot be accepted as prima-facie evidence of a desire for political integration was stressed in 1998 by Max Jakobson, the former Finnish ambassador to the United Nations. He said:

In the referendums of 1994, a majority of Norwegians voted 'no' in order to maintain the independence of their country, while a majority of Finns believed they would enhance their independence by voting 'yes.' The explanation is simple: The Norwegians face the Atlantic, the Finns a 1200 kilometer border with Russia. . . . The new dividing line [in Finland] is not between federalists in Finland—there are no federalists in Finland—but between different concepts of national independence.[39]

European integration cannot, therefore, be uncritically accepted as evidence of the primacy of economic concerns over political ones. By and large, west Europeans have demonstrated a willingness to accept a strong measure of economic integration. Political integration, however, has been elite-driven, with little opportunity for the masses to influence the movement. When given the opportunity to express themselves, large numbers have made their opposition clear. Moreover, those who have expressed support for treaties promoting political integration have often done so for overriding security—not economic—reasons, i.e. as a safeguard against aggression by a resuscitated German or Russian military. In such cases, the basic motivation has been to preserve national independence, not to surrender it to the EU.

A related issue is whether the habits of cooperation brought about by sharing common economic institutions will in time bring about a common frame of mind leading to a desire for political integration. Believers in such a development are known as functionalists, and, at the global level, express the hope that the proliferation of such worldwide organizations as the International Monetary Fund, the World Trade Organization, and the World Bank, etc. might exert some such influence globally. Arrayed against such hopes is the experience of multinational states. A common state-wide currency, banking system, and all the other factors that make up an integrated economy, even when linked to a common legal and political system, did not dissolve the ethno-national identity or the political aspirations of the Armenians, Basques, Croats, Flemings, Letts, Lithuanians, Scots, Welsh, and a myriad of other peoples. A group's sense of relative political deprivation is not eradicated by common economic institutions.

The vision of a world in which nationalism recedes in the face of growing economic integration is not a recent creation. In the *Communist Manifesto* we read:

National differences and antagonisms between peoples are daily more and more vanishing, owing to the development of the bourgeoisie, to freedom of commerce, to the world market, to uniformity in the mode of production and in condition of life corresponding thereto.

Looking back nearly a century later, Carlton Hayes described a history quite at odds with this vision of Marx and Engels:

Many optimists of the present day are convinced that the Industrial Revolution is fundamentally anti-nationalist. . . . the scope of communication is beyond as well as within the frontiers of any particular nation. Each country, each nationality, is becoming more closely linked to others by railways, steamships, motor cars, automobiles, aircraft, postal service, telegraph, telephone, radio, and television. Travel is becoming more international. Information for the newspapers and the press is being gathered and distributed more internationally. Intellectual movements in one country ramify more and more speedily into other countries. . . . We do know that there has been an astounding improvement in the mechanical arts during the past hundred and forty years, involving a veritable industrial revolution. . . . But it is, or should be, apparent also that there have been during the same hundred and forty years . . . a parallel diffusion and intensification of nationalism.[40]

In the more than half a century since these words were penned, the globalizing impact of economic and technological forces has continued to intensify and diffuse. But so have the forces of nationalism. History continues to mock assumptions concerning the likely conquest of national behaviour by economic means.

NOTES

1. A variation on the thesis of relative economic deprivation is that of 'the competition for scarce resources', in relation to which ethno-nationalism is perceived as the product of a decision to mobilize an ethnic group or what, in the context of US politics, is termed a 'pressure group'. A slightly broader variation of the

deprivation thesis is offered by those who introduce the notion of 'status' within the society. Since 'status' is a rather nebulous or amorphous concept, not perfectly equatable with economic standing, its introduction into an analysis offers a measure of protection against a charge of positing an overly simplistic theory of economic causation. In reality, however, describing a nation in terms of a lower status group and maintaining that their nationalism is the result of frustration at being denied higher status does not vary significantly from analyses that describe a nation as an economically deprived class and nationalism as the product of deprivation.

The internal colonial model, the split-labour theory, and the rational-choice model, as applied to the behaviour of ethno-national groups, are also currently popular analytical frameworks that reflect a high regard for the explanatory power of economic motivation. Moreover, those who associate the rise or fall of ethnic nationalism with a specific economic stage ('industrial' or 'post-industrial') or with 'modernization' also thereby make ethnic nationalism subservient to material considerations.

Given all this, it is evident that most social scientists writing on ethnic nationalism could be included on a list of those who ascribe great significance to the explanatory power of economic forces. For those who would like specific names, see J. Ross, 'A Test of Ethnicity and Economics as Contrasting Explanations of Collective Political Behavior', *Plural Societies*, 9 (Winter 1978), esp. 69–71, and J. Fishman, 'The Rise and Fall of the Ethnic Revival in the USA', in W. Connor (ed.), *Mexican Americans in Comparative Perspective* (Washington: Urban Institute Press, 1985). The former's list includes such luminaries as J. S. Furnivall and M. G. Smith. The latter's list is extremely extensive; he traces the tendency to seek economic explanations to the work of Karl Deutsch.

2. There are also more abstract elements involving the cultural traditions of the local people, including their work habits, predispositions towards urban versus rural life, their yardstick for 'the good life', their general aptitude for business, etc.

3. The Irish and non-Irish of Northern Ireland are also less territorially segregated from one another than are most ethno-national groups.

4. See W. Connor, *Ethnonationalism: The Quest for Understanding* (Princeton: Princeton University Press, 1994).

5. State borders can correspond with sharp economic differentials because of the form of state economy (that is, where the two systems fall on the laissez faire–state monopoly spectrum), as well as the imposition of tariffs, immigration laws, and other restraints upon free economic intercourse across the border. Even in free-trade areas (such as within the European Union), borders may correspond with sharp differentials in living standards because of differences in the levels of welfare-statism conducted by the two state governments.

6. See e.g. V. Kusin, 'Czechs and Slovaks: The Road to the Current Debate', *Report on Eastern Europe*, 1/5 (Oct. 1990), 4–13. The Czechs and Slovaks did divide into two separate states in 1993, but the parting had little to do with economic concerns. The division was elite-driven and was opposed by a majority of both peoples. See A. J. Innes, 'The Partition of Czechoslovakia', Ph.D. diss., London School of Economics, 1997.

7. P. Dabin, 'Community Friction in Belgium: 1830–1980', in W. Philipps Davison and L. Gordenker (eds.), *Resolving Nationality Conflicts: The Role of Public Opinion Research* (New York: Praeger, 1980), 71.

8. Ibid. 72.

9. See e.g. K. O'Sullivan See, *First World Nationalisms: Class and Ethnic Politics in Northern Ireland and Quebec* (Chicago: University of Chicago Press, 1968), 146–7.

10. W. Connor, *The National Question in Marxist–Leninist Theory and Strategy* (Princeton: Princeton University Press, 1984), 501, 526.
11. S. Castles and G. Kosack, *Immigrant Workers and Class Structure in Western Europe* (London: Oxford University Press, 1973), 168. See also A. Rose, *Migrants in Europe* (Minneapolis: University of Minnesota Press, 1969), 110, where 51% of West Germans are reported to have replied affirmatively to a similar question.
12. *Neue Presse* (Hanover), 15 July 1982.
13. See *International Herald Tribune*, 3 Apr. 1990.
14. In 1992 alone more than 2,000 acts of violence were committed against aliens within Germany. For an account of such attacks within Sweden, see *International Herald Tribune*, 21 June 1990. Attacks against Africans in Florence and elsewhere in Italy were also broadly reported about the same time.
15. *International Herald Tribune*, 20–1 Dec. 1997.
16. *New York Times*, 11 Mar. 1998.
17. See *Keesing's Record of World Events*, 34 (1988), 36047–8.
18. 'The Talk of the Town', *New Yorker*, 19 Nov. 1984.
19. The analysis that follows does not pertain, therefore, either to diasporas or to members of multi-ethnic, essentially non-homeland, immigrant societies such as the United States.
20. R. Clark, *The Basque Insurgents: ETA, 1952–1980* (Madison: University of Wisconsin Press, 1984), 171. This figure would be substantially higher, however, if restricted to those of ethnically Basque background.
21. The survey is reproduced in L. Bennie, J. Brand, and J. Mitchell, *How Scotland Votes* (Manchester: Manchester University Press, 1997), 155. There had been remarkably little change in separatist sentiment between 1982 and 1992. See the survey reported in the *New York Times*, 24 Mar. 1982.
22. The reason for the abrupt change in 1990 is discussed below. For an analysis of earlier separatist sentiment in Quebec, see R. Hamilton and M. Pinard, 'The Bases of Parti Québécois Support in recent Quebec Elections', *Canadian Journal of Political Science*, 11 (1976), 1–26.
23. H. D. Forbes, *Nationalism, Ethnocentrism, and Personality: Social Science and Critical Theory* (Chicago: University of Chicago Press, 1985), 200–1.
24. Kusin, 'Czechs and Slovaks: The Road to the Current Debate', 6.
25. Forbes, *Nationalism, Ethnocentrism, and Personality*, 201.
26. See e.g. the results of a poll in L. LeDuc, 'Canadian Attitudes towards Quebec Independence', *Public Opinion Quarterly*, 41 (Fall 1977), esp. 352–3. Canada, however, was held in lower esteem within Quebec than it was in the other provinces.
27. R. Gunther, *A Comparative Study of Regionalism in Spain* (Toronto: Society for Spanish and Portuguese Historical Studies, 1981). See also the table in G. Shabad and R. Gunther, 'Language, Nationalism, and Political Conflict in Spain', *Comparative Politics* (July 1982), 449.
28. Bennie *et al.*, *How Scotland Votes*, 155. It is against the backdrop of such data that the results of opinion polls conducted within the Soviet Union during its last years starkly underline the lack of affection for that state. A poll conducted in Oct. 1990, for example, indicated that 91% of the three Baltic nations and 92% of all Georgians favoured secession. See V. Tolz, 'The USSR this Week', *Report on the USSR*, 2/26 (Oct. 1990), 30.
29. The relative success that Switzerland has enjoyed in peacefully accommodating ethnic heterogeneity should not lull one into presuming that a single Swiss identity has supplanted ethnic identity. Thus 11.5% of French Swiss secondary students stated that being a Swiss citizen 'was not very important' and another 8.8%

felt it was 'not at all important'. Among their German Swiss counterparts, the responses were 9.8% and 4.7% respectively. Moreover, a majority (56%) of the French Swiss felt that they were very dissimilar from the German Swiss, while feeling quite similar to the French of France (61%). See C. Schmid, *Conflict and Consensus in Switzerland* (Berkeley: University of California Press, 1981), 91, 95.

30. Clark, *The Basque Insurgents*, 172.
31. R. Clark, 'The Basques, Madrid and Regional Autonomy', MS, 1986.
32. For the views of Scots towards the EU, see James Mitchell and Michael Cavanagh (Ch. 12 in this volume).
33. De Gaulle has been widely but incorrectly cited as calling for a Europe des patries (a Europe of fatherlands), although in interviews he twice tried to correct this misperception.
34. W. Connor, 'The Political Significance of Ethnonationalism within Western Europe', in A. Said and L. Simmons (eds.), *Ethnicity in an International Context* (New Brunswick: Transaction Books, 1976).
35. A. Thomas, 'Denmark', *Western Europe 1993* (London: Europa, 1994).
36. In a follow-up referendum, an affirmative vote was achieved, but at the expense of further deleting nearly all supranational commitments from the treaty.
37. *International Herald Tribune*, 20 May 1993.
38. *New York Times*, 14 June 1999.
39. *International Herald Tribune*, 3 Mar. 1998.
40. C. Hayes, *The Historical Evolution of Modern Nationalism* (New York: Russell & Russell, 1931), 234–7.

PART II

CASE-STUDIES

CHAPTER 7

Switzerland and the European Union: A Puzzle

Jürg Steiner

The relationship between Switzerland and the European Union (EU) poses a puzzle. On the one hand, Switzerland is often presented as a model for the EU in the sense that, despite its cultural diversity, it seems to enjoy a high level of political stability. On the other hand, Switzerland has not yet joined the EU. This chapter addresses this puzzle. When I write of Swiss cultural diversity, I mean primarily the linguistic diversity of the country.[1] Occasionally, I will also touch on other aspects of Swiss cultural diversity, in particular religious, cantonal, and regional diversities.

The Historical Development of the Language Issue

There are four official languages mentioned in the Swiss constitution: German, French, Italian, and Romansch. How have these language groups managed to live relatively peacefully together? It is important to note that at the very beginning of Swiss history language was not an issue since at that time Switzerland was linguistically homogeneous. The three mountain cantons in central Switzerland, Uri, Schwyz, and Unterwalden, which in the thirteenth century founded the Swiss Confederation, were all German-speaking. It was not until the sixteenth century that they were joined by ten other cantons; eight of these were exclusively German-speaking, while two, Berne and Freiburg, had a French-speaking minority but were predominantly German-speaking. This confederation of the thirteen 'old' cantons lasted until the Napoleonic invasion of 1798. It was an extremely loose political system; perhaps we should not even call it a political system but a system of alliances.[2] There were no central authorities except a Diet, where the delegates appointed by the cantons met. Decisions of the Diet had to be unanimous, and concerned mainly foreign policy and military matters. There was much religious strife in the Old Swiss Confederation, and four religious civil wars took place between the fifteenth and the eighteenth centuries. At times there were separate Diets for Catholic and Protestant cantons.

When Napoleon's armies invaded Switzerland, the old regime abruptly broke apart, and France imposed a centralized regime according to the ideas of the French Revolution. It was only then that Switzerland really became multilingual. French-speaking Vaud, for example, which formerly belonged to Berne, became a canton on its own. Geneva, which before was in only a loose alliance with the Swiss Confederation, joined as a full canton. It was also at that time that the Italian-speaking canton of Ticino and the trilingual canton of Graubünden (German, Italian, and Romansch) joined Switzerland. The figures for the four language groups have remained about the same over the last 200 years: about 70 per cent German-speaking, 20 per cent French, 10 per cent Italian, and less than 1 per cent Romansch.[3]

At the Congress of Vienna in 1815, the old order with its largely autonomous cantons, was to a large extent re-established in Switzerland. So once again language was no longer a major issue since most important decisions were made in the individual cantons, which were nearly all linguistically homogeneous. It was only in 1848 that language really became an issue. In the previous year the progressive cantons had won a short civil war against the conservative cantons. The victorious progressive forces established a modern constitution with federal institutions, in particular a federal parliament, a federal cabinet, and a federal court. So for the first time in their history the Swiss had to prove whether they were able to live peacefully together in a multilingual country with central political authorities.

In the last 150 years there have been many conflicts among the language groups, but generally speaking these conflicts were managed quite smoothly.[4] The greatest potential point of conflict has been between German and French speakers. Tensions between them were particularly high during the First World War, when French speakers sided with France and German speakers with Germany and one could speak in term of a trench (*Graben*) dividing Switzerland. The most severe language problem arose not at the national level but within the bilingual canton of Berne, which is predominantly German-speaking but has a French-speaking minority in the Jura. The issue of the Jura will be dealt with in the next section, where it will be shown that the language issue has very different characteristics in the canton of Berne than at the national level.

So why are language relations at the national level relatively harmonious? A possible explanation is that Switzerland practises a pattern of consociationalism among the language groups. Conceptually, consociationalism is at one extreme of a continuum that has, at its other extreme inter-group competitiveness.[5] One important consociational element in the relationship among the Swiss language groups is that the three major groups are usually represented in the federal cabinet. It is a peculiar feature of the Swiss political system that the number of seats in the cabinet, the Federal Council, is set in the constitution. The number is seven, and there is no prime minister, only a yearly rotating chair with the order based on seniority. When modern Switzerland was founded in 1848, the federal parliament elected five German speakers, one French speaker, and one Italian speaker to the Federal Council. This distribution of seats gave the two minority language groups combined roughly a proportional share of the seats in the Federal Council. More recently, the minority language groups have been over-represented, with two French speakers and one Italian speaker on the Council. When, in 1998, one of the two French speakers retired for health reasons, there was absolutely no question in the public discourse that he should be replaced with another French speaker. However, in 1999, an interesting situation developed when the Italian speaker in the Federal Council retired. He was replaced with a French speaker, which shows the flexibility of the Swiss system. The Italian speakers are numerically too weak to have a claim to permanent representation in the Council. Thus, occasionally, they may have to yield their seat to one of the two other language groups.

The principle of linguistic proportionality is applied not only to the Federal Council but to all aspects of the Swiss political system. At the top of the Swiss army, for example, there are seven three-star generals, and usually four of them are German speakers, two are French speakers, and one is an Italian speaker. In the top positions of the federal bureaucracy great care is taken that the linguistic minorities have proportional representation. Outside the political arena the principle of linguistic proportionality has great importance, too. In the executive committee of the Swiss Political Science Association, for example, the minority language groups always have their proportional representation.

Another consociational element in the Swiss political system is a rule that the linguistic minorities be able to exercise power in matters of vital interest to them. This rule has been broken occasionally but in general it has been upheld. The difficulty with the rule is that there may be disagreements among the political actors on whether an issue is really of vital interest to a linguistic minority. Such disagreements occurred, for example, when Swissair wanted to cut international flights to Geneva. Many politicians in the French-speaking region claimed that such a measure violated the vital interest of their region, but in this particular case the claim was not accepted and the cuts were implemented.

Finally, decentralization is an important consociational element. Of all the public expenditures, only about a third occur at the federal level, the other two at the cantonal and communal level. Matters that are closely linked to language, in particular education and culture, are to a large extent handled at the cantonal level. Of the twenty-six cantons, only four are linguistically mixed. The others have a sole official language, and newcomers from other language regions have to adapt, in particular for schooling. A German-speaking family moving from Zurich to Lausanne, for example, must send their children to a French-speaking school. With this great cantonal autonomy in educational and cultural matters many potentially explosive linguistic conflicts are withdrawn from the federal level.

Are these various consociational elements the cause of the relative linguistic harmony at the national level? One can certainly make a plausible argument to this effect. If we take a counterfactual situation with the German-speaking majority behaving in a competitive way, one could expect that the language situation in Switzerland would be much worse. It would be like in Northern Ireland, where the Protestant majority always imposed its will until Catholics rebelled. In a similar way, the linguistic minorities in Switzerland would most likely not have accepted their permanent exclusion from positions of power. Besides this counterfactual argument, the consociational explanation is also supported by the case of the Jura; as we will see in the next section, for a long time the German-speaking majority of the canton of Berne was not willing to practise consociationalism towards the French-speaking minority in the Jura, and this lack of consociationalism was an important cause of the strife there.

Although it is plausible to claim that consociationalism helped to stabilize relations among the Swiss language groups, causality is probably more complex. One could even argue that causality flowed the other way in the sense that relative harmony among the language groups allowed a consociational pattern to take place. What would then explain linguistic harmony? Several potential factors are discussed in the literature.[6] One could argue, for example, that the economic wealth of the country and the relatively equal distribution of this wealth among the language groups contributed to linguistic harmony. If Switzerland had been economically less well-off and if, in addition, there had been great economic inequality among the language groups, linguistic conflicts would have been more severe. The fact that the major religious and linguistic cleavages cross-cut each other may be another factor contributing to linguistic harmony. There are French-speaking Catholics and French-speaking Protestants, German-speaking Catholics and German-speaking Protestants (Italian speakers are nearly all Catholics). Thus, the two major language groups are not always pitted against each other since for some issues French-speaking Catholics, for example, have more in common with German-speaking Catholics than with other French speakers. It may also have helped linguistic harmony that the two major language groups have been divided into cantons that have their own strong identities. Furthermore, there are three bilingual cantons between the main French-speaking and German-speaking regions. This fluid border, together with the cantonal segmentation within the language groups, is another reason that the language groups are not so sharply pitted against each other.

Is linguistic consociationalism then an epiphenomenon of linguistic harmony, which in turn can be explained by other powerful factors? My reading of the history of Swiss language groups is that all the factors mentioned above are causally linked in a complex way with many positive feedback loops. Consociationalism has helped harmony, which in turn has helped consociationalism; economic wealth contributed to both of these factors and was helped by the interplay of the two factors; and so on. There is an entire package of factors reinforcing each other and contributing to linguistic harmony at the national level.

The Problem of the Jura

Although at the national level relations among the language groups have been relatively smooth, this has not been the case within the canton of Berne. Berne joined the Swiss Confederation in 1353. Under the old regime up to 1798 it had a powerful position with a proud cantonal identity and military might. At the Congress of Vienna in 1815 the

French-speaking Jura was considered a masterless territory and was given to German-speaking Berne as compensation for territories that the latter lost after its defeat by the armies of Napoleon. Berne was not enthusiastic about the arrangement, and in the Jura itself there was strong opposition to the annexation. Relations between the Jura and the majority of the canton were stormy in the nineteenth century and continued to be so up to the 1960s; occasionally, there were even violent incidents.

The German-speaking majority of the canton of Berne did not practise consociationalism in its relations with the French-speaking minority in the Jura. Typical in this respect was an incident in 1947 when a job managing the cantonal Department of Public Works was denied to a French speaker with the justification that the department was too important to be run by a French speaker. It seems plausible that relations between the language groups in the canton would have been less stormy if the German-speaking majority had been more willing to practise consociationalism with the Jura. But here, too, causality is more complex. It is important to note that the Jura was economically poorer than the rest of the canton. This was particularly true for the most northerly part of the Jura, which was on the French border and farthest away from the centre of the canton. This area was also Catholic, in contrast to the southern Jura and German-speaking Berne, which were both Protestant. Thus, the northern Jura was disadvantaged in two respects: it was economically deprived and in a religious minority. These structural conditions plausibly explain why resistance against government by Berne was greatest here. The absence of consociationalism may be due not only to a lack of will on the part of the Bernese authorities but also to structural reasons. One could argue that the lack of consociationalism has been not only a cause but also a consequence of the severe problems in the Jura.

After the 1960s tensions were greatly reduced with regard to the Jura problem, although the issue lingers on. To resolve the problem, heavy use was made of the referendum. In an influential review article in the consociational literature Brian Barry argued that since the referendum by definition is based on the majority principle it is contrary to the consociational model.[7] It is true that in Switzerland there are many instances in which a referendum has been used by a majority to outvote minorities. The Jura issue shows, however, that the referendum can also be used in a consociational manner. This can be done by using not a single referendum but a whole series of referendums. At first the populace of the entire canton of Berne accepted a constitutional amendment that allowed the question of Jura's separation to be put to a referendum in the Jura districts. In a second step the Jura decided by a narrow margin for separation. In a third referendum the districts of the Jura bordering the rest of the canton decided not to join the new canton but to remain within Berne. Fourthly, individual communities along the new frontier between the canton of Berne and the canton of Jura were allowed to decide whether they wished to change their district and consequently also the canton. Finally, it was decided in a nationwide referendum to accept the Jura as a new canton, which then began to function on 1 January 1979.

Religion played an important role in the outcome of the various referendums. As noted, the German-speaking majority of the canton of Berne was Protestant, the northern Jura Catholic, and the southern Jura Protestant. The series of referendums allowed the French-speaking Catholics to create a new canton and the French-speaking Protestants to stay within the old canton. This outcome corresponded pretty much to a consociational pattern as arrived at by elite accommodation. Despite the importance of the referendum, the elites were important, too, because it was on account of their ingenuity that the cascade of referendums took place to begin with. The example of the Jura shows that thanks to the referendum it is possible to include ordinary citizens in consociational decision-making.

When the elites negotiated the exact form of the Jura referendums, many issues were highly controversial, in particular, who should have the right to vote. The Jura separatists argued that Jurassians living in other cantons and even abroad should have the right to vote on this vital issue, whereas immigrants from the German-speaking majority of the canton of Berne should be excluded. An advisory committee of so-called 'wise men' from both French- and German-speaking cantons mediated the issue; it came down against the position of the Jura separatists and for the principle of territoriality advocated by the Bernese authorities. The Jura separatists at first threatened to boycott any referendum based on the principle of territoriality, but finally they advised their supporters to take part in the referendums. They never accepted, however, that some districts of the Jura be allowed to stay within the canton of Berne, and they made a commitment to continue the fight for a unified and independent canton of Jura. After the intermediate goal of an independent canton in at least some Jura districts was reached, however, the tone of confrontation became much more moderate. Currently negotiations between the two cantons go on in a rather consociational spirit. Different solutions are considered, such as giving more autonomy to the Jura districts that stayed within the canton of Berne and the establishment of common authorities for the two parts of the Jura.[8] Although it may still be a long time before a definite solution is reached, the Jura problem may well have been removed as an explosive issue in Swiss politics.

The Drifting Apart of the Language Groups

With the Jura problem largely out of the way, one might expect that language has become less of an issue in Switzerland. But this is not true at all. On the contrary, in recent years the language cleavage has become more important in Swiss politics. That the language cleavage is currently of high salience has been revealed in a recent study about the use of the referendum.[9] This investigated the fifty-one referendums that took place at the federal level from December 1992 until September 1997, comparing the percentage of the yes votes in the 184 districts of the country. Altogether the statistical model employed fourteen variables, two of which had to do with language. The study captured the importance of the cleavage between German and French speakers with a variable for which in each district the number of German speakers was divided by the number of French speakers. This ratio turned out to be the most important variable in our investigation, being statistically significant for thirty-five of the fifty-one referendums. We captured the importance of Italian as a language in looking at the percentage of Italian speakers per district. This was the third most important variable, being significant for twenty-seven of the fifty-one referendums. The second most important variable was social class. All other variables, such as the religious composition of a district or its rural versus urban character, were less important than the two language variables.

With regard to language, consociationalism is used more carefully than ever before in relations among the language groups. So why has language become a more important issue despite continued and even increased consociationalism among the language groups? Has consociationalism lost its healing effect? I don't think so. I wish to argue that today the language issue would be even more explosive if consociationalism had been reduced or given up altogether. According to my reading of recent Swiss history, some powerful factors have made the language issue more salient.

Among these factors is, first, the decreased importance of religion in Swiss politics. In the referendums study, religion ranked only ninth among the fourteen variables included in the model. As discussed earlier, religious and language cleavages cross-cut each other. With the religious cleavage having lost most of its importance, the language groups are now much more clearly pitted against each other.

A second reason for the increased importance of the language cleavage is the decreased salience of neutrality as a foreign-policy device. Today Switzerland has a much more active foreign policy than before, which has the consequence that the different foreign-policy approaches of the language groups have become much more manifest. The French speakers tend to prefer an open foreign policy and support, in particular, membership of the United Nations and the EU. German speakers tend to be more reluctant to join such international organizations, and, thanks to their majority status, are able to outvote the French speakers in referendums on these questions. Losing in key foreign-policy referendums has increased the perception among French speakers that they have different interests than the German speakers.

A third reason why language has become more important in Swiss politics is that cantonal borders have become less important. This is particularly true for the French-speaking cantons. The two largest of them, Geneva and Vaud, traditionally had their own very special identities, and there was much rivalry between these two proud cantons. Now there is talk of merging the universities of the two cantons and even of merging these cantons altogether. Although the latter may never happen, the mere talk of it indicates that the cantonal borders in the French-speaking region have become less important, which contributes further to the perception of a common French-speaking identity.

A fourth factor contributing to increased linguistic segmentation has to do with the increased use of television for political discourse. The three major language groups now have their own programmes. Efforts to broadcast trilingual programmes failed, as the public simply did not watch. Political discourse in Switzerland has always taken place to a large extent within the individual language groups; recently this has become even more the case. A similar effect of television on relations between language groups has been noted in Belgium.[10]

As a consequence of these four factors, the language groups are much more clearly delimited against each other than in former times. A useful metaphor is that they stand with their back to each other. Their view is more towards the outside, and here again television plays an important role. German speakers watch German television in great numbers, French speakers French television, and Italian speakers Italian television. Within Switzerland, interactions across language borders have become less frequent. The traditional year that German speakers spent in a French-speaking canton after the end of mandatory schooling has become almost completely a thing of the past. Contributing to the lack of interactions across the language borders is the phenomenon that English has become so popular among young people that learning another national language has become less attractive. What does all this mean for consociationalism among the language groups? In my view, consociationalism is more important than ever if Switzerland wants to stay together. The risk is not that Switzerland will suddenly break apart, but that the language groups will more and more *drift* apart.

Why is Switzerland not a Member of the European Union?

The chapter has now laid the groundwork for an explanation of why Switzerland is not a member of the EU. It has much to do with the drifting apart of its language groups. French and German speakers, in particular, have developed very different perceptions of Swiss identity.[11] The French-speaking Swiss tend to see Switzerland as part of Europe, whereas many among the German-speaking Swiss see Europe as a danger. The more the French speakers want to be part of Europe, the greater the fear of many German speakers that Switzerland is falling apart. That the German speakers are particularly fearful that Switzerland is falling apart is related to their much longer roots in Swiss history. As noted earlier, the Swiss Confederation was founded in the thirteenth century in German-speaking Switzerland, whereas the other language groups, for the most part, joined only around 1800. Many German speakers fear that the French speakers have never really understood the *idea* of Switzerland and are therefore willing to abandon it recklessly. According to the traditional view, Switzerland was always threatened by external enemies, the Habsburgs, Napoleon, Hitler, and many others. Given these permanent threats, Switzerland had constantly to fight to keep its independence. The best way to stay independent was to fortify the mountains and to remain neutral in international affairs. This myth of Swiss history is strongest in German-speaking Switzerland, especially in the mountain valleys where Switzerland was founded.

In recent years traditional Swiss identity has been threatened not only by the wish of the French speakers to join the EU, but also by bad economic times and a harsh international critique of the behaviour of Switzerland during the Second World War. For many years Switzerland took great pride in its economic success. More recently, however, economic growth has been slow or even negative, and the Swiss have encountered problems of unemployment to which they are unaccustomed. Even more troubling is that the good image of Switzerland has been eroded by revelations about collaboration with the Nazis during the Second World War. The banks are criticized for accepting Nazi gold, even gold stolen in concentration camps. They are also criticized for not cooperating in giving access to accounts belonging to Nazi victims. Swiss refugee policy during the Second World War has been attacked for sending many Jewish asylum-seekers to certain death in concentration camps. Switzerland has also been blamed for having sold weapons and ammunition to Nazi Germany.

Difficult economic times and this international criticism have strengthened among many Swiss the perception that the country is once again in danger from external enemies. A charismatic politician from Zurich, Christoph Blocher, has founded an organization named Action for a Neutral and Independent Switzerland to express these fears. Its supporters come mainly from German-speaking Switzerland. The organization claims that this time the danger for Swiss neutrality and independence comes from Brussels. Parallels are even drawn with the Nazi era: as Switzerland had to defend itself against the Nazis, today, it is said, it has to defend itself against the bureaucrats and the judges of the EU. The threat of being ruled by foreign judges goes back to the foundation of the Swiss Confederation, when Habsburg judges were expelled from Swiss territory, so it strikes at the heart of Swiss historical myth when Christoph Blocher exclaims that Switzerland will never allow itself to be ruled by foreign judges. Politically, the Swiss People's Party (one of the governing parties) is close to Action for a Neutral and Independent Switzerland. And here again it is important to note that this party has its main support in German-speaking Switzerland.

What we see, then, is a clash between two perceptions of the place of Switzerland in Europe. One is that Switzerland is a typical small European country and that it should take its place in the EU like other small countries. The other perception builds on the historical myth that Switzerland was always a special case (*Sonderfall*) in the sense that its very existence was constantly endangered and that it must therefore continue to be vigilant against potential threats to its neutrality and independence. Furthermore, it must defend its direct democracy by extensive citizen participation in referenda.

Which perception is going to prevail? If it was a clash between German speakers and the linguistic minorities, entry into the EU would never happen, since German speakers are in a clear majority.

But the picture concerning the two identities is more complex. Not all German speakers adhere to the traditional Swiss identity. There are, in particular, many young, highly educated, urban German speakers who support membership of the EU. In the two German-speaking cantons of Basel-Stadt and Basel-Land supporters of entry into the EU even have a clear majority. In Switzerland at large, polls indicate that support for entry into the EU is close to a majority. But the real issue is support not in the country at large but in the individual cantons. Membership of the EU would need a change in the constitution, and, as with other constitutional changes, a majority of both the national electorate and the cantons is needed. Including the six half-cantons, there are twenty-three full cantons. Therefore, entry to the EU is possible only if the voters in twelve cantons are in support, and this is far from being the case. Most of the small rural cantons in German-speaking Switzerland are adamantly opposed to membership of the EU. As support for membership seems to grow in the Swiss electorate at large, the opposition in these cantons becomes even stronger. Thus, for the time being there is little chance that Switzerland will become a member. The clause that constitutional changes need a majority of the cantons was designed by the constitution-builders to protect minorities. In the case of membership of the EU this works exactly as planned, and the beneficiaries are the small, rural cantons in German-speaking Switzerland. The irony is that, in this case, it works against other minorities, in particular the French speakers.

The deadlock over Swiss membership of the EU will most likely have the consequence that the French speakers will drift further apart. There will be increasing cooperation among the French-speaking cantons, which will try more and more to resolve political problems on their own. They will also increasingly exploit every constitutional opportunity to cooperate with France. When the Swiss constitution was written in 1848, the cantons received a fair amount of authority to deal with other countries, in particular in matters involving border issues. The French-speaking cantons have already begun increasingly to use this authority. In the border region between the canton Neuchâtel and France, for example, some hospitals are run on a common basis across the border. In the region of Geneva there is even more intensive cross-border cooperation on a large number of issues. Many people work in Geneva but live across the border in France, which means that many issues such as taxes, social security, and health insurance have to be resolved across the border.

Italian speakers in the canton of Ticino and in the southern valleys of the canton of Graubünden are also likely to drift further apart from the rest of Switzerland. Economically, Italian-speaking Switzerland is already to some extent part of the greater Milan region. The newly created (and first) university in Italian-speaking Switzerland is likely to reinforce the drifting-apart of this language region. Before this, Italian speakers had to study either in German- or French-speaking Switzerland, which bonded them to the rest of the country. This kind of bonding will continue to some extent because the newly founded university does not encompass all the faculties. On the other hand, it will attract students from Italy, which will reinforce the orientation of Italian-speaking Switzerland towards Italy.

In German-speaking Switzerland there is also increasing cross-border cooperation. This is particularly true in the region of Basel, where France, Germany, and Switzerland come together. Cross-border cooperation in Basel is institutionalized in the form of the Regio Basiliensis. The conglomeration of Basel extends so far into France and Germany that it is hardly visible in everyday life where one country ends and another begins. The airport is in France, and Germany has its railway station on Swiss territory.

Cantons may use their authority to deal with other countries not only for cross-border issues, but also for issues relating to the EU. Recently Switzerland reached a bilateral agreement with the EU on a large number of issues such as transportation, research, and the labour market. It is conceivable that some cantons, especially in French-speaking Switzerland, will make additional arrangements with the EU that go further, for example for the exchange of students and for other more technical matters.

Do all these developments mean that Switzerland will slowly cease to exist as a state? When, in 1991, the 700th birthday of the Swiss Confederation was celebrated, some artists and intellectuals only half-jokingly coined the motto '700 Jahre sind genug' ('700 years are enough'). Shortly afterwards, at the world exposition in Seville, the official Swiss booth had the theme 'La Suisse n'existe pas' ('Switzerland does not exist'). Recently a federal councillor speculated that sometime in the twenty-first century Switzerland may cease to exist. The idea has been floated that Geneva should separate from Switzerland and, analogous to Monaco, become its own country. All this has been said or written in order to provoke, and should therefore not be taken too seriously, but it is nevertheless noteworthy that the very existence of Switzerland has become a theme of public discourse. In the thirteenth-century treaty that laid the foundations of the Swiss Confederation, it was solemnly stated that the treaty should be eternally valid. In the current political culture of Switzerland it has become difficult for many people, especially the young, highly educated, and urban, to see the existence of Switzerland in terms of eternity. Old songs glorifying its eternity are shrugged off by many.

For all practical purposes, however, Switzerland will probably endure for a long time. There will continue to be a Swiss national soccer team, and the Swiss social security system will continue to pay benefits. But the Swiss nation-state will lose its importance. Instead, the regions will become more important, and some of these regions will cross the Swiss national border. For many younger and highly educated Swiss, a European identity will become more and more important. In the remainder of the chapter, I will argue from a normative position that such a development is desirable.

Normative Implications and Further Research

My normative position is based on an ethics of discourse.[12] As Melissa Orlie puts it, we should attempt to imagine other's views and be willing 'to deliberate, to listen and respond to others' claim about our effects and possibly to modify them'.[13] Following Kristen Renwick Monroe, I reject 'the view of human nature as exclusively self-interested, acquisitive, aggressive, and individualistic'.[14] Politics should, in the words of Orlie, be more than 'thoughtless assertion of power'. As an ideal to strive for, politics in a democracy should be an arena where we are willing to listen to each other and to consider also the interests of others. Of course, we never quite know what the interests of others are because we can never *transcend* our own self; but we can make efforts to understand the interests of others and to *transfigure* our ways of life in the sense that we consider not only our own interests but also the interests of others.

The classical nation-state as it has developed in the last 400 years in Europe is not hospitable to such an ethics of discourse. It is characterized by the superimposition of political, economic, military, and cultural boundaries. As a consequence, the boundaries of the classical nation-state are firmly set and do not allow easy exit.[15] Either one is German or French, Italian or Spanish, and so on. The interests of one's nation-state tend to be seen as in conflict with the interests of other nation-states. If the others win, we lose. Living in such a political environment makes it hard to consider the interests of people outside one's own nation-state. As we know from European history in the last four centuries, an international system based on the classical nation-state easily leads to war. People outside the boundaries of one's own state are easily seen as enemies and not as other human beings whose interests one should also consider.

In my view, a multi-layered political system with fluid borders is more hospitable to an ethics of discourse. In such a political environment people activate different identities. Such multiple identities should help people to imagine identities outside the set of their own identities. To imagine other identities does not necessarily mean that one is willing to consider the interests of the people with these other identities, but the chances are better that one will do so.

Let me illustrate this argument with the example of a woman from the French-speaking Swiss canton of Neuchâtel, who works as a doctor in one of the cross-border hospitals that I mentioned before. Because many political issues are handled at the cantonal level, this woman often activates her identity as Neuchâteloise. Other issues are handled in common by the French-speaking cantons, so that the woman often also displays an identity as Romande (French-speaking Swiss). The Swiss nation-state has lost some of its importance, but it is still very strong, so that for many issues the woman from Neuchâtel has a Swiss identity. If it comes to hospital issues, her role as a doctor becomes salient, and she identifies as a member of the cross-border hospital region. Being highly educated and French-speaking, she is likely to support the entry of Switzerland into the EU, so that sometimes she activates a European identity.

How do these multiple identities help to imagine other identities, and how do they strengthen the willingness to consider the interests of the people holding these other identities? Let me begin with the relation of our woman from Neuchâtel with other French-speaking cantons. The canton of Neuchâtel may, for example, be in conflict with the canton of Geneva; but since for other issues the two cantons have the same interests as French-speaking cantons, it is relatively easy for our Neuchâteloise to imagine the interests of the people from Geneva and to add their interests to her own. There is, of course, no guarantee that she will do so, but the chances are higher than if the two cantons were classical nation-states with firm boundaries.

In a conflict between French- and German-speaking Switzerland, the woman from Neuchâtel might also be willing to consider the interests of the German speakers since for other issues the two language groups have common interests as Swiss. We can extend this argument to the relation of this woman towards France. Working on a daily basis with French women and men in the cross-border hospital, she may be willing to consider the interests of France in any conflict between the two countries.

Considering the interests of other groups may lead to a learning process whereby it becomes a *habit* to imagine other identities and to consider the interests of the people who hold these other identities. This habit may allow the woman from Neuchâtel to consider the interests of other European countries, especially if she also has a European identity. In a further phase of the learning process she may even be willing to consider the interests of people from outside Europe, for example, of refugees from Africa. Such a process will not necessarily happen, but if it does, we are on the path to an ethics of discourse.

However, there are also severe risks if a country takes this path. As Stefano Bartolini has shown,[16] fluid boundaries with easy exit opportunities weaken domestic political structures, which, in turn, may lead to feelings of insecurity among many citizens. They feel at a loss and long for the well-established order of the classical nation-state with its firmly set boundaries. It is precisely such a backlash that is currently occurring in Switzerland. It explains the strengthened position of the Swiss People's Party and the prominent role of such organizations as the Action for a Neutral and Independent Switzerland. From the perspective of an ethics of discourse, I am concerned about this backlash, and it is not easy to know what to do about it. The only option that I see is to teach more intensively an ethics of discourse in schools and universities. In a recent book I tried to show what such teaching would involve in practical terms.[17] As political scientists we should be more concerned not only with what we research but also with what we teach our students.

With increased Europeanization and globalization, the political order is in rapid transition. This transition has put severe strains on the classical nation-state, and because of its strong multiculturalism, Switzerland is particularly vulnerable to such strains. But since multiculturalism is gaining strength in other nation-states as well, similar strains are appearing there too. The main strain is between forces that wish to keep the classical nation-state and forces that strive for a multi-layered order where the nation-state is only one layer among others. An important research task for the future is to investigate this conflict between the classical nation-state and a multi-layered political order. One way to get a better understanding of it is to study public political discourse. How does it construct the political world? Whose interests are put at the forefront? What are the terms in which the common good is defined? Is it exclusively the common good of the nation-state? Or is it also the common good of subnational regions or transnational regions, or the common good of Europe or the global society?

In my current research I am trying to find answers to these questions on a cross-national basis.[18] Besides Switzerland I am studying its four neighbours—Austria, France, Germany, and Italy—and am including also the United States, the United Kingdom, Canada, Belgium, and the Netherlands. For each of the ten countries our research groups are studying parliamentary debates over the last forty years, and to what extent these debates are framed in terms of special interests or the common good. With regard to the latter, we are interested in whether it refers to the nation-state, a subnational region, a transnational region, Europe, or the global society. We expect to find cross-national and temporal variation in how the common good is defined, and such variation will need explanation. One set of explanatory variables has to do with Europeanization and globalization. To what extent is a country integrated into the European and the global market? What is the influence of such integration on how the common good is defined in the parliamentary discourse? Probably this influence will be mediated by other variables, in particular the history of a country, its culture, and its institutions.

Why should we care how the common good is defined? My answer is that the way the common good is defined is likely to influence policy outcomes, for example with regard to refugee and environmental issues. If the common good is almost exclusively defined in terms of the nation-state, I expect refugee policies to be restrictive and environmental policies to be narrowly limited to national borders. Ultimately I am interested in explaining policy outcomes in terms of the 'good life' in a philosophical sense. The degree to which policy outcomes come close to this ideal may very well depend on how we define who we are. This question of identity is a crucial issue to the Swiss. Do they emphasize their independence and neutrality, and strict borders around the country? Or do they see themselves as an open country with fluid borders and multiple identities? After the end of the cold war this may be the key question which not only Switzerland, but every country, has to deal with.

NOTES

I wrote this chapter while I was a visiting fellow at the European University Institute, Florence.

1. For Swiss cultural diversity, see also W. Linder, *Swiss Democracy: Possible Solutions to Conflicts in Multicultural Societies* (London: Macmillan, 1994).
2. See for this concept, see B. Mesmer, 'Reformbedarf im Innern—Druck von

aussen. Die Helvetik im historischen Kontext', *Neue Zürcher Zeitung*, 21–2 (Feb. 1998), 67.

3. These figures vary somewhat depending on whether the foreign population is included.

4. On conflict resolution in Swiss history, see J. Steiner, *Amicable Agreement versus Majority Rule: Conflict Resolution in Switzerland* (Chapel Hill: University of North Carolina Press, 1974).

5. For the concept of consociationalism see the corresponding chapter in J. Steiner, *European Democracies*, 4th edn. (New York: Longman, 1998). See also J. Steiner, 'The Consociational Theory and Switzerland', Paper presented to the Conference on the Fate of Consociationalism, Center for European Studies, Harvard University, 2–31 May 1998.

6. Linder, *Swiss Democracy*.

7. B. Barry, 'Political Accommodation and Consociational Democracy', *British Journal of Political Science*, 5 (Oct. 1975), 477–505.

8. Note the similarities to the plans for Northern Ireland.

9. W. Linder, H. Riedwyl, and J. Steiner, 'Wie gut können eidgenössische Abstimmungen durch Aggregatsdaten auf Bezirksebene erklärt werden?', MS, Berne, 1998.

10. K. Deprez, 'Belgium: A Post-National State?', Paper presented to the Conference of the Swiss National Science Foundation on Nation and National Identities, 29–30 Oct. 1998.

11. Italian speakers seem to take a middle position, but they are often not numerous enough in surveys for valid conclusions about their identities.

12. For a full development of my normative position, see J. Steiner, *Conscience in Politics: An Empirical Investigation of Swiss Decision Cases* (New York: Garland, 1996).

13. M. A. Orlie, 'Thoughtless Assertion and Political Deliberation', *American Political Science Review*, 88 (Sept. 1994), 693.

14. K. Renwick Monroe, 'John Donne's People: Explaining Differences between Rational Actors and Altruists through Cognitive Frameworks', *Journal of Politics*, 53 (May 1991), 396.

15. On the question of boundaries and exit options in the classical nation-state, see S. Bartolini, 'Exit Options, Boundary Building, Political Structuring', MS, European University Institute, Florence, Oct. 1997.

16. Ibid.

17. Steiner, *Conscience in Politics*.

18. The project, entitled 'The Consociational Theory and Ethics in the Public Discourse', is funded by the Swiss National Science Foundation.

CHAPTER 8

Civil Society, Media, and Globalization in Catalonia

MIREYA FOLCH-SERRA AND JOAN NOGUE-FONT

Globalization has become prevalent as an explanatory tool for a variety of world phenomena. Treated as a prime cause and a derivative consequence, an ongoing process, and a final outcome, globalization is viewed as erasing differences, discontinuities, and divisions, whether they are economic, cultural, or political. It is also perceived, however, as a force increasing differentiation between places through the spread of unevenness in its personal linkages and relations of social power and domination. Regardless of which one of these antagonistic interpretations is supported, the transformative consequences of globalization cannot be ignored.[1]

In this chapter we consider the impact of globalization on the capacity to establish and maintain public space in a specific setting. In particular, we ponder the effect of globalization on the development of Catalan civil society, through an evaluation of its media from a spatial and historical perspective. We explore local responses to global change. We incorporate the notion of civil society within the context of national identity and globalization. Traits of civil society such as the dialogue established by individuals and institutions, the incorporation of individuals into groups through institutions, and the political spaces enclosing cultural, religious, and social alliances are represented and discussed in the Catalan local media. In turn, the media's network of communication and information strengthens, shapes, and instils vitality into the civil society. Our main objective is to assess, against the backdrop of current district and municipal publications dating from the 1800s to 1997, the role played by the press in the formation and preservation of local identity in Catalonia.

The Nature of Civil Society

The institutions of civil society affect the immediate reality of individuals when they assemble, associate, speak, and reason together. Individuals become part of a group through these institutions and, in turn, groups of individuals forge public spaces that encircle cultural, religious, and social alliances. These relations facilitate conversations within and between households, neighbourhoods, districts, and regions within the wider space of a nation. Together, institutions and voluntary organizations such as churches, unions, citizens' associations, and cultural circles are the embodiment of civil society, and provide a network of communication and information, the ultimate outcome of which is the expression of a national community.

These institutions of civil society, whose political role is not directly related to the control or conquest of power but to the generation of influence through the life of democratic associations and unconstrained discussion in the cultural public sphere, are logically inscribed in a dialogical framework, which is to say, a democratic form of argumentation. Members of civil society are always engaged in dialogue and interpersonal relations, and this situation necessarily implies a particular space where the communicative action takes place. Its function, therefore, is contingent on the place *where* it is established, and must be located within a border. However, the delimitation of a place does not have to involve closure and segregation, but instead may represent a cultural frontier that opens to outside influences and is permeable and porous.

The geography of civil society indicates the possibility of a position in space, whether that position is personal, political, cultural, or social. A conceptual border is not the same as a barrier. It imparts a sense of place and solidarity with other members of society because social relations react to and are conditioned by the constraints of time and space, for example those that take place in a 'busy, transient but ever-renewed *social space* . . . established by the pattern of interactions: the regular timetabled meetings, the informal consultations, the periodic social events, the fundraising activities'.[2] It is within such a context that the opportunity arises to develop bonds of attachment between individuals, organizations, and specific places. Thus, social interactions within the institutions of civil society may produce 'the identity of a place—its social structure, its political character, its "local" culture'.[3] In our example, this character of local culture is shown through the web of Catalan district and municipal publications.

According to the local prevailing conditions, civil society can always become more just, more democratic, more dialogical.[4] In theory, civil societies are the sphere of social interaction composed of voluntary associations seen as the context and product of self-constituting collective actors.[5] In practice, they exist within a geographical framework, are specific to particular national identities, and should not be lumped together with the state and the economy. Some authors have looked into the notion of civil society in relation to the state and the nation.[6] In fact, the strength of civil society in a particular enclave is often measured against the institutional penetration of the state.[7]

The juxtaposition of voluntary associations in the state are well known: society *against* state, nations *against* state, social order *against* political system, private life *against* public power, public life *against* state.[8] Contemporary examples of the opposition of civil society and state abound in relation to the pre- and post-1989 east European 'revolutions',[9] and in the civic struggles of nations without states like Scotland, Catalonia, Quebec, Wales, the Basque Country, and countless others.[10] Civil society, in brief, is an instrument of dialogue, and constitutes the means by which a nation unites for a common end outside the parameters delineated by the state. As Giner and Arbós remark, for the state, demarcation is an end, whilst for civil society it is ambiguity, or what we call porous boundaries.[11] All in all, civil society is the glue that holds together the identity of the members of a nation through civic, religious, and cultural institutions. Catalan identity has been shaped through time by its civil society institutions.

Identity

But what is meant by 'identity', that most charged of concepts? Nation and identity have been amply discussed in academic and popular writing. The latter has been associated not only with personal characteristics such as gender, ethnicity, and class, but also with geographical space. One comes from a specific place, and one is born into a culture. G. Dijkink has argued that each human being yearns for a sensible pattern of people, things, and behaviour in the world, the standards of which are 'acquired during one's youth through exposure to events and objects in the environment and through becoming a member of an interpretive community'.[12] Even the children of immigrants and refugees are given a point of reference and are instilled with memories of place through tales and lullabies. To these children, exile and displacement do not mean being beyond time and space. The

FIG. 8.1. Catalonia

materiality of their geographies is made tangible by the cultural context within the household in spite of the virtual and real cosmopolitanism of their condition. Along these lines, Woolard has provided an
analysis of bilingualism and the politics of ethnicity in Catalonia.[13] In
her account, Castilian-speaking immigrants have for the most part

chosen to protect their Castilian identity within Catalonia. Native Catalans have also continued to maintain their own cultural identity in spite of having become a minority, for the first time in history, within the Barcelona metropolitan regions. (See Figure 8.2.)

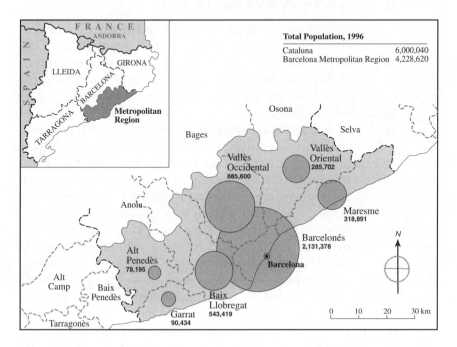

FIG. 8.2. Population of the Barcelona Metropolitan Region 1996

Some people in Barcelona yearn for their faraway Castilian culture, while others struggle to preserve their Catalan heritage *in situ*. One way or the other, people need social interaction to foster their cultural identity, because the image of self is grounded in a particular place, whether this place is a nostalgic narration or the actual site where everyday life unfolds. As Bakhtin has remarked, 'At first I am conscious of myself only through others: they give me the words, the forms, and the tonality that constitute my first image of myself.'[14] It is precisely through others' image of the self that people's interactions are constituted. But these interactions, which foster personal conditions of time and space, take place within and between the institutions of civil society. Massey calls these coordinates 'envelopes of space-time in which and between which we live and move and have our "Being"'.[15] Identity then is linked to the place we must *inhabit* to communicate with one another, with the group, with the text, with the culture, and so on.[16]

The Tug-of-War over Nation and Identity

The current discourse surrounding the nation and identity is not neutral. Most studies of nationalism have criticized it, generally associating the search for nationhood with segregation, stagnation, and fear of the other. Accordingly, some authors have asserted that the quest for identity is nothing less than the construct of 'nationalist ideologues and misplaced symbolism',[17] or as Woolard states in her analysis of class and identity in Barcelona, a form of 'double talk'.[18] A recoil from writing about minority identities, traditions, and cultures is advocated, and theorists are advised to focus on the majority and mainstream: 'to do otherwise is to risk merely reproducing—or worse yet, celebrating in a scientistic jargon that too frequently legitimizes what it names—an ideology of identity from which we should, I believe, distance ourselves'.[19] This task involves debunking 'the politics of memory, identity, and heritage' and focusing instead on scientific records of actual occurrences that took place in the past.[20] Although there is nothing intrinsically wrong with discovering 'scientific records', they must, nonetheless, be interpreted by contemporary scholars. The hermeneutics of meaning cannot be avoided. In the fact-finding campaign, however, meaning has no 'meaning' because it is not a matter of frequencies and statistics, and, like identity, is profoundly unstable. An interpretive community is not easily pinned down. Pierre Nora observes that 'modern memory is, above all, archival'. It relies entirely on the materiality of the trace, the immediacy of the recording, the visibility of the image.'[21] But oral history also plays an important role in the making of modern memory.

Homi Bhabha, on the other hand, has suggested a way of overcoming this essentialist position that turns Territory into Tradition and the People into One by looking at the 'liminality of the nation-space . . . [that allows] the national subject [to] split in the ethnographic perspective of culture's contemporaneity and provides both a theoretical position and a narrative authority for marginal voices or minority discourse'.[22] In the book *Identity in Question*, the authors engage in an examination of how meanings of identity have been determined, and categories fixed.[23] Aranowitz, for example, sees identities formed in social movements as not only many-sided, but also politically 'heteronomous'.[24] Thus minority identity can be conceived not as a given, monolithic, traditional identity, but rather as a multifaceted, unpredictable force that serves to problematize and recompose traditions, and in doing so opens the 'culture' to new possibilities, new subjectivities. This positive assessment, however, is not shared by all.

Some fear that the search for identity can lead to schizophrenia. Using his own life as an example, Todorov has perceived a dialogical tension between his two languages, French and Bulgarian, a tension also present in the possibility of his position in space. He ponders: 'Though I am French and Bulgarian at the same time, I can only be in Paris or Sofia at any given moment. Ubiquity is not yet within my reach. The tenor of my remarks is too dependent upon their place of utterance for my whereabouts to be irrelevant.'[25] Thus two elements of identity, language (culture) and place (geography), multiply and magnify the conflict, and lead Todorov to refuse the notion that one who belongs to two cultures loses his soul, while doubting at the same time that having two voices, two languages, is a privilege guaranteeing access to modernity.[26] After an unsettling experience in his country of origin, Todorov seems to have found the key to a balanced bilingual self in a clear articulation between his two linguistic and cultural identities. However, other 'sufferers' of dual identities are not so fortunate. In some cases, the historico-political context is burdensome, the cultural conflict is painfully alive. Savin's example of Chicano poets clearly shows the impossibility of keeping two identities in separate compartments.[27] Their only route is to mix elements of both cultures in a move towards a hybrid, border identity. In Catalonia this is further complicated because cultural identity is intermingled with class relations and Catalan language is perceived as a 'potential weapon of oppression' by the Castilian-speaking community in Woolard's account.[28]

As we stated, while the rhetoric of globality becomes all-embracing, there emerges a discourse of community that provides a moral measure against which transnational *cultural* claims are measured. What Bhabha proposes is a cosmopolitan community envisaged in a *marginal* relation between the patriotic and the cosmopolitan, the home and the world. It is precisely this border—narrower than the human horizon— that attracts him. 'It is a space that somehow falls short of the transcendent human universal, and for that very reason provides an ethical entitlement to, and enactment of, the sense of community.'[29] Thus the language of borders, liminality, and community, associated with identity and nation, is very different from the one used by the theorists of nationalism, who advocate notions of cultural and national coherence inscribed in a political map of the world made of nation-states.

Coherence is extolled at the expense of porous, permeable boundaries of identity; and the fusion of opposites is advocated as an ideal dialectical model. But the dialogue between minorities and the majority must take place in a space filled with different identities, where 'We appraise ourselves from the point of view of others . . . [where] constantly and intensely, we oversee and apprehend the reflections of our life in the plane of consciousness of other men.'[30] National identity implies the necessity of space–time coordinates (chronotopical borders) for the establishment of dialogue (global or at any other geographical scale), because dialogue can only be brought about through the possibility of difference.

Catalan Civil Society

It is this possibility of difference that was the inspiration for a renewed cultural movement at the turn of the century in Catalonia. Catalans decided to celebrate their cultural differences, which had been systematically suppressed through the centuries. From the years between 1888, when the Universal Exposition took place in Barcelona, to 1906 a nationalist movement seized the opportunity presented by the crisis of the Spanish state (divided between the war with the United States and the loss of Cuba, its last American colony) to build a strong sense of identity on the basis of the recognition that Spain was the state and Catalonia the nation.[31] The outcome of this movement was the foundation of civil associations reflecting a renewed impetus of Catalanism. (See figure 8.3.) This movement became a representation of nationalism by associating the nation with civil society, rather than by associating the nation with economic or class interests. The process was not entirely unprecedented. In the medieval period civil society had to fight against the state on two different fronts, to have its autonomy recognized against feudal regulations, and to avoid impingement or domination from neighbouring states. Even the city-states of that period could become relatively autonomous if they had a strong civil society, Barcelona being an example.[32] In the centuries that followed the medieval period Catalonia's autonomous political institutions would be abolished and its body politic incorporated into the Spanish crown by 1713. At that moment a weakened Catalan civil society and the Spanish state became completely separated. Thus, the incipient Catalanist movement at the turn of the century can be interpreted as a conscious attempt to restore the strength of civil society.

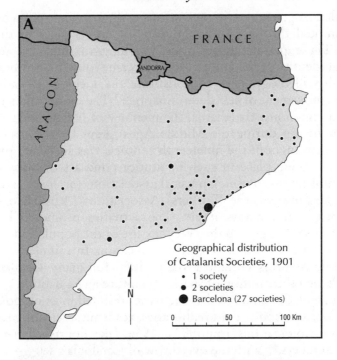

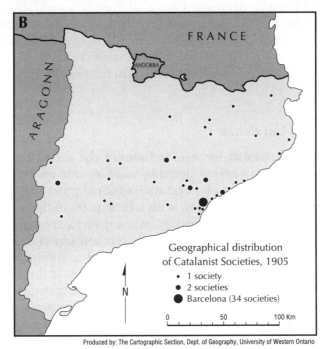

FIG. 8.3. Geographical distribution of the Catalanists associations, 1901 and 1905

Catalan language and literature, music, the arts, and sports began to be promoted through the institutions of civil society in the early 1800s. These private associations, working to impart a sense of national identity at the cultural level, became fully fledged bearers of nationalist ideology, later to constitute the ideological basis for a political movement of self-determination.[33] The more or less residual national consciousness (that is, the memory of having been an independent nation during the Middle Ages), kept by the majority of Catalans throughout the nineteenth century, was sustained by active processes taking place in such institutions and associations such as sport clubs (*excursionisme*), musical associations (*orfeons*), traditional dance (*sardanisme*), the Workers' Associations (Agrupació Obrera Catalanista), and many others. The activities promoted by these associations impinged on the everyday life of the population and provided a means of interpersonal communication. In a similar way, reading the local press became a daily ritual for many Catalans, and strengthened their notion of sharing a culture and a nation.

The cumulative effect of these activities resulted in an outpouring of institutions of popular culture, libraries, academics, scientific societies, and private foundations from 1900 to 1936. They flourished in unprecedented numbers.[34] With the overthrow of Catalonia's self-government by General Franco's decree in 1939 it all came to an end. But the suppression of political autonomy and civil institutions did not completely erase the sense of national identity in Catalonia. Although several decades were to pass before the institutions were restored, the hiatus only served to conceal their continuity into the present time.[35]

The Press in Catalonia

The press in Catalonia has evolved within the social, cultural, and political climate of a nation defining itself against multiple circumstances. The coexistence of a regional–national press that covers the Catalan territory in its entirety, with a local press indigenous to each geographic zone (province, district, municipality), constitutes at present its distinctive trait.[36] Authors Alberch and Huertas, and before them Guillamet, documented the instance of a robust number of municipal and district publications of local character flourishing side by side with the main Barcelona dailies.[37] This trend originated in the seventeenth century, when the first publications of a periodical nature appeared generally by the name of *Gazette*, *Account*, *Letter*, *Note*, or *Mercury*, as in other European countries.[38]

It was during the nineteenth century that the first publications exalting Catalanism appeared. This trend culminated in the second half of the century with a range of newspapers and magazines published in Catalan which served as both mouthpiece and support for the so-called *renaixença*, or renaissance, which was the name given to the cultural movement that gave rise to institutions promoting Catalan language and the arts, in spite of Castilian being imposed as the language of administration and justice in the region.[39] The first newspaper written completely in Catalan was the *Diari Català*, founded in Barcelona in 1879. It only lasted for about two years, but others came in its place and, by the end of the Civil War in 1939, twenty-five different newspapers were being published in the Catalan language, all of them in Barcelona.[40] Yet strict censorship was imposed during the 1940s and all publications had to adhere to the new political order, effectively suppressing freedom of expression. By that time, however, some of the regions of Catalonia had begun to see the resurgence of a local press with a strong nationalist content.

Characteristics of the Regional Press

Municipal and district publications, which had been widely diffused and distributed prior to Franco's dictatorship (1939–75), did not resurface with renewed vigour until the late 1960s.[41] (See Figure 8.4.) This resurgence was favoured in part by the Press and Printing Law of 1966. After this the local press became a notable witness and protagonist of the political and social tensions of the dictatorship's last years, yet legal support for freedom of expression was still very limited. Publications usually survived only due to the complicity and support of the civil society manifested through Catholic parishes and cultural and recreational associations. It was only during the period of democratic transition (1975–9) that a very intense movement of appearance and disappearance of periodicals, magazines, and some dailies took place. Noticeably, four years after Franco's death, in 1979, municipal and district publications had increased to 201: 8 were dailies, 39 were periodicals, and 154 were magazines. In 1979 out of 944 municipalities there were 159 with their own press, compared to 204 in 1939 before the fascist repression. By 1986 publications had increased to 221 (10 dailies, 37 periodicals, and 174 magazines) encompassing 185 municipalities with their own press.[42]

At present most municipalities with several thousand inhabitants have a privately owned press produced in the town either monthly,

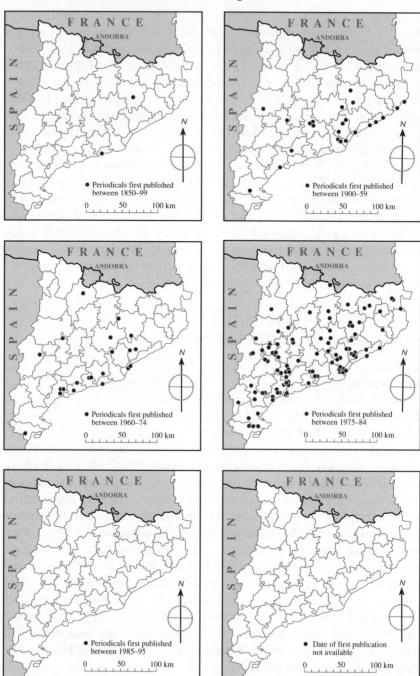

FIG. 8.4. Chronology and location of district and municipal publications

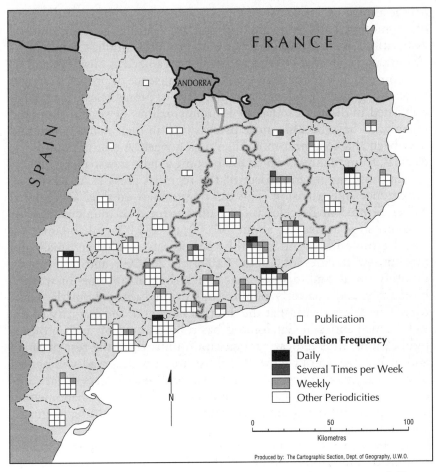

FIG. 8.5. Frequency of publication of periodicals, including major dailies

bi-monthly, weekly, or daily. (See Figure 8.5.) These publications are often distributed throughout the entire region or several regions. Similarly, many of the smaller municipalities in Catalonia also have smaller, less frequent magazines (every other month or quarterly) which are published by cultural or civic associations or by non-professional collectives—again corroborating the strength of provincial civil society. These media form a virtual communications and information network that provide a large amount of news and informative matters of local interest not picked up in the press, radio, or television with wider circulation. Some of the main characteristic features of the district and municipal press that should be pointed out are:

(*a*) the almost exclusive use of Catalan language; (*b*) its large diversity of promoters, such as neighbourhood associations, schools, cultural associations, recreational groups, youth groups, Catholic Church institutions, and collectives of journalists not organized as business; and (*c*) as a consequence of the above, a common absence of proper strategies to obtain greater frequency and circulation. Nonetheless, magazines published in district capitals or in municipalities of several thousand inhabitants have become more professional in their management and have been able to appear more than once a week. A case in point is the *Regió 7*, from Manresa, which has become a daily newspaper.

The most significant aspect of the regional press is its territorial coexistence and extension. This can be summarized thus: (*a*) regional dailies printed in Barcelona; (*b*) dailies printed in municipalities or medium-sized cities of about 50,000 to 250,000 inhabitants; (*c*) weekly, bimonthly, and monthly periodicals printed in small and medium-sized cities of about 10,000 to 200,000; and (*d*) mostly monthly local and district magazines, but also some bi-weekly, bimonthly, and quarterly publications printed throughout the territory. These data reveal that the internal market of the majority of the 944 municipalities in Catalonia is basically covered by autochtonous publications, thus indicating a situation unusual in the rest of Spain and in Europe. In our view, this illustrates a widespread willingness to read the Catalan press. Local news, local newsmakers, local readers, and local journalists are part and parcel of the same phenomenon: an interpretative (signifying) community united by culture, language, and human agency.

In 1986 experts in communication studies engaged by the Council of Europe undertook a study of the district of Penedès in order to analyse its system of local communication. The 'system', they observed, consists of the district press, the municipal press, the district radio, the municipal radio, and the local (regional) and district television. It may seem paradoxical that such a coherent conglomerate of local media has developed in an age of uniformity and mass communication that leaves little space for the re-creation of local identity. Yet, in fact, globalization and the political and economic logic of large-scale systems of government have had the contrary effect of delimiting the bounds of similarity, and drawing new borders that respond to the need of individual identity within more meaningful collectivities. As David Laitin demonstrates (Chapter 5 in this volume), 'regional language groups, politically dead for centuries, have become mobilized and mobilizable'. According to this thesis, a 'constellation' of languages could become the alternative to language rationalization strategies traditionally employed by nation-states to superimpose a hegemonic language over their multilingual population.

The district and municipal press in Catalonia has been greatly favoured by a factor that, if not totally determining, has been at least influential: this is the fact that the metropolitan dailies (printed in Barcelona) have not made a serious effort to include district and municipal news and information. These dailies have assumed the role either of regional informants (*Avui, El Periódico de Catalunya*), or of disseminators of the news of the Spanish state (*La Vanguardia*). The district and municipal press, therefore, has not had to deal with serious competitors, as has been the case in France and Germany. In France, for example, many regional dailies offer extended district and municipal editions. In Germany some of the district dailies have formed associations to produce supplements common to all areas. In Catalonia this latter variant was intended, without success, by *El Correo Catalán* in the late 1960s with a special edition for the districts of Vallès Occidental and Vallès Oriental. More recently (1993 and 1994) *El Nou Diari* also tried and failed. In the past, as in the present, the creation of dailies in Barcelona has been associated with the idea of covering the whole of the Catalan territory, thus endeavouring to reach both the cosmopolitan urban population and the population of small cities and rural enclaves. This aim entails two different functions and approaches to information (providing local information for two sets of readers with different interests and needs), but nonetheless it was supposed to work by printing supplements with local news. Before the revival of the district and municipal press some Barcelona regional dailies could have assumed, in part, the role of the former, penetrated the market, and prevented the future publication of new district dailies. After the explosion of the local press, however, the regional Barcelona press cannot possibly hope to rival the district and municipal press, sustainable and well entrenched as it is in its territories.

But the demographic weight of the metropolitan region, with close to three-quarters of the principality's population (4.2 million), cannot be ignored. In it more than half the population (53 per cent) are Castilian speakers. In the rest of the Catalan territory, Catalan speakers are bilingual. They have to be because they need to access services that are provided solely in Castilian. For example, only about 5 per cent of justice administration is provided in Catalan—even driving licences are in Castilian. According to a survey done to compare language use between the years 1990 and 1995, it has become evident that the metropolitan region is clearly divided along linguistic borders. For example, in 1990 the regular use of Catalan was 35.8 per cent and in

1995 36.3 per cent in the metropolitan region. But there is a caveat in these figures because, in the city proper, the regular use of Catalan was 42.3 per cent in 1990 and 44.2 per cent in 1995. However, in what city planners call *primera corona* it was 22.9 per cent, while in the *segona corona* it was 42.6 per cent. Thus the survey considered not two, but three, different areas in the metropolitan region: the city, and the inner and outer urban belts.[43]

These figures are telling because the particular distribution and consumption of publications in Catalan are made to fit this 'linguistic segregation'. Obviously, whoever does not speak Catalan will not patronize publications in that language. So what has to be acknowledged is the large population of Castilian speakers who have lived in the metropolitan region for several decades now (since the later 1940s). They can live and work in Castilian, no matter how hard the Generalitat (the Catalan provincial government) works on the implementation of a linguistic programme. As McRoberts remarks, the Generalitat 'could not even bring Catalan up to a position of equality with Castilian'.[44] But in spite of this situation, the district and municipal press is almost all written in Catalan, even though the demographic weight is not on its side. Lately, however, some of Barcelona's dailies have made concessions to the Catalan language. One of the papers written in Castilian, *El Periódico*, now publishes a Catalan version (since 28 October 1997), which has almost as much readership as its Castilian version.[45]

Barcelona, like Toronto, Vancouver, New York, and Los Angeles, has become a site of international flows of capital and labour, which have been widely discussed as an economic issue. But if we consider the other side of the global city, its political culture, which in this case is a product of an ancient cultural continuity, then the drive towards globalization and homogeneity may have to be reconsidered. For a contemporary city is simultaneously a locale, where social relations are created; a location where global economic processes impinge;[46] and a place where the particular qualities of a culture are experienced by the inhabitants.[47] The Catalan-speaking citizens of Barcelona are still affecting the fate of their city through their cultural preferences, as the concession made by *El Periódico* shows.

Another issue that bears consideration is the difference between the legal and the cultural use of the language. Of course, one reinforces the other, but in some instances one or the other must predominate. In Catalonia the cultural use of Catalan in publications, as language of instruction in education, and language of popular culture was banned between 1939 and 1975. Its legal implementation began only with the Generalitat's new language law in 1977, which, according to McRoberts, seems quite limited when compared to programmes adopted in some other settings, such as Quebec.[48] Is time a factor that can affect the social use of Catalan in all its legal and cultural aspects? As McRoberts demonstrates, Castilian is the first or preferred language of close to half the population in Catalonia, 'and will likely stay that way'.[49] This would make Catalan speakers and, by the same token, Catalan culture a minority in the principality. However, the cultural drive and persistence of a linguistic culture may not be so easily overpowered by purely demographic weight.[50] On the whole, support for the language will have to come from an altogether different environment. As Danielle Provansal has stated, 'in what concerns civil society, the groups speaking Castilian have become minority groups within a Catalan cultural majority'. If this is the case, the demographic picture does not conform to the cultural significance of the civil society in Catalonia. [51]

The District and Municipal Press and the 'fet nacional'

The regional press (that is the press covering the whole principality) is represented by *Avui, El Periódico, La Vanguardia* (all printed in Barcelona) and the state dailies published in Madrid, with their Catalan versions.[52] Of these, the only daily published in Catalan is *Avui* (and lately a version of *El Periódico*), a journalistic enterprise politically linked to the Catalan government via its party, *Convèrgencia i Unió*, and heavily subsidized by the Generalitat. Its poor financial situation can be attributed, in part, to the fact that it has become a political project rather than a journalistic one. At the beginning of 1996 *Avui* had accumulated more than 4,000 million pesetas of debt. In Table 8.1 we show the circulation of daily newspapers edited in Catalonia (including Barcelona and the provinces) from 1984 to 1992. It is interesting to note that eight out of eleven are written in Catalan, and while the only daily whose circulation has decreased is *Avui*, the general trend has been an increase in circulation. From the three written in Castilian, two are published in Barcelona, and one in the city of Lleida, in the province of the same name. The large sales of the dailies written in Castilian and published in Barcelona reflect the demographic composition of the city, which since the 1960s has accommodated a population from other regions of Spain where Catalan is not spoken, making the case of Barcelona a unique instance in relation to the rest of the territory, where the majority are Catalan

TABLE 8.1. *Circulation of daily newspapers edited in Catalonia, 1984–1992* (no. of copies)

Title	Place of publication	Sales		
		1984	1986	1992
La Vanguardia	Barcelona	194,189	194,553	206,829
El Periódico	Barcelona	127,775	150,912	180,992
Avui	Barcelona	40,452	40,232	35,432
Punt Diari	Girona	10,694	10,878	16,297
Diari de Girona	Girona	5,270	6,910	7,501
Diari de Tarragona	Tarragona	n/a	7,007	12,145
Segre	Lleida	6,950	6,498	10,695
Diari de Sabadell	Sabadell	6,111	6,255	7,874
Diari de Terrasa	Terrasa	5,352	5,184	5,727
La Mañana	Lleida	n/a	5,063	8,032
Regió 7	Manresa	3,542	4,575	8,070

Note: n/a = not available.

Source: J. M. Corbella, *General Survey of the 1980s: Social Communication in Catalonia* (Barcelona: Generalitat de Catalunya, 1988), 16; *Anuari de la Informació de Catalunya, 1994–1995* (Barcelona: Fundació Centre Internacional de Premsa).

speakers. The four Catalan provinces are represented in the table, as well as some of the districts (see table 8.1).

With the noted exception of the districts of metropolitan Barcelona, the district and municipal press has not only been linguistically 'normalized', but it has become economically self-sufficient with no need of subsidies. Data collected in 1985 demonstrated that of 217 district publications, 158 were completely written in Catalan, 28 had a small amount of Castilian, 23 were bilingual, 7 were bilingual with predominance of Castilian, and only *one* was totally Castilian.[53] In relation to the above table, the proportion that is Castilian is minimal outside the metropolitan area. This study was conducted barely ten years after the use of Catalan had been forbidden for about four decades, leaving the younger generations without the writing and reading skills necessary to function in the language. At the time of writing, the 200-plus district and municipal periodicals are almost all written in Catalan, close to 85 per cent.[54] These publications are read by an estimated readership of 2 million people, according to data gathered by Ricard Rafecas, president of La Associació Catalana de Prensa Comarcal.[55]

The healthy financial condition of the district press is demonstrated by a daily, *El Punt*—issued in 1979 in Girona—which has been steadily increasing its circulation, and also its profits, year after year. Two other district dailies, *El 9 Nou* and *Regió 7*, are following the trend established by *El Punt*: they have achieved a healthy financial state, and the costs of production and distribution are much lower than those from Barcelona's publishing firms. In fact, they are generating enough profits to allow for an expansion of circulation and territorial reach. *El Punt*, for example, is on the verge of a spectacular expansion into the faraway districts of Tarragona and Reus. These are the first steps towards the formation of a regional daily written in Catalan covering the whole principality, and published outside Barcelona. It looks like the reverse of the top-down process followed by *Avui*. Indeed, the diffusion of written Catalan is now a reality without the need for subsidies, thanks to the district press in the Girona region, and in the central zone of the interior, where the city of Manresa functions as a nucleus. (See table 8.1.)

The district and municipal press is steadily becoming a source of influence and inspiration for the so-called linguistic normalization of Catalonia. It is also true that public radio and television broadcast in Catalan throughout the whole region. Yet these are different media and fulfil different functions. Thus, it is difficult to compare them. Furthermore, Catalan television, even if it covers the entirety of the territory, has its headquarters in Barcelona. Its programming is aimed at the metropolitan population, and it extends this cosmopolitan focus to the rest of the region. On the other hand, the district and municipal press is radically different: it has multiple headquarters and is produced from multiple viewpoints. It represents better than any other media the dialogical nature of civil society: a universe of many discourses and multiple uses of social and cultural spaces—each 'animating each other'.[56]

Figures 8.4 and 8.5 show not only the frequency of publication, but the number and location of periodicals and their first date of publication. It is noticeable that the chronology and location of periodical publications (fig. 8.4) also provide a rough impression of population distribution in the region. As can be observed, the most heavily populated area is the coastal plain, with clusters around Barcelona and Tarragona. Barcelona acts as the centre of an urban system which extends to the surrounding districts and serves about 70 per cent of the population. This metropolitan area includes most of the cities with more than 50,000 inhabitants. In the remainder of the territory only the other provincial capitals (Girona, Lleida, and Tarragona) and the cities of Reus and Manresa have more than 50,000 inhabitants. The population is thus unevenly concentrated in the coastal districts, with a much lighter density in the interior. This distribution also explains the spatial pattern of older publications concentrated in the more urbanized areas of the principality. A historical pattern, too, can be discerned. During the period 1975–84 ninety-two periodicals were published for the first time. This is the highest number in relation to the other periods shown in Figure 8.4. A boom of this order could be attributed to the arrival of democracy, and the public demand for publications written in Catalan. The other noticeable trait is the flipside of the former: before 1975 the number of publications was less than half, probably reflecting the nature of political repression. All in all, the tally of the plotted 296 publications is as follows: 2 in 1850–99; 24 in 1900–59; 20 in 1960–74; 88 in 1985–95; and 70 non-dated.[57]

The frequency of publication, represented by the squares (Fig. 8.5) follows a slightly different pattern. But the main consideration here is to show the location of the publisher. Each square represents a single publication, and the shading reflects the frequency—from daily publications, to several times per week, to weekly and beyond. The map does not show circulation (illustrated in table 8.1), thus the Barcelona dailies, which presumably are read throughout the principality, are shown only on their site of publication. The point made through the maps goes beyond these spatial characteristics. What we hope to convey, rather, is a process of communication that involves a population unevenly distributed in a land surface of about 32,000 square kilometres. Those who live in or near rural communities and provincial capitals (Girona, Tarragona, and Lleida) are consistently reading 296 district and municipal publications, mostly written in Catalan, to know more about their immediate social and physical environment.

Conclusion

Our case shows that the singularity of some places may disrupt the ostensible universalizing force of globalization. Through the everyday act of living in a locality and actively seeking information about local news, Catalan speakers in Catalonia delineate a distinct outcome of their particular historical, cultural, and territorial circumstances. This exploit confirms a conception of nationalism as a place-specific phenomenon—transformed by the processes of globalization, and yet not engulfed by the same processes. Rather, 'nationalism has an ideological core which is, to a certain extent, autonomous and independent of the structures of modernity; in other words, nationalism is a long historical precipitate and not a byproduct of modernity, even if the latter might have given it a larger than life image'.[58] Because it is place-specific, nationalism *depends* on the bonds established by a community of agreement (a signifying community), which leads to a greater or lesser shared identity of interest in the society.

The initiative of reading the Catalan popular press, taken consciously by the population as a whole, can be contrasted with initiatives promoted by the political–intellectual bourgeoisie through subsidized publication. The project of reading in Catalan is developed and furthered by local publications dealing with local issues reflecting the everyday-life aspect of the culture. This illustrates that national identity must be rooted in civil society, and cannot be carried by government institutions alone. As Gillis states, 'in this era of plural identities, we need civil times and civil spaces more than ever, for these are essential to the democratic processes by which individuals and groups come together to discuss, debate, and negotiate the past, and through this process, define the future'.[59] It follows from this that national identity is directly linked to the everyday deeds of individuals establishing social alliances through the networks of communication and information.

Municipal and district publications show one instance of this pragmatic function of civil society. They also illustrate attachment to language, culture, and place, thus linking civil society and the media. There are many more instances that could and should be observed and analysed in order to draw wider conclusions and more results about the manifestations of the civil society and their contribution to national identity in Catalonia. Further studies should engage other forms of communication, and draw comparisons with one another. An analysis of the content of publications would also contribute to understanding the topics that interest Catalan readers. Yet we believe that the practical engagement of the population in supporting the existence of these publications is in itself worth revealing.

NOTES

We would like to thank Roger King for his suggestions on the representation of data in our maps, and for his helpful comments on the first draft. Also, our appreciation goes to David Mercer and Trish Chalk for their fine cartographic work.

1. The consequences of globalization are considered by a variety of authors. Some of the latest discussions include the works of A. Amin and N. Thrift (eds.),

Globalization, Institutions, and Regional Development in Europe (Oxford: Oxford University Press, 1994), on globalization and regional development in Europe; the collection of articles in K. R. Cox (ed.), *Spaces of Globalization: Reasserting the Power of the Local* (New York: Guilford Press, 1997), dealing with the spaces of globalization and how they impact on local enclaves; the links between nationalism, globalization, and modernity discussed by J. P. Arnason, 'Nationalism, Globalization and Modernity', *Theory, Culture and Society*, 7 (1990), 207–36; A. Scott, *Regions and the World Economy* (Oxford: Oxford University Press, 1998), on the coming shape of global production; and James Laxer's critique of globalization *False God: How the Globalization Myth has Impoverished Canada* (Toronto: Lester, 1993).

2. E. K. Teather, 'Voluntary Organizations as Agents in the Becoming of Place', *Canadian Geographer*, 41/3 (1997), 231.
3. D. Massey, *Space, Place and Gender* (Minneapolis: University of Minnesota Press, 1994), 120.
4. As M. Bakhtin alludes to in *Toward a Philosophy of the Act* (Austin: University of Texas Press, 1993), the text–context relations of social action are contingent: they act in response to the time-space conditions of possibility.
5. J. L. Cohen and A. Arato, *Civil Society and Political Theory* (Cambridge, Mass.: MIT Press, 1994).
6. A. Shanks, *Civil Society: Civil Religion* (Oxford: Blackwell, 1995); C. Hann and E. Dunn (eds.), *Civil Society: Challenging Western Models* (New York: Routledge, 1996); J. Keane, *Civil Society and the State* (New York: Verso, 1988); R. Dahrendorf, *After 1989: Morals, Revolution and Civil Society* (Oxford: St Anthony's College, 1997); M. Shaw, *Civil Society and Media in Global Crisis* (New York: Pinter, 1996); S. Giner and X. Arbós, *La governabilitat i l'esdevenidor de les societats modernes* (Barcelona: Edicions 62, 1990).
7. Although the systematic study of civil society is a relatively recent field of inquiry, there are antecedents, such as the controversial classic first published in 1767: A. Ferguson, *An Essay on the History of Civil Society* (London: Transaction Books, 1980), which has become required reading for those interested in the evolutionary history of society; and, of course, Gramsci's works reversing the reductionist trend of the Marxist analysis that stresses the negative aspects of civil society. A. Gramsci, *Prison Notebooks* (New York: Columbia University Press, 1992).
8. M. Keating, *Nations against the State: The New Politics of Nationalism in Quebec, Catalonia and Scotland* (London: Macmillan, 1996); Cohen and Arato, *Civil Society and Political Theory*.
9. Keane, *Civil Society and the State*; Dahrendorf, *After 1989*; Hann and Dunn (eds.), *Civil Society*.
10. W. Connor, *Ethnonationalism: The Quest for Understanding* (Princeton: Princeton University Press, 1994).
11. Giner and Arbos, *La governabilitat*, 44. In some instances, though, it should be recognized that state and civil society may share the same goals.
12. G. Dijkink, *National Identity and Geopolitical Visions* (New York: Routledge, 1996), 15–16.
13. K. A. Woolard, *Double Talk: Bilingualism and the Politics of Ethnicity in Catalonia* (Stanford, Calif.: Stanford University Press, 1989). The study was conducted solely in the capital city, Barcelona. But it would be interesting to compare Catalonia with Quebec's situation. The fact that in Quebec it is possible to live in English alone (Montreal), or French alone (Montreal and all around the province), makes a difference. In Catalonia it is unthinkable to speak Catalan only. Catalan

speakers are all bilingual, although the odd occurrence of Catalan monolingualism may happen, as mentioned by David Laitin (Ch. 5 in this volume).

14. Cited in T. Todorov, *On Human Diversity: Nationalism, Racism, and Exoticism in French Thought* (Cambridge, Mass.: Harvard University Press, 1993).
15. Massey, *Space, Place and Gender*, 122.
16. Even technological communication is grounded in a place as long as we humans have to lead a body-bounded existence.
17. R. Handler, 'Is "Identity" a Useful Concept?', in J. R. Gillis (ed.), *Commemorations: The Politics of National Identity* (Princeton: Princeton University Press, 1994), 30.
18. Woolard, *Double Talk*.
19. Handler, 'Is "Identity" a Useful Concept?', 38.
20. See Gillis (ed.), *Commemorations*, where the authors discuss the problem of identity and memory, memory in the construction of national identities, and the politics of memory and identity.
21. Cited ibid. 15.
22. H. Bhabha, 'DissemiNation: Time, Narrative and the Margins of the Modern Nation', in H. Bhabha (ed.), *Nation and Narration* (New York: Routledge, 1990), 301.
23. J. Rajchman, *Identity in Question* (New York: Routledge, 1995).
24. Ibid. 111.
25. T. Todorov, 'Dialogism and Schizophrenia', in A. Arteaga (ed.), *An Other Tongue* (Durham, NC: Duke University Press, 1994), 211.
26. Ibid. 214.
27. Cited in Artega (ed.), *An Other Tongue*.
28. Woolard, *Double Talk*, 142. This 'border' identity, however, is open to multiple possibilities. The border is not necessarily a barrier, and it indicates rather the conditions of possibility and of a position in space that may be enriching. But then, issues of identity are highly subjective, as some of the children of Castilian immigrants can attest when they choose to become part of the Catalan-speaking community.
29. H. Bhabha, 'Unsatisfied: Notes on Vernacular Cosmopolitanism', in L. Garcia-Moreno and P. C. Pfeiffer (eds.), *Text and Nation* (Columbia: Camden House, 1996), 195.
30. Bakhtin, cited in Todorov, *On Human Diversity*, 94.
31. J. L. Marfany, *La cultura del Catalanisme* (Barcelona: Editorial Empúries, 1995).
32. P. Fernandez Albaladejo, 'Cities and the State in Spain', in C. Tilly and W. P. Blockmans (eds.), *Cities and the Rise of States in Europe*, AD *1000 to 1800* (Boulder, Colo.: Westview Press, 1994), 169.
33. J. R. Llobera, *The God of Modernity: The Development of Nationalism in Western Europe* (Providence, RI: Berg, 1994), 131.
34. A. Gali, *Historia de las institucions i del movement cultural a Catalunya 1900–1930*, 20 vols. (Barcelona: Fundació Alexandre Gali, 1983).
35. D. Conversi, *The Basques, the Catalans, and Spain* (London: Hurst, 1997), 266, notes that the 'dictatorship prolonged a highly abnormal situation: the language was alive and widely spoken in many walks of life, but its public use was strictly forbidden . . . the vitality of the civil society [, however,] turned it into one of the most creative non-official languages in Europe'.
36. It has been corroborated by the curators of the exhibition entitled 'Two Hundred Years of Catalan Press'.
37. R. Alberch and J. M. Huertas (eds.), *Dos-cents anys de premsa catalana* (Barcelona: Institut Municipal d'Història i Fundació Caixa d'Estalvis de

Catalunya, 1995). J. Guillamet, *La premsa comarcal: Un model català de periodisme popular* (Barcelona: Department de Cultura de la Generalitat de Catalunya, 1984); J. Guillamet, *La premsa a Catalunya* (Barcelona: Diputació de Barcelona, 1988). The Barcelona dailies are *La Vanguardia*, *Avui*, and *El Periódico*.

38. The most prominent of these diverse publications was the *Gazeta de Barcelona* appearing in May 1641, but what was really considered to be the first daily in the Iberian peninsula was the *Diario de Barcelona*, published in 1792 (*The Press*, 1988).

39. Marfany, *La cultura del Catalanisme*.

40. *The Press*, 1988.

41. A district, or *comarca*, is a group of neighbouring municipalities that share a common history, tradition, market, or service network, and between the inhabitants of which there are constant relations and movements. In 1987 the Generalitat re-established the territorial organization of districts which had been ratified in 1936 and then abolished by the Franco regime (which maintained the division of Spain into provinces). Catalonia is presently divided into forty-one districts.

42. Guillamet, *La premsa a Catalunya*, 38.

43. The survey was done by the Ínstitut d'Estudis Metropolitans de Barcelona.

44. K. McRoberts, 'Catalan Language and Culture', MS, 1998.

45. The Castilian edition prints 267,228 issues, while the new Catalan edition prints 147,531.

46. According to one recent study, of the world's 100 largest economies, fifty-one are corporations. Wal-Mart, for example, has greater revenues than the gross domestic product of 161 countries, including Poland. P. C. Newman, *Maclean's, Canada's Weekly Magazine* (1998), 60.

47. J. A. Agnew, 'The Devaluation of Place in Social Science', in J. A. Agnew and J. S. Duncan (eds.), *The Power of Place* (Boston: Unwin Hyman, 1989).

48. McRoberts, 'Catalan Language and Culture'.

49. Ibid.

50. As it happens, a whole generation of Castilian speakers in Catalonia were raised in Castilian when Catalan was a forbidden language of education. This cohort, now in their late thirties and forties, are sending their children to be schooled in Catalan. Thus these children may in the future become a bilingual generation.

51. D. Provansal, 'Le Role des productions culturelles dans la construction de l'identité et de l'altérité: L'Exemple de la Catalogne', in H.-G. Haupt *et al.* (eds.), *Regional and National Identities in the* xixth *and* xxth *Centuries* (Boston: Kluwer Law International, 1998) 71.

52. *El Pais, ABC, El Mundo, Diario 16* are all written in Castilian. 'Fet nacional', loosely translated, means 'national fact'.

53. Guillamet, *La premsa a Catalunya*, 41.

54. *Anuari de la informació de Catalunya, 1994–1995* (Barcelona: Fundació Centre Internacional de Premsa de Barcelona).

55. *El Periódico*, 2 Jan. 1996, 20.

56. M. Folch-Serra, 'Place, Voice and Space: Mikhail Bakhtin's Dialogical Landscape', *Society and Space: Environment and Planning*, 8 (1990), 255–74.

57. The number of publications in the period 1850–99 does not mean that in that period there were only two publications in Catalonia. They are the ones that have survived until today.

58. Llobera, *The God of Modernity*, 132.

59. Gillis (ed.), *Commemorations*, 20.

CHAPTER 9

Globalization in a Very Small Place: From Ethnic to Civic Nationalism in Quebec

Daniel Latouche

After the disaster in Yugoslavia, nationalism, especially when coupled with repeated calls for yet another ethnically based nation-state, remains a suspicious proposition. Indeed, events everywhere, from Indonesia to Kosovo, seem to confirm that love of nation can bring out the worst in people.

How can we best explain this apparently insatiable thirst for a state of one's own design, even when it poses great risks for the very community whose future supposedly depends on achieving a measure of sovereignty? What lies behind this obsession for statehood? Is it a failure to accommodate oneself to a changing world? Will the aspiration to independence go away with the passage of time or as subnational communities are integrated in federal and quasi-federal state forms? Are all nationalisms condemned, especially when they encounter difficulties on the political battlefield, to move towards intolerance? Will modernization work its usual magic and transform even the most dynamic of nationalisms into another tamed player on the post-modern scene?

The array of persistent questions is of course different, depending on the geopolitical and historical conditions under which these national aspirations have surfaced and evolved over the years. Not all nationalisms are created equal, and one of the unexpected results of globalization has been to increase divergences within the nationalist family. It is no longer sufficient to proclaim that the end of the cold war, and the increase in transnational interactions, have proven a bonanza for local identities in search of a cause. One has to explain why so many territorially-based nationalist movements put forward such different programmes, each with its own vision of the best electoral tactic to follow, its own mixture of openness and closure, and a different version of what the 'Nation' can achieve. While the dynamics of globalization may push certain disfranchised groups in the direction of exclusion and xenophobia, the same forces are also causing other ethno-cultural movements to follow another, less incendiary, path.

This chapter examines one such case, that of Quebec nationalism. Its demise has often been predicted, but it seems to be enjoying another of its periodic revivals. How can the idea of a Quebec nation-state still mobilize the vast majority of an ebullient civil society, a group not especially known for its tribalism? Is it yet another case of a 'lost cause' peddling its romantic appeal among constantly anxious intellectuals and social activists? How can they continue to make use of historical grievances against the Anglo-Canadian majority when for all practical purposes the socio-economic gap between the two communities has been eradicated, even to the point that it is now English-speaking Quebeckers who complain of discrimination and cultural assimilation—certainly a unique case in a world where English is seen everywhere as the great cultural threat?

If it were only a question of intellectuals, this might not matter, since they have been known to be wrong before. But what should be made of the electoral ups and downs of the Parti Québécois, the principal political expression of this nationalism? How can a political party whose *raison d'être* is to achieve sovereignty continue to enjoy significant support—around 45 per cent of the overall electorate and close to 60 per cent of francophone voters—even though it has yet to deliver on its central promise?

Success at the polls may be the result of an incoherent electoral system rather than the expression of a persistent popular will.[1] More difficult to understand is the fact that having succeeded in maintaining the essentials of a social democratic agenda—a significant achievement in itself—the Parti Québécois has been at the forefront of recent attempts to redirect Quebec nationalism away from its former ethno-cultural territory into a more civic and inclusive one.

How can the very idea of a distinct Quebec nation-state still mobilize a majority of the French-speaking population while its promoters insist on this state having an open, non-ethnic, and multicultural character? Can a nationalist party win at the polls without any reference to past ethnically-based grievances and a good measure of Québécois pride?

As this chapter shows, many pieces of the puzzle are closely linked, and, to some extent, the consequences of the overall pattern of globalization and its more specific North American variations. Globalization, I will argue, is neither the trustworthy ally nor the arch-enemy of sub-state nationalist movements.

Nationalism: The Still Dominant 'Medical' Paradigm

The apparent success of certain nationalist movements in transforming themselves, thus ensuring their survival, is surprising only from the somewhat distorted view with which most analysts, in both the English- and French-speaking worlds, have considered the phenomenon. Students of nationalism have succeeded in replenishing their reservoir of grand explanations, elaborate typologies, and forceful causal schemes because of their conviction that the 'era' of nations was indeed coming to an end. Apparently, theoretical thinking is made easier when the end is in sight.[2] As the end has failed to materialize, many of the prophets of its demise have shifted to suggesting that nationalism will become but a minor nuisance in a world bent on meeting more important challenges than group identity. Nationalism will not entirely disappear, claims E. J. Hobsbawm, but it will maintain itself 'in subordinate, and often rather minor roles'.[3] 'Nationalism', concludes John Breuilly 'is a declining force.'[4]

This obstinacy has led to the association of nationalism with the image of a periodic plague, one which is triggered when the conditions are ripe. So contagious is nationalism, warned Hobsbawm, that theorists should take care not to come too close. 'I cannot but add that no serious historian of nations and nationalism can be a committed nationalist.' Why? Because nationalism 'requires too much belief in what is patently not so'.[5] Nationalism, it is recommended, is to be understood from the outside and at a safe distance. Writers, it is said, can thrive on identity issues, but not historians or political scientists.

Some have tried to explain nationalism's bad reputation by the behaviour of nationalists. This has not always been above suspicion—to say the least—but neither have most other -isms in whose name millions of people have suffered.[6] Although nationalism has been recognized 'as the most successful political ideology in human history', it suffers, according to Anthony Birch, from having no founder and no single official history.[7] The lines of its historical development have to be redrawn each time one attempts a new interpretation. As Benedict Anderson points out, nationalism, 'unlike most other isms, has never produced its own grand thinkers: no Hobbeses, Tocquevilles, Marxes, or Webers.'[8] For a political and intellectual schema so intent on historical continuity, this lack of a founding moment is a serious shortcoming indeed.

Nationalism also suffers from being too popular for its own ideological good. As we get to celebrate (or mourn) the end of the *grands textes*, nationalism-bashing often remains the only intellectual game left to play. What other idea is still considered dangerous and corrosive? In Canada, for example, only the prospect of a victory by Quebec sovereignists can succeed in mobilizing both the Anglo-Canadian financial community and the trade union movement. In North America, where nationalism is 'always conceived as a deep, horizontal comradeship best understood in terms of male fraternity, bondage and patriarchy', the nation is further suspected for being on the wrong side of the gender divide.[9] Scholarship rarely flourishes in such an environment.

For the last fifty years this medical vision of nationalism as an illness has remained the dominant one as nationalism continues to be seen as the result of a mass psychology run amok.[10] At best, nationalism might be acceptable as a temporary defence mechanism against the disturbing impact of 'outside' forces. With proper care, it is hoped, it can be overcome and individuals suffering from the affliction reassured sufficiently so as to live non-nationalist and productive lives.[11]

Traditionally, industrialization, and then the more encompassing phenomenon of political and socio-economic modernization were considered the most plausible suspects for the popularity of nationalism. Incapable of adapting to the demands of a rapidly changing world, individuals and communities resorted to nationalist rhetoric as a way to reconstitute a world gone by. The exact working of the modernity–nationalism duo varies, of course, but the notion of a rupture between two worlds remains the unifying theme in perspectives as varied as those of Ernest Gellner, Tom Nairn, and Karl Deutsch. In Quebec the so-called 'quiet revolution' of the 1960s has been analysed essentially in terms of before and after. Many of the attempts to explain the resurgence of nationalist movements in Scotland, Catalonia, Slovakia, and other sub-state or stateless situations still share in this before–after vision, although globalization has now replaced modernization or industrialization as the Great Divider.

Some students of nationalism reject the dominant 'rupture' approach in favour of a more primordialist vision of ethnicity and nationality. For Anthony Smith and Clifford Geertz, the idea of rupture explains very little, as nationalism, in its sub-state or nation-state incarnations, has tended to occur with very little respect for the pre-modern/modern/post-modern agenda. It would seem, as Marco Martiniello suggests, that most European thinkers cannot help but see ethnicity as a pre-modern category.[12]

Whatever their shortcomings, primordialists—'perennialists' would be a more appropriate term to describe this group—nevertheless have succeeded in catching an important and usually forgotten element of the ethnic–symbolic complex, the sense of absolute 'normalcy' and 'ordinariness' with which the vast majority of people accept their membership in national communities. True, we are not yet at the stage where it is possible to suggest, as Jean Baechler has recently done concerning democracy, that *la nation* is the natural form of socio-cultural organization. Yet there are some signs that, in the absence of violent repression and demographic degradation, ethnic groups will 'naturally' seek the status of nation and eventually of nation-states.[13]

Although they would certainly object to this rapprochement, primordialists share with those who see nationalism mainly in terms of its capacity to mobilize political resources a more instrumentalist perspective, which somewhat lessens the dysfunctional dimension so prevalent in the rupture approach. By stressing the links between various forms of cultural identity (religious, linguistic, national) and their territorial anchoring (*enracinement*) Stein Rokkan has shown how effective the nation can be in dislodging medieval forms of authority and in making effective use of the resources offered by the emerging state. For Rokkan, nationalism is best understood by considering interlocking historical, geographic, and cultural maps in order to figure out how certain groups succeed better than others in constructing a sensible vision of the world that allows for an effective mass mobilization around a number of socio-economic objectives. Many of Rokkan's 'explanations' are off the mark when applied to non-European nations, but his insistence on making culture and identity the core elements of the remaking of the geopolitical map is worth revisiting.[14] Strategy here is the keyword.

Of course, this threefold classification—rupture, primordialism, and instrumentalism—is both incomplete and unfair. Its sole purpose is to suggest that as the study of nationalism moves away from a strictly time-oriented and historical frame stressing rupture, instability, and anxiety, nationalism acquires a more strategic dimension. It serves not so much to reassure—although this dimension is never completely absent—as to infuse our shaken welfare state democracies with a much needed dose of solidarity and compassion as well as a more coherent definition of what the public domain is all about.

Without a sense of the civic community, communities and individuals cannot hope to find the necessary common ground to help them transcend their opposing interests.

In this sense, globalization has provided ethno-cultural movements not only with an additional threat to their survival, but also with an opportunity to establish their efficiency as effective social, economic, and political equalizers.

Quebec Nationalism and Globalization: The Geopolitical Argument

Much has been said on the impact of globalization—the French word *mondialisation* is perhaps more appropriate—on the re-emergence of nationalist movements both in developed and in developing areas of the world. The Quebec situation is often presented as a case in point. The best-known incarnation of the 'globalization-as-godmother' argument relates to the presumed weakening of the state component in the nation–state partnership. It is said that both governments and states are being threatened from below and from above at the same time: from below, by pressures for decentralization, regionalization, and devolution, and from above, by the rise of supra-state agreements of the European Union (EU) or North American Free Trade Agreement (NAFTA) variety, not to mention Mercosur or the Association of South East Asian Nations. The presumed workings of this double bind are well known. As they agree to major redefinition of their constitutional architecture, nation-states have made it legitimate for subnational groups to ask for a further architectural shake-up. If Great Britain, Spain, and Canada find it acceptable to transfer important elements of sovereignty to supra-state organizations while claiming that their distinct identity is being reinforced by such transfer, what is there to prevent Scotland, Catalonia, and Quebec from asking for a similar transfer of legislative and constitutional authority, but this time in their direction? Supra-state organizations are also said to provide smaller and weaker states direct access to markets without having to pay a political price for this security. Once Austria, Greece, and Finland have joined the EU, no amount of pressures or indirect barriers can prevent products from those countries from reaching European markets.

As Quebec nationalists argued repeatedly during the 1995 referendum campaign, the United States and Canada would have little choice but to accept a sovereign Quebec in their exclusive club. To do otherwise would be to fall foul of an elaborate set of rules governing regional trading groups that prevent discrimination against potential members if they satisfy entry conditions. Of course, the issue of what the United States would or would not do in the case of a Quebec declaration of sovereignty was the topic of much debate during the 1995 referendum exercise. The United States was careful not to commit itself one way or the other except to say that this issue was one to be resolved by Canadians in Canada. But whatever the legal value of their claim, there is no doubt that the sovereignty movement benefited from the existence of NAFTA. It alleviated one of the persistent fears prevalent among Quebeckers, that of being left out in the cold following a decision in favour of sovereignty. On this issue at least, the argument that supra-state agreements work in favour of nationalist movements has credibility, mostly because it allows those aspiring to statehood to show off their credentials as new-style internationalists.[15] In Quebec it is rare for a finance minister's speech not to mention the strong level of support given by Quebeckers of all political persuasions to the free-trade agreement first with the United States and then with Mexico.[16] While the electoral pay-offs of a 'free Scotland in a united Europe' remain to be seen, globalization and the responses it has elicited everywhere has provided nationalist movements not only with tactical arguments but also with a refutation of what had long been a devastating observation, that the nation-state and the very concept of border on which it is founded was disappearing.[17]

Both the Gulf and Kosovo Wars, to name but two recent examples of the new internationalism, had to do with nations wanting to obtain or retain statehood. The war effort might have been international, but its aims were purely 'national' in both cases. The reshaping of the global order has also confirmed that the desire of many nationalist movements to add to the 'border' heritage of the world is not necessarily sailing at a cross-current to history. Frontiers everywhere are disappearing, only to reconstitute themselves better. Leaving out the turbulence in former Yugoslavia, forty-six new international borders were created in Europe between 1989 and 1994, a net gain of forty-three, if we take into account the disappearance of the borders of the old German Democratic Republic. So borders no longer frighten, and the proposals of Quebec, Catalonia, or Flanders to modify their own are no longer regarded as risible.

Another element in the equation is the growing acceptance that local and regional frameworks of economic governance may be more efficient than so-called national ones, and that they must and should be accompanied by new forms of political government. So in proposing smaller-scale frameworks for belonging and for the elaboration of public policies, the sovereignty movements claim to be favouring both efficiency and democratic control. Their analysis is that, corresponding to the new economic spaces, there must rapidly develop a constellation of political territories, with the 'region' and other medium-scale units occupying the main place. The important issue, as the nationalist leaders in Quebec constantly proclaim, is to participate in a large commercial space, but at the same time direct a smaller territorial economy, better integrated and presumably better able to resist and to take advantage of the turbulence of the global economy.[18]

What should we make of these arguments? How much do they explain the resurgence of nationalisms based on ethno-cultural factors? We can certainly accept that the new dominant discourse tends to see national sovereignty as coming to an end. Kenichi Ohmae has recently announced the era of the regional state. Taking the argument to its extreme conclusion, he thinks that the nation-state will be obliged to give way to sub-state regions (such as Quebec or Lombardy) or to supranational ones like Europe or North America.[19] But this argument has now collapsed under the weight of its exaggerated claims. Transfers of sovereignty have not meant the end of the nation-state or the emergence of supranational or regional states. It also seems that the electoral appeal of the North American and European reference has been overstated. Certainly the argument was not enough to swing the Quebec referendum of 1995; indeed none of the new nationalisms has managed to attain sovereignty in this way. The argument about the irresistible rise of the region is also constestable. In spite of all the efforts to the contrary, in Europe as in Canada the regional state is above all seen as a branch of the nation-state. At the electoral level the America of the Regions and the Europe of the Regions are elusive notions.[20]

One could even reverse the argument that the rise of regional states is one of the decisive factors in the success of regional nationalisms. It may be that these supranational agreements have permitted local nationalisms to express their differences, but in several cases their immediate and unanticipated effect is to revive the flame of state nationalism. In some cases this reaction has hampered transfers of sovereignty and the erosion of the national 'fortress'. After the trauma of the adoption of NAFTA, it is unlikely that Canada will accept further similar accords with the United States or other countries of the hemisphere. Indeed it was only reluctantly, and under pressure from the United States, that Canada accepted the expansion of the free-trade agreement to include Mexico.

The paradox must be underlined. Precisely at the moment when they have come to accept that the scope of exclusive nationality and political identity must be reduced, many 'nations' are rediscovering a 'national interest' and even a 'national consciousness'. So we have the astonishing spectacle of supposedly anti-nationalist politicians in France insisting on the need for a strong Europe for the greatness of France or talking of Europe as France's last chance. Europe is thus presented as a continuation of French national interest or as the best defence for 'French ideas' and 'French values'. One need hardly stress that the pretensions of some French politicians to appropriate the European idea is ill received in other European countries, and can only serve to nurture discord in the future.

As for the argument about the greater adaptability of small integrated economies, we should be sceptical about the electoral appeal of such geo-strategic arguments. Besides, there is room for doubt about the supposedly superior performance of territorially embedded, closely integrated economies. Small may often be more beautiful, but it is not always better.[21] So while it is right to underline the connection between the new electoral success of certain territorially based nationalist parties and their ability to place their demands in a more global and reassuring context, this is no more than a tactical argument that cannot explain the nationalist resurgence. In the short term the argument could even be turned against the nationalist parties, as their actions are seen as inappropriate in the context of rising tensions among the member states of supra-state unions.

Nationalism as a Response to Globalization: The Strategic Argument

The globalization argument is not limited to the difficulties, however exaggerated, of the nation-state and the emergence of transnational economic spaces that would facilitate nationalist movements. Globalization, it is too often forgotten, is also about the relationship with the world (the globe). As Alain Touraine has pointed out, we are in danger of reducing globalization to an economic phenomenon, ignoring its cultural and political aspects. Seen purely from an economic perspective, it is a homogenizing force, fostering a spirit of discouragement, powerlessness, and resignation.[22] Yet this logic is not inescapable. Globalization can also encourage more pluralist forms of nation-building. People can affirm their own specific identity as the basis and the very justification for their insertion into the global arena. This is what we call the logic of embedding.

At the heart of globalization we also find a dynamic of incorporation, which some describe as enclosure or compression of the world. This is not new. The geographic, then the economic and cultural, insertion of the American continent in the global system of the sixteenth century constituted one of the defining moments of the expansion of the planet. What distinguishes the present situation is the vigour and definitive character of the process. Incorporation expands like a gas that rapidly fills the space of its container. Each new development occupies the whole of a space, which itself appears infinitely expandable. So all societies are incorporated, in spite of themselves, into a universe in which they are the components and the actors.

After the forced march of modernity, which required all societies to join 'modern times', this enclosure of the world marks the arrival of a time in which it is more and more difficult to live outside of space. The era of enclaves and exceptions is coming to an end, and the world is on the way to becoming a finished system. Quebec and other societies operating in the same space-time dimension are forced to join in this process of enclosure if they are not to disappear into a non-world. This feeling of urgency has in large part replaced the fear of the 'other' as the basis for nationalism.

Globalization also includes a dynamic of consciousness. Without constant media coverage this simultaneous pursuit of the infinitely small and the infinitely large which characterizes globalization would be a mere will-o'-the-wisp. Without the possibility of seeing them in action with the rapidity and brutality that satellite images permit, these dynamics of enclosure, of interpenetration, of hollowing, and of recomposition, which I have mentioned, would not have the combined impact that they have.[23] Globalization, it has often been said, is also an imagined fact. At the extreme, one could even say that consciousness is the engine of globalization. Indeed it is in those sectors where exchanges are least material, that is in information and communications, that globalization is advancing most rapidly. Journalists and broadcasters have thus become the carriers of globalization, so that perhaps we should talk of world consciousness or world communication in the same way that we talk of the world economy or world society.[24]

These four dynamics—embedding, incorporation, enclosure, and consciousness—combine to create a situation of permanent uncertainty and indeterminacy. This situation seems to me to provide a better explanation for the persistence and reorientation of Quebec nationalism than do popular theories about the inevitable fragmentation of big units.

It seems as though many of the phenomena associated with globalization push in all directions at the same time, with perverse effects that combine to contradict the original dynamic. It is as though we have a situation of permanent bifurcation. This concept, coined by Poincaré and recently popularized by Prigogine, implies that the tendencies to centralization and decentralization, to the reinforcement and withering away of states, to change and continuity, will continue to run through the global system without producing a definitive outcome.[25] So the existence of a world system allows all tendencies, however opposed, to coexist. History is not finished, and has no need to come to a definite end-point. Even backward moves and sharp changes in direction are possible. This new climate of permanent uncertainty, indeterminacy, and ceaseless renewal is the real novelty of geopolitics at the end of the millennium. We can say, generally, that it allows many organizations, including stateless nations, to emerge, but it does not guarantee their permanence or success.

It is evident in this situation that the Canadian federal state and the 'national' identity which it promotes are ever less able to reduce uncertainty for Quebec. This inability is one of the most important sources for the 'new' Quebec nationalism and its opening to a plurality of identities. So multiculturalism, one of the pillars of Canadian state policy in promoting its own identity, is seen in Quebec as an attempt to reduce Quebec's national identity to the level of ethnic folklore on the lines of the 'ethnic groups' in the United States. In refusing to consider itself as a multinational and not merely multicultural state, Canada deprives itself of an important argument in its efforts to secure recognition of cultural exceptions in international trade law.[26]

One of the unforeseen effects of the new global geopolitical environment is that it has become more difficult to revise the Canadian constitution and thereby accommodate the specificity of Quebec within the framework of Canada. Hitherto, unspoken understandings, informal arrangements, and improvisations were the essential elements of the Canadian model of accommodation. This allowed opposing forces and contradictory interpretations to coexist in unforeseen ways. This feature of permanent improvisation certainly produced a lot of incoherence, but it also facilitated compromise and the acceptance of situations which at first sight appeared impossible. The attempts to reduce the turbulence described earlier threaten this tradition of laxity and the fluidity of the Canadian political architecture. It is now believed that, to confront an ever more complex external environment, Canada must simplify its internal functioning. The country needs, we are repeatedly told, a coherent vision of itself, of its identity and its place in the world. Without this internal solidity the Canadian political system will continue to waste precious energy in sulphurous but futile battles over the division of competences. The rules must not only be the same for all, but they must be recognized as such. In sum, Canada must become a 'nation' like the others and enjoy the advantages that stem from the existence of an integrated national community. On the one hand, nothing must be left to chance, as the recent reference to the Supreme Court to 'clarify' the existence of the right of self-determination shows. On the other hand, there is the search to codify as far as possible the whole functioning of the federation and the relations among its communities. Since 1982 this search for formalization has been accelerated, with the Charter of Rights and an amending formula whose complexity prevents any fundamental change in the federation. There has been an effort to codify everything, as if the multiplication of rules and the generalization of norms could in themselves replace the symbols and unspoken understandings that are the foundation of all citizenship. Nothing illustrates better this pursuit of formalization than the recent efforts to obtain identical definitions in each language of the concept of 'distinct society'. Faced with the impossibility of a common definition, Canada's leaders abandoned the attempt to find a code that could satisfy all actors.

By multiplying supranational agreements, whether multilateral or regional, countries are constantly losing a part of their sovereignty; this merely reinforces their need to preserve at any cost what remains of the rest and of the identity that is attached to it. This pursuit of external agreements merely accelerates the push to internal codification and uniformity. The interpenetration of two juridical orders, the traditional national order and the new supranational order, restrain, if not prevent, the juridical recognition of internal specificities. The new constraints in which nation-states must operate make forms of internal accommodation such as devolution of legislative powers, or constitutional asymmetry, more difficult. Quebec is particularly liable to be penalized by this fact.

This pursuit of normalization will increasingly prevent Canada and Quebec from arriving at a satisfactory and original compromise for their constitutional dispute. Having passed on sovereignty association, and then on the 'distinct society' option, it is difficult to see what other intermediate solution could serve as a basis for compromise. At a time when constitutional clarity and transparency is valued above all, one might expect Quebec to become either a nation-state or a province like all the others. The middle ground will have disappeared. Canada is prisoner of a logic that pushes it to conform with the norms of a hyperactive international society that is not prepared to allow countries to renege on their international obligations by hiding behind the special arrangements made for internal minorities; it is likely therefore to insist that Quebec rejoin the ranks.[27]

Quebec and the Rise of a more Civic Nationalism

Globalization already means that Quebec cannot escape the gaze of outsiders. It can no longer hide behind the 'privilege of historic backwardness' which served it well in the past. The difficulties of the Canadian state, which has not even consolidated itself properly, prevent Quebec looking for protection from that quarter. Yet while these difficulties facilitate some of the sovereigntists' arguments, they make their task more difficult by polarizing the debate between two intransigent positions. This outside exposure has, however, had some benign effects on Quebec nationalism and its evolving political project, notably in regard to the place of Quebec's minority communities. The dynamics of globalization by their indeterminate quality have two effects. They facilitate the expression of the exclusive characteristics of the community, such as origins or language. Yet they also insert the society in a more universal process of self-determination. Rather than seeing nationalism as a mechanism for going back in time the better to appropriate history and so confirm that one exists, we should see it as a way of organizing space on the basis of territory. It is no longer the historical anchorings that matter but those founded in a place where one leaves one's traces and which permits us to link to the universal. The universal in turn is itself no more than the sum of those localisms that participate in the project. This is what has been called civic nationalism.

At the core of the civic nationalist outlook one finds a stated preference for inclusion and openness as well as the belief that appeals to the nation only make sense if they are joined with propositions concerning the effective entrenchment of differences in a non-Jacobin form of republic. Seen in this light, nationalism can lead to more rather than less citizenship, moreover a citizenship not limited to formal political rights but that also includes more intangible rights such as the right to one's own history and the right to share in the building of a 'new' history.

These, as I mentioned, are preferences, and as such they are not necessarily shared by all members of the community and those who speak in its name. The fact that significant segments of the Quebec national-ist leadership and of the general population still harbour anti-immigrant, anti-aboriginal, and anti-English sentiments should not be ignored, even though most surveys indicate that Quebeckers as a group are generally more tolerant of diversity and open to immigra-tion than the rest of Canada. Nevertheless, the degree of intolerance and anti-immigrant (or anti-Semitic) feeling in Quebec is still hotly debated and is part of the ongoing struggle between pro- and anti-sovereignty forces. Many on the federalist and anti-nationalist side have suggested that the Quebec version of pluralism is but a form of ideological bricolage, an unconscious and unworkable accommoda-tion of contrary impulses.[28] Others have pointed out the absolute incompatibility between Québécois nationalism and democracy.[29] A few have seized on the reorientation of the Parti Québécois as further proof that without a strong anchorage in a pan-Canadian progressive movement, Quebec nationalism will necessarily return to its old mes-sianistic, clerical, and culturalist traditions.[30]

These positions share in a long tradition of considering Quebec intellectual elites as prisoners of a tradition of resentment typical of clerical and especially Catholic milieus. Even among those Anglo-Canadian intellectuals who consider themselves sympathetic to the Quebec nationalist struggle there is still a widely held conviction that the Québécois need to be protected against their own excesses. 'Is Québec Nationalism Just?' was the intriguing title of a recent collec-tion of essays by a group of Anglo-Canadian philosophers who, obli-vious to the paternalism of their research programme, felt the need to transform themselves into a tribunal, albeit a sympathetic one. One is also reminded of another suggestion coming from progressive Anglo-Canadian circles that Quebec cannot go it alone because Canada as a whole needs the Quebec sense of ethno-national difference if it is to remain distinct from the United States.[31]

The intellectual challenge lies not with these recurrences of ethno-centricism, which repeatedly come back to haunt Quebec nationalism, or with the almost total lack of support for the idea of Quebec sover-eignty among even the most 'progressive' segments of Anglo-Canadian opinion. It lies with the rapid generalization of the more civic and inclusive vision of Quebec identity and what it means to be a Québécois.[32] When reviewing the recent Quebec (political, sociolo-gical, and philosophical) literature on the various variants of the nation–nationality–nationalism triangle, one is struck by the diversity and intensity of opinions on the significance and implications of this renewed quest on one part and its insertion in the ongoing dialogue on the fragmentation and coexistence of identities.[33] Civic nationalism, or the civic nation, can be defined as that form of collective identity and action that stresses those elements of individuality based principally although not exclusively on a territorially bounded public sphere rather than on the exclusive combination of certain ethno-cultural markers and historical experiences.

Defined in those terms, civic nationalism clearly remains within the family of those communities, imagined or not, that seek to put the nation at the core of the identity project. As such, civic nationalism shares a number of characteristics with most other forms of 'national' identification, characteristics which are clearly anathema to those who reject all forms of collective action based on a 'we–them' dichotomy or even the mere concept of identity-based difference as a way of access to authenticity. Contrary to those who share in a form of anti-communitarian *déracinement* either in its nomadic ('we belong nowhere') or neo-cosmopolitan ('we belong everywhere') version, proponents of a more civic form of nationalism argue that an open individuality can indeed be achieved through a recognition that the 'other' (*l'Autre*) and its own multiple fragmented identities contributes equally to a public domain that defines the boundaries of a tolerant citizenship.[34] Without the recognition of one's own 'strangeness', writes Julia Kristeva, a French psychoanalytic writer, there can be no acceptance that the strangeness of others contributes positively to the richness of the community. A civic definition of the nation is the only way out of the 'identity trap'.[35] It is also the only way to free oneself from the domination of a so-called 'civil society' and, as Tom Nairn recently suggested, 'resume business as political society'.[36]

Civic nationalism takes many forms. For example, some have argued that sovereignty is a necessary although not a sufficient condition for the emergence of a truly multicultural society.[37] Others have argued that the almost fanatical rejection of ethnicity that is at the core of one form of the civic discourse leads to the exclusion from the citizenry of groups like the aboriginal nations and certain ethno-religious groups, who define their sense of belonging in strict ethnic terms.[38] Indeed the debate about the proper place of ethnicity in the public domain has become one of the most challenging in nationalist circles as people argue that many of the institutions that define this domain are indeed ethno-culturally defined.

The relationship between nationalism, identity, and liberalism is still intensively debated, with some arguing that the state of permanent political ambivalence which has come to characterize Quebec is not the sign of an identity crisis but the signal that ambivalence, hesitation, and the permanent refusal to choose are the stuff of which future post-modern national identities will be made.[39] As expected, the precise political programme to incarnate this civic orientation has been the topic of intense discussion. While the majority of civic nationalists still adhere to the idea of sovereignty, although with a serious realignment of its core programme in the direction of pluralism,[40] others have argued for the transformation of Canada into a multinational state, a proposal which finds close to zero support in anglophone Canada.[41] Although Charles Taylor can be considered the philosophical father of this variety of Quebec nationalism, his almost visceral opposition to the sovereignty option and his willingness to ally himself with many of the most retrograde elements in the anti-Quebec struggle have left a deep scar among his followers and testify to the near impossibility of two competing nationalisms coexisting on the same territory.[42]

What holds these various takes on the 'civic nation' together is a critique of the pretensions of neo-liberalism to found democracy exclusively on values such as personal accomplishment, individual freedoms, and the predominance of the subjective. It requires a fundamental change in the old idea in which the State maintained its hegemony because the Nation provided it with the cement (or glue), making its pretensions to universal authority legitimate in the eyes of the majority, even if not welcomed by all. The concept of civic nationalism calls into question the traditional opposition and division of labour between nation and state. More and more the state is being called upon to provide various groups and communities with the means, judicial and others, to support their specificities. The nation provides individuals with the possibility of sharing in the construction of a community based not exclusively on the imaginary construction and reconstruction of a pre-ordained *nous* but on imperatives of organizing the coexistence of their multiple identities.

In the Quebec case, this needed *recomposition identitaire* (identity recomposition) has led to some rather astonishing remodelling of the intellectual landscape, notably with regard to the British and American components of the Quebec public space.[43] As is often the case, this reassessment has increased rather than reduced tensions between Canadian and Quebec nationalisms. For the central government and opponents of Quebec sovereignty, this *américanité* so loudly proclaimed by Quebec nationalists is but a direct attack on the intellectual integrity of Canada, whose very existence rests on maintaining an arm's-length relationship with the United States.

Globalization, it is argued here, is the major force pushing for this coexistence, not so much because of a primordialist impulse or the need to come to terms with a gap or a rupture in the modernization process, but because such multiple identities are now an 'objective' component of this sense of *nous*. While multiculturalism, as practised in Canada and the United States, is but a form—albeit a less domineering one—of managing cultural diversity, civic nationalism allows for a more intercultural (or transcultural) approach to a diversity which is not seen as a problem to be managed but as a resource which adds to the social capital of the community.[44]

Is Civic Nationalism Irreversible?

Civic nationalism constitutes, as I have noted, a strategic response to an ever more globalized geopolitical environment. It is not, however, the only possible response, and even the best strategies can lose their cutting-edge because of the lack of combatants and, above all, the lack of results. There are already signs that this might be the situation in Quebec. The federal government continues to deny the right of self-determination to Quebec and hides behind a legalistic position, which regards any referendum as illegitimate unless it itself has determined the terms and the consequences. This plays into the hands of those elements within the sovereigntist movement who only accepted the democratic route after more 'muscular' approaches had failed. Certainly, a recent decision of the Supreme Court found that Quebec did not have the right under the Canadian constitution to declare sovereignty unilaterally. Yet the clarifications it provided about the exercise of this non-right served to cool the more ardent anti-nationalist fervours of the federal government. Apart from reminding the government that the question of Quebec sovereignty was a political rather than a juridical issue, the court declared that, if there was a clear majority in favour, the government of Quebec would have the legitimacy to carry this through and the Canadian government would have to respond in good faith. This, unfortunately, did not have the calming effect hoped for, since the federal government immediately insisted on a stratospheric threshold for a referendum victory. On several occasions the minister for intergovernmental affairs has let it be known that he regards a threshold of 66 per cent as a reasonable basis for the federal government to agree to negotiate a transition to sovereignty with the government of Quebec. Such obvious bad faith makes it difficult to maintain a discourse based on tolerance and openness. This is exacerbated by the rather surprising demands made by certain ethno-linguistic (minority) leaders in Quebec who, strongly attached

to their Canadian citizenship, have been pushing the idea of partition-
ing Quebec, by force if necessary, in the event of a positive referendum
vote. The partitionist movement, which is extremely francophobe, has
fortunately found little echo among the ethno-linguistic communities
concerned, mainly concentrated in Montreal. Its principal organization, Alliance Québec, however, continues to receive financial support
from the federal government under its programme of support for
minority communities and defence of individual rights. The task of the
partisans of dialogue and intercultural understanding is not facilitated
by the emergence of this unforeseen ethno-cultural extremism.

The question of the relationship between Quebec civic nationalism
and the other ethno-linguistic communities living in the same territories is also a prickly one. The decision of Quebec's aboriginal nations
to support the central state against any form of Québécois nationalism
or sovereignty makes the acceptance of the aboriginal's own project by
Quebec nationalists—already too feeble—even more difficult. The
poor electoral record of the Parti Québécois among immigrant
groups, whose 'official' leaders have declared war on the 'separatists',
also puts civic nationalism at risk.[45]

A new referendum failure, or simply the continuation of the federal
government's present policy of letting the situation stagnate, could also
serve to discourage civic nationalists incapable of demonstrating any
gains from their willingness to open up. So they risk letting the discourse on the nation and on identity be monopolized by the partisans
of a rediscovered ethno-linguistic purity. In a similar way, the French
left's abandonment of anything to do with the defence of the nation to
the extreme right, in order to force the mainstream conservative parties
to join forces with the National Front and so discredit themselves in
public opinion, may have gained electoral dividends; but it has not
favoured the emergence of attitudes of tolerance and openness.

While Canada could, with some difficulty, accommodate two competing state-building projects, it does not have room for two strategic
states. Yet this is precisely what is required of governments in the new
global conditions. The redefinition of the role of the state leads
inevitably to the reinforcing of its central structures, especially those
linked to the outside world. Decisions and arbitration are thus taken
up to the highest levels and, while this centralization may not necessarily be disastrous for Quebec, it certainly forces it to rethink its
strategy in dealing with the central government. Cooperative federalism may give way to a clientelistic federalism, in which partisan
fidelity and electoral alliances replace functionalism or the balance of
power as the criteria for allocating governmental responsibilities. All

levels of government risk being affected by this tendency. In so far as
Canadian strategy is to become a spoke to the American hub,
Quebec's room for manoeuvre is likely to be reduced, since Canada
will not permit this to be used against its own strategy.

There is no doubt that the capacity of nation-states and governments to regulate economic activities and actors in their territory has
diminished considerably in recent decades. This failure, like many
others, has convinced many regional governments that they could do
more, but that to do this they need to control the levers of economic
development. It is questionable, however, whether they have in fact
done any better. This confirms the already 'old' analysis of Michael
Keating, to the effect that the new global context will permit some
sub-state collectivities to increase their margin of autonomy, while
others will be reduced to new forms of dependence.[46] The collectivities that will see real improvements in their margin of manoeuvre are
those without a defined territorial base and whose institutions do
not take state-like forms. Ethnic, religious, linguistic, cultural, and
lifestyle communities will thus be the winners; in short it will be the
era of disaporas.[47]

If this should prove to be the case, civic nationalism will have been
no more than an epiphenomenon, and it will be necessary to think of
new forms for the governance of ethnicity. Perhaps it is here that the
future of nationalism lies. After all, wherever there is the nation, there
is the possibility, or even a strategic necessity, to use it to make sense
of the world.

NOTES

This chapter takes on what previous works left out: 'Le Québec: See under Canada.
Québec Nationalism in the New Global Age', in A. Gagnon (ed.), *Québec: State and
Society*, 2nd edn. (Scarborough: Nelson, Canada, 1993); 'Quebec in the Emerging
North American Configuration', in R. L. Earle and J. D. Wirth (eds.), *Identities in
North America* (Stanford, Calif.: Stanford University Press, 1995); 'Le Canada et le
Québec: L'Heure de la globalisation et de l'incertitude', in A. Gagnon and A. Noel
(eds.), *L'Espace québécois* (Montreal: Québec-Amérique, 1995).

1. In the 1998 election the Parti Québécois received 42.8% of the vote (and 76 seats
   out of 125), behind the Liberal Party with 43.5% (but only 48 seats). In 1994 the
   equivalent figures were 44.7% for the Parti Québécois (77 seats) and 44.4% for
   the Liberal Party (47 seats). For an extensive and longitudinal study of Quebec
   voting patterns, see P. Drouilly, 'Les Tendances du vote, 1985–1995', and R.
   Nadeau and É. Bélanger, ' L'Appui aux partis politiques québécois, 1989–1998',
   both in R. Boily (ed.), *L'Année politique au Québec, 1997–1998* (Montreal: Les
   Presses de l'Université de Montréal, 1998).

2. For a useful presentation of this conceptual apparatus, one which unfortunately still shares the medical metaphor, see A. Von Busekist, *Nations et nationalismes, xixe et xxe siècle* (Paris: Armand Colin, 1998).

3. E. J. Hobsbawm, *Nations and Nationalism since 1780: Program, Myth, Reality* (New York: Cambridge University Press, 1990), 182.

4. J. Breuilly, *Nationalism and the State*, 2nd edn. (Chicago: University of Chicago Press, 1994), 422.

5. Hobsbawm, *Nations and Nationalism since 1780*, 12.

6. It would seem that patriotism is most often associated with the idea of dying for one's nation while nationalism is reserved for those who choose to kill for it.

7. A. H. Birch, *Nationalism and National Integration* (London: Unwin Hyman, 1989), 3.

8. B. Anderson, *Imagined Communities: Reflections on the Origin and Spread of Nationalism* (New York: Verso, 1991), 5.

9. Ibid. 7. The 'dialogue' between the nationality and gender literatures is particularly rich as both insist on the 'other' as a potentially useful construct. See G. L. Mosse, *Nationalism and Sexuality: Middle-Class Morality and Sexual Norms in Modern Europe* (Madison: University of Wisconsin Press, 1985). Curiously, in French, *la nation*, like Marianne, is clearly feminine.

10. A majority of selections included in recent readers on nationalism share in this view of nationalism-as-a-dysfunction. See J. Hutchinson and A. D. Smith (eds.), *Nationalism* (New York: Oxford University Press, 1994); J. G. Kellas, *The Politics of Nationalism and Ethnicity* (New York: St Martin's Press, 1998).

11. A sampling of recent 'analysis' of nationalism reveals the extent of this medical metaphor. See, among many others, D. Kecmanovic, *The Mass Psychology of Ethnonationalism* (New York: Plenum, 1996). Fortunately, suggests B. Badie, the two foundations of any nationalism, territory and sovereignty, are 'dead': See his *La Fin des territoires* (Paris: Fayard, 1995) and *Un monde sans souveraineté* (Paris: Fayard, 1999).

12. In *L'Ethnicité dans les sciences sociales contemporaines* (Paris: Presses Universitaires de France, 1995). In his book on ethno-politics *L'ethnopolitique* (Paris: Presses Universitaires de France, 1995) R. Breton leaves no doubt as to where this recent fascination with ethnicity can lead: concentration camps, genocides, deportations, exterminations.

13. See his interview to *Le Monde*, 16 Feb. 1999: 'La démocratie est le régime politique naturel de l'espèce humaine'.

14. Rokkan made little use of his initial intuition, which is summarily condensed into a centre-periphery argument in S. Rokkan and D. Urwin *Economy, Territory, Identity: Politics of West European Peripheries* (London: Sage, 1983).

15. Curiously, those political economists concerned with various aspects of the rise of supranational regionalism rarely mention intra-state regionalism as a consequence. See the contributions to two recent readers: E. D. Mansfield and H. V. Milner (eds.), *The Political Economy of Regionalism* (New York: Columbia University Press, 1997) and W. D. Coleman and G. R. D. Underhill (eds.), *Global Economic Integration: Europe, Asia and the Americas* (London: Routledge, 1998).

16. Empirical studies show that Quebec nationalists are strong supporters of continental economic integration. See P. Martin, 'When Nationalism Meets Continentalism: The Politics of Free Trade in Quebec', *Regional and Federal Studies*, 5/1 (1995), 1–27. P. Bakvis, 'Free Trade in North America: Divergent Perspectives between Quebec and English Canada', *Quebec Studies*, 16 (1993), 39–48, shows that Quebeckers, especially the more 'progressive' and left-wing, have tended to be less suspicious of American intentions than their Canadian

counterparts. Anti-Americanism is simply not a central element of the socialist discourse in Quebec.

17. The argument is well developed in M. Keating, *Nations against the State: The New Politics of Nationalism in Quebec, Catalonia and Scotland* (London: Macmillan, 1996). For a more detailed electoral and political perspective, see G. Leydier, *La Question écossaise* (Rennes: Presses Universitaires de Rennes, 1998).

18. For a more 'economic' presentation of this argument, see P-P. Proulx, 'L'Intégration économique dans les Amériques: Quelles Stratégies pour tenter d'assurer l'américanité plutôt que l'américanisation du Québec', *Politique et Sociétés*, 18/1 (1999), 129–50.

19. K. Ohmae, *The End of the Nation-State: The Rise of Regional Economies* (New York: Free Press, 1995).

20. This argument is present in a number of assessments of Europe of the regions in action. See E. Négrier's introductory chapter 'Que gouvernent les régions d'Europe? Change politique territorialisé et mobilisations régionales', in E. Négrier and B. Jouve (eds.), *Que gouvernent les régions d'Europe* (Paris: L'Harmattan, 1998). Not much would seem to be the answer of most contributions to this work. This is also my conclusion in 'Do Regions Make a Difference? The Case of Science and Technology Policies in Québec', in H.-J. Braczyk, P. Cooke, and M. Heiden-Reich (eds.), *Regional Innovation Systems* (London: UCL Press, 1998). Similar conclusions with specific references to the region as a *trompe l'œil* or an imaginary construction are to be found in P. Le Galès and C. Lequesne (eds.), *Regions in Europe* (London: Routledge, 1998).

21. I have examined this issue in 'Do Regions Make a Difference?'.

22. Cited in D. Salée, 'La Mondialisation et la construction de l'identité au Québec', in M. Elbaz, A. Fortin, and G. Laforest (eds.), *Les Frontières de l'identité: Modernité et postmodernisme* (Sainte-Foy: Les Presses de l'Université Laval, 1996). For a rare anti-sovereigntist perspective on the *mondialisation*–identity linkage, see A. Burelle, *Le Droit et la différence de l'heure de la globalisation: Le Cas du Québec et du Canada* (Montreal: Éditions Fides, 1996).

23. The expression is borrowed from F. Balle, cited in 'La Mondialisation des médias', *Cahiers Français*, 263 (1993), 59. The idea of consciousness as the essential element in globalization is borrowed from R. Robertson, *Globalization: Social Theory and Global Culture* (Newbury Park, Calif.: Sage, 1992), 8.

24. The image of world communication is taken from A. Mattelart, *La Communication-monde: Histoire des idées et des stratégies* (Paris: La Découverte, 1992).

25. The mathematical indeterminacy of Poincaré with his infinite number of stable solutions has been taken up by Ilya Prigogine. As one gets away from the initial conditions of equilibrium, there appear multiple bifurcations to other equilibria. In the critical zones weak internal or external fluctuations are enough to produce changes in direction. *Ex post facto*, the new path effectively constitutes an acceptable solution for the initial indetermination. See I. Prigogine and I. Stengers, *La Nouvelle alliance* (Paris: Gallimard, 1987).

26. At times this refusal produces some odd situations, like the decision of the federal minister of national heritage, Sheila Copps, in 1999 to boycott a working group convened by France on the theme of cultural diversity because a Quebec government minister had been invited to give the Quebec view on diversity.

27. The same pursuit of formalization distinguished the US–Canada Free Trade Agreement from its successor, NAFTA. On several occasions the Canadian government presented the multiplication of rules and mechanisms as a victory for the country.

28. See R. Robin, 'L'Impossible Québec pluriel: La Fascination de la souche', in M. Elbaz, A. Fortin, and G. Laforest (eds.), *Les Frontières de l'identité: Modernité et post-modernisme* (Sainte-Foy: Les Presses de l'Université Laval, 1996).

29. This view is defended by J.-P. Derriennic, *Nationalisme et démocratie: Réflexion sur les illusions des indépendantistes* (Montreal: Boréal, 1995). For an even more antagonistic statement, see M. Angenot, *Les Idéologies du ressentiment* (Montreal: Éditions XYZ, 1996).

30. The works of Philip Resnick can be said to be representative of this orientation. See his *Letter to a Québécois Friend* (Montreal: McGill–Queen's University Press, 1991) and his more recent *Thinking English Canada* (Toronto: Stoddart, 1994). For a traditional Anglo-Canadian anti-nationalist perspective, see R. Cook (ed.), *Canada, Quebec, and the Uses of Nationalism* (Toronto: McClelland & Stewart, 1995).

31. A statement that is tantamount to suggesting to the Scots that England needs their 'Scottishness' in order to feel more European and less British.

32. One is struck by the obvious difference between how the Catalan, Quebec, and Scottish national 'questions', as they are usually referred to, are received by the intellectual and political elites of the dominant group.

33. For an overview (in English) of this new civic nationalism, see L. Balthazar, 'Towards a New Citizenship: The Dynamics of Multi-Ethnicity in French-Speaking Quebec', in J. A. Laponce and W. Safran (eds.), *Ethnicity and Citizenship: The Canadian Case* (Portland, Oreg.: Frank Cass, 1996); J. Couture, K. Nielson, and M. Seymour (eds.), *Rethinking Nationalism* (Calgary: University of Calgary Press, 1996).

34. One will have recognized here James Clifford's forceful rejection of 'nomadology' and its pretentious rejection of all that is local and anchored. See his *Routes: Travel and Translation in the Late Twentieth Century* (Cambridge, Mass.: Harvard University Press, 1997). For an elaboration on this theme and an imaginative presentation of civic nationalism and the quest for authenticity, see J. Maclure, 'Authenticités québécoises: Le Québec et la fragmentation contemporaine de l'identité', *Globe: Revue Internationale d'Études Québécoises*, 1/1 (1998), 9–36.

35. See J. Kristeva, *Étrangers nous-mèmes* (Paris: Fayard, 1988).

36. T. Nairn, *Faces of Nationalism* (London: Verso, 1997), 68. Nationalism within a province, suggests Nairn, is the worst which could happen to nationalist and neo-nationalist movements alike: 'On its own, cut off from normal or "high politics", civil society itself can amount to a kind of ailment, a practically pathological condition of claustrophobia, cringing parochialism and dismal self-absorption. No one would claim such symptoms are confined to Scotland, of course; sink-bottom "provincialism" has been a common feature of modern development, frequently pilloried in its literature. However, chosen provinciality is worse' (pp. 68–9). This perspective is shared by Julia Kristeva, who recently publicly turned down the possibility of moving to Quebec because, as she said, although it constitutes a fascinating laboratory for the emergence of a new, more civic definition of the collective self, as long as these attempts were confined to a 'province', they were bound to lead nowhere.

37. This position is well argued by D. Lamoureux, 'L'Autodétermination comme condition du multiculturalisme québécois', *Politique et Sociétés*, 28 (1995), 53–69; M. Labelle, F. Rocher, and G. Rocher, 'Pluriethnicité, citoyenneté et intégration: De la souveraineté pour lever les obstacles et les ambiguités', *Cahiers de Recherche Sociologique*, 25 (1995), 213–45.

38. See D. Juteau, *Ni essence, ni illusion: L'Ethnicité et ses frontières* (Montreal: Les Presses de l'Université de Montréal, 1998); G. Bouthillier, *L'Obsession ethnique*

(Montreal: Lanctôt Éditeur, 1997); G. Bourque and J. Duchastel, *L'Identité fragmentée* (Montreal: Fides, 1996).

39. This position has been articulated by J. Letourneau in his 'Impenser le pays et toujours l'aimer', *Cahiers Internationaux de Sociologie*, 45 (1998), 361–82. See also the contributions to J.-M. Fecteau, G. Breton, and J. Létourneau (eds.), *La Condition québécoise: Enjeux et horizons d'une société en devenir* (Montreal: VLB Éditeur, 1994).

40. J. Beauchemin, 'La Question de la souveraineté: Redéfinition des enjeux et nouveaux argumentaires', *Globe: Revue Internationale d'Études Québécoises*, 1/1 (1998), 53–75.

41. W. Kymlicka, *Finding our Way: Rethinking Ethnocultural Relations in Canada* (Toronto: Oxford University Press, 1998); F. Rocher, 'Repenser le Québec dans un Canada multinational: Pour un modèle fonctionnel de la citoyenneté', *Globe: Revue Internationale d'Études Québécoises*, 1/1 (1998), 77–109. A.-G. Gagnon, 'Fédéralisme et identitée nationales: Le Passage obligé de l'État-nation à l'État plurinational', in P. Soldatos and J.-C. Masclet (eds.), *L'État-nation au tournant du siècle: Les Enseignements de l'expérience canadienne et européenne* (Montreal: Presses de l'Université de Montréal, 1997).

42. Guy Laforest is the most eloquent interpreter of Charles Taylor's thinking and an influential proponent of civic nationalism in his own right. See G. Laforest and P. de Lara (eds.), *Charles Taylor et l'interprétation de l'identité moderne* (Sainte-Foy: Les Presses de l'Université Laval, 1998) and *De l'urgence* (Montreal: Boréal, 1995).

43. Following the work of Inglehart and others—R. Inglehart, N. Nevitte, and M. Basanez, *The North American Trajectory: Cultural, Political and Economic Ties among the United States, Canada and Mexico* (New York: Aldine de Gruyter, 1996)—members of the Groupe de Recherche sur l'Américanité have published a number of studies indicating that Quebeckers make a difference between 'Americanization' and 'Americanity'. See G. Lachapelle, 'L'Américanité des Québécois, ou, L'Émergence d'une identité supranationale', in M. Seymour (ed.), *Nationalité, citoyenneté et solidarité* (Montreal: Éditions Liber, 1999); Y. Lamonde, 'Pourquoi repenser l'américanité du Québec?', *Politique et Sociétés*, 18/1 (1999), 93–107; *Ni avec eux, ni sans eux: Le Québec et les États-Unis* (Montreal: Nuit Blanche, 1996). On the rediscovery of the 'British' component of Quebec political identity, see Y. Lamonde, 'Le Lion, le coq et la fleur de lys: L'Angleterre et la France dans la culture politique du Québec', in Y. Lamonde and G. Bouchard (eds.), *La Nation dans tous ses États: Le Québec en comparaison* (Paris: L'Harmattan, 1997).

44. The idea that Canada has espoused a 'mosaic' rather than a 'melting-pot' vision of cultural diversity is still prevalent, although there is no empirical support for this idea. See J. G. Reiz and R. Breton, *The Illusion of Difference: Realities of Ethnicity in Canada and the United States* (Toronto: C. D. Howe Institute, 1994). As suggested by the authors, outside Quebec Canada is more of a melting-pot than the United States, while only Quebec can seriously be considered to be approaching the cultural mosaic model.

45. Apparently new data have shown that immigrant communities are slowly warming to the Parti Québécois and even to the sovereignty option. Linguistic integration (and not socio-economic factors) appears to be the key variable. According to Pierre Seré and Nathalie Lavoie, six of the eleven ridings won by the Parti Québécois on the island of Montreal in 1989 and 1994 were the result of a significant contribution (more than 20%) by 'non-Québécois-de-souche' ('non-Quebec stock') voters. See their 'Le Comportement électoral des Québécois

d'origine immigrante dans la région de Montréal, 1986–1998', in Boily (ed.), *L'Année politique au Québec.*

46. M. Keating, 'Regional Autonomy and the Changing State Order: A Framework of Analysis', *Regional Politics and Society*, 2/3 (1992), 45–61.
47. See J. Kotkin, *Tribes: How Race, Religion and Identity Determine Success in the New Global Economy* (New York: Random House, 1993).

CHAPTER 10

The Lure of Economic Prosperity versus Ethno-Nationalism: Turkish Cypriots, the European Union Option, and the Resolution of Ethnic Conflict in Cyprus

Tozun Bahcheli

Ever since it emerged in the international arena more than forty years ago, the Cyprus conflict has frustrated parties interested in resolving it. As the consent of Greece and Turkey are essential to any settlement negotiated between the Greek and Turkish communities, mediators have had to deal with both the internal and the external elements of the Cyprus conflict. Indeed, it has been the regional dimension (namely, the danger of the Cyprus dispute provoking a war between Greece and Turkey) that has ensured the sustained, decades-old involvement of such third parties as the United States and the United Nations (UN) and—to a lesser extent—the United Kingdom. But while a Greek–Turkish war has been averted, a Cyprus settlement remains elusive.

It is against this inauspicious background that the European Union (EU) has—with considerable reluctance on the part of some of its members, and somewhat unwittingly—assumed a key role in Cyprus. In spite of objections by Turkish Cypriots and Turkey that membership should await the settlement of the island's ethnic dispute, the EU has offered Cyprus the prospect of joining the Union, and began accession talks with the Greek Cypriot-controlled Republic of Cyprus on 31 March 1998.

While intervening directly in Cyprus, the EU has also pledged to support both UN and US endeavours for a settlement on the island. The EU hopes that the prospect of membership will give both Cypriot communities an incentive to settle their differences. Since the Greek majority is convinced of the benefits of membership, primarily for security reasons, the EU has sought to overcome Turkish Cypriot resistance by emphasizing the considerable economic benefits that membership would bring to the island's poorer Turkish community. Furthermore, in response to Turkish Cypriots' fears of domination by the Greek Cypriot majority, EU officials have pointed out several opportunities available to national minorities to protect their interests within the EU.

This chapter will illustrate the limits of economic incentives and of membership in supranational organizations as a way of overcoming the Turkish minority's desire for self-rule. It will also argue that a realistic bid to settle the Cyprus issue has to address both the regional (i.e. Greek–Turkish) as well as the communal dimensions of the dispute. The EU's failure to do so became evident in the aftermath of its Luxembourg summit of 12–13 December 1997, which placed Cyprus on a fast track for accession while rejecting Turkey's bid for inclusion in the list of (eleven) countries that are eligible for membership.[1] Turkish leaders responded angrily to the Brussels declaration and, in response to the EU's backing of the Greek Cypriot bid for accession, threatened to integrate the self-declared Turkish Republic of Northern Cyprus (TRNC) with Turkey. For its part, in a decision backed by Ankara, the Turkish Cypriot leadership retaliated against the EU move, by demanding that the future talks between Greek and Turkish Cypriots be conducted on a state-by-state basis.

While these set-backs have been discouraging, thanks to the improvement in relations in the aftermath of the earthquakes in both countries during the summer of 1999, the EU has regained some of the clout it lost after Luxembourg. It did so by affirming Turkey's eligibility to become an EU member at the Helsinki summit on 10 December 1999. The Turkish political establishment has eagerly sought EU membership for many years. This has caused some anxiety among Turkish Cypriots that they may be pressured by the Turkish government to make major concessions to Greek Cypriots in order to smooth Turkey's entry into the EU. However, it is far from certain that the prospect of Turkey's EU membership will help to overcome the obstacles that have impeded a Cyprus settlement for many years.

The European Union and Cyprus: From Observer to Interlocutor

The EU's decision to begin accession negotiations for Cyprus in 1998 has catapulted Brussels into a key role. On the other hand, it is fair to say that the European states remained wary of involvement in Cypriot affairs for many years. In addition, it should be noted that the majority of EU states have no particularly large stake in Cyprus itself, or indeed in other issues that divide Greece and Turkey. But the Cyprus-EU membership issue is a priority matter for Greece, which sees Cypriot membership as helping its strategic goal of reducing (if not removing) Turkey's influence in the island.

Cyprus and the EU (known then as the European Community) first signed an association agreement in 1972. This agreement was prompted by economic considerations, namely the desire to protect Cypriot agricultural exports to the British market in view of Britain's approaching accession. Unlike the Community's association agreements with Greece and Turkey, the 1972 accord envisaged not full membership, but rather a customs union after a ten-year transitional period.

When the war of 1974 divided the island into two ethnic zones, the European states adopted a cautious approach, particularly after the failure of the EU's brief attempt at mediation between the island's communities. According to Redmond, 'EU efforts to mediate in 1974 had been the first real application of its European Political Cooperation procedure and had effectively been a failure. The EU had been reduced simply to falling in line behind US- and UN-led endeavours to resolve the conflict.'[2] There was a widespread assumption among EU states that the upgrading of the association agreement with Cyprus to the level of membership would have to await the settlement of the island's communal dispute.

However, by the time the Republic of Cyprus submitted its application for membership in 1990, European resistance to consider Cyprus's membership had softened. This was largely due to the influence that Greece has been able to exercise since becoming an EU member in 1981. In addition, numerous EU states have commended the Greek Cypriot leaders for the skilful management of their economy, and also for their greater willingness to reunite the island and pursue a policy of reconciliation with the Turkish community. Even though the EU displayed a greater receptivity towards Greek Cypriots, the Commission's 1993 opinion on the Republic's application fell short of a commitment on accession. In fact, the Commission cited the need for a political settlement on the island before accession talks could proceed, but, in a significant concession to Greek Cypriots, agreed to reconsider Cypriot membership by January 1995 if no communal settlement emerged.[3] Ultimately Greece was able to secure a commitment that Brussels would open negotiations on Cypriot membership within six months of the conclusion of the 1996 intergovernmental conference as a quid pro quo for lifting its veto on the EU–Turkey customs union agreement of 1995. In effect, then, Greece swayed the rest of the EU states on the Cyprus membership issue because they wanted to advance EU–Turkish relations by proceeding with the customs union agreement with Turkey.

The Promises of European Union Membership for Greek Cypriots

In pursuing EU membership the Greek Cypriot leadership has encountered resistance and cynicism from the Turkish Cypriot leaders and various segments of the Turkish Cypriot population. However, within the Greek community, support for EU membership has been strong, even though the Progressive Party of the Working People (AKEL) initially opposed the membership application in 1990 because of fears that Cyprus's non-aligned status would be compromised; by the mid-1990s AKEL changed course in favour of membership. There exists an impressive consensus within the Greek community that EU membership will provide enormous benefits and carries no significant risks. Greek Cypriots hope that the prospect for EU accession will serve as a catalyst to reach a settlement with Turkish Cypriots and reunite the island. However, they would be content to see the Republic of Cyprus join the EU alone, in the belief (or hope) that the attraction of EU membership benefits would encourage the bulk of Turkish Cypriots to join subsequently. In this connection, many Greek Cypriots cite the analogy of Germany, with East Germany following West Germany into membership after the country remained divided for many years.

Greek Cypriots' enthusiasm for the EU is also related to their awareness that the UN's thirty-five-year mission to reach a settlement in Cyprus has achieved little. Inasmuch as Greek Cypriots are disillusioned with the United Nations' ability to help reunify the island, they remain keen to sustain its continued involvement, including the United Nations Peacekeeping Force in Cyprus (Unficyp). The principal utility of Unficyp's presence is that it ensures the uninterrupted involvement of the world body (and more specifically the Security Council) in the Cyprus problem. This approach is part of the general Greek Cypriot policy of internationalizing the Cyprus issue as a means of exerting pressure both on the Turkish Cypriots and on Turkey. Greek Cypriots' pursuit of the EU option can be seen as another concerted attempt to facilitate the engagement of third parties that are credible and sympathetic to the Greek Cypriot desire to unite Cyprus.

Even though both the UN and the EU assert their impartiality, both have conferred a considerable advantage on the Greek side by recognizing the Greek Cypriot-controlled Republic of Cyprus as the legitimate government of the entire island. This has been consistent with the position adopted by the UN Security Council, since it authorized the deployment of Unficyp in 1964. By contrast, both organizations have dealt with the Turkish Cypriots merely as a 'community'. This has angered the Turkish Cypriot leader, Denktash, who has complained of being deprived of the capacity to act in the international arena enjoyed by his Greek Cypriot counterparts. Both the EU and the UN have been careful about Greek Cypriot sensitivities by refraining from conferring any legitimacy on the TRNC.

Greece's veto within the EU has ensured that it has been even less accommodating than the UN of the Turkish Cypriots' desire to be treated on an equal fooring with their Greek Cypriot counterparts. Brussels has accepted the Greek Cypriot government, currently led by Glafcos Clerides, as its sole Cypriot interlocutor. Whereas the UN 'Set of Ideas' of 1992 provided that EU membership for Cyprus should follow a political settlement, the EU gave in to Greek pressure to fast-track Cyprus's accession process. Thus Agenda 2000 stated: 'If progress towards a settlement is not made before the [accession] negotiations are due to begin, they should be opened with the government of the Republic of Cyprus, as the only authority recognized by international law.'[4]

In addition to the other advantages, Greek Cypriots expect that EU rules would favour their negotiating position with Turkish Cypriots on several key issues. In the aftermath of the 1974 war in Cyprus the leaders of both communities agreed to seek a bi-zonal, bi-communal federal solution for the island. However, Greek Cypriots have sought to create a federation with a central government whose writ would extend to the entire island and not the loose federation or confederation espoused by Turkish Cypriots. Accordingly, Greek Cypriot negotiators have stated that any new settlement ought to provide for the much debated 'three freedoms': freedom to travel, freedom to settle, and freedom of property. Greek Cypriots are comforted by the belief that EU rules would secure these freedoms, even though temporary derogations might postpone the exercise of property rights to a later date.

Greek Cypriots are also confident that full membership will offer economic benefits to Cyprus. Most of Cyprus's trade is conducted with the EU. While Greek Cypriots have achieved a reasonably high level of prosperity outside the EU, they want to achieve more secure access for Cypriot exports and, with additional financial assistance from the EU, to promote even greater levels of economic growth. The Republic of Cyprus is already more prosperous than countries such as Greece, Spain, and Portugal. There are no significant economic problems standing in the way of Greek Cyprus's accession to the EU. Indeed, unlike several members of the EU (including Greece), Greek Cyprus already meets the convergence criteria set for participation in the third stage of economic and monetary union.

However, political and security considerations (rather than economic ones) have been the overriding considerations in the Greek Cypriot desire for EU membership. Most importantly, Greek Cypriots hope that, as EU members, they would enjoy greater security in relation to Turkey. Once Cyprus, or Greek Cyprus alone, becomes an EU country, it could call upon the solidarity of other members in its relations with Turkey. Greek Cypriots calculate that, in any post-accession crisis, Turkey would be restrained from taking armed action against Greek Cypriots.

Turkish Cypriots: The Risks of EU Membership

Given the depth of mistrust between the two communities in Cyprus, it would be surprising if Turkish Cypriots were not suspicious of anything that Greek Cypriots seek. In general, Turkish Cypriot perceptions of EU membership are the direct opposite of Greek Cypriots'. Both communities care most of all about how EU membership would affect their security. Turkish Cypriots, who have been outnumbered by four to one for most of the century, also fear political domination if they give up their own state. There is a general belief among Turkish Cypriots that Greek Cypriots remain committed to the Hellenization of Cyprus in spite of the difficulties this has caused in the past.

In many respects, the post-1974 political conditions in Cyprus (that is, the *de facto* partition) have suited Turkish Cypriots because they have been able to exercise self-government in their own state, and to enjoy the security provided by Turkey's substantial military presence in the TRNC. Accordingly, they have been sceptical of any third-party initiative that has sought to alter the status quo. This has presented a great challenge to both the United Nations and the United States, who have sought to be peacemakers in Cyprus for over thirty-five years. But the task facing the EU is even more difficult because of the Turkish Cypriot (and Turkish) perception that Brussels is heavily biased in favour of Greece and Greek Cypriots.

Even before the EU's decision to open the door for accession talks with Cyprus, Turkish Cypriots had been troubled by what they viewed as European solidarity with the Greek Cypriot government. In August 1994 Greek Cypriot attempts to curtail Turkish Cypriot exports to the EU culminated in a decision of the European Court of Justice that exports from the north were illegal if they did not have the necessary certificates of the Republic (that is, of the Greek Cypriot authorities).[5] Given that the EU, and particularly Britain, is the TRNC's largest export market (the main commodities being citrus, potatoes, and clothing), this ruling was a substantial blow to the north's economy.[6] European officials have responded to Turkish Cypriot protests by pointing out that the European Court of Justice based its decision on legal, not political, considerations. However, among Turkish Cypriots (and Ankara) this was seen as yet another instance of EU states giving in to Greek Cypriot and Greek pressures to penalize the Turkish community in Cyprus and weaken its bargaining position with the Greek community.

Turkish Cypriots insist that the EU accept that there is contested sovereignty on Cyprus, and that there are two legitimate authorities on the island. Accordingly, Turkish Cypriots have rejected the notion that the Greek Cypriot government—acting as the Republic of Cyprus—has any legal authority to represent the entire island on any EU-related issues (or indeed on any other issue). By the same token, they have insisted that the EU does not have the right to negotiate or reach agreements pertaining to Cyprus without the Turkish Cypriot authorities having an equal say with their Greek Cypriot counterparts.

Thus, Turkish Cypriots have strenuously objected to outsiders' characterization of them as a minority; they have insisted on the principle of political equality for both communities. For many years Denktash has sought to have this principle acknowledged by both Greek Cypriots and the international community. He has achieved only limited success, and only within the framework of intercommunal negotiations. Thus, in his *Report of the Secretary General on his*

Mission of Good Offices in Cyprus, UN Secretary-General Boutros Boutros-Ghali stated that 'Cyprus is the common home of the Greek Cypriot community and of the Turkish Cypriot community. Their relationship is not one of majority and minority, but one of two communities in the State of Cyprus.'[7]

The Greek Cypriot leadership is concerned that accepting such a principle would enable Turkish Cypriots to veto or otherwise frustrate the will of the Greek Cypriot majority. However, Turkish Cypriots are convinced that Greek Cypriots are bent on applying a majoritarian solution on the island and, furthermore, that the EU has accepted the merit of the Greek Cypriot position. Thus, Denktash has angrily reacted to the statement of the EU external affairs commissioner, Hans van den Broek, that the EU 'could not indefinitely ignore the aspirations of the majority of the population to be an EU member'.[8] Denktash also contends that membership in the EU violates the 1960 constitution that established the Republic of Cyprus, which states that the island cannot join any body of which Greece and Turkey are not members. However, EU officials reject this view. One observer has stated that 'this restriction does not apply to a *sui generis* organism such as the EU, any more than a similar provision in Austria's 1955 State Treaty [to prevent a reunion of Austria with Germany] stopped Austria from joining the EU'.[9]

In addition to questioning the legal basis of the Greek Cypriot recourse to the EU, Turkish Cypriot authorities have regularly complained that European officials have been insensitive and arrogant in their dealings with the TRNC. EU officials have repeatedly encouraged Turkish Cypriot officials to display statesmanship, to look to the future rather than the past, and to be prepared to bury the hatchet with Greek Cypriots (as did France and Germany after the Second World War). While the EU approach in promoting reconciliation between the two communities is well-intentioned, many Turkish Cypriots have been left with the impression that Europeans do not appreciate the suffering they endured at the hands of Greek Cypriots during the 1963–74 period, and of their resolve to avoid placing themselves in a position of vulnerability again.

Turkish Cypriot officials are also troubled by EU officials' emphasis on economic factors, rather than security issues; and the Turkish Cypriot leadership has complained that EU officials have exaggerated the interest among the Turkish community in EU membership. In this connection, the Denktash government is upset by what it has seen as EU encouragement of the two opposition centre-left parties, which support EU membership. Both the Republican Turkish Party (CTP) and the Communal Liberation Party (TKP) would like to see Turkish Cypriots become EU members as part of a bi-zonal federation of the type promoted by the UN and broadly consistent with EU hopes; these two parties have accused Denktash of being too intransigent on the EU issue and, generally, in negotiating the terms of a new settlement with Greek Cypriot leaders.[10]

Whether or not the EU has been insensitive, it has been unsuccessful in addressing the security concerns of large segments of the Turkish Cypriot community. When discussing any new settlement, most Turkish Cypriots dwell on instances of mistreatment and threats to their physical security posed by Greek Cypriots when the latter enjoyed military and political dominance during the 1963–74 period. Most Turkish Cypriots fear that any settlement on Cyprus (whether promoted by the EU or the UN) would entail the substantial or total withdrawal of the Turkish troops stationed in the TRNC, and that this would be exploited by the more numerous Greek Cypriots to threaten the Turkish community in the future. EU officials have responded to these fears by stating that Turkey's rights as a guarantor in Cyprus would not be affected by the accession of the island. However, many Turkish Cypriots are sceptical about these assurances; instead they attach greater credibility to the Greek Cypriot leaders' claim that EU membership would curb Turkey's ability to act on the island.

Most Turkish Cypriots prefer to have their own state in order to secure their future, even as they realize that lack of recognition and isolation has impeded economic development in the TRNC. Accordingly, even though EU membership is expected to bring some economic benefits to the Turkish community, there is a fear that this will severely circumscribe their political independence.

Even though the demographic balance on the island has shifted in their favour because of the influx of settlers from Turkey, Turkish Cypriots are outnumbered by Greek Cypriots by a ratio of slightly more than three to one.[11] One of the largest concerns in the north is that, just as a citizen of any EU country has the right to settle in any one of the member countries, this right will be utilized by many Greek Cypriots to 'swamp' the north. Turkish Cypriot officials have not been swayed by the prospect of EU derogations as an effective measure to limit Greek Cypriot settlement in the north. Fears have also been expressed in the north that EU membership would encourage large numbers of Turkish Cypriots to emigrate to other EU countries in search of better economic conditions.[12] The Turkish Cypriot leadership is worried by such a prospect, given its resolve to maintain a preponderant ethnic majority in the north, and also to protect the island-wide demographic balance with Greek Cypriots. By comparison, there are no evident concerns of population loss in Greek Cyprus, where living standards are higher than in some EU countries.[13] In the long run it is possible that economic development in the north will increase incomes to the level of Greek Cypriots.

In addition, Turkish Cypriots fear that, with the application of the EU's *acquis communautaire*, Greek Cypriots will be able to buy the properties of the poorer Turkish Cypriots. These anxieties are related to the fact that the per capita income of Greek Cypriots is about three times that of Turkish Cypriots.[14] EU derogations of the Åland Islands variety could provide a solution for this dilemma, but there are doubts among TRNC officials whether such arrangements will be sufficient to protect Turkish Cypriot interests in the long run.[15] On the other hand, the prospect of Turkey's EU membership may ease the fears of Greek Cypriot 'swamping', and encourage a more favourable consideration of derogations concerning land ownership.

All of these concerns contribute to the abiding fear among Turkish Cypriots that they risk becoming a vulnerable minority again in a reunited island. Most Turkish Cypriots believe that the majority of Greek Cypriots consider Cyprus to be a Greek island with a Turkish minority; they suspect that Greek Cypriot political forces are resolved to restablish their dominance over Turkish Cypriots and to re-establish Hellenism in the north. This explains why many Turkish Cypriots have preferred the continued division of the island, rather than face the risks of a new settlement.

Overcoming Turkish Cypriot Resistance?

In spite of the strong opposition among many Turkish Cypriots to EU membership, Brussels has not abandoned its hopes of garnering support in the north for the eventual accession of a unified, federal Cyprus. There is a hope that, as the accession process with Greek Cypriots advances and the benefits are publicized, Turkish Cypriots will want to board the EU train.

EU officials may have been encouraged by two surveys conducted in the TRNC, which showed a huge majority of the respondents supporting EU accession.[16] However, a majority of those polled stated that joining the EU should come after a Cyprus solution. Ever since the accession of Cyprus emerged as a possibility, several Turkish Cypriot organizations have endorsed EU membership. In particular, the two centre-left parties, the CTP and the TKP, have consistently supported EU membership for Turkish Cypriots in a reunited federal Cyprus. In addition, some trade unions in the north have also spoken in favour of EU membership. The main attractions for these groups are the prospect of economic growth in the north and the belief that this will stem Turkish Cypriot emigration.[17]

Clearly, there is an expectation among Turkish Cypriots that EU membership will bring some economic benefits. At the very least, the much resented Greek Cypriot economic embargo will be lifted:[18] Turkish Cypriot exports will reach European markets more easily and European tourists will visit the north without hindrance. In addition, although there is scant familiarity among Turkish Cypriots regarding specific EU programmes, it is believed that the north will be entitled to development assistance to help overcome its relative poverty.

Inasmuch as the general receptivity of Turkish Cypriots to the promises of economic benefits is apparent, there are additional, political, explanations for the attraction of the EU option. Both the CTP and the TKP have articulated widespread Turkish Cypriot concern that immigration from Turkey since 1974 has diluted the 'Cypriotness' of the society in the north. The majority of Turkish settlers came to Cyprus from poor rural areas of Turkey; they are more religiously observant and socially conservative than most Turkish Cypriots. As a result, their integration in Turkish Cypriot society has not been smooth. Turkish Cypriots consider themselves more 'modern' than mainland Turks: they are better educated, more secular, and view themselves as better equipped than Turkish settlers to become European citizens. By exposing northern Cyprus (along with the rest of the island) to European norms and laws, many Turkish Cypriots hope to limit the influence of Turkish settlers in their society. In addition, the centre-left parties would like to see a reduction of Turkey's influence in the TRNC; they hope that Cyprus's membership in the EU will help secure that, by ending the economic reliance of Turkish Cypriots on Ankara.

On the other hand, security concerns dominate the Turkish Cypriot approach. In responding to these, European officials (and Greek Cypriot authorities) have argued that EU membership would not compromise Turkish Cypriot security. Specifically, given the Turkish Cypriot anxiety that Turkey's rights as a guarantor remain unchanged, EU officials have insisted that no EU law could take precedence over the 1960 Treaty of Guarantee. However, even as EU and Greek Cypriot officials have sought to promote the multiple benefits of membership, they have especially appealed to the economic interests of Turkish Cypriots. This is based on the calculation that with only a third of the per capita income of the Greek Cypriots, and with perennial economic problems, the majority of Turkish Cypriots would welcome an improvement in their living standards.

It is already apparent, however, that political considerations have prevailed over economic ones among Turkish Cypriots. In the course of their conflict, the Greek and Turkish communities have quarrelled mostly about political and security issues, and only rarely about economic matters. Moreover, the economic gap between the two communities has existed for several decades.

Since 1974 the gap between Greek and Turkish Cypriots has widened substantially. But at the same time Turkish Cypriot living standards have increased significantly. Thus, according to figures provided by Turkish Cypriot authorities, the per capita income of Turkish Cypriots was $1,444 in 1977, but this figure more than doubled to $3,447 by 1990; and the figure increased to $4,222 in 1996.[19] Some Turkish Cypriot commentators have argued that with its substantial 'grey economy', the TRNC has provided a higher standard of living than is indicated by GDP statistics.[20]

In addition, Turkish Cypriots have benefited from Turkey's willingness to bolster their economy. In order to maintain living standards, and to protect their interests, Turkish governments have been willing to allocate large amounts of aid to the region; indeed, the per capita income in the TRNC is higher than that in Turkey.[21] Since the TRNC is unrecognized internationally, it has been ineligible to receive the aid that the Greek Cypriot government has received from a number of states and international bodies such as the World Bank and the EU. Accordingly, Turkey has invested in several infrastructure projects in the TRNC, and has provided credits and other forms of development aid. It was Turkey, too, that assumed the large costs associated with re-exporting Turkish Cypriot citrus and clothing when the European Court of Justice ruled in 1994 that EU countries could not receive goods from northern Cyprus without the export licences issued by the Republic of Cyprus. More recently, in 1998, Turkey began to alleviate chronic water shortages experienced by Turkish Cypriots by shipping water to the TRNC; these shipments will be accelerated with the planned construction of a water pipeline from Turkey to northern Cyprus.[22]

In the course of their struggle with Greek Cypriots since the 1960s Turkish Cypriots have rejected political terms deemed threatening to their security, even when it was clearly in their economic interests to accept them. Turkish Cypriots acknowledge the economic benefits (namely, from increased tourism and unhindered trade) that would result from the lifting of the economic embargo on the TRNC, although they might disagree with Greek Cypriots—and EU or UN officials—on the extent of such benefits. However, there is no compelling reason to expect that the EU's economic incentives will prove any weightier than those offered by Greek Cypriot leaders in the past. As for the embargo, after nearly a quarter-century Turkish Cypriots have adjusted to it, however much they may blame it for many of their economic ills.

The case of the Turkish Cypriots is not unlike that of other ethnic groups that have achieved *de facto* independence at considerable economic cost: Chechens, Armenians of Nagorno Karabakh, and Abkhaz are cases in point. All of these ethnic groups have been prepared to pay a heavy economic price in order to achieve independent statehood; all have rejected a wide measure of autonomy short of independence. By comparison with these cases, considerably better economic conditions prevail in the TRNC, and living standards have improved gradually.[23] In addition, there is every expectation that Turkey will continue to provide substantial subsidies to Turkish Cypriots. The economic cost borne by Turkey for its Cyprus commitment is relatively light: Ankara has exploited its strategic relationship with the United States and key European countries in order to minimize the political–diplomatic burden of its policy of maintaining its military presence in, and support of, the TRNC.

The European Union's Challenge: Balancing Greece and Turkey

Both Greece and Turkey have been primarily motivated by strategic considerations in Cyprus. Greek leaders see in Cyprus's EU membership the best assurance for the long-term protection of Greek Cypriots from Turkey, and for limiting the latter's influence on the island. This belief is based on the expectation that Turkey will be obliged to withdraw the bulk of its troops from Cyprus once the island becomes an EU member. In addition, with the sovereignty of Cyprus fortified by EU membership, Greeks (and Greek Cypriots) hope that Turkey could not justify military intervention in the future. For Turkey the biggest danger is that, with Cyprus admitted as a member prior to a settlement, Cyprus will become an EU–Turkish issue and not just a Greek–Turkish dispute. Ankara anticipates that Cypriot EU membership would increase pressures for Turkey's withdrawal of forces from the island, even though Turkish leaders can be expected to resist such withdrawal without first securing Turkish and Turkish Cypriot interests. There is also the potential threat that unless EU rules on veto rights were to be revised, with Greek Cyprus admitted as a member, there would be two 'Greek' vetoes on Turkey's future membership. Consequently, Ankara has been opposed to the island's membership unless Turkey itself is also assured of joining the EU.

Greece and Turkey have had serious differences not only in Cyprus, but also over sovereign rights in the Aegean, particularly over the delineation of the continental shelf. During the cold war years the United States was instrumental in averting military clashes between its NATO allies on several occasions. However, United States and NATO clout over Turkey and Greece may have declined since the end of the cold war. In addition, before the warming of Greek–Turkish relations in late 1999 there were fears of clashes in the Aegean or Cyprus.

Before lifting its veto on Turkey's candidacy in December 1999, Athens tried to garner the support of its EU partners both to pressure Ankara for a Cyprus settlement, and also to support Greece against perceived Turkish threats to its sovereign rights in the Aegean. As an EU insider, Athens has clearly enjoyed an important advantage over Ankara in advancing its interests in relation to Turkey, including the Cyprus question. When its EU partners have disagreed with its policies, Athens has used its veto powers, as shown by its blocking of EU aid earmarked for Turkey under the association and customs union agreements. This not only angered Turkey, but also taxed the patience of Greece's EU partners. The European states often felt obliged to cater to Greece, but they have also endeavoured to maintain good relations with Turkey, an associate member of the EU since 1963. However, even after the Helsinki summit's endorsement of Turkey's candidacy in 1999, there are doubts among many Turks (and Europeans) over whether Turkey will qualify for admission in the foreseeable future: this is due, in part, to the magnitude of the internal reforms that Ankara will be required to make, not least in the way it manages the Kurdish issue.

Turkey is also a major trading partner of many EU countries. Moreover, it has shared membership in virtually all European institutions with the EU countries, and is considered by many Europeans as having vital strategic assets. In addition, as one observer has explained,

Turkey seems to be at something of a crossroads in terms of its future political and strategic direction and the EU does not wish to do anything that could encourage it to turn away from the West and towards the East and Islamism. [This] is partly because Turkey is seen as a possible bridge between the West on the one side and both Islamism and the Arab countries of the Middle East on the other.[24]

For all of these reasons, EU states are reluctant to support Greece to the point where they would damage their relations with Turkey.

Turkey has been troubled by Greece's success in getting the accession talks started between Greek Cyprus and the EU, against Turkish–Turkish Cypriot objections. But for many years Turkish leaders have hoped that Turkey would itself be able to join the EU, and thus balance Greek influence in Brussels. This is why the Turkish government raised no serious objections when the EU acceded to the Greek demand for a commitment to begin accession talks with Cyprus in return for lifting its veto on the EU–Turkey customs union agreement in 1995.

However, Turkey's leaders have rejected any linkage between its membership and the Cyprus dispute, and have also insisted that the Cypriot communities be left alone to negotiate a settlement on an equal basis. One of the critical challenges facing any Turkish government is the electoral risk that it would incur in accepting a settlement involving large territorial concessions in Cyprus and the forsaking of TRNC independence. There is a consensus in Turkey that the Cyprus issue was settled in 1974, when Turkey intervened in response to the Greek junta's coup and partitioned the island. In effect then, even though successive Turkish governments have backed UN negotiations between the two Cypriot communities on the basis of a bi-zonal, bi-communal federation, since August 1998 they have revised this policy in favour of a two-state confederation as demanded by Denktash.

As Turkey has long sought after EU membership, the other parties with a stake in the Cyprus issue have expected that Turkish governments would display sufficient flexibility and cooperation (and pressure the Turkish Cypriots to do the same) in order to help create a federal state on the island with a single sovereignty. It is widely believed in Europe that a Cyprus settlement would remove a major obstacle to Turkey's membership of the EU. However, Cyprus is by no means the only issue that has created an impediment to Turkey's EU aspirations. Ankara's poor human rights record (particularly the treatment of its substantial Kurdish minority), and the comparatively poor state of its economy, represent additional, weighty factors that weaken Turkey's prospects.

Turkish leaders have claimed that other European governments often refrain from expressing their resistance to Turkey's membership while conveniently letting Greece spearhead such opposition. It is well known in Turkey that other EU members (particularly German administrations under former Chancellor Helmut Kohl) have had strong misgivings regarding Turkish membership, and that these are not merely related to the well-known human rights problems in Turkey. German governments have been anxious that Turkey's membership would encourage large numbers of poor Turks to move to German cities in search of jobs and social benefits, thereby creating major economic and social problems for Germany.

These anxieties are related to the presence of more than 2 million ethnic Turks (and Turkish Kurds) in Germany. Most Germans believe that these Turks (and Kurds) have not integrated well into the German social fabric. There are also fears in Germany and elsewhere in Europe that the ideal of creating European political and cultural unity would be jeopardized by the admission of Islamic Turkey with its large population. Turkey's population of 63 million (in 1998) is expected to become the largest in Europe by the year 2010. During a meeting of European Christian Democrats in March 1997 Wilfried Martens, a prominent Christian Democrat in the European Parliament, bluntly stated that 'the EU is in the process of building a civilization in which Turkey has no place'.[25] This clearly offended many Turks, who believe that many Europeans hold the same views as Martens but are reluctant to state them publicly. On the other hand, the German government of Chancellor Schröder has assumed a more sympathetic approach to Turkey, and this was a helpful factor in the EU's decision at Helsinki in December 1999 to offer membership status to Turkey.

Helping secure a Cyprus settlement will not be enough to gain Turkish entry into the EU. On the other hand, many Western officials believe that—since EU membership is so highly prized by Turkish leaders—Ankara would agree to a negotiated Cyprus settlement along federal lines if it were given a clear timetable for accession. It was on this premise that Richard Holbrooke, the United States envoy for Cyprus, tried to secure a Cyprus settlement in 1997. Washington has long promoted Turkey's EU membership not just to advance a Cyprus settlement, but also to help secure Turkey's political integration with Europe. However, Holbrooke failed to persuade European governments to include Turkey among the designated candidates for accession during 1997. Nevertheless, United States diplomacy subsequently helped secure a reversal of the EU position on Turkish candidacy at the Helsinki summit in 1999.[26]

Pulled in opposite directions by Greece and the Greek Cypriots on the one hand, and Turkey and the Turkish Cypriots on the other, Brussels has faced a dilemma on the Cyprus EU membership issue.

Greece threatened to veto the EU's plans to admit new members if the accession talks with Greek Cyprus did not go forward, whereas Turkey threatened to integrate with the TRNC, thereby ending any realistic hopes for the island's future reunification. Thanks to the Helsinki summit decision, the EU has now recovered some of the clout that it lost when it shunned both Turkey and the Turkish Cypriots with its Luxembourg summit decision in 1997.

Conclusions

The Cyprus conflict has proved to be one of the most intractable and internationalized disputes of recent years. It has frustrated many third parties that have tried to resolve it. Given this record, there was no assurance that the EU would do better than its predecessors when it became an interlocutor in Cyprus in the mid-1990s. Indeed, when the EU was prodded by Greece to offer membership to Cyprus in the mid-1990s, it complicated rather than helped the prospects for a settlement by antagonizing Turkish Cypriots and Turkey.

Turkish Cypriots are an embittered minority who have exercised self-rule and enjoyed security for more than a quarter-century. They have proved resistant to the lure of economic prosperity offered by EU membership. In this respect, they are like the many other ethnic communities, including the Irish before 1921, Slovaks in 1993, and Chechens today, who have placed their identity and political concerns ahead of materialism. The belief that Turkish Cypriots could be persuaded to embrace a single Cyprus because of its economic advantages is just one more example of what Walker Connor has described as an unwarranted exaggeration of the importance of materialism in human affairs.[27] Rather than calculating how much better off they will be, Turkish Cypriots have instead focused on the political costs of a single Cyprus in the EU.

However, the warming of Greek–Turkish relations in late 1999 has paved the way for the EU's granting of candidate status to Turkey. With Turkey as a prospective EU member, Turkish Cypriot fears regarding their security will ease. However, not all Turkish Cypriot anxieties about becoming a vulnerable minority in a reunited island can be easily put to rest. There are widespread concerns in the TRNC that Turkish Cypriots' independence may be sacrificed to overcome Greece's veto and secure Turkey's EU accession. Whereas news of the EU's decision on Turkish candidacy generated much enthusiasm in Turkey, it has been greeted with caution and scepticism in the TRNC.

All the parties involved in the conflict appreciate that Turkey's EU candidacy has introduced a new dynamic for Cyprus, giving Turkey an important reason to settle the Cyprus problem. However, there are still a number of difficult issues to be resolved: refugees and their right of return, security arrangements, territorial adjustments, and whether a federation or a two-state confederation ought to be established on the island. Greek Cypriot leaders have rejected the Turkish Cypriot insistence that a confederation of two sovereign states be created: this issue, together with the extent of Turkish Cypriot territorial concessions to Greek Cypriots, will be especially hard to resolve. Mediators may find some wording that would be acceptable to both sides, perhaps by providing for an implicit rather than an explicit recognition of a Turkish Cypriot state that would form a union with its Greek Cypriot counterpart. Clearly, Ankara's influence on Turkish Cypriots will be paramount in any consideration of possible compromises. On the other hand, Denktash's resolve to achieve recognition or acknowledgement should not be underestimated, nor should his capacity to reject pressures from Turkish governments.

NOTES

I would like to thank the United States Institute of Peace in Washington, DC, for a grant that helped with researching this chapter. For helpful comments and criticisms on earlier drafts, I am grateful to John McGarry and Will McKercher.

1. At the Luxembourg summit in 1997 the European Council invited Cyprus, together with the Czech Republic, Hungary, Poland, Estonia, and Slovenia, to begin negotiations for EU membership on 30 Mar. 1998. A second group of applicant countries—Latvia, Lithuania, Bulgaria, Romania and Slovakia—were judged eligible for membership but not yet ready to begin accession talks. The European Council added Turkey to the list of candidates at its Helsinki summit on 10 Dec. 1999.
2. J. Redmond, 'From Association towards the Application for Full Membership: Cyprus' Relations with the European Union', in H. J. Axt and H. Brey (eds.), *Cyprus and the European Union: New Chances for Solving an Old Conflict?* (Munich: Sudosteuropa-Gesellschaft, 1997), 95.
3. According to Redmond, 'this was intended to prevent the Turkish Cypriots from effectively having the power of veto, that is, they would be able to veto Cypriot accession to the EU simply by refusing to agree to an internal settlement with the Greek Cypriots' (Redmond, 'From Association towards Full Membership', 97).
4. Cited by N. Nugent, 'Cyprus and the European Union: A Particularly Difficult Membership Application', *Mediterranean Politics*, 1/3 (Winter 1997), 69.
5. As Redmond notes, 'As the EU did not recognize the TRNC then it could not technically accept Turkish Cypriot documentation' (Redmond, 'From Association towards Full Membership', 97).

6. According to a report, the ruling cut the TRNC production of potatoes and fruit in half. See the *Inter Press Service*, 9 Oct. 1997.
7. United Nations Security Council Document S/21183, 8 Mar. 1990, 2.
8. Reported by Reuters, 16 Mar. 1996.
9. See *Financial Times*, 5 Jan. 1998.
10. The centre-left parties between them won 26.6% of the votes in the elections to the TRNC assembly in Dec. 1998, capturing 13 of the 50 seats; by comparison, the right-wing–nationalist parties won 44% of the total vote and 37 seats (*Economist Intelligence Unit Country Report*, Cyprus, 1st Quarter (1999), 28).
11. In 1960, the last year when an island-wide census was taken, the Turkish Cypriot population comprised roughly 20% of the island total of 571,500 (Statistics and Research Department, Republic of Cyprus, *Statistical Abstract* (Cyprus, 1963), 22). It is widely assumed that the population ratio between Greek and Turkish Cypriots did not change significantly during 1960–74. However, the census taken by Turkish Cypriot authorities on 15 Dec. 1996 reported a population of 200,587 (Turkish Republic of Northern Cyprus, Statistics and Research Department, *State Planning Organization, Census of Population, Social and Economic Characteristics of Population* (Cyprus, 1999), 10). Figures provided by the Republic of Cyprus indicate the Greek Cypriot population to be 645,300 (Republic of Cyprus, *The Almanac of Cyprus: 1988* (Cyprus: Press and Information Office, 1998), 8). These figures show that the Turkish Cypriot proportion of the population has increased roughly from 20% to 31% since 1974. This increase has been primarily due to the settlement of immigrants from Turkey since the island's division. Although there are no reliable statistics on the Turkish settlers, two researchers have estimated that they represent about 40% of the population in the TRNC (H. Brey and G. Heinritz, 'Ethnicity and Demographic Changes in Cyprus: In the Statistical Fog', *Geographica Slavonica*, 24 (1993), 218).
12. This is based on interviews conducted by me in Cyprus in Apr. 1998.
13. Greek Cypriot per capita gross domestic product (GDP) of $13,000 is comparable with Spain's but is higher than those in Greece and Portugal.
14. See K. Kyle, *Cyprus: In Search of Peace* (London: Minority Groups International Report, 1997), 37. Greek Cypriot GDP per head was reported to be $13,000, and Turkish Cypriot GDP per head, $4,158 (*Economist Intelligence Unit Country Report*, Cyprus, 3rd Quarter (1998), 7, 29).
15. Only citizens of the Åland Islands 'may acquire, possess, or lease lands in the islands without the need for special permission from the provincial [i.e. Ålands] government' (R. Lapidoth, *Autonomy: Flexible Solutions to Ethnic Conflicts* (Washington: United States Institute of Peace, 1997), 75). The EU, prior to Finland's accession in 1995, endorsed these exceptions, or derogations. The islands have a population of about 25,000 Swedish speakers. While the Ålands are technically a province of Finland, they have enjoyed a wide measure of autonomy for over seventy-five years.
16. The survey, conducted by the polling agency COMAR, found that over 80% of the respondents supported EU membership, as reported in *Kibris*, 24 Nov. 1997. The poll led EU officials and the Turkish Cypriot leaders to offer contrasting interpretations of the results: the EU welcomed the findings as confirming overwhelming support for EU membership, whereas Denktash asserted that the vast majority of Turkish Cypriots rejected EU membership until the Cyprus conflict was resolved. A similar poll conducted during the first week of Dec. 1999 also showed huge Turkish Cypriot support for EU accession; as in the 1997 poll, a majority wanted a political settlement first before achieving EU membership (*Kibris*, 27 Dec. 1999).

17. There are no reliable statistics of the number of Turkish Cypriots who have emigrated since 1974. Greek Cypriot official sources estimate 45,000 without indicating the basis of the estimate (*Almanac of Cyprus:* 1988, 9). The author of a recent article reported that 'some 20,000 Turkish Cypriots' emigrated since 1974, but offered no accounting for his estimate either (C. de Bellaigue, 'Conciliation in Cyprus?', *Washington Quarterly*, 22/2, 191).

18. Since 1974 the Republic of Cyprus has boycotted goods produced in the TRNC, and has succeeded in preventing many other states from trading with Turkish Cypriots. As a result of effective Greek Cypriot pressures, European governments do not permit scheduled flights to the TRNC. This has hurt tourism, which is 'the Turkish Cypriots' main source of income with net earnings from the sector estimated to be more than 40% of GDP in 1997' (*Economist Intelligence Unit Country Report*, Cyprus, 1st Quarter (1999), 32). It is widely believed that tourism would expand greatly if the economic embargo on the TRNC was lifted.

19. State Planning Organization (Turkish Republic of Northern Cyprus), *Economic and Social Indicators for 1996* (Oct. 1997), 1.

20. There are 125,219 motor vehicles registered in the TRNC (*Kibris*, 24 Jan. 2000), most of which are passenger cars; this shows that there is, on average, one car per two residents in the TRNC.

21. The Turkish government estimated the per capita GDP for Turkey at $3,339 for the year 2000. This was reported by Turkey's official news agency, Anadolu Ajansi, on 3 Jan. 2000; cited in Foreign Broadcast Information Service (West Europe), *FBIS-WEU*, 3 Jan. 2000.

22. *Economist Intelligence Unit Country Report*, Cyprus, 1st Quarter (1998), 25.

23. The TRNC GDP grew by 3.9% in 1997 and 6.3% in 1998 (*Economist Intelligence Unit Country Report*, Cyprus, 3rd Quarter (1999), 34).

24. Nugent, 'Cyprus and the European Union', 59.

25. *The Economist*, 15 Mar. 1997.

26. An American analyst argued as follows: 'It is doubtful that the EU would have acted . . . had not Washington vigorously lobbied for Turkey's candidacy. The United States used three main arguments to persuade and, to some extent, to shame the Europeans into including Turkey: the strategic importance of anchoring Turkey to the West, the boost that the EU candidacy would give to the professed EU goal of democratization in Turkey, and the important role the EU has in promoting values of tolerance and diversity toward the Muslim world. Whether persuaded or shamed, the EU came around' (A. Makovsky, 'Turkey: Europe Bound?', *Policywatch*, no. 429 (Washington, DC: Washington Institute for Near East Policy, 15 Dec. 1999), 2).

27. See Connor, Ch. 6 in this volume.

CHAPTER 11

Nationalism and a Critique of European Integration: Questions from the Flemish Parties

Janet Laible

Although analysts of European integration debate the extent to which states have ceded sovereignty to European Union (EU) institutions,[1] there is a general agreement that significant powers once under the control of state governments now rest at the European level.[2] In the past decade nationalist parties in EU member states have thus increasingly debated the merits of independence in an integrating Europe. Will self-government within the EU increase the capacity of the nation or region to manage its affairs, or is 'sovereignty' in the contemporary European order increasingly devoid of meaningful content? Some nationalists debate the challenges of European integration with a focus on the relationship of sovereignty 'in Europe' to national welfare and economic development.[3] With projects such as Economic and Monetary Union requiring extensive centralization of decision-making power in European institutions, the linkage of national sovereignty and economic welfare has emerged as a dominant theme in debate over the future of Europe and its states.

Yet just as polities do not concentrate solely on promoting economic welfare, nationalists do not focus exclusively on the relationship between sovereignty and economy in their considerations of European integration. State government institutions have historically served to form and articulate national culture and identity, and nationalists recognize the potential for the European polity to influence the development of their national cultures. Some, such as Welsh and

Catalan nationalists, see Europe as a more positive and tolerant context for the expression of regional culture than have proven their respective states. Others, however, view the relationship of European integration, sovereignty, and national culture as deeply problematic and believe that only with a major transformation of the constitution of Europe will their linguistic and cultural interests be protected. Culture therefore becomes one lens through which to examine questions of legitimate governance in the EU.

This chapter explores how Flemish nationalists raise questions about the impact of European integration on the cultural rights of their nation, the members of which have struggled for a century and a half to assert themselves against the political and cultural hegemony of French language interests in Belgium. I discuss why Flemish nationalists perceive threats to their culture from European integration, why they believe this reflects larger problems of sovereignty for weak actors in a centralizing Europe, and how they attempt to formulate responses to these problems. Two nationalist parties, the Volksunie (People's Union) and the Vlaams Blok (Flemish Bloc) present very different visions of the Flemish nation and of the appropriate political order they wish to see emerge at the level of Europe. Long the central concerns of the Flemish movement, language and culture are placed by both the Volksunie and Vlaams Blok at the heart of their 'European' politics. Yet although members of each party seek to resolve differently the problems they perceive in European governance, their criticisms of the EU that emerge from cultural issues are strikingly similar. There is agreement that 'culture' legitimately lies under the jurisdiction of the Flemish 'polity', and that European integration is infringing upon this jurisdiction.

I argue that the Flemish nationalist reaction to European integration is inspired by actual and potential losses of institutional power and constitutional protection for Flemish culture. I explore claims by Volksunie and Vlaams Blok activists that the EU threatens political arrangements that support Flemish culture as well as the *future* capacity of the Flemish nation to preserve its autonomy and to protect its cultural interests. Culture is not the only issue of concern to Flemish nationalists in contemporary Europe. But through the concepts of *nation* and *state* articulated by their respective parties, Flemish nationalists explicitly link the transformation of domestic institutions by European integration to questions concerning the survival of their culture, and hence to considerations of power exercised by the EU. Political power in the area of cultural policy is seen to be shifting from domestic institutions that are explicitly empowered with cultural functions under Belgian law towards an 'undemocratic' European arena.

By positing that cultural issues are fundamental to Flemish nationalist criticisms of the legitimacy of European governance, this chapter challenges more widely accepted views of European integration and cultural politics. Lynch and Leslie argue that because the EU lacks policy responsibility in culture and does not possess a potentially hegemonic national or linguistic culture, Europe is not likely to become a target for the discontent of minority nationalists.[4] On this view, nationalists might question numerous aspects of European integration, but culture will not itself prove a point of contention. Another perspective holds that Europe *de facto* does participate in cultural politics, and that this may contribute to nationalist support for Europe. In their study of constitutional nationalism in Northern Ireland, Scotland, and Wales, Mitchell and Cavanagh argue that the inclusion of regional actors in EU decision-making processes, and the positive orientation of the Commission and the European Parliament to minority languages and cultures, have helped to generate a favourable response on the part of these nationalist parties towards Europe.[5]

However, evidence from Flemish nationalism suggests not only that culture has become a contested field in an integrating Europe, but that nationalists may perceive themselves to be at odds with European institutions on cultural issues and on the political questions raised thereby. Whereas the EU may help nationalists in some member states, such as the United Kingdom, to sidestep or challenge a central state that is viewed as obstructing the nationalist agenda, the relationship of Europe with Flemish nationalists appears more complex. Both Flemish nationalist parties promote the further weakening of the central state, but both recognize that regional and community government can and do act in the nationalists' interests. Furthermore, for many Flemish, the capacity of sub-state government to promote and protect Flemish interests, particularly in the domains of culture and language, is a hard-fought accomplishment that they are loath to see diminished by government at a higher level. Indeed, I demonstrate that both the Volksunie and Vlaams Blok believe that Europe has infringed upon these powers and is subsequently regarded not as an ally in the nationalist struggle, but as a problematic partner and even as a threat. In addition, both parties suggest that the disrespect for their national culture within European institutions reveals deeper problems of democracy in the EU; small or weak polities are endangered by centralization of the EU but at the same time have insufficient institutional means to articulate their concerns. Ultimately, it is no longer sufficient that the state can be changed to protect Flemish interests, as these interests will only be protected and promoted in a radically restructured Europe.

I first outline the constitutional developments in Belgium and the EU that have altered the context in which regional actors, including nationalists, engage with European integration. I then explore how each party links its particular vision of nation and state to this context of institutional transformation. European integration is revealed to conflict with party ideals of Flemish autonomy, and autonomy is shown to be inextricably linked with cultural and linguistic rights. I conclude with illustrations drawn from interviews with party officials that demonstrate how the Vlaams Blok and Volksunie link the impact of Europe on Flemish cultural politics to larger problems of participation and accountability in a centralizing European polity. With a focus on the weak institutional capacity of Flanders, officials from these two distinct nationalist parties arrive at a similar radical critique of the European project.

A Changing Belgium in an Integrating Europe

Nationalist critiques of Europe should be considered in the context of the relationship of Belgium and its regions to the EU, a relationship that has been dramatically transformed in the past decade. Recent constitutional reforms have significantly empowered the Belgian regions with respect to the central state.[6] The impact of European legislation has grown considerably since the passage of the Single European Act, and European institutions and policy-making processes have increasingly been opened to participation by regional actors. However, the weakness of Belgium in an integrating Europe, where the role of the regions is far from well established, has created an imbalance between the jurisdictions that the regions claim under the Belgian constitution, and their capacity to act effectively in these areas at the European level. In this environment, questioning the constitutional design of the EU has become politically relevant for Flemish nationalists.

Belgium is divided into three regions: Flanders, Wallonia, and Brussels, and three communities: Dutch-, French-, and German-speaking; bilingualism is the official policy of Brussels.[7] Reforms of the state have left the federal government with relatively few powers, primarily in areas of 'high politics' such as defence and foreign affairs, as well as federal finance, justice, internal security, social security, and some aspects of public health. The regional jurisdictions include land use and planning, environment, transport, and agriculture; the jurisdictions of the communities include culture, education, media, use of languages, and the protection of young people.[8] The regions have made inroads even in policy areas traditionally reserved for the central governments of states: the new constitution grants them the capacity to make treaties with foreign countries, provided the substance of the treaties falls under those powers belonging to the regions.[9] With control over monetary policy recently transferred to the European level, social security may be the most significant policy area still under the jurisdiction of the central government.

Yet demands to reform the state by devolving additional powers away from the centre have not ceased and are voiced not only by radical separatist parties but by the largest parties in the country, including the largest Flemish party, the Christelijke Volkspartij (Christian People's Party, the CVP). The CVP leader in Flanders, Luc van den Brande, has called for such significant policy areas as social security, and other residual federal powers in foreign trade and fiscal policy, to be transferred to the regions. Van den Brande has also been keen to promote Flemish economic and cultural interests internationally, including pushing closer cooperation between the Netherlands and Flanders.[10] Furthermore, the cause of increased autonomy, in particular in Flanders, has widespread appeal based on perceptions that Walloon welfare is overly dependent on Flemish wealth, and that greater control over taxation and spending would benefit Flemish economic performance.[11] Belgian constitutional reforms have not only granted significant powers to the regions, but also led many to question what constitutes legitimate governance for the regions and communities of Belgium with respect to the centre.

Accompanying changes for regions within the state have been shift in the relationship between the regions and the EU. Developments over the past decade of European integration have increased the scope of involvement for regions in numerous policy areas, among which structural fund policy-making and implementation have been widely discussed.[12] Attempts to protect and develop the competitiveness of regional economies in the wake of Single Market legislation have led many regional and local governments to participate informally in European politics by establishing information and lobbying offices in Brussels.[13] Belgian regions have recognized the importance of communicating their interests to the Commission and have established their own official delegations to the EU to lobby and speak on behalf of the respective region in all areas under its jurisdiction. The Treaty on European Union provided some mechanisms to meet the demands of stronger regions, such as the German *Länder*, to have formal representation in the institutions of Europe. The Committee of the Regions institutionalized a role for regions and local authorities in numerous areas of the consultative processes of policy design; and a modification to voting rights in the Council of Ministers now permits regional ministers to represent their states in Council votes.[14]

Yet the creation of bodies for regional representation in Europe has raised as many questions about participation in the EU and the legitimacy of governance as it has supposedly answered. The role of the Belgian regions in Europe is particularly complicated, even with respect to the Council of Ministers, where Article 146 of the Maastricht Treaty was intended to foster a stronger sense of participation by regions in EU decision-making.[15] However, regional ministers are prevented from speaking for their respective regional constituencies; they must speak with a collective voice. Furthermore, the question of whether Belgian regions are *effective* when they participate in the Council of Ministers remains open.[16] Belgian regions may 'on paper' be among the most powerful sub-state actors in European institutions, but their inclusion in European institutions can imply accepting the watering-down of their specific interests to forge agreements with their colleagues in the Council, and allowing themselves to be placed on equal status with local authorities and metropolitan executives in the Committee of the Regions.

Institutional and legislative reform has brought the regions into increased contact with European policy-making and with the impact of EU decisions. But the consequent weakening of the Belgian state implies that a void exists with respect to the representation of regional and communal interest in Europe, where states continue to be the privileged actors. The regions are excluded from decision-making in several policy areas that have a significant impact on them: they do not legislate in monetary policy but have felt the impact of the European Monetary System (EMS), as the fiscal restraints imposed on Belgium by the EMS reduced the capacity of the central state to respond to Flemish and Walloon economic concerns.[17] The introduction of the single currency in 1999 caused the Belgian central state to lose control of one of the few policy areas that it had retained from the regions, and, despite the weakening of the Belgian state in the European arena, the regions will not be concomitantly empowered. Regional actors may bear the economic and political brunt of deflationary readjustments in many states that adopt the euro, but as of yet they appear unlikely to be granted any further capacity to act, at the European level, to have their grievances addressed.[18]

Leaders of the Belgian regions, with significant resources and authority in their hands domestically, are increasingly operating in a European environment in which the power of the central state to make decisions and implement them appears to be ever decreasing. Yet despite the growing significance of the European level in the politics and economics of the regions, these apparently powerful leaders have not found themselves with significantly increased capacity to act in the EU. The Belgian state remains a juridical equal with its EU counterparts, but this equality is increasingly a fiction, and the powers that the state has lost to its regions are not being reflected in the power relations among these domestic actors at the European level. Regional politics in Belgium is therefore operating not only in a 'capacity gap' with respect to Europe, but with the increasing potential for a 'legitimacy gap' as power evolves upward towards the supranational level with few new mechanisms to provide for participation by, and accountability to, regional actors.

However, the existence of the *potential* for problems with legitimacy does not imply that actual criticism will emerge. Some parties in Belgium, such as the CVP, trumpet the advantages created for regions by European integration. For others, however, defining elements of their philosophies provide them with compelling reasons to question the legitimacy of a political system in which the capacity gap endures. The background of Flemish political nationalism reveals how the notions of sovereignty and national identity embraced by two modern nationalist parties lead them into a contentious relationship with the EU. Despite major differences between the parties, domestic constitutional reform to protect national interests is a legacy of Flemish social mobilization that cannot be easily compromised by either nationalist party.

The Diverging Paths of Flemish Nationalism

Post-war Flemish nationalism exhibits conflict over defining the Flemish nation and finding appropriate strategies to protect it. In 1954 the Volksunie was founded to advance the political goals of the Flemish movement: support for the Dutch language was critical to the agenda of the party, but its platform came to contain support for federalism and a greater emphases on social and economic development for Flanders. By the late 1970s the party had achieved sufficient strength to be invited to participate in drafting proposals for the first round of significant devolution to the Belgian regions in 1978. But disputes emerged within the Volksunie over its perceived compromises with French language interests. Of particular sensitivity was the status of Brussels and new voting rights for French speakers in the Flemish periphery of the city, which were interpreted as a sell-out by Flemish nationalists concerned to protect the interests of Dutch speakers in the capital and to safeguard the linguistic border established in 1963. Defectors from the Volksunie formed two new Flemish nationalist parties, the Vlaams-Nationale Partij (Flemish National Party, VNP) and the Vlaamse Volkspartij (Flemish People's Party, VVP), which joined in coalition to compete in the 1978 elections as the Vlaams Blok. The Vlaams Blok party was formally established to replace the VNP and the VVP in 1979.

The Vlaams Blok initially was not primarily concerned with a right-wing agenda. The party was founded to continue the struggle for radical constitutional reform, that is, independence for Flanders. Only in the mid-1980s, with the arrival of Filip Dewinter, the former president of the party youth wing with an interest in immigration questions, did the party turn decisively towards the right and shift the focus of its election campaigns towards immigration issues.[19] Much of the party programme is now devoted to issues other than the constitutional one: the return of immigrants and political refugees is part of a platform that also includes an emphasis on Catholic family life and values, action against crime and drugs, reducing the role of the state in society, rejecting the Maastricht Treaty-based EU and an end to political corruption.[20] The Vlaams Blok continues to place 'an independent Flanders' at the beginning of its electoral programme, but it has clearly found a vote-winning strategy with its anti-immigration and anti-foreigner policies, and has carved itself a niche in the extreme right of the political spectrum.[21]

Although the Volksunie participated in government in 1978–9 and again in 1988–91, the 1991 general elections were a disappointment for the party: it was eclipsed by the Vlaams Blok for the first time and sank to 9.4 per cent of the Flemish vote, compared to 10.5 per cent for the Blok. In the May 1995 general elections the Volksunie won only 4.7 per cent of the Flemish vote for the federal Chamber of Representatives and five seats, whereas the Vlaams Blok won 7.8 per cent of the vote and eleven seats.[22] In the direct elections to the Flemish regional parliament the strength of the Blok was evident: it won 12.3 per cent of the vote and fifteen seats, compared to 9 per cent and nine seats for the Volksunie. Election results from June 1999 suggest that the slide of the Volksunie may have been halted. In an election in which food and health scandals contributed to big losses for the governing parties, the Vlaams Blok increased its vote to 9.9 per cent in the federal Chamber of Representatives and gained four seats, to bring its total to fifteen in the 150-seat Chamber. The Volksunie, running under a new VU-ID21 ticket, saw its share of the vote rise to 5.6 per cent and gained three seats to hold eight. In the Flemish Parliament the Vlaams Blok grew to 15.5 per cent, securing the party twenty seats and making it the third-largest party in Flanders, slightly ahead of the Socialist Party. The VU-ID21 ticket won 9.3 per cent of the vote and eleven seats, a slight improvement on the 1995 results for the Volksunie.[23]

The increasing devolution of powers to the regions of Belgium has led to serious questioning about the purpose of the Volksunie, even from within its own ranks. Under newer and younger leadership the party has sought in the 1990s to redefine itself as the socially progressive, tolerant face of Flemish nationalism. Yet debate over the constitutional question continues: the party officially advocates a 'confederal' Belgium in which the federal state retains minimal powers in areas such as defence and foreign policy, but individual party members speak openly of total independence and this latter may be the position of the party in future talks on constitutional reform. There is little enthusiasm for Belgium, but it seems unlikely that an official policy of total separatism will be taken up by the Volksunie until the tricky question of the status of Brussels is solved: resolving the 'Brussels question' has been described as a step without which separatism could not be imagined.[24] Although there are ambiguities in party policy about the structure of a Brussels–Flanders–Wallonia confederation, what is clear is that the party presenting a moderate form of Flemish nationalism has lost ground to the Vlaams Blok.

Flemish Nationalism and the European Union

From two diverging strategies of promoting the interests of Flanders emerged two radically different parties: ideological and constitutional opponents, they have also adopted different approaches to participation in the institutions of the EU, an arena of political activity that has grown all the more salient in Flemish politics in the past decade. The European dimension of Flemish nationalism places in stark relief the different conceptualizations of the Flemish nation that the two parties articulate; ideas of both nation and state contribute to the understanding of legitimate governance that each the Volksunie and Vlaams Blok bring to Europe. Yet despite the differences between the parties, striking similarities emerge in party responses to European integration.

Protection of the nation, ultimately, requires an examination of democracy in the EU, and, according to Flemish nationalists across the ideological spectrum, a reassessment of the constitution of the European polity so as better to represent the interests of its weaker constituent parts. Each party has a vision of the nation that it believes is compromised by European integration; furthermore, the constitutional demands of the parties draw them into conflict with a Europe that is seen to be depriving the Flemish of the powers for which they have long struggled.

The Vlaams Blok: The Ethnic State in Europe

The Vlaams Blok conception of the ethnic nation forms the basis of the party's vision of Europe. The party presents a solidaristic view of society based on the *volk*: membership in the nation is based on blood, or Flemish descent, not language (a strategy by which the party can claim that the French speakers of Brussels, if descended from Flemings, are actually 'Flemish'), and cannot be acquired from birth in Flemish territory or by marriage. Describing the structuring principle of Flemish society in the view of the Vlaams Blok as the organic solidarism favoured by the proto-fascist Flemish movements of the 1930s, Swyngedouw refers to the party's *Principles of the Vlaams Blok*: 'This [solidarism] implies that whoever "truly experiences the natural ethnic commitment" will reject the class system and the class struggle'; the model presented by the Vlaams Blok is one of harmony within a homogeneous ethnic group, in which social conflict does not exist.[25] The legitimate polity is that which is coterminous with the ethnic nation; only in this way can social order be maintained and the culture of the national group be protected.

It is this vision of the ethnic nation-state that the Vlaams Blok projects onto the EU. Just as Belgium is 'artificial' because it seeks to regulate the relations of different 'peoples' within a single political entity, so can the legitimate political order of Europe only be that which is based on the *volk*-state. For the Vlaams Blok, there can be no distinction between a 'Europe of the States' and a 'Europe of the Peoples', although, in the words of the 1995 party election programme, 'This is not to agree with and not to lapse into a narrow sort of provincialism . . . Each people has a right to its cultural uniqueness. In this manner we come to a cultural Europe, a people's Europe.'[26] The EU in its entirety must be composed of ethnic states, and the Vlaams Blok asserts its solidarity with other nationalist movements in Europe that seek to destroy artificial states and replace them with a 'natural

order'.[27] It is therefore apparent that certain forms of political governance must be ruled out: federalism or other power-sharing devices by
which one ethnic group would govern another, or in which ethnicity
would not be the organizing principle, are construed as philosophically out of order, either at the European or at the domestic level. A
Europe of the peoples is a confederal Europe, in which sovereignty
ultimately remains at the level of the nation.[28]

But the Vlaams Blok has a rather instrumental notion of 'sovereignty' and does indeed see the EU as serving a useful purpose if constructed in the appropriate manner. Party leaders recognize that an
independent Flanders will be a small and relatively weak state, and that
economic interdependence with neighbouring states will be high. The
neo-liberal economic philosophy of the party makes the idea of
participation in the free market attractive. Furthermore, party members assert that certain tasks should be delegated to the European level:
a common European defence and foreign policy are the most rational
means to cope with potential threats from Russia and east European
states; a common European army is the most efficient means of implementing European-wide military decisions.[29] Hence the Vlaams Blok
view of the modern state is one where interdependence is recognized
as a reality in numerous policy areas. 'Sovereignty' must ultimately
remain with the nation-state, but the party recognizes that the Flemish
state would be small and weak. Military and economic cooperation, to
the extent that Flemish ethno-national interests are advanced and not
compromised in an EU confederation, are an acceptable component of
European integration.

Conceptualizing the state as an ethnic national state frames the
appropriate political order that the Vlaams Blok sees for the EU as
well as how the party currently chooses to participate in that order.
Whereas numerous nationalist parties across the EU member states
have members in the Committee of the Regions, the consultative body
to the European Commission, the Vlaams Blok has categorically
refused to participate in the institution. The idea of a Committee of the
'Regions' is repugnant to a party that views its constituents as forming
a nation and an embryonic state: 'We are not Barcelona, we are not a
"region" . . . We are more than that! We are not London or something.
We are, and we should be, a state.'[30] Participation in the European
Parliament is viewed as an opportunity for the party to publicize its
programme, in particular during the European election campaigns,
and to gain resources, especially financial, that can be used to promote
the goals of the party. More importantly, the European Parliament is
seen as a forum in which the party can protest what it sees as the

increasingly federalist tendencies of the EU. The Vlaams Blok view of Europe is a product both of the constitutional goals of the party and of their particular definition of the nation. A 'Europe of the States' is the only form of European polity that will allow the interests of the European citizens to be protected, but only a specific notion of the state prevails in the party. Tendencies in the EU that would appear to infringe on the sovereignty either of states *or of nations* represent, therefore, dangerous developments that the Vlaams Blok will protest.

The Volksunie: The Region as a Privileged Actor in Europe

The official ideology of the Volksunie reveals a sense of Flemish nationhood very different from that of the Vlaams Blok. As a party of the Flemish movement, the Volksunie has always had an interest in defending and promoting Flemish culture and the Dutch language, but the view of culture articulated by the party is not the exclusive ethnic culture described by the Vlaams Blok. The profile of the party since the late 1970s as socially progressive and tolerant has taken on a new importance in how the Volksunie seeks to define Flemish nationalism in the 1990s. This is not simply a reaction to the threat from the Vlaams Blok to monopolize a definition of the Flemish nation: the leadership of the Volksunie has consistently affirmed that the party should be the expression of democratic *volksnationalisme* (popular nationalism), emphasizing pluralism, tolerance, social justice, and pacifism.[31] Although the Flemish identity as conceived by the Volksunie contains a linguistic and cultural component, these cultural aspects exist within a framework of a more broadly defined civic identity.

The implications for the appropriate structure of the state are radically different from the ethnic state of Vlaams Blok; the more inclusive notion of Flemish identity set forth by the Volksunie can be seen in the party preferences for domestic and European-level governance. In the 1970s Volksunie leaders rejected separatism in favour of autonomy or confederalism within the Belgian state, out of the belief that some policy areas were best left under federal government jurisdiction and that no adequate solution to the 'Brussels question' had yet been found. A recognition that a skeletal Belgian state might prove some use for protecting Flemish interests in a three-region confederation has meant that party sentiment towards Belgium is more nuanced than the explicit rejection of the polity articulated by the Vlaams Blok. Indeed, the language that party activists use to describe their emotions towards Belgium reflects a high degree of indifference, rather than antipathy: the former vice-premier Hugo Schiltz remarked that Belgium 'wasn't a problem posed to "Flemish autonomy"', and former Volksunie Youth president Gilbert Lambert has more recently stated that Belgium 'may exist; it doesn't bother us'.[32] Belgium is accepted by many in the Volksunie as a temporary state: useful until the question of Brussels is resolved and, perhaps, not likely to survive further European integration as the central state, losing some of its remaining powers to the EU, is increasingly irrelevant.

While the state continues to exist, with Flanders as a powerful region, the implications for how the Volksunie confronts the EU differ from those of the Vlaams Blok, for whom the state is utterly illegitimate with no practical function. Rather than an ethnic national basis to the constitutional preferences of the party, the Volksunie vision of an ideal EU is shaped by the current domestic constitutional status of Flanders. The party actively supports a 'Europe of the Regions and the Peoples', although it is far more vague on who, precisely, constitutes 'a people' than is the Vlaams Blok. What is key to the Volksunie idea of the EU, however, is the notion that, in so far as regions ought to play a critical role in domestic politics, they should equally be endowed with sufficient powers at the European level to protect and promote their interests. Lambert, now assistant to Volksunie European parliamentarian Jaak Vandemeulebroucke, states: 'We don't believe in a Europe of states. We don't want Europe to be constituted as it is at the moment, of the fifteen nation-states. But we would like the regions. . .to take part in the decision-making of Europe,' emphasizing that the goal is for Flanders to be a full participant in the European arena.[33] The structure of European institutions that the Volksunie would like to see involves the collapse of the Committee of the Regions and the Council of Ministers into a single body in which regions would possess formal voting rights; the second chamber of the EU would be the European Parliament, in which citizens have a direct vote: these two chambers would elect the executive of Europe (the Commission). The EU would represent the third level of political life, above regions, and above cities and villages; states as presently constituted would wither away.[34] For Volksunie, Europe can only be legitimately constituted when its institutions provide regions with full participatory rights.

Participation by the Volksunie in the institutions of the presently constructed EU reflects the interests of a party that seeks to exploit all possible opportunities for regions to the maximum benefit, while using European institutions as a platform from which to advocate a more radical ideal vision of the EU. The legitimacy of the region as an organizational entity is demonstrated with the acceptance by the

Volksunie of the Committee of the Regions as a fledgling institution with the potential to evolve into a more powerful body. Furthermore, the Volksunie has for the past two decades participated in the European Free Alliance (EFA), a non-EU body that unites numerous regional nationalist movements of varying ideological and constitutional stripe from across Europe in efforts to support their electoral campaigns, primarily at the European level. Their membership of the EFA reveals the commitment of the Volksunie to constitutional change, as opposed to ethnic politics. Similarly, the European Parliament has proven an arena in which the party can build on these relations, in the (left progressive) Rainbow coalition in the 1980s and the left-liberal European Radical Alliance of the 1994–9 Parliament. In the European Parliament the party can promote its social agenda as well as publicize its constitutional goals, work for constituency interests, and attempt to combat the negative image of Flemish nationalism that the Volksunie MEPs believe the Vlaams Blok are propagating.[35]

The differences between the Volksunie and Vlaams Blok appear stark: one bases its constitutional philosophy on the legitimacy of the ethnic state; the other seeks constitutional outcomes that will enable the regional nation, more broadly defined, to protect its interests. As the EU has come to impinge on the nationalist struggle, the nationalists themselves have sought to envision the European order that best serves their respective views of the nation and of the role Flanders should play in international life. But despite their differences, the parties share common interests emerging from their shared history as political manifestations of the Flemish movement. Furthermore, underlying what appear to be cultural critiques of European institutions lie deeper challenges: to the nature of participatory democracy as currently practised in the EU, and to the appropriate order of governance across the evolving European polity.

Language, Culture, and a Constitutional Critique of European Governance

Cultural issues for Flemish nationalists have themselves become the subject of contention in the European context, and have also become magnifying lenses for more fundamental questions posed by the parties about the legitimacy of European governance. For Flemish nationalists, issues of language and culture reveal how the EU intrudes too far into spheres of authority that they claim rightfully should remain with Flanders, whether as a region in the view of the Volksunie or as an independent state in the philosophy of the Vlaams Blok. European institutions intervene both 'actively', through legislation and official activism to whittle away at the right of the Flemish people to control their cultural interests, and 'passively', by neglecting to protect the Dutch language and Flemish culture. Two main areas of criticism by the nationalists emerge from an exploration of Flemish cultural politics in Europe. First is the perception of the exclusion of minority cultures from equal status in European institutions; this exclusion is seen as both formal and normative. The second area of criticism is the intervention of Europe into cultural politics believed rightfully to fall under the jurisdiction of Flanders: the degradation of Flemish sovereignty. Several examples illustrate broader difficulties perceived by the nationalists in the relationship of nation, cultural policy, and European integration.

Both the Volksunie and Vlaams Blok are highly critical of European legislation and official policies that they believe are designed intentionally to weaken the position of the Dutch language as an official language of the EU, and to create incentives for French language interests to gain a foothold in Flemish and Brussels regional politics. A major point of contention for the nationalist parties derives from the belief that the European Commission refuses to provide sufficient resources for Dutch language interpretation. Members of the European Parliament from the Flemish nationalist parties have demanded explanations from Commissioners when Dutch interpretation is not available at official meetings or when documentation is not translated into Dutch; Vlaams Blok MEP Frank Vanhecke claims to have tabled 'hundreds' of written questions to the Commission concerning its neglect of Dutch, and he describes the response he receives as unhelpful.[36] Furthermore, European-level activists in each party believe that this represents an *intentional* effort on the part of the Commission to create a polity where the 'smaller' member state languages are slowly being marginalized in an effort to create a more efficient European polity that will function primarily in French, German, and English. This apparent inequality among the official languages of the member states reinforces the fear among some nationalists, in the Vlaams Blok in particular, that even where, legally, equal status exists, the Commission is not only able to ride roughshod over minority interests but will do so when in the interests of efficient government.[37] Belgian political practices of respecting as equals even the weakest linguistic cultures are apparently not the norm in the European arena; in addition, the EU itself seems to contribute to the erosion of this norm in the *domestic* arena.

Alongside this neglect of the linguistic interests of Flanders in Europe, specific legislation and treaty provisions that would effectively alter the linguistic balance in Brussels, and its 'commuter suburbs' in Flemish Brabant, are viewed by the Vlaams Blok as an overt attempt by the signatories to Maastricht and the Commission to encourage French language interests in these areas. Long a highly sensitive subject in Belgium, disputes over the status of individuals living on the 'wrong side' of the linguistic border have even led to the fall of governments. Perceptions that EU politics is significantly shifting the balance of local power in favour of French language interests upsets domestic conventions of egalitarian solutions to linguistic disputes. The Vlaams Blok is particularly concerned with provisions in the Maastricht Treaty to allow citizens from any EU member state to vote in the local elections of the area in which they reside. Although the party claimed success in having pressured the Belgian state to seek, and eventually win, a 'reprieve' on this issue until the year 2000,[38] it stated that this policy would lead to the gradual creation of French-speaking villages within the Flemish region, and that the continuing use of Brussels as the seat of European institutions was already encouraging the intrusion of French into Flemish Brabant.[39]

Beyond the question of language itself, however, are issues of jurisdiction and political control. Constitutionally within Belgium, the communities have sole responsibility for policies concerning language and culture. Flemish nationalists bemoan the unwillingness of their Belgian and Dutch colleagues to take the lead in promoting their linguistic interests in the European arena;[40] yet the Belgian state itself has little or no formal power to act in such areas. Perceived infringement by European-level forces upon sensitive linguistic and cultural areas are therefore interpreted not only as offensive to the national interest, but as constitutional challenges. In the words of Karim van Overmeire, the EU is seeking to reverse what it took the Flemish movement 150 years to accomplish.[41] Flanders is exposed to legislation at the European level that may impinge significantly on the jurisdictions of a region with little power to respond, and little likelihood, as the nationalists see it, to gain such power while Belgium continues to exist: 'On the European level . . . Flanders is a prisoner in the Belgian state,' notes Gerolf Annemans of the Vlaams Blok.[42]

Members of the Volksunie and Vlaams Blok respond to the constitutional quandary of Flanders by suggesting that, if the EU were to apply rigorously its vaunted principle of subsidiarity, the results would go far to address their concerns about linguistic and cultural questions.[43] Yet neither party believes that the EU has gone far enough, and both fear that if the European polity continues to evolve along the path set at Maastricht and Amsterdam, little will change in favour of Flanders. As indicated above, both the Vlaams Blok and Volksunie dismiss the Committee of the Regions as an insufficient measure to right the constitutional balance, although Volksunie members are more hopeful for the potential development of the body and in less of a hurry to dismiss the intentions behind its establishment. Volksunie MEP Jaak Vandemeulebroucke has been an ardent advocate of increasing the powers of the Committee, but some of his colleagues find problematic the inclusion of local and municipal authorities on the Committee; they believe that meaningful participation by the regions in the EU must imply a recognition of their distinctiveness as actors in European politics.[44] Contrary to Belgian politics, which privileges regional and communal identities over local or municipal ones, European politics is seen as failing to recognize the unique role played in domestic social relations by regional identities. The Vlaams Blok is more scathing in its rejection of the Committee of the Regions as a sufficient mechanism for Flemish representation in Europe, pointing out that the 'centralizing vision' of Maastricht and the 1996 intergovernmental conference will prevail, with the Committee lacking the strength to provide any countervailing force.[45] The Flemish nationalist parties agree that if the state cannot protect linguistic and cultural interests at the European level, and if 'Europe' is unwilling or unable to do so, the only solution is to empower Flanders itself to take up this role in Europe.

Concerns over the representation of cultural interests in the EU, and over which actors do, or should, possess the capacity to take decisions in these areas, support and amplify the demands of each party to restructure European governance. The interests of the Volksunie and the Vlaams Blok in creating a Flemish polity with significant powers at the European level are frequently presented in the context not simply of improving the status of Flanders, but of contributing to the legitimacy of the EU itself. Indeed, the lack of appropriate representative structures for Flemish interests is cited as both undemocratic and a potential threat to the viability of the continuing European project. Both parties view Flemish control over language and cultural policy as central to creating or maintaining support for the EU at the popular level. Gilbert Lambert has pointed out that 'It's one of the main things of democracy, that people can discuss and understand in their own language what [the EU] is all about,' adding that he felt that Euro-scepticism was starting to be felt in traditionally Euro-enthusiastic Flanders.[46] The Vlaams Blok are similarly adamant about the role language and national culture play in legitimizing a polity (as noted regarding their definition of the ethnic nation, above). For Flemish nationalists, linguistic and cultural issues have been at the heart of political struggle since the founding of the Belgian state. The perceived increase in the infringement of regional powers by European actors requires solutions at the European level. Yet whether in the Vlaams Blok vision of a Europe of ethnic states, or the Volksunie preference for a Europe of regions and peoples, Flanders has not yet achieved sufficient power in the EU that its people can claim to exercise on the European level those powers that they already possess on the domestic level.

Conclusion

Changes in the relationship between regions and the federal government in Belgium have already had a significant impact on the strategies and practices of the country's political parties. The interaction of Belgian domestic politics with the dynamics of European integration has forced political actors in the Belgian regions to think prospectively about their constitutional position in an integrating EU, and to consider a future in which the political institutions in which they operate are likely to be radically transformed no matter what the actions they take may be.

Taking advantage of potential opportunities requires that politicians identify the institutional structures that will be of primary importance in a future Europe and seek to position their parties accordingly. Does one attempt to be a strong regional player, with a view towards gaining influence in a 'Europe of the Regions', or does one accept the view that *states* will be the privileged actors in the EU? For Belgian political parties, an emphasis on the strength of regions within the EU matters while Belgium still exists as a state: in this case, upgrading the status of regions in European institutions to match the powers that domestic regional administrations possess is the key to addressing the legitimacy gap. But what if Belgium ceases to exist? There seems little use in promoting the role of 'regions' in the EU if the regions are, *de facto*, small states; what then becomes critical is protecting the powers of small states within the EU and ensuring that they continue to be able to function as equal partners in decision-making.

What distinguishes the nationalist parties of Flanders from their electoral opponents is the demand that the constitutional structure of the EU address the legitimacy gap in either one or the other respect, that is, with respect to improving the status of powerful regions in the

EU, or ensuring that the rights of small states will not be circumscribed. The two nationalist parties reject that the status quo is acceptable or that it can be maintained in the context of future European integration. The leaders of both parties argue that if the interests of Flanders—however these may be defined—are to be protected and advanced, it no longer serves any useful purpose simply to criticize the relationship of the central state to the regions, or to use the time-honoured Belgian strategy of carving up the centre in order to win more power for the regions. The Belgian state no longer controls those policy areas with which the nationalists are concerned, but neither do the Flemish executives: for Flemish nationalists, the true point of contention has become the relationship of Flanders with Europe.

Multi-level governance approaches to European integration have suggested that central state governments no longer perform the 'gate-keeper' function of controlling access by subnational authorities to the international arena.[47] Domestic constitutional reform in Belgium contributed to removing this traditional role from the state, even before the recent institutional innovations of Maastricht introduced new regional and local political players into the institutions of the EU. But proponents of multi-level governance approaches have focused on shifts in relative power among actors nested within the state, and across the levels of policy-making in the EU. There is little disagreement that the role of the Flemish region with respect to Europe has been transformed in the past decade. But perhaps a more compelling set of questions now includes asking how actors with differing views of regional identity will face similar challenges to participate in, and respond to, developments at the supranational level. Some regional actors in EU member states, including nationalists, have found that Europe provides economic, cultural, and political opportunities long denied them by their domestic governments. Mitchell and Cavanagh argue in this volume (Chapter 12) that different nationalist parties recognize diverse possibilities in the new opportunity structure created by European integration. Constitutional nationalists in unitary states, in states that officially recognize a dominant language, culture, or religion, or in states the dominant ideology of which allows for no fulfilment of nationalist aspirations, may find that the decline of the state gatekeeper in the European arena allows them to pursue some of their goals with sympathetic European partners. However, the case of Belgium illustrates how the gate swings in two directions: regions may have greater access to Europe as the state weakens, but the decline of the gatekeeper also implies that the state loses the capacity to protect regions against the impact of the international arena.

We thus return to the argument made by Keating concerning why nationalism is re-emerging as a force in western Europe: it serves a need for collective action in an era of weakened states.[48] The very weakness of the Belgian state makes it all the more important to pose questions about legitimate governance by European institutions: there is little left to buffer the regions of Belgium from EU decisions in which they have little say, and over which the central state has little authority to act. Unlike the other parties of Flanders, nationalists are confronting broad questions about participation and power in the EU: what is and should be the role of weak actors, be they regions in a system designed for states, or small and highly interdependent states? Questioning the political order of Europe is a rational response by actors who believe themselves disadvantaged or endangered by integration, and who believe that their marginalization or exposure is likely to increase, whether or not they achieve their domestic constitutional goals. Flemish nationalism operates in a context in which it is a long-standing practice of political parties to question the legitimacy of the political order, and in which the evolving European polity is rendering it critical that they continue to do so.

NOTES

I would like to thank Sean Duffy, Mark Emery, Soo Yeon Kim and Kathryn McDermott for comments on earlier drafts. Any errors are my sole responsibility.

1. The European Union came into existence as a result of the Maastrict Treaty (1992). In this chapter I will follow the convention of referring to the European polity as the EU, recognizing that this is not always the technically correct term.
2. Even the 'intergovernmentalists' recognize that many aspects of European policy-making have supranational elements, although they argue that such elements are the product of bargaining among states and ultimately reflect the preferences of state governmental actors. See R. O. Keohane and S. Hoffman (eds.), *The New European Community: Decisionmaking and Institutional Change* (Boulder, Colo.: Westview Press, 1991), and A. S. Milward, *The European Rescue of the Nation State* (London: Routledge, 1992).
3. See e.g. the general election manifestos of the Scottish National Party for 1992 and 1997, respectively: *Independence in Europe: Make it Happen Now!* (Edinburgh: Scottish National Party, 1994) and *Yes We Can Win the Best for Scotland* (Edinburgh: Scottish National Party, 1997).
4. P. Lynch, *Minority Nationalism and European Integration* (Cardiff: University of Wales Press, 1996), 16; P. Leslie, 'The Cultural Dimension', in J. Jens Hesse and Vincent Wright (eds.), *Federalizing Europe?* (Oxford: Oxford University Press, 1996), 143.
5. See J. Mitchell and M. Cavanagh, 'Context and Contingency: Constitutional Nationalists and Europe' (Ch. 12 in this volume).

6. The constitution was revised in May 1993 and came into effect in Feb. 1994; the first elections to the regional and federal parliaments under the new constitution were held in May 1994.
7. Dutch speakers are in the majority in Belgium—about 60% of the population. Approximately 68,000 German speakers live in eastern Wallonia. As most Dutch speakers live within the Flemish region, the administrations of the community and region fused into a single entity for purposes of governance; Brussels, however, contains a significant amount of the French-speaking population of Belgium, and therefore the Walloon region and the French language community have remained distinct political entities.
8. Current particulars concerning the regions, communities and 'linguistic regions' of Belgium are found in the 1994 constitution, *Constitution de la Belgique*, (Brussels: Bruylant, 1994), title III, ch. IV.
9. See ibid., sect. II, art. 127.
10. Van den Brande was minister president of Flanders until the elections of June 1999; at the time of writing his future position is not yet clear. 'Could Flanders be Reinvented?', *The Economist*, 20 Sept. 1997, 54.
11. For example, see 'Belgium's Melting Fudge', *The Economist*, 16 Mar. 1996, 50, and 'Belgium: The Next Identity Crisis', *The Economist*, 22 Feb. 1997, 59. For recent Flemish debate over the regionalization of health insurance, see D. Durand de Bousingen, 'Belgium Faces Health Insurance Split in 1999', *Lancet*, 349 (1997), 783.
12. See the discussion in L. Hooghe (ed.), *Cohesion Policy and European Integration* (Oxford: Oxford University Press, 1996); and B. Jones and M. Keating (eds.), *The European Union and the Regions* (Oxford: Clarendon Press, 1995).
13. These offices are intended to alert regional governments to developments in European Commission proposals for legislation that may have an impact on the interests of the region, and to communicate the interests of the region to relevant European officials in order to secure the most favourable treatment possible.
14. Article 146 of the Maastricht Treaty. This article should be taken at its face value, i.e. regional ministers vote in the name of their *states*, not their respective regions.
15. In some policy areas, only regional ministers may vote in the Council; in others, a federal minister may vote, but must consult colleagues from the regions and include their notes in his or her decision; in a very few matters, only the federal-level minister votes. For a summary of regional and federal powers in Europe and a discussion of regional and federal actors in four sectors of European policy-making, see L. Wouters and S. De Rynck, 'Subnational Autonomy in the European Integration Process: The Belgian Case', in J. J. Hesse (ed.), *Regions in Europe*, (Baden-Baden: Nomos, 1996).
16. Wouters and De Rynck (ibid. 145) indicate that although the impact of the Belgian regions in the Council will likely increase in the policy areas under their jurisdiction, it remains difficult for the regions to influence agenda-setting and decision-making processes in Europe: the impact of the regions at the European level is limited. Hooghe notes that no forum exists for systematic coordination of regional or communal policy positions among the Belgian regions, which may allow EU institutions to gain influence in areas of Council voting where the regional and cultural ministers must develop a joint position (L. Hooghe, 'Belgian Federalism and the European Community', in Jones and Keating (eds.), *The European Union and the Regions*, 154).
17. See P. Kurzer, 'Decline or Preservation of Executive Capacity? Political and Economic Integration Revisited', *Journal of Common Market Studies*, 35/1 (1997), 31–56.

18. Furthermore, proposed enlargement of the EU to include several central and east European states will require a massive overhaul of the structural fund programme, to the detriment of many regions currently receiving funding. See Commission of the European Communities, *Agenda 2000, i: For a Stronger and Wider Union*, COM(97) 2000 final, pt. 1, sect. II 4 (Luxembourg: Office for Official Publications of the European Community, 1997).

19. The shift in the party was sufficiently extreme that Jaak Peeters, the Vlaams Blok general secretary, resigned in 1988 because he disagreed with the party's moving its focus away from the reorganization of the state.

20. Vlaams Blok, *Facts and Objectives* (Brussels: Vlaams Blok, 1995).

21. Studies of Flemish voting behaviour reveal that the main reasons for voting Vlaams Blok in the 1995 general elections were the party's 'anti-foreigner' policies. See e.g. M. Swyngedouw, 'Scientific Electoral Studies—A Democratic Assessment: Announcing and Documenting Political Changes in Belgium', Paper presented to the Maison Française, Oxford, July 1997.

22. These were the first direct elections to the regional and communal assemblies. All parties in Belgium organize on a regional, not state-wide, basis; figures for the federal Chamber of Representatives show Flemish vote shares from Flanders and the Brussels Capital region.

23. Election results from 1999 available at http://www/standaard.be/verkiezingen99.

24. See S. Govaert, *La Volksunie*, Courrier Hebdomadaire du CRISP, no. 1416–17 (Brussels: Centre de Recherche et d'Information Sociopolitiques, 1993), 67.

25. M. Swyngedouw, 'The Extreme Right in Belgium: Of a Non-existent Front National and an Omnipresent Vlaams Blok', in H. G. Betz and S. Immerfall (eds.), *The New Politics of the Right: Neo-Populist Parties and Movements in Established Democracies* (New York: St Martin's Press, 1998), 65.

26. Vlaams Blok, *Verkiezingsprogramma 1995* (Brussels: Vlaams Blok, 1995), 53; my trans.

27. Interview with Karim van Overmeire, leader of the Vlaams Blok parliamentary party in the Flemish Parliament, 7 Feb. 1996.

28. Interview with Gerolf Annemans, 7 Feb. 1996.

29. Interview with Overmeire, 7 Feb. 1996.

30. Interview with Annemans, 7 Feb. 1996.

31. This characterization of the party was put forward by former Volksunie president Vic Anciaux in 1992; see the discussion of his position in Govaert, *La Volksunie*, 61. The inclusiveness of the Flemish nation has been seen by some party members as a means of bridging the gaps between traditional cleavages in Belgian politics; in the early 1990s a permanent 'fusion' with the Flemish Liberal Party was considered by some Volksunie members, revealing the extent to which Flemish national identity was not considered synonymous with religious identity or economic ideology.

32. Schiltz, quoted ibid. 48; interview with Gilbert Lambert, Brussels, 29 May 1996.

33. Interview with Lambert, 29 May 1996.

34. Ibid.

35. Ibid.

36. I was able to locate references to only about a dozen written questions; official documentation of written questions from the Parliament is notoriously difficult to track. Interview with Frank Vanhecke, MEP for the Vlaams Blok, 7 Feb. 1996.

37. This point was emphasized by Vanhecke, 7 Feb. 1996.

38. Interview with Annemans, 7 Feb. 1996.

39. Vlaams Blok, *Verkiezingsprogramma 1995*, 16.

40. Interview with Lambert, 29 May 1996, and Vanhecke, 7 Feb. 1996. Karel Dillen, the second Vlaams Blok MEP, also frequently takes note of other Flemish MEPs' non-use of the Dutch language in the plenary sessions of the European Parliament.

41. Interview with Overmeire, 7 Feb. 1996.

42. Interview with Annemans, 7 Feb. 1996.

43. Frank Vanhecke of the Vlaams Blok even acknowledges that if subsidiarity were 'recognized as the most important principle, more important than any other article of the [Maastricht] Treaty . . . I believe our problems would be solved' (interview with Vanhecke, 7 Feb. 1996).

44. The 'problem' of the Committee of the Regions including representatives of local authorities was highlighted in the interview with Lambert, 29 May 1996.

45. Interview with Annemans, 7 Feb. 1996.

46. Interview with Lambert, 29 May 1996.

47. See e.g. L. Hooghe, 'Subnational Mobilisation in the European Union', *West European Politics*, 18/3 (1995), 179; also G. Marks, L. Hooghe, and K. Blank, 'European Integration from the 1980s: State-Centric v. Multi-Level Governance', *Journal of Common Market Studies*, 34/3 (1996), 372.

48. M. Keating, 'Stateless Nation Building: Quebec, Catalonia and Scotland in the Changing State System', *Nations and Nationalism*, 3/4 (1997), 689–717.

CHAPTER 12

Context and Contingency: Constitutional Nationalists and Europe

JAMES MITCHELL AND MICHAEL CAVANAGH

This chapter compares the European policies of three constitutional nationalist parties within the United Kingdom: the Scottish National Party (SNP), Plaid Cymru, and the Social Democratic and Labour Party (SDLP). These three quite different nationalist parties now find themselves in broad agreement, supporting European integration, a process which seems to contradict a basic tenet of nationalism. As Gellner has maintained, nationalism is 'primarily a political principle, which holds that the political and national unit should be congruent'.[1] How do we explain the phenomenon of nationalist parties supporting institutions that would remove power from the nation, in which the political and national units are no longer congruent? These three nationalist parties now have policies that are more positive about 'ever closer union' than putatively non-nationalist parties, including the United Kingdom Conservative and Labour Parties. Indeed, in the context of European integration the rhetoric familiarly associated with nationalism is more often heard within these supposedly non-nationalist parties.

This raises questions about the nature of nationalism. There are a number of ways to explain this phenomenon. It could be that nationalism is the ideology which dares not speak its name within the Labour and Conservative Parties and that state (United Kingdom or British) nationalism is a pervasive component of the ideological make-up of these parties and, indeed, politics in the United Kingdom. It could also be that the SNP, Plaid, and SDLP have, to some degree, abandoned nationalism. Are these parties in some sense 'post-nationalist', while putatvely non-nationalist or even 'anti-nationalist' parties have become nationalist? Another explanation is that each of the constitutional nationalist parties has redefined its nationalism to take account of the changing contexts. Each seeks nation-state congruence in a pragmatic way to the greatest extent possible in an increasingly globalized world. If the last is correct, then we might wonder why this has happened. Is it easier for regional or sub-state nationalist movements to come to terms with globalization, the interdependent nature of contemporary politics, or that nationalisms encompassing smaller nations find it easier to come to terms with the modern world? Or indeed is there some other factor which predicates an acceptance of integration and interdependence?

Globalization and Nationalism

In his essay on globalization Zygmunt Bauman makes a point about the relationship between globalization and the traditional political paradigm: 'There is a new asymmetry emerging between the extra-teritorial nature of power and the continuing territoriality of the "whole life"—which the now unanchored power, able to move at short notice or without warning, is free to exploit and abandon to the consequences of that exploitation.'[2]

As others have argued, the processes wrapped up in the term 'globalization' amount less to the 'end of history' than to the 'end of geography'.[3] In Europe and inside the three nationalist parties being discussed in this chapter, the most relevant processes have been associated with European integration. It is not so much that power is extra-territorial as that the territory which has assumed increased political relevance is neither the nation which is aspiring to govern itself nor even the state which is being challenged by these nationalists. An early critic of European integration warned that European integration would merely create a super-nation that would be even less conducive to maintaining international peace.[4]

The nature of European integration will determine the response of nationalists. There is no agreement on the nature of the European Union (EU) or the course of European integration. Two schools of thought exist that highlight the difficulties nationalists have in responding to Europe. One school of thought, the intergovernmentalist school, maintains that European integration is state-centric and that the process has occurred in the interests of states.[5] On the other hand, a multi-level governance perspective views the process as allowing non-state actors, including regions and nations within states, considerable input into decision-making.[6]

From a nationalist perspective, it is possible to support European integration whether it is viewed as state-centric or multi-level governance. A state-centric viewpoint would be acceptable so long as the nation and state are congruent. If not, the EU would be viewed as a polity in which stateless nations are distant from power. However, nationalists who view the EU as involving multi-level governance might see opportunities within it for the articulation of stateless nation' interests. Therefore, at issue is not only how the EU and European integration is perceived but also the nature of nationalism subscribed to. A hard-line nationalist would be reluctant to share power over her nation with any others, and would be critical of a state-centric Europe, even if her nation was one of the states involved in decision-making, and would be even more critical of a Europe in which her nation was stateless. When viewed as multi-level governance, the EU might be attractive to stateless nations as offering some limited means of articulating the interests of the nation, but would be less attractive than a nation that is congruent with the state.

Origins of the Parties

The three parties have quite different histories, and contact between each has varied over time, but they have rarely been intimate. Closest contact takes place in the House of Commons among MPs from the parties. SNP and Plaid have had joint meetings and have attempted to operate as one party for parliamentary purposes, but the SDLP's membership of the Socialist grouping in the European Parliament and its close relationship with the Labour Party has meant that it has had a more distant relationship from the SNP and Plaid. Indeed, interviews with senior members of these parties suggest not only that there has been remarkably little formal contact between the SDLP and the other two nationalist parties but that there is a remarkable degree of ignorance of the origins and nature of the parties amongst elites in the other parties, especially between the SNP and SDLP. Each of the three parties was formed by a coalition of different groups, interests, and ideologies, and some of the current tensions within each party relate back to its origins. The SNP and Plaid were founded in the inter-war period outside Parliament and, with the brief exception of an SNP by-election victory in 1945, only gained parliamentary representation in the 1960s. The SDLP was formed more recently, although constitutional nationalism has existed throughout Northern Ireland's history.

Plaid originated in campaigns in support of the Welsh language, and concerns for the language have been at the forefront of its campaigns. The Welsh language has provided an electoral base for the party, but offers a limited pool of potential support.[7] The priority attached to support for the language lies at the heart of Plaid's dilemma. The SNP was founded after the failure of home rule measures in the 1920s. A key tension throughout the party's history has been between its fundamentalist and pragmatist wings, the former fearing distractions from the primary objective of independence.[8] The SDLP emerged from the civil rights movement of the 1960s as well as out of socialist and constitutional nationalist parties in Northern Ireland. Officially launched in August 1970, it comprised six Stormont MPs and one Stormont senator. John Hume, leader of the SDLP since 1979, was one of three Independent MPs who joined the new party, while Austin Currie came to it from the Nationalist Party. The original leader of the party, Gerry Fitt, was one of two former Republican Labour members, and Paddy Devlin came from the Northern Ireland Labour Party.[9] The socialist–nationalist mix has been important in the party's evolution.

In terms of left–right politics, the three parties have had quite different histories, though all have come to adopt broadly similar positions on the left of politics. The SNP primarily attracted left-wing support initially, but a significant right-wing contingent of disaffected Liberals came into the party early in its history. For much of the postwar period the party attempted to portray itself as above left–right politics in a conventional nationalist manner. 'Put Scotland First', a slogan from the 1960s, summed this up well. Plaid was generally a left-wing party, but it harboured some distinctly conservative elements. In both cases, the parties attracted some crypto-fascist elements which are now a source of embarrassment. As its name suggests, the SDLP was always an avowedly left-of-centre party, though the relationship between its nationalist and socialist tendencies has not always been easy.

The SDLP was formed on the basis that it would offer an anti-sectarian approach to politics within 'radical left-of-centre principles': the fostering of short-term cooperation with the Republic of Ireland with a long term objective of achieving reunification through the consent of the people of Northern Ireland and the Republic.[10] Clause 2 of the constitution of the SDLP details the party's main objectives, which include: to maintain a socialist party in Northern Ireland; to cooperate with the Irish Congress of Trade Unions in joint political action; to promote the cause of Irish unity based upon the consent of the majority of the people of Northern Ireland; and to cooperate with other social-democratic parties on an international level.[11] It was later amended to include a sub-clause explicitly in favour of European integration: 'To promote unity and harmony among the peoples of Europe, to work to end divisions based on religion, ethnic origin or perceived national identity and to promote a new international order of peace and justice throughout the world.'

The relationship each party has had with established institutions has been ambiguous and at times a source of internal tension. The SNP's fundamentalist–pragmatist tension meant that devolution proposals coming from other parties were a source of friction and viewed with suspicion by fundamentalists while usually welcomed by more pragmatic elements. However, there was little support at any stage in its history for abstentionism, even though the party found it difficult to establish itself as a serious electoral force for the first thirty years of its existence. The SNP has been a remarkably constitutional party, supporting civil disobedience on rare occasions. Plaid's activities in support of the Welsh language led it to support civil disobedience either explicitly or tacitly. Electoral politics have not dominated the party's approach to politics to the same extent as in the SNP. This difference between the parties partly reflects their ambitions and social base.

In Northern Ireland the lack of attention to, or even awareness of, European integration on the part of the Nationalist Party, a forerunner of the SDLP, is best understood by the party's ability to survive without developing a party organization, never mind a coherent position in relation to developments on the continent of Europe. The absence of other constitutional nationalist rivals meant that there was little electoral pressure on the Nationalist Party and therefore little pressure for developing an internal coherence or clearly definable policies beyond those relating to the issue of the reunification of Ireland. In addition, the lack of party organization and the strong sectarian context of Northern Irish politics meant that the Nationalist Party and constitutional nationalism were confined to those constituencies where there was a clear Catholic majority. This position of unrivalled constitutional representation of the nationalist community was paralleled by the Nationalist Party policy of abstention from parliamentary politics. The policy of abstention resulted in the party refusing to be defined as the official opposition to the Unionists in Stormont until 1965.[12]

The development of political responses to the malaise in nationalist politics in Northern Ireland emerged in the 1960s. The National Democratic Party and Republican Labour Party developed as alternatives to the Nationalist Party. Both parties deliberately avoided encroaching on the Nationalist Party's rural strongholds, instead concentrating upon the Belfast area. As a result both parties had limited opportunities for electoral success, urban Northern Ireland being then predominantly Protestant.[13] In addition, new pressure groups arguing for basic civil rights for the minority Catholic community emerged.[14]

What the new nationalist parties and civil rights protesters offered was a shift away from non-cooperation and a concern only with constitutional and border issues. It is in this context that the SDLP emerged as a nationalist party with a strong focus on the social and political inequalities within Northern Ireland. It recognized the existence of Northern Ireland, a significant shift in the nationalist politics of the region.

The SDLP went further than previous constitutional nationalist parties, taking part in the short-lived power-sharing executive of 1974. The party maintained its long-term aim of achieving a united Ireland, and refrained from giving unconditional support to the security forces. However, the significant factor related to the power-sharing exercise was that it achieved a precedent for cooperation between the nationalist and unionist parties and raised the possibility for a resolution of the sectarian and constitutional divisions concerned with Northern Ireland. Central to SDLP thinking was the belief that any solution must be in the context of the island as a whole.[15] This emphasis on the island and this determination to mobilize support beyond nationalists' traditional heartlands were important in the development of its European policy. Nevertheless, its involvement in power-sharing indicated a degree of pragmatism in its nationalism.

The three parties differed, often more than just in degree, in terms of their aims, objectives, histories, and strategies. All opposed the constitutional arrangements of the United Kingdom: the SNP primarily sought Scottish independence, Plaid primarily sought to defend the Welsh language, and the SDLP sought the reunification of Ireland. The social bases of the parties differed. Plaid was predominantly the party of Welsh-speaking Wales, the SDLP was a constitutional nationalist Catholic party, though it aimed to widen its appeal, while the SNP had cast a wider socio-economic net in pursuit of support. From these differences, however, a degree of agreement emerged on the need for membership of the EU.

Contingent and Contextual Nationalism

Students of nationalism have long noted its contingent nature. It is a 'thin' ideology in the sense that it is one that is 'limited in ideational ambitions and scope'.[16] The core is the prioritization of the nation and, as Freeden maintains, a desire to give it 'politico-institutional expression'.[17] However, what is striking is that there is little coherence across different nationalisms or within the same nationalism over time as to the nature of politico-institutional expression. Nationalism's contingent nature is a theme which runs throughout Ernest Gellner's writings. The politico-institutional form which this congruence takes alters with time. Two sets of explanations can be given for the contingent nature of nationalism. Both relate to the general question of how identities are formed. One set of explanations focuses on the context in which national identities are formed; the other focuses on the role of nationalist leaders in devising strategies to develop or even create national identities and to mobilize these for political ends. It is not always easy to separate the two. Changes in the social, political, or economic context offer a new opportunity structure in which nationalist leaderships operate.

The process of European integration offered a new opportunity structure within which the parties could operate. However, recognizing the opportunities which this presented differed initially within each party. SNP and Plaid paid little attention to the emerging European polity until the 1960s. Both parties had occasionally noted the process that was taking place, and even gave support to it before then, but European integration was no more salient in Scottish and Welsh politics than Scottish and Welsh nationalism were salient in British politics prior to the 1960s. Occasional, unsustained agitation for home rule and references to a new political order in Europe punctuated early post-war politics, but these were episodic and rarely thought to be related. In the late 1940s, at the height of agitation for a Scottish Parliament, the Attlee Labour government dismissed the opportunity to join the original six member states founding the European Coal and Steel Community. These two developments occurred in splendid isolation. Welsh language activists often looked to other minority language communities in similar positions in Europe and generally gave more support to developing links with these than they did to supporting the integration of European states. A state like France, which was in the vanguard of European integration, with its reputation for assimilating local communities and undermining linguistic minorities, was unlikely to be seen to be a role model for Plaid. Plaid members, much more so than SNP members, in the early stages of the parties' existence, saw themselves as European but without the connotations later associated with the term.

There were a few voices within each party who supported European integration, who could, given the small size of the parties, sound as if they spoke for the party as a whole. Given also that the issue was of low salience, and therefore unlikely to provoke a strong response, it was possible for occasional pro-European integration positions to be adopted. These have subsequently helped each party anchor its current enthusiasms for Europe into its past. Nationalism's tendency to invent or redefine its past has been evident in the histories of the parties, as in the histories of the nations. Plaid's involvement in establishing the International Congress of European Communities and Regions following the Hague Congress in 1948 (at which Churchill famously talked of a 'United States of Europe') and SNP conference resolutions in 1943 and 1948 supporting Scottish membership of a European confederation have become more significant for each party in recent years than they were at the time.

In the 1960s, as the UK applied for membership of the European Economic Community (EEC), both SNP and Plaid were becoming serious electoral forces. It was inevitable in this new context that the parties would have to express opinions on Europe. Previous support gave way to hostility to the European project. Influxes of new members, especially following by-election victories in Carmarthen for Plaid in 1966 and Hamilton for the SNP in 1967, altered the parties almost beyond recognition. Even accounting for exaggerated claims, the old membership of the SNP became a minority, though still significant, after Hamilton. The early 1960s had also seen the rise of the Campaign for Nuclear Disarmament, and both Plaid and the SNP were influenced by the 'peace movement'. The Labour Party's volte-face on unilateral nuclear disarmament was an opportunity to exploit the fears of many Labour supporters, and there has always been a strong pacifist element in the SNP, as in Plaid. The association of European integration with defence, nuclear weapons, and the cold war influenced the two parties.

Added to this was a view that European integration involved the creation of a gigantic, centralized super-state, which ran contrary to notions of self-determination and of community, particularly in the case of Plaid.[18] A populist dimension must also be taken into account. Public opinion was opposed to Europe, and the prospect of Scotland and Wales opposing European integration while England supported it offered opportunities for the parties. The constitutional nationalist case against Europe that developed in the 1960s was a mixture of opportunism and crude interpretation. On the other hand, there was little emanating from Europe at this time to disabuse the parties of their notions of European integration. The EEC's fairly unambiguous status as an intergovernmental institution in which the central governments of member states were dominant did little to dislodge the impression that 'Europe' lacked sympathy for the aspirations of minority nationalists.

A referendum had been held in the Irish Republic, under the terms of its constitution, prior to membership, which had endorsed the recommendation of the government to join. Ireland had followed the United Kingdom's difficult relations with the EEC with much interest and had been greatly influenced by these developments. The early vision of Irish nationalism had been de Valera's: 'The Ireland we dreamed of would be the home of a people who valued material wealth only as a basis of a right living people who were satisfied with a frugal comfort and devoted their leisure to things of the spirit. It would, in one word, be the home of a people living the life that God desired men to live.'[19]

Seán Lemass, who succeeded de Valera as Taoiseach, abandoned this autarkic (and theological) nationalism. His view was that Ireland was 'too small to influence others' and that the link with England was a priority with regard to EEC entry in the late 1950s.[20] However, by the mid-1970s a more independent line was adopted. Ireland would remain a member of the EEC even if the United Kingdom left. This influenced SDLP thinking.

The 1975 referendum was a watershed in the politics of Scotland, Wales, and Northern Ireland as well as the United Kingdom as a whole. The hostility to Europe inside the SNP and Plaid was carried through to the debates on membership of the EEC in the early 1970s and the 1975 referendum on continued membership after the United Kingdom had joined. However, there were tensions below the surface, and some figures in each party were reluctant to oppose membership outright especially after the United Kingdom had acceded to membership in January 1973. As the referendum approached, the prospect of the United Kingdom dividing by constituent nation on continued membership offered an opportunity for the SNP and Plaid to exploit. The best result for each party would have been a positive endorsement of membership from England while Scotland and Wales voted 'no'.

The SDLP has consistently supported membership of the EU. The SDLP supported the entry of the Republic of Ireland in the 1972 referendum as well as the United Kingdom's continued membership in the referendum in 1975. The party has consistently included references to EU participation in the resolution of divisions in Northern Ireland since their contribution to the Sunningdale Conference in December 1973.[21] In large measure, the SDLP shadowed the developments in the Republic. Butler and Kitzinger note that the party supported continuing UK membership, but did not want to emphasize any potential economic significance of the border with the Republic.[22] Europe offered the Irish Republic a means of breaking free of its dependence on the United Kingdom which was bound to be attractive to the SDLP. The SDLP mirrored the Republic's attitude towards Europe, just as unionists in Northern Ireland mirrored British attitudes.

Publicly, both SNP and Plaid were opposed to membership of the EEC but each harboured elements who succeeded in watering down opposition. The oppositionalist dilemma is always a central issue for constitutional nationalist parties: should the party exploit an issue for electoral purposes even though this might create problems should it ever attain its goal and come to power? For some in the SNP and Plaid, independent membership of the EEC for Scotland and Wales was desirable, but the opportunity to exploit public hostility to membership was too great. The circle was squared, though it is doubtful that the subtleties were appreciated by the public at large, by arguing for 'No, on anyone else's terms'. The implication was that an independent Scotland or Wales might negotiate more favourable terms of entry. George Reid, then an SNP MP, and Daffyd Wigley, then a Plaid MP and later its leader, were caught in this dilemma. However, the dilemma did not exist for all party members. In each party there were those who were quite simply opposed to European integration. It would take little effort to undermine the careful balance involved in arguing for 'No, on anyone else's terms'. Fear that the Scottish fishing industry would be damaged by continued membership of the EEC was important, as the SNP held a number of seats covering fishing communities. The 'Norwegian model' of a small, oil-rich state successfully operating outside the EEC (and having held a referendum to confirm this position in 1972) was attractive to substantial elements in the SNP. The impression was created that each party, especially the SNP, made no concession and opposed membership on anyone's terms.

The result of the referendum was disappointing for the Scottish and Welsh nationalists but welcomed by the SDLP (see Table 12.1). There was not the usual high turnout recorded in Northern Ireland, suggesting that EC membership had relatively low salience there. The SNP and Plaid were losing momentum, and by the time of the 1979 general

TABLE 12.1. *Results of the 1975 referendum on membership of the European Communities* (%)

Area	Turnout	Yes	No
England	64.6	68.7	31.3
Scotland	61.7	58.4	41.6
Wales	66.7	64.8	35.2
Northern Ireland	47.5	52.1	47.9
United Kingdom	64.0	67.2	32.8

Source: F. W. S. Craig, *British Electoral Facts, 1885–1975* (London: Macmillan, 1976), 170–1.

election the issue of Scottish and Welsh nationalism had declined. Both parties became introspective, and divisions emerged that would take time to heal. Significantly, Europe was not a major source of tension within either party.

Changing Contexts: The Rise of Europe

The 'relaunch' of Europe in the mid-1980s had a considerable impact on each of the constitutional nationalist parties, but it would be wrong to suggest that any of the parties made a dramatic and sudden change of policy in response. There was a change of emphasis and a greater focus on European matters, but a more positive engagement with Europe had been evolving or had already been established in each. The SDLP had long been pro-EC, but the new emphasis on European affairs allowed it to place its long-established credentials both in favour of European integration and political cooperation in a new context. Plaid and the SNP edged towards support for European integration in the early 1980s. The issue did not have high salience inside the parties, and changes took place that were largely unnoticed.

Europe was in the UK news in the early 1980s primarily because of controversy surrounding the United Kingdom's budgetary contributions. This matter was resolved, after much wrangling, at Fontaine-bleau in 1984, removing a significant barrier to European integration. The appointment of Jacques Delors as president of the Commission the following year gave the process of integration a dynamic and charismatic leader just at the point when the main stumbling-block towards 'ever closer union' had been removed. The high public profile attached to Europe and the '1992 campaign' ensured that each party's European policy would become more significant. In addition, the model of integration that was emerging was in one important respect quite different from that of the mid-1970s. The state-centric model was giving way to one in which other actors played a more significant part. Regions within member states were becoming more important, and regional policy was accorded greater resources. European institutions, including the Commission and Parliament, sponsored minority languages and cultures. European integration was beginning to appear not only less threatening to minority nationalists but as a potentially positive force, at least so long as these nations remained stateless. The emphasis on 'subsidiarity', however imprecise its definition, suggested a greater role for sub-state nations and regions. Under the Single European Act, the implementation of European policies, including the completion of the single market, were to take account of social and economic cohesion. This was developed further under the terms of the Maastricht Treaty. Maastricht also permitted member states to be represented in Council of Ministers meetings by regional politicians. A Committee of the Regions was set up, and regional and national diversity were acknowledged. The model of integration was perceived to have become one in which cultural and linguistic diversity was encouraged while simultaneously encouraging economic and social cohesion. The EU was no longer seen by many constitutional nationalists as a threat but as an ally. Divisions within the Thatcher government helped further, and Mrs Thatcher's shrill hostility to the process in the latter stages of her premiership provided further reason for nationalists to support it.

The relaunch of Europe in the late 1980s created a new and potentially difficult environment in which the constitutional nationalists had to operate. The potential problem lay in perceptions that the trend towards integration directly contradicted the direction in which the nationalists were heading, the former suggesting bringing barriers down and the latter suggesting resurrecting old divisions. In fact, each party was able to take advantage of the changes which were taking place. Each appeared more relevant in the emerging environment.

Leadership and Electoral Strategy

Key figures have played a significant role in the development of each party's European policy. The most significant case is John Hume in the SDLP. Neither the SNP nor Plaid has had an individual who has played such a singular role in the development of the party's European policy, but key figures can be identified in each. In each case, figures who had formerly been hostile to European integration were important in changing their party's European policy.

Hume was early in seeing that Europe offered a model for those seeking a way out of the entrenched, sectarian politics of Northern Ireland. In February 1971 he wrote an article in which he drew lessons from European integration for Ireland. A theme which became part of his hallmark appeared in this article:

It must be quite astonishing and puzzling to outsiders to note that while countries like France and Germany, who only twenty-five years ago were engaged in mutual carnage, are today building bonds of friendship, in Ireland there is little or no sign of the communities coming together. It seems somewhat contradictory that each part of Ireland seems willing to participate separately in the planned integration of Europe, but not in the planned integration of this little island.[23]

This theme has been well rehearsed by Hume in speeches over many years, to the point that critics have called it his 'single transferable speech', though supporters see it as evidence of Hume's remarkable prescience and consistency.

Hume's experience as an MEP since 1979 was preceded by a period as policy adviser to Richard Burke, the former Fine Gael minister for education, who was European commissioner for consumer affairs. Burke's responsibility from 1977 was related to preparations for the first direct elections to the European Parliament in 1979. It was at this time that Hume made 'a lot of very powerful contacts in the European Commission'.[24] By 1979 he was a successful candidate in the European parliamentary elections, polling the second-highest number of votes under the single transferable voting system, behind Ian Paisley. His willingness to utilize the legal and political processes of the European arena demonstrated a clear awareness of the significance of the EU for the political, economic, and social situation in Northern Ireland. Within six months of taking his seat he had successfully lobbied within the socialist group to commission a report, subsequently adopted by the Regional Policy Committee, of which Hume was a member, recommending substantial aid for Northern Ireland. In addition, between 1978 and 1981 successful lobbying led to visits to Northern Ireland from European commissioners or their aides, including Hume's former boss, Richard Burke.[25]

Notably, it is as a model of conflict resolution that Europe excites most interest for the SDLP leader. Hume's comments in recent years are similar to those he used in 1971:

Europe has been central to my political thinking. I regard Europe as the best example in the history of the world of conflict resolution. Areas of conflict everywhere should study how it was done. Consider the bitterness of the European conflict over the centuries, and the 35 million dead in 1945; yet fifty years later there is a European Union. But the Germans are still German and the French are still French . . . How did they do it? Exactly as I am trying to do here, by building institutions that respect their differences, gave no victory to either side, but allowed them to work together in their common interest, to spill their sweat, not their blood, and thereby break down the barriers of centuries. As a result of that, a real healing process began. The divisions of centuries cannot be healed in one decade, in Ireland or anywhere else. There has to be a healing process and the task of politicians is to create the framework in which that process can take place.[26]

The SDLP vision of a political process leading to a solution to divisions in Northern Ireland and the island of Ireland itself has developed a definite EU dimension. This growing significance of the EU has been assisted by developments within the EU. The growing competence of the EU and the developments in power distribution, policy-making, and voting procedures through the Single European Act and the Maastricht Treaty have facilitated the SDLP strategy by establishing an alternative focus for political activity, as well as a source for financial assistance for the improvement of social and economic deprivation in Northern Ireland.[27]

Some unionist opponents of the SDLP in Northern Ireland suspect that Hume's Europhilia is merely a covering for his primary objective of a united Ireland. This would suggest that Hume's leadership on Europe has been entirely cynical, indeed dishonest. The Cadogan Group, a unionist think tank formed in 1991, argued that the European Community (EC) was a union of states with no plans to create a Europe of the Regions and emphasized the limitations of what can be achieved for Northern Ireland in that context.[28] The European 'region', coincidentally, which Northern Ireland finds itself in is the island of Ireland. An alternative view is that the SDLP's thinking on Europe has been influenced by a critique of traditional nationalism as 'outdated territorial nationalism'.[29] Unlike the SNP, the SDLP's view of a Europe of the Regions is far removed from a Europe of States.

Winnie Ewing, SNP member of the European Parliament since 1979, had been a staunch critic of the EC during her period as Westminster MP for the fishing constituency of Moray between 1974 and 1979. However, she became a strong supporter of European integration after serving as an elected MEP after 1979. Jim Sillars, who had been a leading advocate of a 'no' vote in the 1975 referendum as a

Labour MP, became a leading supporter of Scottish independence in the EC after he joined the SNP in 1981. The combination of Ewing and Sillars proved important, especially as they came from very different backgrounds and in the early 1980s found themselves on either side of bitter divisions inside the SNP.

Europe cut across the deep divisions which afflicted the SNP in the early 1980s and played a part in uniting the party in the late 1980s. Sillars was the leading figure arguing the case for independence in Europe. In the early 1970s he concluded that if the United Kingdom decided to join and remained a member of the EC, then independent Scottish membership was more attractive than membership as part of the United Kingdom. His decision to leave the Labour Party and found a new party, the Scottish Labour Party, which supported independence in Europe, was in part made as a result of the 1975 referendum. The SNP, which Sillars joined in 1980, had been edging towards support for European integration during the 1980s, but under Sillars's leadership the issue came to the fore at the 1988 annual conference. The party overwhelmingly endorsed the policy, and it became central to its thinking thereafter. Though he was later to disavow his enthusiasm for Europe after he lost the Govan constituency in 1992, won in a by-election in 1988, Sillars left his mark, and the party remains committed to European integration.

The need to confront the accusation that the SNP were 'narrow nationalists' appears to have been an important motivation behind the SNP conversion. In his book *The Case for Optimism* Sillars explicitly tackles this, and argues that support for European integration made independence both economically viable and electorally possible.[30] The extent to which economic calculation played its part is difficult to assess, but there can be little doubt that 'Independence in Europe' was an important consideration for the party and for those elements in the leadership intent on devising a successful electoral strategy.

Dafydd Wigley and Dafydd Elis Thomas had previously adopted different positions on Europe in the 1970s. The former had been a staunch critic of the EC, while the latter preferred to keep open the possibility of supporting membership on terms favourable to Wales. However, Elis Thomas came to be a leading advocate of membership during the 1980s during his period as leader, a position which was maintained after Wigley resumed the leadership in 1991. There was a significant difference in the European policy supported by the two during the 1980s. Elis Thomas had a more radical vision of Europe and supported a Europe of the Regions, involving a major overhaul of European institutions as well as major changes in the United

Kingdom's constitution. This was closer to the policy supported by John Hume. Wigley, on the other hand, preferred the SNP model of independence in Europe with member states continuing to be the basic building-block in Europe.

Conclusion: A Post-Nationalist Vision?

Each of the parties has developed a pro-European integration position, but the aims and objectives of each differ in important respects. Each has abandoned absolutist notions of nationalism. If, as Gellner suggested, nationalism is a doctrine arguing for the congruence of 'political and national units', then none of these parties could strictly speaking be described as nationalist. Indeed, the Conservative Party appears to fit this definition better than any of the three constitutional nationalist parties discussed here, though, of course, the 'nation' in question is different. Indeed, even the Labour Party and the Liberal Democrats conform more to this nationalist definition than the SDLP and perhaps also the SNP and Plaid Cymru.

The SDLP has travelled furthest in this respect. The focus of the SDLP vision of the Europe of the future is, as we have seen, that of a Europe of the Regions. This view of Europe is one that plays down the significance of the 'nation-state' in favour of a recognition of cultural diversities between and within national boundaries. As Denis Haughey of the SDLP notes:

I think it's right that we haven't allowed the nation-state to be the last word in polity creation and in international political development. What we have in the European sense is a 'pooling' of sovereignty . . . We, in the SDLP, look on it as not diluting sovereignty but dilating democracy because the fact is that we live in an age now where the forces and factors that have a direct effect on people's lives and well-being are not forces and factors that can be controlled or regulated by nation-state instruments.[31]

However, the SDLP has not abandoned the idea of the island of Ireland as a political unit. It is this that raises doubts about the nature of the SDLP's 'Europhilia' in the minds of their unionist opponents.

The context in which the SDLP operates differs markedly from that of the SNP and Plaid Cymru. The nationalism of the SDLP is one that seeks unification while the nationalism of the other parties seeks break-up. The state which SDLP members wish to join is one that has already embraced European integration but this seems only a part of the explanation for that party's European policy. The socialist dimension of the SDLP's ideology has played a part in diluting its nationalism, but again this is unlikely to be a satisfactory explanation for its policy. The party's experiences in the harsh world of politics in Northern Ireland, and its support for power-sharing and opposition to hard-line nationalism, have affected its views on Europe. In this sense, the SDLP is the most post-nationalist of the three constitution-alist nationalist parties discussed here.

Something similar, though less urgent, has been evident within the SNP and Plaid Cymru. Electoral opportunism, combined with the belief that European integration is inevitable, has encouraged these two parties to develop much more positive attitudes towards Europe than any of the main British parties. A changing context has con-tributed to an evolving view of European integration. In each case, it has not so much been the various processes of globalization, viewed as the de-territorialization of politics, as Europeanization, and the increased importance of a new regional level of governance, that have been most influential in the development of the politics of constitu-tional nationalism in the constituent nations of the United Kingdom. The context in which the parties operate has been important in each case. This suggests that in other circumstances these parties, like those discussed by Janet Laible in Chapter 11 of this volume, could adopt an antagonistic attitude towards European integration.

NOTES

1. E. Gellner, *Nations and Nationalism* (Oxford: Blackwell, 1983), 1.
2. Z. Bauman, *Globalization: The Human Consequences* (Cambridge: Polity Press, 1998), 9.
3. R. O'Brien, *Global Financial Integration: The End of Geography* (London: Chatham House–Pinter, 1992).
4. D. Mitrany, *A Working Peace System: An Argument for the Functional Development of International Organization* (London: Oxford University Press, 1943).
5. A. Moravcsik, *The Choice for Europe* (London: UCL Press, 1998).
6. G. Marks, 'Structural Policy in the European Community', in A. Sbragia (ed.), *Euro-Politics: Institutions and Policy-Making in the 'New' European Union* (Washington, DC: Brookings Institute, 1992).
7. D. Balsom, P. J. Madgwick, and D. Van Mechelen, 'The Red and the Green: Patterns of Partisan Choice in Wales', *British Journal of Political Science*, 13 (1983), 299–326.
8. J. Mitchell, 'Factions, Tendencies and Consensus in the SNP', *Scottish Government Yearbook* (1990), 49–61.
9. I. McAllister, *The Northern Ireland Social Democratic and Labour Party: Political Opposition in a Divided Society* (London: Macmillan, 1977).

10. S. Elliott, 'Voting Systems and Political Parties in Northern Ireland', in B. Hadfield (ed.), *Northern Ireland: Politics and the Constitution* (Buckingham: Open University Press, 1992), 87–8.
11. McAllister, *The Northern Ireland Social Democratic and Labour Party*, 168.
12. Ibid. 15.
13. Ibid. 19–20.
14. B. Purdie, *Politics in the Streets: The Origins of the Civil Rights Movement in Northern Ireland* (Belfast: Blackstaff, 1990).
15. P. O'Malley, *Ireland: Uncivil Wars* (Belfast: Blackstaff Press, 1983), 100.
16. M. Freeden, 'Is Nationalism a Distinct Ideology?', *Political Studies*, 46 (1998), 750.
17. Ibid. 752.
18. I. McAllister, 'The Political Ideology of Welsh Nationalism', *Government and Opposition*, 23 (1998), 497–517.
19. J. K. Jacobsen, *Chasing Progress in the Irish Republic* (Cambridge: Cambridge University Press, 1994), 1.
20. Ibid. 70.
21. B. White, *John Hume: Statesman of the Troubles* (London: Blackstaff Press, 1984), 229.
22. D. Butler and U. Kitzinger, *The 1975 Referendum* (London: Macmillan, 1976), 156.
23. Hume cited in G. Drower, *John Hume: Peacemaker* (London: Victor Gollancz, 1995), 58.
24. P. Routledge, *John Hume: A Biography* (London: HarperCollins, 1997), 154.
25. P. Hainsworth, 'Northern Ireland: A European Role?', *Journal of Common Market Studies*, 2 (1981), 2.
26. Routledge, *John Hume*, 155.
27. C. McCall, 'Intimations of Postmodernity: Structural Change and Communal Identities in Northern Ireland', Ph.D. diss., University of Strathclyde, 1997.
28. G. Murray, *John Hume and the SDLP: Impact and Survival in Northern Ireland* (Dublin: Irish Academic Press, 1998), 219.
29. Quoted in Murray, *John Hume and the SDLP*, 215.
30. J. Sillars, *Scotland: The Case for Optimism* (Edinburgh: Polygon, 1989).
31. McCall, *Intimations of Postmodernity*, 114.

CHAPTER 13

Projecting Sovereignty in Post-Soviet Russia: Tatarstan in the International Arena

KATHERINE E. GRANEY

The end of the cold war has precipitated a new wave of interest in one of the most enduring questions in international relations—how the norm of state sovereignty is constructed and gains meaning in practice.[1] Recent works addressing this question have explored the changing nature of the norm of state sovereignty by looking at three significant aspects of the post-cold war world. The first concerns the relationship between state sovereignty and increasing instances of international intervention.[2] The second is focused on how the evolution of all-European institutions affects the norm of state sovereignty.[3] Finally, there is the attempt to determine the criteria for the recognition of sovereign statehood in the post-cold war era by re-examining the relationship between self-determination, nationalism, and the norm of state sovereignty in light of the creation of the successor states to the former Yugoslavia and the Soviet Union.[4]

This chapter seeks to contribute to these debates by addressing a question generated by the third line of enquiry identified above— exploring what new opportunities for the practice of state sovereignty the post-cold war international system affords to actors which are nominally sub-state member units of another state.[5] In particular, it is concerned with understanding how both sub-state units in Russia and the Russian central state have responded to the opportunities and challenges facing them as they seek to negotiate the post-cold war international system. Within the universe of sub-state entities making claims to state sovereignty of various scope and intensity, which includes Quebec, Scotland, and various of the Spanish autonomies, a particularly intriguing new case is the Republic of Tatarstan, a nominally constituent unit of the Russian Federation which declared itself to be a 'sovereign democratic state' in August 1990.[6] Tatarstan, a multi-ethnic republic whose population is about 49 per cent ethnic Tatar and 39 per cent ethnic Russian, was one of the first member units of the Russian Federation to make a claim to sovereign statehood in the post-Soviet era.[7] Tatars are a Muslim, Turkic people with a strong national linguistic and literary tradition who were incorporated into the Russian state in 1552 when Tsar Ivan Grozny forcibly captured the Kazan' khanate, a Golden Horde successor state located on the territory of modern-day Tatarstan.[8]

Tatarstan's political elites have attempted to fulfil the republic's post-Soviet claims to state sovereignty by probing for new economic and political spaces in the international arena within which the republic can project itself as 'a sovereign state'. These efforts have taken the form of what could be called a *sovereignty project*—a coherent, multifaceted effort aimed at fulfilling a claim of sovereign statehood by investing that claim with empirical and discursive meaning. Describing efforts to construct sovereignty as a project is useful in a dual sense. The first is that sovereignty is constructed through the continuous work of political actors who mount a concerted 'project' towards this end that consists of both material and discursive efforts.[9] Secondly, these efforts aim to bring sovereignty to life by 'projecting' performances of the sovereign state for those external and internal audiences without whose recognition and complicity sovereignty does not exist.[10]

For all states, the construction of sovereignty involves gaining recognition of their claims to sovereignty from both external audiences (the international community) and internal audiences (their domestic populations).[11] However, like Quebec, Scotland, and the Spanish autonomies, Tatarstan is a sub-state actor which is nominally a member unit of the Russian Federation. Therefore its claim to sovereign statehood must be negotiated with and validated by an additional audience—the Russian Federation. Tatarstan's efforts to project sovereignty thus are being carried out simultaneously in three arenas: the international community, the Russian Federation, and the domestic realm.

This chapter explores how Tatarstan has attempted to construct a sovereign presence in the international arena in the post-Soviet period. Since declaring Tatarstan to be a sovereign state in 1990, its political elites have mounted a coherent project that aspires to occupy some of the international political spaces formerly monopolized by the Soviet state. Furthermore, Tatarstan's efforts are situated in a discourse that asserts a commitment to the long-term process of fulfilling the declared status of the Republic as a 'sovereign state' by achieving some form of membership for Tatarstan in the international community. While largely avoiding the inflammatory language of secession, which is generally condemned in international law and in the international community,[12] Tatarstan's sovereignty project nonetheless embodies claims and posits goals that are explicitly aimed at securing an independent political presence for the Republic in the post-cold war international community.

Tatarstan's political leaders have pursued the international sovereignty project in two ways. First, they have sought to increase the Republic's direct and unmediated political and economic activities in the international arena by establishing bilateral relations with individual states and by participating in international organizations and transnational political and economic networks. The Tatarstani leadership has found a particularly receptive audience to their sovereignty project among those all-European institutions dealing with regional or sub-state issues, such as the Assembly of European Regions, which has actively sought to involve Russian federal member states like Tatarstan in their activities alongside their European counterparts in the post-Soviet era. Second, Tatarstani elites have attempted to gain the complicity of the international community in their sovereignty project by pursuing a type of 'anticipatory adaptation',[13] wherein the Republic has made unilateral efforts to align itself with the dominant norms of the international community in the hopes of achieving new levels of 'international personality'.[14]

While Tatarstan's political elites have attempted to carve out an independent international presence for the Republic in the name of sovereignty, they have not been able to ignore the reality of their status as a nominal member unit of the Russian Federation. The prevalence of the norm of the territorial integrity of states, the general lack of support in the international community for sub-state claims to autonomy, and the basic fact of Tatarstan's location within the territorial and economic boundaries of Russia all dictate that Tatarstan's efforts to project a sovereign international presence will be mediated by the Russian Federation to some degree. Thus Tatarstan's international sovereignty project is the result of negotiations with Russia concerning how the two political entities will share participation in the international community in the post-cold war era—a process which exhibits elements both of cooperation and of contention.

On the one hand, eager to promote those parts of the Tatarstani sovereignty project that contribute to the overall development of the Russian Federation, Moscow has proven itself willing to share significant amounts of economic sovereignty with Tatarstan in the international arena. In the post-cold war international system, which is characterized by the increasing globalization of economic and political networks, state survival necessitates devolving some sovereignty up to transnational networks and some sovereignty down to sub-state units.[15] Accordingly, Russia's economic survival after communism depends on it becoming more 'post-modern' and deepening its overall integration into the transnational networks of the world economy by transferring some rights of economic sovereignty to its regions, one of the most economically promising of which is Tatarstan.[16] Thus the Russian central government has encouraged Tatarstan to find new foreign economic partners while attempting to secure a portion of the profits from Tatarstan's new international economic relationships for the Russian central state.

Despite evidence of willingness to devolve sovereignty to sub-state units such as Tatarstan in the international economic sphere, the Russian central government has also demonstrated that there are firm limits to the amount of *political* sovereignty that it will devolve to or share with Tatarstan and other member units of the Russian Federation in the international arena in the post-Soviet period. In practice this has meant Moscow has made efforts to limit or contain the political aspects of Tatarstan's international sovereignty project within those all-European institutions that are specifically geared towards regional or sub-state units. Again in this instance, the Russian central state has attempted to co-opt the desire of sovereignty-seeking sub-state member units such as Tatarstan to join transnational political and economic institutions in order to help integrate the Russian state *as a whole* more fully into Europe and the rest of the international community in the post-Soviet era. However, Tatarstani political elites have consistently challenged these efforts at co-optation and the boundaries set by Moscow for their political participation in the international arena, and have pursued their own vision of the type of sovereign political presence Tatarstan can and should have.

The evolving relationship between Tatarstan, Russia, and the international community illustrates the elasticity and facility of the claim of 'state sovereignty' as an organizing principle for sub-state units seeking new levels of autonomy within their host states and extant to them, especially in the post-cold war international context. Because statehood and sovereignty are themselves contested norms, using them as the basis for negotiation with host states provides significant material and discursive spaces for sub-state actors within which they can manoeuvre to achieve significant, if ambiguous, levels of 'international personality'. The preliminary result of Tatarstan's international sovereignty project is a situation of sovereignty-sharing between Tatarstan and Russia in the international arena that is not unlike that currently evolving in Europe, where European states and their sub-state member units both occupy some international political and economic spaces.[17] The necessity of devising types of creative sovereignty-sharing regimes is becoming more apparent in the increasingly interdependent and plurilateral post-cold war world, where transnational political institutions such as those of the European Union (EU) and increasingly globalized economic networks provide new opportunities for nominally sub-state actors such as Tatarstan to project themselves as 'sovereign' in the international arena.[18]

Furthermore, the case of Tatarstan illustrates that sub-state claims to sovereignty and statehood are informed in significant ways by international discourses about these norms.[19] Tatarstan has justified its quest for international sovereignty using a nationalist discourse which claims that sovereignty for the modern-day state of Tatarstan fulfils the ethnic Tatar nation's historical rights to statehood. However, this nationalist sentiment has been moderated by the employ of another discourse which emphasizes Tatarstan's *empirical* fitness for sovereign statehood, wherein the criteria for empirical sovereignty include, principally, adherence to democratic norms and human rights conventions, especially a commitment to civic multiculturalism. The competing discourses employed by Tatarstan in their sovereignty project reflect the ambiguity in the international community over which criteria to use in legitimizing claims to sovereignty in the post-cold war period.[20] They also highlight the peculiar character of many sub-state nationalisms in a time of increasing globalization, where civic and ethnic elements coexist uneasily as the bases for claims to self-determination and state sovereignty.[21]

Tatarstan's experience in the international arena in the post-Soviet period forces us to recognize the variety and degrees of sovereign statehood as it is practised by those actors claiming to possess it or those actors who are actively pursuing it. It also leads us to recognize that there are now significant spaces for the projection of state sovereignty by nominally sub-state actors in the international system. In particular, transnational economic networks and political institutions like those of the EU have offered ample opportunity for sub-state units in Russia such as Tatarstan to 'act like a state'. Tatarstan's leadership has proven itself to be both extremely interested in and remarkably adept at finding and exploiting those opportunities. In this sense, the international system now appears to tolerate and even encourage the emergence of various types of shared sovereignty or simultaneous statehoods for sub-state units.[22] At the same time, however, these transnational economic and political networks also provide potentially useful ways for the Russian central state to transform itself into a functional post-communist state and to integrate itself more deeply into the economic and political life of both Europe and the international community. Thus Russia has attempted to control the participation of Tatarstan in these networks and institutions. Therefore, the key dynamic between Tatarstan, Russia, and the international community now and in the foreseeable future is the attempt to balance and reconcile Tatarstan's own sovereignty ambitions with Moscow's desire to use Tatarstan's participation for its own purposes. Indeed, this is the key dynamic facing all central state governments and their constituent sub-state units in the post-cold war world.

My discussion of these issues is organized into two parts. First I examine the theoretical importance of Tatarstan's international sovereignty project. Next I describe and analyse Tatarstan's efforts to project sovereignty in the international arena in the post-cold war era, focusing in turn on how the Republic's leadership has negotiated its international sovereignty project with the Russian state and the international community.

Theoretical Context of the Analysis

It is useful to situate this discussion in social-constructivist discussions of sovereignty. Constructivists argue that sovereignty exists 'by virtue of certain intersubjective understandings and expectations'.[23] That is, state sovereignty comes into existence when a particular political community forwards a claim to sovereign statehood and the relevant external and internal audiences to that claim validate it by recognizing and responding to it. Sovereignty, and by extension the sovereign state, is thus understood as 'a struggle'; 'a play'; 'a work of art'; 'an on-going dynamic'; 'a claim'; 'a cultivated habit'; and an 'on-going, all-consuming project'.[24]

Because the 'textual and contextual prescriptions' of what a state must do to be recognized as sovereign are produced by the international community through its practice of recognizing and legitimizing sovereign states,[25] it is necessary to understand the nature of the international system within which Tatarstan is attempting to project sovereignty. This section discusses two aspects of that system; the first concerns the confused nature of the norms of state sovereignty and self-determination in the post-cold war era, while the second concerns more structural changes in the international system, especially the expansion of transnational political and economic networks.

The constitutive rules about state sovereignty that are produced in the international community vary over time and are subject to reinterpretation during periods of major systemic crisis. In particular, international sovereignty regimes tend to oscillate between the recognition of either statehood (understood as empirical fitness for statehood) or nationality (understood as ethnic claims to national self-determination) as the legitimate basis for sovereign statehood and international enfranchisement.[26] The end of the cold war marked the beginning of a period of systemic crisis in which the international sovereignty regime that evolved during the process of decolonization after the Second World War is currently being reconstituted.

The post-Second World War sovereignty regime that emerged from decolonization supported a limited right of national self-determination for former colonies in Africa and Asia. The United Nations (UN), representing the existing community of sovereign states, conferred juridical sovereignty upon a select group of post-colonial states modelled on the basis of former colonial boundaries. The domestic communities within these states were envisioned as explicitly civic and multinational, not ethnic.[27] After the creation of this limited number of new sovereign states the international community turned its energies towards consolidating and protecting the territorial integrity of existing states, and rebuffed most later claims to statehood, especially those forwarded with explicitly ethnic claims to national self-determination. Despite this fact, the norm of ethnically inspired national self-determination has remained a powerful political force across the globe.

It is unclear what role the norm of national self-determination will play in legitimizing claims to state sovereignty in the post-cold war world. The international community has recognized some claims to statehood based on ethnic arguments for national self-determination in the former Yugoslavia and former Soviet Union, although these claims were recognized only after assurances of adequate protections for minorities and provision of democratic norms were received.[28] One prominent author has argued that the norm of self-determination has been 'revitalized' in the international community in the post-cold war period and that state boundaries now seem more 'adjustable' than before the cold war.[29] Another author has suggested that since the collapse of communism there has been 'a detectable shift in emphasis away from an absolute, unconditional right to political sovereignty and territorial integrity, towards more flexible, less statist positions'.[30]

Others disagree, arguing that in the wake of the Yugoslav fiasco the international community is wary of any claims to self-determination and fearful of inciting new ethnic conflicts. Rather than embracing self-determination in the post-Soviet period, they argue, the international community now considers the main component of the emerging international sovereignty regime to be a sufficient level of *empirical sovereignty*, characterized by the ability to provide good governance, democracy, and respect for human rights.[31] Thus the international climate in which Tatarstan has undertaken its sovereignty project is one that is undecided about how to respond to sub-state claims to statehood.

Structurally, the post-cold war international system may be described as a plurilateralist one where state sovereignty is less a 'territorially defined barrier' than a 'bargaining resource' to be used in an international arena where political and economic power is increasingly diffused both upwards to transnational actors and downwards to the subnational level.[32] This increasingly dense network of transnational economic and political networks, which is most evident in the Organization for Economic Cooperation and Development countries, appears to afford increased opportunities for sub-state units to project sovereignty internationally—the increased activity in the EU by Europe's regions is the most prominent example of this phenomenon.[33] Thus the international system within which Tatarstan is seeking to project itself as 'sovereign' is one which may afford it new and expanded opportunities to accomplish exactly that.

In the following section I outline the contours of Tatarstan's efforts to project sovereignty in the international sphere and discuss how the Republic's international sovereignty project has been negotiated with the Russian Federation. Then I examine how Tatarstan has attempted to gain the complicity of the international community in its sovereignty project, focusing on how competing international norms and discourses about sovereignty and statehood have informed the Republic's efforts.

The Tatarstani Sovereignty Project in the International Arena

The essence of Tatarstan's international sovereignty project is the claim that Tatarstan is 'a sovereign state and a subject of international law, which bases its relations with the Russian Federation and other republics on the basis of equal agreements'.[34] By forwarding a claim to sovereignty that embodies both statehood and international legal subjecthood, Tatarstan's political elites make it clear they aspire to something beyond the mere achievement of new levels of political and economic autonomy *within* the Russian Federation. By formulating the claim to sovereignty in this way, the desire for some form of membership in the international community is made explicit. And yet these claims are also ambiguously presented: it remains unclear what the 'sovereign statehood' Tatarstan has declared really amounts to in practice, while the claim to 'international subjecthood' is similarly vague. Tatarstan's claim to sovereignty seems to have been formulated with the intent to cast as wide a net as possible for the potential development of the Tatarstani sovereignty project, especially in the international arena, while also not alienating the Russian Federation or the international community with inflammatory secessionist claims.

Having forwarded these sweeping, if vague, claims to sovereignty and statehood, Tatarstan's leadership has been faced with the task of bringing them to life. They have pursued this goal in a variety of ways, including both unilateral domestic policy moves and policies that have been negotiated with the Russian Federation. These efforts include attempts to codify legally Tatarstan's status as a sovereign state and subject of international law, making direct political and economic overtures to the international community and foreign states, and mounting discursive efforts aimed at differentiating Tatarstan's identity as an international actor from that of the Russian Federation.

The first attempt by the government of Tatarstan to codify legally their claims to sovereignty in the international arena came in March 1992. Tatarstani officials refused to sign the new draft of the Russian Federal Treaty, claiming that the treaty had not taken into account Tatarstan's declared status as a sovereign state.[35] Tatarstani officials then proceeded to hold a referendum to determine public support for the Republic's declared status as 'a sovereign state and subject of international law'. The referendum was held in the hope of demonstrating the degree to which claims to sovereignty had public support in Tatarstan, thus increasing Tatarstan's leverage against the Russian Federation as it pursued contentious new levels of sovereignty in the post-Soviet period. The referendum also allowed the leadership of Tatarstan to demonstrate to Russia and the international community that its sovereignty project was being conducted in accordance with internationally accepted democratic procedures.[36]

It is significant that in announcing the referendum, the Presidium of the Supreme Soviet of Tatarstan justified Tatarstan's claims to 'international legal subjecthood' by arguing that 'the existing ties between Tatarstan and the CIS countries in a legal sense practically are already of an international nature'.[37] In other words, the Republic's leadership argued that because Tatarstan was already a *de facto* international actor by virtue of its relations with Commonwealth of Independent States (CIS) countries, the Republic's claim to occupy its own international space in the post-Soviet era was legitimate.

After the referendum passed in the Republic, having received affirmative votes from 61.4 per cent of the 82 per cent of eligible voters who participated, the government of Tatarstan issued a decree that appealed to 'states and international organizations' to build relations with Tatarstan 'according to her new status' as a sovereign state and subject of international law.[38] This decree demonstrates an understanding that only the international community could validate Tatarstan's post-Soviet claims to sovereign statehood and international legal subjecthood, and an awareness that direct ties to the international community would provide powerful legitimization of Tatarstan's claims to sovereignty in the face of Russian and domestic opposition to those claims.

The results of the March 1992 referendum were later codified in the constitution of the Republic of Tatarstan, which was adopted in November 1992.[39] Articles 61 and 62 of the constitution reaffirm Tatarstan's status as a sovereign state and subject of international law and enumerate Tatarstan's specific rights and responsibilities in the international sphere. These include the right to enter into relations with other states, to exchange diplomats and other representatives with other states, and to participate in the activity of international organizations. Article 62 of the Tatarstani constitution also seeks to link the Republic more closely with the international community by asserting that international law has precedence on the territory of Tatarstan. Since its adoption Tatarstani political elites have consistently legitimized their right to pursue an independent foreign policy through recourse to the constitution of Tatarstan.

In February 1994 the Russian Federation recognized some of Tatarstan's claims to international juridical sovereignty when it signed the ground-breaking Agreement on the Delimitation of Powers and Authorities with the Republic.[40] While this agreement, which will be discussed in more detail later, did not explicitly refer to Tatarstan as a sovereign state, it did recognize Tatarstan's claimed status as 'an international actor'. Article 11 of the Agreement gave Tatarstan the right to: 'participate in international relations, establish relations with foreign states and conclude treaties which do not contradict the Constitution

or international obligation of the Russian Federation, the Constitution of the Republic of Tatarstan, or the present agreement, and to participate in the activity of international organizations'.[41] Furthermore,
Articles 12 and 13 of the Agreement gave Tatarstan the right to create
its own national bank, and to 'conduct foreign economic activity
independently'.[42]

Besides these efforts to codify legally their right to a sovereign international presence, Tatarstani political elites have also attempted to
increase their political and economic participation in the international
arena. In the political realm Tatarstan has initiated contacts with
several international organizations, including the UN (mainly through
the UN Educational, Scientific, and Cultural Organization (UNESCO)
and the World Federation Association at the UN), various all-European
organizations, and the League of Arab States.

As membership in the UN is generally considered to be the clearest
hallmark of sovereign statehood and membership in the international
community,[43] Tatarstan's efforts to establish close contacts with it are
a particularly important aspect of its overall sovereignty project. In
September 1993, it hosted a UNESCO conference on the culture of
young cities. The publications prepared for the conference by the
government of Tatarstan reflect the Republic's aspiration to an international presence and perhaps even membership of the UN. The government argued that being chosen to host a UNESCO conference
indicates the Republic is 'realistically destined for international legal
recognition', and called the conference a crucial step towards the goal
of 'strengthening Tatarstan's ties with UNESCO and the whole system of the UN in general'.[44]

In November 1994 the assistant secretary-general of the UN,
Joseph Verner Reed, paid an official visit to Kazan' to announce the
opening of a UN information and resource centre in Tatarstan called
the Association for Cooperation with the UN. Reed praised
Tatarstan's attempts to resolve autonomy conflicts in the Russian
Federation and expressed his hope that cooperation between the UN
and Tatarstan would continue to grow. President Mintimer Shaimiyev
used the occasion to inform Reed that Tatarstan had 'laid the political
legal bases for sovereign statehood', and noted the important role of
the international community in helping Tatarstan to evolve as a democratic state in the post-Soviet period.[45] In March 1996 another
UNESCO conference was held in Tatarstan to address the problem of
ethnic schools in a multicultural environment.

Since 1990 Tatarstan has also deepened its involvement with
European political structures. Tatarstani elites have interpreted their

participation in the regional institutions of the EU as strengthening the Republic's declared 'state sovereignty' and have used their new EU contacts in negotiations with Moscow over certain contentious political issues. In October 1996 Tatarstan and the EU sponsored an international conference on the budgetary and tax problems of federal systems in Europe and the former Soviet Union.[46] The next month in Moscow Tatarstan's vice-president, Vasili Likhachev, chaired a meeting of the Congress of Local and Regional Organs of Power in Europe, aimed at increasing ties between Russia's regions and Europe, in order 'to allow Russia's regions to make a real contribution to the architecture of Europe and the EU in the 21st century'.[47] In 1997 Tatarstan hosted a related conference sponsored by the EU entitled 'Democracy at the Local Level', and was made a member of the Assembly of the European Regions.[48]

In spring 1998 a conflict between Tatarstan and Russia arose, in which Tatarstani elites attempted to use their new-found contacts with EU and other transnational institutions to challenge the Russian central state in Moscow over the issue of a Tatarstani law on citizenship. The Tatarstani citizenship law was adopted in April 1998 as a protest against the new Russian Federation internal passports, which eliminated the category of the carrier's nationality. The Tatarstani citizenship law provided for the issue of separate Tatarstani passports, automatically gave residents of Tatarstan dual citizenship in Tatarstan and the Russian Federation, and allowed anyone whose grandparents were born in Tatarstan to apply for citizenship.[49] While the creation of an independent Tatarstani citizenship and the idea of independent Tatarstani passports are certainly provocative challenges to the Russian central state, what is also interesting here is how Tatarstani officials have attempted to use their new connections with European and international institutions to strengthen their own position in the conflict with Russia over this new law. More specifically, Tatarstan's vice-president, Likhachev, has attempted to legitimize the controversial law by arguing that it conforms to international legal standards, and has even brought the text of the law to the legal department of the Parliament of the Council of Europe in Strasbourg to have its democratic and international legal credentials verified.[50]

Significantly, in May 1998 Likhachev was named the Russian Federation's permanent representative to the EU in Strasbourg. This appointment reflects both the important role that Tatarstan has begun to play in European politics in the post-Soviet period and the seriousness with which Russia regards Tatarstan's international sovereignty project. However, appointing Likhachev to this important post appears most of all to be an attempt by Yeltsin to co-opt him and Tatarstan's quest for membership in the international community. Moscow seeks to contain the Republic's drive towards internationalization within European *regional* frameworks and the opportunities for sub-state participation within them. By giving Tatarstan's vice-president such a prestigious post, it appears Yeltsin also hoped to increase Russia's overall integration into European political and economic institutions. However, in accepting the position, Likhachev vowed that one of the most important parts of his job would be to represent the interests of Tatarstan and other Russian regions at the EU.[51]

Besides these efforts to increase its participation in the international community through international organizations, Tatarstan's leadership has also attempted to develop direct bilateral ties with foreign countries.[52] In the early years of the sovereignty project (1990–3) Tatarstan established official political and economic contacts with all of the CIS states, much of the former Soviet bloc, and Europe (especially Hungary, the Czech Republic, Germany and France), as well as with Turkey, Canada, and the United States.[53] On many of these visits the Tatarstani president, Mintimer Shaimiyev, signed general agreements pledging to increase 'trade-economic, scientific-technical and cultural' trade cooperation between Tatarstan and the various other polities.[54] During these years Tatarstan also hosted foreign economic and business delegations from the United States and various European countries including Sweden, Hungary, and Germany.

Tatarstan has continued to pursue independent economic and political initiatives in the international arena in the wake of the February 1994 Agreement with the Russian Federation. From 1994 to 1997 official delegations from Tatarstan were received in Iraq, Iran, Malaysia, Azerbaijan, and Egypt, as well as in the United States and France. President Shaimiyev represented Tatarstan at the January 1995 Davos World Economic Forum, emphasizing in his news conferences that Tatarstan had been invited to the forum 'as an independent actor'.[55] Later in 1995, claiming that 'whether Russia or the CIS likes it or not, Tatarstan is located in international economic space', the government of Tatarstan hired an American consulting firm to do a comprehensive survey of the Republic's economy and to devise a programme for its long-term economic development and integration into the world economy.[56] The firm's recommendations, which included using the Republic's hefty oil revenues to propel the country out of its reliance on raw material exports and towards a more investment- and innovation-driven economy, became the basis for a new

Programme for Social and Economic Progress in Tatarstan.[57] In a further effort to increase its contacts with the international economy, Tatarstan has adopted some of the most liberal and generous legislation governing foreign investment anywhere in Russia.[58]

Tatarstan has also made domestic-policy moves to support its independent political and economic forays into the international community. In 1993 it created its own Ministry of Foreign Economic Affairs, and articulated its own *Conception of the Foreign Economic Policy of Tatarstan*. This document includes plans to increase foreign investment in Tatarstan, to diversify Tatarstan's exports, to create a 'fully internationally integrated information system to support international business', and to prepare qualified personnel to carry out Tatarstani foreign economic policy.[59] To help realize this plan, the Cabinet of Ministers of Tatarstan issued a decree creating a special programme for the training of foreign policy and foreign economic policy personnel.[60] In conjunction with this programme a department of international relations was opened at Kazan' State University in March 1995, which was charged with producing 'representatives of Tatarstan for the world stage'.[61]

These domestic policy efforts culminated with the creation of the Department of Foreign and CIS Affairs of the President's Office of Tatarstan in August 1995. This entity was created to 'help Tatarstan realize her sovereignty in practice in the sphere of international relations'.[62] It is also responsible for providing a unified conception of the foreign policy of Tatarstan and coordinating the activity of the representatives of Tatarstan in other countries. Thus it functions much as a Ministry of Foreign Affairs for Tatarstan, but is located wholly within the president's office. The trend towards consolidating foreign policy-making power in the executive branch continued in the summer of 1997, when the Ministry of Foreign Economic Activity was reorganized and subsumed into the Department of Foreign and CIS Affairs of the President of Tatarstan.[63]

Tatarstani officials have also attempted to demarcate discursively the boundaries of Tatarstan's international personality from those of Russia in the post-Soviet period, and to 'cultivate the habit' among Tatarstani and Russian citizens of viewing the Republic's international activities as legitimate and normal.[64] Visits by President Shaimiyev to foreign countries and the reception of foreign dignitaries in Kazan' are inevitably referred to by Tatarstani officials and Tatarstan's media as being examples of Tatarstan's 'bilateral' or 'inter-state' ties. The fact that some of these events may have involved the participation of the Russian Federation Ministry of Foreign Affairs is not often acknowledged.

Instead, the emphasis is on creating the impression of Tatarstan as a state that engages in unmediated bilateral agreements with other states, that the Republic's foreign relations are truly of an 'inter-state' nature and not just subsidiary to Russia's foreign policy.

Similarly, when addressing Tatarstan's foreign-policy activities, Republican officials and the local press stress Tatarstan's legal right to manage its own foreign affairs independently, as is codified in the Tatarstani constitution and the February 1994 Agreement with Russia. For example, the visit of a Tatarstani delegation to Iraq in July 1995 was referred to by Tatarstan's deputy prime minister, Ravil Muratov, as a 'realization of Tatarstan's right to an independent foreign policy', which nevertheless was 'wholly within the channel of Russia's policy in Iraq'.[65] Similarly, when French prime minister Alain Juppé went to Kazan' in February 1996, Tatarstan's local media proudly congratulated the Republic for hosting such a prestigious foreign visitor and noted that it was a foreign policy precedent that 'the Russian Federation must reckon with for the future'.[66]

In addition to emphasizing the bilateral and inter-state quality of their foreign economic and political relations, Tatarstani officials have also attempted to differentiate the Republic's identity as a sovereign international actor by stressing the *unmediated* quality of its ties with international organizations. In an interview given in June 1997 President Shaimiyev stressed proudly that Tatarstan had become a participant in the European and international legal fields 'in the most direct unmediated way'.[67] He added that, owing to this new political reality, the Republic of Tatarstan would soon move unilaterally to align itself with all-European charters and conventions. By positioning the Republic as a state that is moving to join European multilateral conventions (while conveniently avoiding the question of whether or not they have been invited to do so), Shaimiyev is attempting to make the notion of Tatarstan as an independent international actor seem a natural reality.

To further demarcate and publicize the boundaries of its international sovereignty project the government of Tatarstan has also invested heavily in what might be called 'sovereignty propaganda'. These are publications aimed at foreign governments and businesspeople which advertise Tatarstan's claims to state sovereignty and international economic independence and explain the legal bases of these claims (namely the constitution of Tatarstan and the 1994 Agreement with the Russian Federation). The government has funded advertisements about the Republic in foreign newspapers, as well as two high-quality brochures and several books which extol Tatarstan as a stable potential political and economic partner whose right to conduct an independent economic and foreign policy is fully secure and legitimate.[68] At the same time foreign audiences are reassured that Tatarstan is fully integrated within Russia's economic and political space.

Together these various elements indicate that Tatarstan's leadership has a long-term commitment to pursuing some form of sovereign presence in the international community. Some public officials in Tatarstan are more candid than others about the ultimate aims of the international sovereignty project. For example, on the six-month anniversary of the agreement with the Russian Federation, Tatarstani vice-president Likhachev announced: 'for Tatarstan's international recognition it is not enough simply to raise the Republic's flag outside the headquarters of the United Nations or some other international organization. This is a lengthy process and Tatarstan is only taking the first steps.'[69] Furthermore, in late 1996 the assistant chair of Tatarstan's Supreme Soviet publicly declared his belief that Tatarstan could and should attain UN membership in the future.[70]

Yet despite the impressive array of resources Tatarstan's leadership has committed to the construction of a sovereign presence in the international arena, the fact of the Republic's nominal sub-state status as a member unit of the Russian Federation has coloured every aspect of its international sovereignty project, and the international aspirations of Tatarstan have been tempered at every step by the reality of its federal locale. In the next section I explore the effects of this reality and the resulting situation of sovereignty-sharing that has emerged in post-Soviet Russia.

Russian Mediation of Tatarstan's International Sovereignty Project

In pursuing sovereignty in the international arena, Tatarstan's leadership has dealt with its location within the Russian Federation by continuously stressing two seemingly opposing points: first, that Tatarstan is a sovereign state and independent international actor; and second, that the Republic is located wholly within a unified Russian economic and political field. Ignoring the inherent contradictions in these two claims, Tatarstani elites argue that both Russia and Tatarstan can benefit from the Republic's sovereignty project and claim that Tatarstan is not trying to fracture Russia's sovereign presence in the international arena but rather to expand it by adding new Tatarstani spaces of sovereignty in the international system to it.

While it is in Tatarstan's interests to make its international activities more palatable to Russian federal and international audiences by representing them in a win–win fashion, the argument that the Republic's international sovereignty project is not a zero-sum game has theoretical merit as well. Considering the nature of the post-cold war international system and Russia's need to find new ways to act within it, a sovereignty-sharing arrangement between Tatarstan and Russia in the international arena could be beneficial for both parties. While Russian officials have attempted to co-opt the Tatarstani sovereignty project to further Russia's economic development, they are somewhat sceptical of Tatarstan's claim that its sovereignty project does not represent a challenge to Russian sovereignty in the international arena. The Yeltsin administration has thus found itself walking an uneasy path regarding Tatarstan's international presence—on the one hand encouraging Tatarstan's international economic overtures in an attempt to increase the overall economic development of the Russian Federation, but also striving to limit Tatarstan's international political activities and keep them within well-defined boundaries that are mediated by the Russian state. The negotiation between Russia and Tatarstan regarding the Republic's international status is a process that exhibits both cooperative and contentious elements.

While Tatarstan's elites commenced their efforts to build direct political and economic contacts with the international community immediately after the declaration of sovereignty, they soon realized that no foreign state outside the CIS countries was willing to commit fully to economic or diplomatic ties with the Republic while its relationship to Russia was still unclear legally.[71] Tatarstani officials thus needed to convince foreign audiences that Tatarstan's economic and political relationship with Russia was stable and regularized while also attaining the maximum level of foreign policy-making authority and sovereignty for Tatarstan in the international arena. The goal of the Russian federal government, on the other hand, was to encourage the development of the international economic ties of its sub-state units while still attempting to conduct a unified Russian foreign policy and present a unified sovereign presence abroad.[72]

The concept of a bilateral agreement between Tatarstan and Russia that would include international relations powers for Tatarstan far beyond those afforded by the Russian federal treaty became the vehicle for the realization of both sides' goals.[73] The aforementioned February 1994 Agreement achieved an ambiguous, if strategic, alliance between Tatarstan and Russia in the sphere of international political and economic activity. Tatarstan received the right to make foreign economic policy 'independently', to participate in international organizations, and to sign treaties and agreements that do not contradict Russia's constitution or its international agreements. Yet the Agreement also allowed for the preservation of the unity of Russia's transportation, currency, and tariff systems by relegating decisions in these areas to the joint jurisdiction of Russia and Tatarstan. The levels of Tatarstan's yearly oil export levels also fell under joint jurisdiction, while the Russian Federation alone retained the right to make decisions on war and peace.[74]

The February 1994 Agreement allowed Russian officials to declare that the fundamental unity of the Russian state had been preserved, especially in the areas of military and defence policy. It also enabled Tatarstani officials to assure potential foreign economic partners both that Tatarstan possessed the right to conduct its own foreign policy independently *and* that the basic unity of Russian economic and political space was legally ensured.[75] Since the signing of the Agreement Tatarstani officials have characterized their foreign activities as 'fully independent' but still 'coordinated with', and 'in the same channel' as, Russia's foreign policy.[76] These reassurances, which attempt to gloss over the ambiguities present in the February 1994 document, are aimed at both international audiences (potential investors, international organizations) and the Russian federal government.

The ambiguous situation of sovereignty-sharing in the area of foreign economic policy created by the February 1994 Agreement has proven beneficial to both Russia and Tatarstan. For example, in 1996 Tatarstan ranked third behind Moscow and Nizhni Novgorod in terms of levels of foreign investment, and was rated by one survey as having the most favourable climate for foreign investment in the entire Russian Federation.[77] One of the most visible results of the February 1994 Agreement was a series of meetings between Tatarstani officials and US political and economic elites arranged by Russian prime minister Viktor Chernomyrdin, including a meeting between US vice-president Al Gore and Tatarstan's first deputy prime minister, Ravil Muratov, in Washington in September 1996. These contacts led to the opening of a joint General Motors (GM)–Tatarstani auto plant in Tatarstan in December 1996 in which the Russian Federation, Tatarstan, and GM are all equal investors.[78] Muratov directly attributed the success of this venture to the February 1994 Agreement, revealing that Tatarstan had desired a top-level reception in the United States 'for many years' but that such meetings were not deemed possible until after the Russian–Tatarstani agreement, when the United States came to understand that Tatarstan was a 'solid partner' and not 'separatist'.[79]

However, despite economic policy successes such as the GM deal, the February 1994 Agreement has not resolved the basic inherent tensions between Tatarstan and Russia concerning the nature of Tatarstan's international sovereignty project. Especially after Yevgeni Primakov became Russia's minister of foreign affairs in late 1995, Moscow has actively moved to regain control over Tatarstan's *political* ambitions in the international arena. Primakov has stated that, while Russia will 'solicit input' from the regions, and will seek to promote the regions' interests abroad, Russia's regional leaders should follow Moscow's lead in foreign policy and stop 'acting outside their competencies' by conducting independent policies which are in essence illegal and amount to 'international freelancing'.[80]

Inspired by Primakov's hard-line approach, in April 1997 the Russian Federation Duma voted 318 to 10 to adopt the first draft of a law aimed at 'regularizing' the international ties of Russian Federation member units and subjecting them to closer federal control. In introducing the legislation, the chair of the Duma Committee on Foreign Affairs, Vladimir Lukin, specifically targeted Tatarstan, asserting that the Republic's claims to being an independent subject of international law 'didn't really mean anything' and that they were 'just a dream'.[81]

In spite of this growing Russian opposition, Tatarstan has remained committed to finding independent political and spaces for itself in the international arena. Tatarstani response to the Russian Duma's April 1997 legislation has been intense. As if in direct response to Russian attempts to assert more control over Tatarstan's international activities, in April 1997 Tatarstani negotiators signed lucrative contracts to sell Tatarstani-produced helicopters, trucks, and planes to Malaysia and Colombia,[82] while a popular Kazan' newspaper warned that 'Tatarstan would not agree to a ban on acting like a subject of international law', and Tatarstani president Shaimiyev reminded Russia in a public interview in June 1997 that in the post-Soviet era Tatarstan would never again 'take dictation from the centre'.[83]

Russia's insistence that Tatarstan stop its 'international freelancing' and its calls for a more unified Russian foreign policy are clear attempts to enforce limits on Tatarstan's international sovereignty project. Another way Russia has attempted to curb Tatarstan's international ambitions is to channel the Republic's international political ambitions into the EU's regional institutions such as the Assembly of the Regions of Europe. The most clear example of this policy is the appointment of Tatarstan's vice-president, Likhachev, as Russia's permanent representative to the EU in May 1998. By encouraging Tatarstan and other Russian regions to participate in these specifically *regional* European institutions, Russia is hoping to contain Tatarstan's desire for 'sovereign statehood' within Europe, and to curb any international ambitions of Tatarstan beyond those boundaries and institutions.

It is not clear that Tatarstan's leadership will be content to limit its international sovereignty project to increased participation in the EU's regional institutions. Furthermore, conditions of the changing international system, namely the growing need for states to adapt to transnational and plurilateral networks of production and governance, may favour Tatarstan as it continues its international sovereignty project. As is becoming more true for all states, devolving some aspects of state sovereignty by allowing or even encouraging sub-state units like Tatarstan to deepen their participation in transnational economic networks and political institutions, such as those of the EU, may in fact be the only hope that the severely weakened Russian central state has of transforming itself and integrating itself into the post-cold war international system in an effective way. There is cause to believe that situations of 'divided and messy' state sovereignty like that evolving between Tatarstan and Russia will continue to occur with more frequency in the post-cold war era, and that in fact it is precisely these types of shared sovereignty arrangements that will help states to flourish in the new global context.[84] As such, the achievements of Tatarstan's international sovereignty project may be seen as an example of the possibilities that exist for creative international sovereignty regimes in multicultural or federal states. As one author has stated: 'An increasingly diverse set of "sovereign" state structures will not adversely affect formal sovereign equality at the international level, and such diversity is more likely to respond to the needs of the individuals and groups within each state who are theoretically the repository of ultimate sovereign authority.'[85]

Yet, as the reluctance of some elements in the Russian government to allow Tatarstan comfortably to occupy more independent spaces in the international arena indicates, creating spaces of sovereignty for sub-state units and crafting sovereignty-sharing regimes in federated states is a fundamentally contentious process. Several elements of the Tatarstani sovereignty project help to illustrate the factors that complicate this process. They include the role of international norms and the international community's role in motivating sub-state sovereignty projects and producing sub-state sovereignty. These are discussed in the next section.

Engaging the International Community: Discourses of Legitimization in the Tatarstani Sovereignty Project

Tatarstan's efforts to project sovereignty in the international arena undoubtedly have an instrumental aspect, but they are also informed by international normative discourses about sovereign statehood. Here I discuss both these aspects in turn. To understand the instrumental aspects of Tatarstan's actions, it is necessary to remember that because Tatarstan declared itself a sovereign state while still formally a sub-state unit, its elites must simultaneously work to produce sovereignty within the Russian Federation and domestically in Tatarstan, as well as in the international arena. The support of the international community is thus a valuable resource for Tatarstan as it seeks to remake its relationship with the Russian Federation and to consolidate its position over domestic society in Tatarstan, and is also a powerful defence against Russian efforts to dismantle the Tatarstani sovereignty project.[86] As was discussed above, the most prominent example of how Tatarstan is attempting to use its new contacts with the international community to shore up its sovereignty projects in the Russian federal and domestic spheres concerns the newly adopted Tatarstani law on citizenship.

Despite these instrumentalist aspects of the Republic's international sovereignty project, it is clear that Tatarstan is pursuing sovereignty as an end in itself. Tatarstan's project is also clearly a process that is informed by international normative discourses about statehood and self-determination, not just self-interest. Furthermore, the discourses which Tatarstan's leadership has used in relation to the international community reveal the extent to which ethnicity informs Tatarstan's international sovereignty project. By extension, Tatarstan's sovereignty project also highlights the confused nature of the current international sovereignty regime, where the rules governing the legitimization of claims to sovereign statehood are unclear.

Tatarstan's international aspirations are couched both in a nationalist discourse about the right of the ethnic Tatar people to regain their lost statehood and in discourses about Tatarstan's empirical fitness for sovereign statehood. The evidence presented by Tatarstan of its 'empirical fitness' for statehood include proclaimed adherence to democratic norms and international human rights conventions, especially a commitment to civic multiculturalism and the right of the 'entire multi-ethnic people of Tatarstan' to self-determination. This uneasy coexistence between an 'ethnic Tatar' and a 'civic Tatarstani' legitimization for sovereign statehood and international subjecthood reflects the ongoing tension in the international community concerning the normative basis for the recognition of sovereign statehood in the post-cold war era—civic statehood or ethnic nationhood.[87]

The historical memory of an independent ethnic Tatar statehood which existed outside the framework of the Russian state has become an important part of the project to construct international sovereignty for post-Soviet Tatarstan. The history of Tatar statehood, including the state of Great Bulgar (ninth to thirteenth centuries) and the Kazan' khanate, has been consciously evoked by modern-day Tatarstani officials in their performances of international sovereignty.[88] For example, when Tatar president Shaimiyev gave a public address at Harvard University in October 1994, he referred to the legacy of the Kazan' khanate and claimed that Tatarstan was destined to lead the activity of remaking the Russian Federation in the post-Soviet period because 'Tatarstan has always had a very strong statehood.'[89] In 1997 Shaimiyev told Russia and the international community not to forget that a thousand years ago Great Bulgar was considered the 'strongest state in Europe' and that the Tatar people have 'never made peace' with the loss of their ancient statehood to Russia in 1552. Only now, since sovereignty had been declared and was being fulfilled, Shaimiyev argued, 'has history been righted'. He went on to proclaim that, while there was no ethnic discrimination in Tatarstan, Tatarstan was the spiritual homeland of the Tatar people, and as such was the legitimate state with which the Tatar nation could 'make its life as it sees fit'.[90]

These arguments illustrate an understanding of sovereignty and statehood among the political elites of Tatarstan that is predicated on a nationalist interpretation of the norm of self-determination. They reflect the belief that the ethnic Tatar nation has legitimate claims to statehood and participation in the international community through the vehicle of modern-day Tatarstan, and that the sovereignty project in Tatarstan is informed to some degree by ethno-nationalist concerns.

However, Tatarstan has also attempted to legitimize its performance of sovereign statehood for the international community by pursuing a policy of 'anticipatory adaptation'—attempting to identify Tatarstan with the dominant norms governing the most important international institutions in the post-cold war period in the hopes that those institutions will consider Tatarstan for some form of membership or participation.[91] In an effort to stress the Republic's empirical fitness for membership in the international community, its leadership has attempted to link Tatarstan with international norms concerning democracy and human rights, especially by asserting Tatarstan's commitment to civic multiculturalism and arguing that its sovereignty is fundamentally based on the right of the Republic's *multinational* citizenry to self-determination. This discourse also emphasizes Tatarstan's high levels of political and economic development and stability as evidence of their empirical fitness for sovereign statehood.

Tatarstan's political elites have publicly asserted the Republic's commitment to fulfilling international legal norms concerning democracy and human rights on numerous occasions. For example, Article 62 of the constitution of Tatarstan states that international law has precedence on the territory of the Republic of Tatarstan. In a clear example of anticipatory adaptation Tatarstani officials proudly declared at the UNESCO conference in Kazan' in 1993 that Tatarstan, while 'not even being a separate member of international agreements', had already 'taken upon itself' the responsibilities and duty to fulfil internationally accepted normative standards of human rights and democracy.[92] Shaimiyev's assertion in summer 1997 that Tatarstan would unilaterally move to ratify all existing European conventions on democracy and human rights is another example of Tatarstan's attempt to project sovereignty in the international arena through anticipatory adaptation.

Tatarstan has also attempted to highlight its commitment to international norms about democracy and human rights by emphasizing the civic and multicultural nature of its international sovereignty project. The March 1992 referendum concerning Tatarstan's status as a sovereign state and subject of international law was justified as allowing the 'entire people of Tatarstan' to express its will to self-determination.[93] Furthermore, at a round-table discussion between Russian federal and Tatarstani officials in Kazan' in August 1992 Tatarstani vice-president Likhachev asserted that Tatarstan's foreign policy must 'proceed from the broadest interests of Tatarstan's multinational people'.[94] In his many public pronouncements and publications on the subject of Tatarstan's sovereignty, one of Tatarstani president Shaimiyev's closest advisers, Rafael Khakimov, has stated that Tatarstan's claims to sovereign statehood 'are not based on ethnicity or the ethnic idea', but rather on the idea of full self-determination for the entire multinational people of Tatarstan in a democratic state framework.[95]

Tatarstan's political elites have also used arguments about the Republic's empirical fitness for statehood to legitimize its performance of sovereignty for the international community. Vice-President Likhachev has consistently argued that 'according to the objective criteria' used by the UN and other international organizations to determine membership and participation rights, such as economic and political development, Tatarstan has 'undeniable and very legitimate international potential'.[96] Tatarstan's democratic political system and economic stability also play a prominent part in President Shaimiyev's official discourse about sovereignty, making their way into most of his public pronouncements concerning the sovereignty project.[97]

The fact that Tatarstan's political elites have chosen to moderate their ethnic claims to sovereignty and statehood by placing them within a broader claim to empirical sovereignty indicates an understanding that the international community has generally rejected ethnic claims to self-determination when they are couched in demands for territorial statehood based on ethnic criteria.[98] It illustrates the belief that these other normative discourses must supplement the national self-determination argument in Tatarstan's sovereignty project. This lends credence to the argument that in the post-cold war era the international community has grown wary of the tragedies spawned by the failure of post-colonial quasi-states and the proliferation of ethnic claims to statehood (most notably the former Yugoslavia), and suggests that in the post-cold war period the international community will be more receptive to arguments of empirical fitness for statehood than ethnic claims to nationhood when legitimizing claims to state sovereignty.[99]

Conclusions

Like the micro-states of Andorra or Micronesia, or the ambiguous semi-states of Taiwan, Scotland, and Quebec, Tatarstan's international experience in the post-Soviet period forces us to recognize the variety and degrees of sovereign statehood as it is practised by those who claim to possess it or who are actively pursuing it. Tatarstan's example also leads us to recognize that there are substantial new opportunities for sub-states to project both economic and political state sovereignty in the post-cold war international system, particularly in the political institutions of the EU as well as the ever-expanding web of transnational economic networks, and that some Russian sub-state units are eager to take advantage of these opportunities alongside their European regional counterparts. This discussion has also demonstrated that Tatarstan's elites are committed to finding ever more political and economic niches in the international arena within which the Republic can project itself 'as sovereign'. At the same time the chapter has illustrated that Tatarstan's international activism provides Moscow with a potentially useful way to integrate Russia more deeply into Europe and the international community, if federation leaders can find a way to encourage the aspects of Tatarstan's international sovereignty project that benefit the Russian state as a whole, while minimizing the centrifugal tendencies which are always present in sub-state sovereignty-seeking behaviour. Watching the evolution of this complex relationship between the international community, Tatarstan, and Russia more closely will generate important insights into the ongoing debates about how sovereign statehood is produced and practised in the international arena in the post-cold war era, and how Russia will participate in the global community in the wake of communism.

NOTES

1. See generally R. Jackson, *Quasi-States: Sovereignty, International Relations and the Third World* (Cambridge: Cambridge University Press, 1990); A. Wendt, 'Anarchy is What States Make of It', *International Organization*, 46 (1992), 395–429; J. Barkin and B. Cronin, 'The State versus the Nation: Changing Norms and the Rules of Sovereignty in International Relations', *International Organization*, 48/1 (1994), 107–30; J. Bartelson, *A Genealogy of Sovereignty* (Cambridge: Cambridge University Press, 1995); R. Keohane, 'Hobbes's Dilemma and Institutional Change in World Politics: Sovereignty in International Society', in H. H. Holm and G. Sorenson (eds.), *Whose World Order: Uneven Globalization and the End of the Cold War* (Boulder, Colo.: Westview Press, 1995); J. Thomson, 'State Sovereignty in International Relations: Bridging the Gap between Theory and Empirical Research', *International Studies Quarterly*, 39 (1995), 213–33; T. Biersteker and C. Weber (eds.), *State Sovereignty as Social Construct* (Cambridge: Cambridge University Press, 1997); O. Osterud, 'The Narrow Gate: Entry to the Club of Sovereign States', *Review of International Studies*, 23 (1997), 167–84; G. Sorenson, 'An Analysis of Contemporary Statehood: Consequences for Conflict and Cooperation', *Review of International Studies*, 23 (1997), 253–69.
2. See L. F. Damrosch (ed.), *Enforcing Restraint* (New York: Council of Foreign Relations Press, 1993); G. Lyons and M. Mastanduno (eds.), *Beyond Westphalia? State Sovereignty and International Intervention* (Baltimore: Johns Hopkins University Press, 1995); C. Weber, *Simulating Sovereignty: Intervention, the State, and Symbolic Exchange* (Cambridge: Cambridge University Press, 1995).
3. See R. Keohane and S. Hoffman (eds.), *The New European Community* (Boulder, Colo.: Westview Press, 1991); R. Keohane, J. Nye, and S. Hoffman (eds.), *After the Cold War: International Institutions and State Strategies in Europe, 1989–1991* (Cambridge, Mass.: Harvard University Press, 1993); M. Mann, 'Nation-States in Europe and Other Continents: Diversifying, Developing, not Dying', *Daedalus*, 3 (1993), 115–40; J. Habermas, 'The European Nation-State—Its Achievements and its Limits', in G. Balakrishnan (ed.), *Mapping the Nation* (London: Verso 1996); J. Newhouse, 'Europe's Rising Regionalism', *Foreign Affairs*, 76/1 (1997), 64–84; Sorenson, 'Analysis of Contemporary Statehood'.
4. See M. Halperin and D. J. Scheffer, *Self-Determination in the New World Order* (Washington, DC: Carnegie Endowment for International Peace, 1992); G. Gottlieb, *Nation against State* (New York: Council on Foreign Relations

Press, 1993); M. Barnett, 'The New United Nations Politics of Peace: From Juridical Sovereignty to Empirical Sovereignty', *Global Governance*, 1 (1995), 79–97; R. Jackson, 'International Community beyond the Cold War', in Lyons and Mastanduno (eds.), *Beyond Westphalia?*; G. Simpson, 'The Diffusion of Sovereignty: Self-Determination in the Post-Colonial Age', *Stanford Journal of International Law*, 255 (1996), 255–86; D. Horowitz, 'Self-Determination: Politics, Philosophy, and Law', in M. Moore (ed.), *National Self-Determination and Secession* (Oxford: Oxford University Press, 1998).

5. Some notable attempts to address this issue are B. Hocking (ed.), *Foreign Relations and Federal States* (London: St Martin's Press, 1993); B. Jones and M. Keating (eds.), *The European Union and the Regions* (Oxford: Oxford University Press, 1995); H. Hannum, *Autonomy, Sovereignty, and Self-Determination: The Accommodation of Conflicting Rights* (Philadelphia: University of Pennsylvania Press, 1996); M. Keating, *Nations against the State: The New Politics of Nationalism in Quebec, Catalonia, and Scotland* (London: St Martin's Press, 1996).

6. Tatarstan declared sovereignty on 30 Aug. 1990. For the text of this document in English, see *Suverennyi Tatarstan*, ('Sovereign Tatarstan'), F. Mukhametshin and R. Ismailov, (eds.) (Moscow: Plenipotentiary Representation of the Republic of Tatarstan to the Russian Federation and INSAN, 1997), 9–10.

7. During the 'parade of sovereignties' of 1990–1 various of the ethnic and non-ethnic constituent members of the Russian Federation declared themselves to be sovereign states. The Russian Federation is made up of eighty-eight constituent units, eighty-nine if Chechnya is counted. Twenty-one of these units are so-called 'national republics', named for an ethnic titular minority group residing in that group; eleven are 'autonomous *okrugs*', also bearing an ethnic designation; fifty-five units are non-ethnic administrative entities known as *okrugs* and *oblasts*; while the two largest cities of Moscow and St Petersburg enjoy *oblast* status. On the parade of sovereignties, see A. Sheehy, 'Fact Sheet on Sovereignty', *RFE/RL Report on the USSR*, 1/44 (9 Nov. 1990), 23–5.

8. For the best overview of Tatar history currently available in English, see A. A. Rorlich, *The Volga Tatars: A Profile in National Resilience* (Stanford, Calif.: Hoover Institution Press, 1986).

9. M. Barnett, 'Sovereignty, Nationalism, and Regional Order in the Arab States System', in T. Biersteker and C.Weber (eds.), *State Sovereignty as Social Construct* (Cambridge: Cambridge University Press, 1996), 176–7.

10. See C. McNeely, *Constructing the Nation-State* (Westport, Conn.: Greenwood Press, 1995); Biersteker and Weber (eds.), *State Sovereignty as Social Construct*; C. Tilly, 'The State of Nationalism', *Critical Review*, 10/2 (1996), 299–306.

11. That sovereignty has both an internal and external dimension appears to be one of the axiomatic concepts governing the usage of the term. For an interesting overview and discussion of the internal and external dimensions of sovereignty, see Bartelson, *Genealogy of Sovereignty*, ch. 2.

12. I. Lustick, *Unsettled States, Disputed Lands: Britain and Ireland, France and Algeria, Israel and the West Bank–Gaza* (Ithaca, NY: Cornell University Press, 1993), 23–4; Simpson, 'The Diffusion of Sovereignty'.

13. S. Haggard, M. Levy, A. Moravcsik, and K. Nicolaides, 'Integrating the Two Halves of Europe', in Keohane *et al.* (eds.), *After the Cold War*, 182; Keohane, 'Hobbes's Dilemma', 176–7.

14. Hannum, *Autonomy, Sovereignty, and Self-Determination*, 16–17.

15. See P. Cerny, 'Plurilateralism: Structural Differentiation and Functional Conflict in the Post-Cold War World Order', *Millennium*, 22/1 (1993), 27–51; Mann,

'Nation-States in Europe'; Holm and Sorenson (eds.), *Whose World Order*; Keohane, 'Hobbes's Dilemma'; S. Strange, *Retreat of the State*, (Cambridge: Cambridge University Press, 1996); Sorenson, 'Analysis of Contemporary Statehood'.

16. Sorenson, 'Analysis of Contemporary Statehood', 261–4.
17. Jones and Keating (eds.), *European Union and the Regions*; Newhouse, 'Europe's Rising Regionalism'.
18. See n. 15 above.
19. This calls into question the prominent belief that the Russian regions' declarations of sovereignty in the post-Soviet period are motivated only by instrumental concerns. See D. Triesman, 'The Politics of Intergovernmental Transfers in Post-Soviet Russia', *British Journal of Political Science*, 26 (1996), 299–335; D. Triesman, 'Russia's Ethnic Revival: The Separatist Activism of Regional Leaders in a Postcommunist Order', *World Politics*, 49 (1997), 212–49; and D. Triesman, 'Fiscal Redistribution in a Fragile Federation: Moscow and the Regions in 1994', *British Journal of Political Science*, 28 (1998), 185–222.
20. Halperin and Scheffer, *Self-Determination in the New World Order*; Barkin and Cronin, 'State versus the Nation'; Barnett, 'New United Nations Politics of Peace'; Simpson, 'The Diffusion of Sovereignty'; Osterud, 'The Narrow Gate'.
21. Habermas, 'The European Nation-State'; Keating, *Nations against the State*.
22. Mann, 'Nation-States in Europe'; J. Duursma, *Fragmentation and the International Relations of Micro-States* (Cambridge: Cambridge University Press, 1996); Hannum, *Autonomy, Sovereignty and Self-Determination*; Keating, *Nations against the State*.
23. Wendt, 'Anarchy is What States Make of It', 416–17.
24. Weber, *Simulating Sovereignty*, 3; Tilly, 'State of Nationalism', 304–5; Jackson, *Quasi-States*, 3–4 (Jackson is quoting Jacob Burckhardt); J. Migdal, A. Kohli, and V. Shue, 'Introduction: Developing a State-in-Society Perspective', in J. Migdal, A. Kohli, and V. Shue (eds.), *State Power and Social Forces: Domination and Transformation in the Third World* (Cambridge: Cambridge University Press, 1994), 11–12; D. Sayer, 'Everyday Forms of State Formation: Some Dissident Remarks on "Hegemony"', in J. M. Gilbert and D. Nugent (eds.), *Everyday Forms of State Formation* (Durham, NC: Duke University Press, 1994), 371 (Sayer is quoting Philip Abrams); Lustick, *Unsettled States, Disputed Lands*, 34; Barnett, 'Sovereignty, Nationalism, and Regional Order', 176–7.
25. Biersteker and Weber (eds.), *State Sovereignty as Social Construct*, 12.
26. Barkin and Cronin, *State versus the Nation*.
27. Horowitz, 'Self-Determination, Politics, Philosophy, and Law', 437.
28. See Halperin and Scheffer, *Self-Determination in the New World Order*, 33–7.
29. Horowitz, 'Self-Determination, Politics, Philosophy, and Law', 422.
30. Simpson, 'The Diffusion of Sovereignty', 284.
31. Barnett, 'The New United Nations Politics of Peace'; Osterud, 'The Narrow Gate'.
32. Cerny, 'Plurilateralism', 27; Keohane, 'Hobbes's Dilemma', 177; Sorenson, 'Analysis of Contemporary Statehood', 262. Also see Strange, *Retreat of the State*.
33. See nn. 3 and 5 above.
34. This is the wording of the Mar. 1992 referendum on sovereignty in Tatarstan, and has since become the most used description of the goals of the sovereignty project in Tatarstan, appearing in official speeches about sovereignty and in interviews given by prominent Tatarstani elites about the efforts to construct sovereignty. See *Zayavleniye Presiduma Verkhovnogo Soveta Republiki Tatarstan* ('Announcement of the Presidium of the Supreme Soviet of the Republic of

Tatarstan') 6 Mar. 1992; repr. in R. Khakimov (ed.), *Belaya kniga Tatarstana: Put' k suverenitetu 1990–1995* ('White Book of Tatarstan: The Path to Sovereignty 1990–1995'), special issue, *Panorama-Forum*, 5/8 (1996), 14–15.

35. For coverage of Tatarstan's refusal to sign the Russian Federal Treaty and the Tatarstani referendum on sovereignty, see *Current Digest of the Post-Soviet Press*, 11 (1992), 21–2; and 12, 6–8; and *New York Times*, 21 and 23 Mar. 1992. Also see A. Sheehy, 'Tatarstan Asserts its Sovereignty', *RFE/RL Report on the USSR*, 1/14 (3 Apr. 1992), 1–4.

36. It is interesting to note that at the same time Tatarstan was formulating its own plans for a referendum on sovereignty in Mar. 1992, Bosnia-Herzegovina was also conducting a referendum on independence, which had been requested by the European Community (EC) as one of the criteria for Bosnia's recognition as an independent state by the (EC). While I have no evidence linking the two events, it seems likely that the Tatarstani government was aware of the legitimizing potential of such referendums. See Halperin and Scheffer, *Self-Determination in the New World Order*, 35.

37. See *Zayavleniye*, 14–16.

38. See *Postanovleniye Verkhovnogo Soveta Respubliki Tatarstan O merakh po realizatsii gosudarstvennogo suvereniteta Respubliki Tatarstan*. ('Announcement of the Supreme Soviet of the Republic of Tatarstan about Measures for the Realization of the State Sovereignty of the Republic of Tatarstan'), 21 Mar. 1992; repr. in R. Khakimov (ed.), *Belaya kniga Tatarstana*, 15–17.

39. The text of the constitution is available in *Suverennyi Tatarstan*, 241–80.

40. It is significant that in the Tatarstani press the Feb. 1994 Agreement is always referred to as a 'treaty-type' agreement, indicating that it is considered to be an agreement among two sovereign states regulated by international law. On the negotiations surrounding the agreement and the significance of the agreement, see E. Teague, 'Russia and Tatarstan Sign Power-Sharing Treaty', *RFE/RL Research Report*, 3/14 (8 Apr. 1992), 19–27. The text of the agreement is available in English in *Suverennyi Tatarstan*, 40–6.

41. *Suverennyi Tatarstan*, 87.

42. The protocol for Tatarstan's conduct of foreign economic activity was outlined in a separate agreement, also signed on 15 Feb. 1994. In this agreement the two parties agreed to 'coordinate' their formation of foreign economic policy. According to this document, the determination of export quotas, payment credit regimes with foreign partners, and licensing of the sale of Tatarstani products abroad belong to the 'joint authority' of Tatarstan and the Russian Federation. Tatarstan itself has exclusive authority to conclude trade and economic agreements with foreign states; to guarantee and oversee the usage of foreign state, bank, and commercial credits; to form a currency fund of the Republic of Tatarstan; to develop a separate policy of attracting foreign investment to Tatarstan; to participate in the work of international financial organizations; and to establish free economic zones in Tatarstan. See *Suverennyi Tatarstan*, 73–5.

43. See McNeely, *Constructing the Nation-State*.

44. See D. M. Ishakov (ed.), *Tatarstan-Strana gorodov* ('Tatarstan-Country of Cities'), (Naberezhnye Chelny: Krona, 1993), 3–5.

45. *Izvestiya Tatarstan*, 29 Nov. 1994; *Respublika Tatarstan*, 29 Nov. 1994.

46. *Molodezh Tatarstana*, 11 Oct. 1996.

47. *Respublika Tatarstan*, 23 and 26 Nov. 1996.

48. *Vremya i Dengi*, 18 Mar. 1997; *Republika Tatarstan*, 17 June 1997.

49. This clause is presumably for ethnic Tatars who might feel a connection to Tatarstan as the historic homeland of the Tatar people, although it is open to all

nationalities. Tatarstan also announced that it will issue its own internal passports, which will indicate the holder's ethnicity. For more on the history of the Tatarstani citizenship law, see the *Jamestown Monitor On-Line Report*, 9 Feb. 1998, and the *Radio Free Europe/Radio Liberty Newsline On-Line Report*, 26 Feb. 1998.

50. *Radio Free Europe/Radio Liberty Tatar–Bashkir Service*, 21 and 28 Apr. 1998.
51. See the *RFE/RL Newsline* (on-line news report), 2/86, 6 May 1998.
52. See M. Sabirov, 'Market Economy and State Regulation', *Passport to the New World* (Moscow: Mar.–Apr. 1994), 15.
53. For example, two months after the Declaration of Sovereignty, in Oct. 1990, then prime minister of Tatarstan M. G. Sabirov led a delegation from Tatarstan's huge oil conglomerate TATNEFT to the United States to discuss economic cooperation (*Sovetskaya Tatariya*, 31 Oct. 1990, 1).
54. Tatarstan signed the earliest of these agreements with the Baltic countries and Belarus (in late 1992) and signed others with Hungary and Turkey in 1993. For a partial list of these agreements, see Apparat Prezidenta Respubliki Tatarstan, *Tatarskii mir: Informatsionno–statisticheskii spravochnik* ('Tatar World: Informational–Statistical Handbook') (Kazan': 1995), 68–9.
55. *Izvestiya Tatarstan*, 31 Jan. 1995.
56. *Izvestiya Tatarstan*, 16 Mar. 1995; *Vremya i Dengi*, 28 Mar. 1996 and 9 July 1996.
57. See the full Programme on Social and Economic Development as published in F. Mukhametshin (ed.), *Respublika Tatarstan: Vremya bolshikh peremen* ('Republic of Tatarstan: Time of Great Changes') (Kazan': Cabinet of Ministers of the Republic of Tatarstan, 1996).
58. These laws provide large tax breaks to foreign investors, allow foreign partners to own the land that the enterprises they invest in are located on, and provide guarantees against nationalization backed up by Tatarstan's government and national bank. The new laws on foreign investment are reprinted in *Suverennyi Tatarstan*, 190–9.
59. *Izvestiya Tatarstan*, 20 Oct. 1993.
60. *Tatarstan*, Mar.–Apr. 1995, 44–5.
61. *Izvestiya Tatarstan*, 1 Mar. 1995.
62. *Ukaz Prezidenta Respubliki Tatarstan no. 183: O sozdanii Departamenta Vneshnikh Svyazei Prezidenta Respubliki Tatarstan* ('Decree of the President of Tatarstan no. 183: On the Founding of the Department of Foreign Relations of the President of the Republic of Tatarstan'); repr. in *Vedomosti Verkhovnogo Soveta Tatarstana* ('Proceedings of the Supreme Soviet of Tatarstan') (Kazan': Supreme Soviet of Tatarstan, July–Aug. 1995), 31–4.
63. *Ploshchad Svobody*, 15 June 1997, 6–7.
64. See Lustick, *Unsettled States, Disputed Lands*, 38.
65. *Foreign Broadcast Information Service Report on Central Eurasia*, 5 July 1995, 42–3.
66. *Vremya i Dengi*, 20 Feb. 1996.
67. *Respublika Tatarstan*, 17 June 1997. For a discussion of other sub-state participation in all-European structures, see Jones and Keating (eds.), *The European Union and the Regions*; and Newhouse, 'Europe's Rising Regionalism'.
68. The newest of these brochures, printed in London by Flint River Press and jointly published by the Chamber of Commerce of the Republic of Tatarstan, is *Tatarstan: Path-Breaker in Political and Economic Reform* (London: Flint River Press, 1996). Also see the issue of Aeroflot's in-flight magazine devoted to Tatarstan, *Passport to the New World* (Moscow: Mar.–Apr. 1994).
69. *Foreign Broadcast Information Service Report on Central Eurasia*, 19 Aug. 1994, 27.

70. *KRIS*, 1 Nov. 1996.
71. *Current Digest of the Post-Soviet Press*, 37 (1992), 5.
72. Ibid., 46 (1992), 21–2. At a conference about Russian federalism in Kazan' in June 1996, a top official of the Russian Ministry of Foreign Affairs admitted that in the early 1990s the Russian regions had surprised the centre with their vigorous foreign policy initiatives. They, especially Tatarstan, had forced the centre to try to 'make some order' out of the *de facto* independent foreign policies of the regions. See 'Ostrye Grani Federalizma' ('Sharp Edges of Federalism'), *Tatarstan* (Oct. 1996), 15–16.
73. As Tatar vice-president Vasili Likhachev announced in 1992, 'a bi-lateral treaty with Russia will be a powerful impetus for the international recognition of Tatarstan and for the development of foreign economic relations', *Current Digest of the Post-Soviet Press*, 37 (1992), 5.
74. According to one of the related treaties also signed on 15 Feb. 1994, the Tatarstani government is to be consulted about the deployment of Russian Federation troops in Tatarstan and about issues of defence production in Tatarstan.
75. *Izvestiya Tatarstana*, 15 Nov. 1995; *Vremya i Dengi*, 30 Jan. 1996. Also see the address Tatarstan's prime minister Farid Mukhametshin gave to an audience of German businessmen and politicians in Germany in Sept. 1995; repr. in *Tatarstan* (Feb. 1996), 3–11.
76. *Foreign Broadcast Information Service Report on Central Eurasia*, 19 Aug. 1994, 27, and 5 July 1995, 42–3.
77. Survey conducted by the firm Pioneer First, reported in the on-line *OMRI Russian Regional Report*, 1/17 (18 Dec. 1996).
78. *Vremya i Dengi*, 19 and 21 Dec. 1996.
79. Ibid., 19 Sept. 1996; *Respublika Tatarstan*, 19 Sept. 1996.
80. *Monitor On-Line News Report*, 25 Jan. 1996; *OMRI On-Line News Report*, 25 Jan. 1996.
81. *Vremya i Dengi*, 24 May 1997.
82. Ibid., 10 and 17 Apr. 1997.
83. Ibid., 5 May 1997; *Respublika Tatarstan*, 17 June 1997.
84. Mann, 'Nation-States in Europe'.
85. Hannum, *Autonomy, Sovereignty and Self-Determination*, 26.
86. Charles Tilly and Michael Keating note that nationalists in Quebec, Catalonia, and the Basque country have employed the same strategies. See Tilly, 'State of Nationalism', 305, and Keating, *Nations against the State*.
87. Barkin and Cronin, 'State versus the Nation'; Habermas, 'European Nation-State'.
88. For further discussion in English of early Tatar history and the Kazan' khanate, see Rorlich, *The Volga Tatars*.
89. See *Suverennyi Tatarstan*, 53–4.
90. *Respublika Tatarstan*, 17 June 1997.
91. Haggard *et al.*, 'Integrating the Two Halves of Europe'.
92. See Ishakov (ed.), *Tatarstan–Strana gorodov*, 3–5. In an interview given in 1995 Tatarstan's vice-president, Vasili Likhachev, again noted that Tatarstan had 'voluntarily taken upon itself' the responsibilities of statehood by fulfilling international legal norms concerning democracy and human rights. He also stated that while Tatarstan had not yet formally signed any international conventions, it considered such actions 'a step for the future' (*Tatarstan* (Mar.–Apr.1995), 16–18).
93. See *Zayavleniye*, 14–16.
94. *Current Digest of the Post-Soviet Press*, 37 (1992), 5–6.

95. *Izvestiya Tatarstan*, 18 Jan. 1995. Yet Khakimov also admits that the sovereignty project of Tatarstan is informed by the historical legacy of Tatar statehood and the desire to resurrect that legacy. In 1992 he stated that it was true that 'the Tatar people have always lived with the dream of restoring their statehood' (see *Current Digest of the Post-Soviet Press*, 37 (1992), 3).

96. *Sovetskaya Tatariya*, 8 June 1993; also Ishakov (ed.), *Tatarstan–Strana gorodov*, 3–5.

97. Based on a content analysis of the President's speeches given on the anniversaries of the Declaration of Sovereignty (30 Aug.), the signing of the agreement with the Russian Federation (15 Feb.), and the adoption of the Tatarstani constitution (6 Nov.) from 1990 to 1996.

98. See L. Bucheit, *Secession: The Legitimacy of Self-Determination* (New Haven: Yale University Press, 1978); A. Buchanan, *Secession: The Morality of Political Divorce from Ft. Sumter to Lithuania and Quebec* (Boulder, Colo.: Westview Press, 1991); Simpson, 'Diffusion of Sovereignty'; Horowitz, 'Self-Determination: Politics, Philosophy, and Law'.

99. Barnett, 'The New United Nations Politics of Peace'; Osterud, 'The Narrow Gate'.

CHAPTER 14

Globalization, European Integration, and the Northern Ireland Conflict

JOHN MCGARRY

This chapter is concerned with the impact of globalization and European integration on the Northern Ireland conflict and its resolution. By 'globalization', I refer to a number of related phenomena: the development of global communications (satellite television and the internet); the increased mobility of labour, goods, and capital; the new move to integrated economies within regional economic associations (the European Union (EU), North American Free Trade Area, Association of South East Asian Nations (ASEAN), Mercosur); the development of supra-state political institutions (the EU, North Atlantic Treaty Organization (NATO)); the spread of democratic and human rights norms; and an emerging global regime, in which international action in defence of these norms is countenanced against 'sovereign' states. 'European integration' covers aspects of these phenomena that are focused on Europe and that involve European institutions.

There are two broad approaches to answering the question of how these developments affect, or will affect, national conflicts like Northern Ireland's. Some claim that they have identity-transforming or difference-eliminating effects. Others view them as providing a context in which differences can be more effectively managed.[1]

These two approaches are related to an important debate on the development of nationalism. On a modernist conception of the construction of nations and national forms of identity, associated with the work of Gellner, Anderson, and Hobsbawm among others, nations developed in the modern period because they were functional to the economic imperatives of modernization and the large bureaucratic state.[2] In Gellner's formulation of this argument, the modern economy and the accompanying rise of the modern bureaucratic state presupposes mass literacy, and increasingly standardized modes of communication and cultural practices. Whereas, in the pre-modern period, cultural and linguistic communities were politically irrelevant, national forms of identity become important in the modern period, because they are functional to the imperatives of industrialization and modernization. Anderson elaborates on this basic thesis: he claims that vernacular reading communities created through print capitalism came to shape the boundaries of national identities.

This description of the construction of national identities by broad economic and social forces suggests that global economies, and the institutional changes that accompany globalization, will transform nations and national identities. As states give up their powers to suprastate institutions and transnational corporations, we end up in a condition of post-modernity in which national identities become less relevant and dysfunctional and where they are superseded by other kinds of association and identity. This thesis is put forward most starkly by Hobsbawm, who argues that nationalism is largely a nineteenth-century phenomenon, associated with the construction of national economies and of declining relevance in the new economic order: 'The owl of Minerva which brings wisdom, said Hegel, flies out at dusk. It is a good sign that it is now circling around nations and nationalism.'[3]

Another variation of this argument emphasizes the role of globalization in increasing interactions among different peoples, and claims that it is this that leads to a reduction of cultural diversity, to overlapping and multiple identities, and even to the creation of a global cosmopolitan culture.[4] This view has its roots in an older argument, shared by thinkers on the left and right, that industrialization and urbanization would erode regional identities *within* states.[5]

The view that changes associated with globalization and European integration have a difference-eliminating potential is not restricted to intellectuals: it was uppermost in the minds of the statesmen who established the European Common Market. This was constructed not only, or even mainly, for its purported economic benefits, but because it was thought it would erode the rival nationalisms that had produced two world wars.[6]

X   A second and quite different view is that globalization, and especially the institutional structures that accompany it, permits us to *manage* national divisions more effectively. Thus, it has been argued that the construction of the EU has provided national minorities in

Scotland, the Basque Country, and Catalonia with the opportunity to enhance their autonomy by establishing direct links with the EU in Brussels. An increase in regional cooperation across state frontiers has allowed national groups divided by these boundaries to (re-)establish links. A new internationalized rights regime, associated in Europe with the European Court of Human Rights and the European Convention on Human Rights, has made it more difficult, though clearly far from impossible, for states to engage in the repression of minorities. Increasingly, states are becoming signatories to international treaties that commit them to respect a variety of human and minority rights. International non-governmental organizations, such as Amnesty International and Helsinki Watch, aided by technological advances in communications, are becoming more adept at exposing abuses. Multi-governmental organizations such as the Organization for Security and Cooperation in Europe, the EU, and NATO have taken steps to protect the position of particular minorities, the latter two by making respect for minority rights a prerequisite for membership. The United Nations and NATO seem increasingly prepared, in the aftermath of the cold war, to intervene directly in conflict zones, such as Bosnia, the Kurdish area of northern Iraq, and Kosovo, to enforce equitable settlements on warring national communities. Majority–minority relations, it appears, are less likely to be regarded as purely domestic matters.[7]

The view that globalization is primarily a difference-managing device does not presuppose a particular position on the debate about the history of nationalism. It is consistent with the view that nations have pre-modern origins, with roots in ancient *ethnie*.[8] It is also compatible with the modernist view that nationalism is economically functional, as long as it is accepted that its economic utility remains relevant in spite of globalization. Thus Michael Keating, who argues in Chapter 2 of this volume that globalization has several difference-managing benefits, also claims that new or re-emergent nationalisms in places like Scotland, Catalonia, and Quebec are largely attempts to ensure these territories are favourably situated in the global economy.[9] Finally, the difference-managing hypothesis is consistent with the view that globalization has not yet proceeded far enough to have difference-eliminating effects.

This debate about the origins of nationalism, and its relation to modernity and post-modernity, has affected thinking on the Northern Ireland conflict. As elsewhere, there is an influential view that identities are being transformed by the forces of globalization, and by European integration in particular. My goal in this chapter is to show the shortcomings of such thinking and to demonstrate that, while globalization has had no noticeable difference-eliminating effects, it has helped to provide a context in which differences can be more effectively managed.

Globalization and Difference Erosion in Northern Ireland

The argument that globalization and European integration are transforming, or will transform, identities in Northern Ireland, comes in both modernist and post-modernist variants.

Modernist (Irish and British) Accounts

Since the 1950s Irish nationalists have portrayed economic integration as conducive to securing unionist support for a united Ireland. This thinking was outlined by future Taoiseach Liam Cosgrave in a speech to Dáil Éireann in 1954. It played an important part in convincing Taoiseach Séan Lemass to abandon attempts at autarky in the Irish Republic, to sign a free-trade treaty with the United Kingdom, and, in 1965, to meet with Terence O'Neill, Northern Ireland's prime minister, to improve economic cooperation.[10] In a referendum on the United Kingdom's membership of the European Economic Community (EEC) in 1975, many nationalists voted yes because they thought it would weaken the border and bring a united Ireland closer.

To help convert unionists, nationalists routinely argue that European integration has made a united Ireland more attractive from an economic perspective. They claim that Ireland and the United Kingdom's joint membership of the EU means that Protestants can now accept a united Ireland without losing access to British markets, a benefit they could not be assured of when Ireland was partitioned in 1921. It is noted that the disproportionate representation of small states in EU institutions means that the north as a relatively large part of Ireland would fare better in its political capacities than it does as a small and insignificant part of the United Kingdom.[11] It is argued that all-Ireland political institutions would represent Northern Ireland's interests better in Brussels than Whitehall, given that both parts of Ireland have common and important interests in agriculture and regional policy that are not shared by Great Britain.[12] In an attempt to offset Protestant fears about losing the substantial British subvention, it is sometimes added that Europe would be prepared to finance Irish unity.[13]

This thinking was given a boost by the Single European Act of 1986, by the Maastricht Treaty of 1992, and by the recent economic performance of the 'Celtic Tiger'. From the nationalist perspective, Ireland's position on the periphery of an increasingly integrated Europe is making it more worthwhile for both parts of the island to establish all-island political institutions.[14] When, in the early 1990s, the Chair of the Northern Ireland Institute of Directors proposed an integrated 'island economy' in the context of the single market, a nationalist newspaper (the *Irish News*) lauded the plan as 'paving the way for unity'.[15] Nationalists also point to the way in which Northern Ireland's Euro MPs work together at Brussels as evidence they are latently co-nationals.[16]

While nationalists claim that European integration will erode the British identity of unionists, unionists are less optimistic that it will erode the Irish identity of nationalists. Because international public opinion tends to favour a united Ireland, unionists normally see any form of internationalization as aiding their enemies.[17] However, some unionist intellectuals argue that European integration, with its benefits of labour mobility, common European citizenship, and limited cross-border cooperation between adjacent parts of different states, has the potential to reconcile Irish nationalists to a future within the United Kingdom.[18] While an Irish cultural identity would survive, it would be shorn of much of its political nationalist content.

Post-Modernist (Europeanist) Perspectives

The post-modernist argument that continental integration will erode both Irish and British nationalism is made by a number of intellectuals. Elizabeth Meehan argued in her inaugural lecture at Queen's University in Belfast in 1992 that 'a new kind of citizenship is emerging that is neither national or cosmopolitan but which is multiple in enabling the various identities that we all possess to be expressed, and our rights and duties exercised, through an increasingly complex configuration of common institutions, states, national and transnational interest groups and voluntary associations, local or provincial authorities, regions and alliances of regions'.[19] Rupert Taylor claimed recently that 'increasing European integration has led to the erosion of absolutist conceptions of national sovereignty' and that there 'has been an erosion of ethno-nationalism on both sides, a fading of Orange and Green, in favour of a commonality around the need for genuine structures of democracy and justice'.[20] Taylor points, approvingly, to the EU's involvement in the establishment of new 'inclusive' partnerships through its peace and reconciliation programme. This funds collaboration between the voluntary community sector, local councillors, and representatives from trade unions, from both sides of the political divide and from both sides of the border.[21]

Other intellectuals have been more safely future-oriented. Kevin Boyle has expressed a belief that the 'Europeanization of both islands . . . will force a reassessment of all relationships on these islands and in particular of the two principal influences on the present tragedy of Northern Ireland, "Britishness" as an historical integrating force and the reactive tradition of Irish separatism.'[22] Richard Kearney and Robin Wilson argue that European integration will allow Northern Ireland's citizens to evolve beyond nationalism and unionism and irreconcilable loyalties to different nation-states. They envisage Europe evolving into a federation of regions, including Northern Ireland, which will foster allegiances 'both more universal and more particular than the traditional nation-states'.[23] Cathal McCall claims that European integration has the potential to erode unionism and nationalism in Northern Ireland, particularly in the absence of sectarian violence.[24]

These post-modernist arguments also have a strong normative and prescriptive component. They are based on a view of nationalism as a form of tribalism, responsible for conflict, and as a threat to democracy and the universalist values of the Enlightenment. The claim is not only that nationalism is being transcended, but that it should be. Post-modernists champion the process of European integration and globalization because of its nation-eroding powers, and they oppose policies that they see as hindering the removal of national divisions within Northern Ireland. Thus, Taylor strongly opposes the power-sharing institutions in Northern Ireland's Good Friday Agreement, in which both nationalists and unionists are given legislative vetoes, on the basis that this 'reinforces the belief in the centrality of ethno-national politics'.[25]

Dissolving Nationalisms?

As Michael Keating and I argue in our introductory chapter, modernist and post-modernist accounts of the demise of nationalism run up against observed reality. Rather than eroding minority nationalisms, globalization has contributed to their emergence (or re-emergence) in several places, such as Quebec, Scotland, Catalonia, and the Basque Country. In each of these cases, the construction of transnational regimes has provided new reasons why the nation should have its own institutions, whether to take advantage of new economic interests or to protect itself against new dangers of economic dislocation or cultural uniformity.

Globalization has also played a role in the re-emergence of nationalism in Northern Ireland. The civil rights campaign that preceded the 'Troubles' was linked to spreading international norms about human rights, and particularly to the example of the civil rights movement in the United States. The Northern Ireland Civil Rights Association used the same song, 'We shall Overcome'; the same slogan, 'one man, one vote'; the same tactics, marches and civil disobedience; and the same demand, equal rights for everyone, as its US counterpart.[26] The unionist regime's control of the minority was fatally undermined as images of policemen clubbing marchers were carried globally by satellite television.[27] The new circumstances ended Britain's traditional policy of quarantining Northern Ireland. London's intervention, and the eventual implementation of direct rule, was prompted by what Brendan O'Leary and I have described as 'the politics of embarrassment'.[28] It was in this context that Northern Ireland polarized into two rival (Irish and British) camps, as Irish nationalists (and republicans) stepped into the breach left by civil rights campaigners, and the unionist community mobilized in defence. In the resulting violence, over 3,200 people have been killed and many thousands seriously injured.

Given this violent 'inter-national' conflict, it would have been surprising if the simultaneous, often abstract, process of European integration had been able to dilute either side's national identity. That it did not is clear from evidence provided by opinion surveys and election results. The first significant survey of national identities in 1967 showed Protestants splitting between a British identity (39 per cent), an Ulster identity (32 per cent), and an Irish identity (20 per cent). Another major survey in 1978 recorded a significant increase in Protestants' Britishness, with 67 per cent choosing a British identity, compared to an Ulster identity (20 per cent) or an Irish identity (8 per cent). A third survey in 1989 showed no significant change from 1978 (68 per cent British, 10 per cent Ulster, 16 per cent Northern Irish, and 3 per cent Irish).[29] In other words, British national identity strengthened among Protestants during this period, probably as a result of the threat posed by violent Irish republicanism. Among Catholics, these surveys show consistently high support for an Irish identity. Seventy-six per cent of Catholics claimed an Irish identity in 1967 and 69 per cent did so in 1978. The proportion dropped to 60 per cent in the 1989 survey, but this was largely because a new category of 'Northern Irish' was introduced, which 25 per cent of Catholics chose.[30] A series of further surveys conducted in the 1990s show broadly similar results for both Protestants and Catholics.[31]

Northern Ireland's politics have been dominated throughout this period by nationalist and unionist political parties, as the election results in figure 14.1 indicate. Contrary to what the post-modernist thesis would suggest, the share of the vote won by parties outside the two ethno-national blocs has declined. The most important of these parties, the Alliance Party of Northern Ireland, averaged 8.4 per cent of the vote in its first five (Northern Ireland-wide) election campaigns (1973–5), but only 6 per cent in its last five election campaigns (1997–9). During the last two regional elections in 1996 and 1998, the total vote of parties outside the ethno-national blocs (Alliance, the Northern Ireland Women's Coalition, and the Labour Party) amounted to only 8.4 per cent on both occasions. While nationalist and unionist parties won an average of 82 per cent of the vote during the five elections that were held between 1973 and 1975, they have received an average of 90.6 per cent in Northern Ireland's last five elections.[32] Non-ethnic parties do poorly in all types of election including those that are based on PR-STV, an electoral system that provides more openings for small and new parties than its main alternative, the single-member plurality (SMP) system.[33]

Nor is there any evidence from electoral data of softening identities *within* either of Northern Ireland's two ethno-national communities. Before 1982 the nationalist electoral bloc was dominated by the relatively moderate Social Democratic and Labour Party (SDLP), although largely because the more radical Sinn Féin boycotted elections. Since Sinn Féin began to contest elections after the 1981 hunger strikes, however, its share of the total nationalist vote has increased noticeably. In its first five election campaigns (1982–7) it won an average of 37.3 per cent of the nationalist vote, but in its last five campaigns (1996–9) it achieved an average of 41.8 per cent.[34] As the nationalist share of Northern Ireland's vote has expanded throughout this period, Sinn Féin's success means that it is also winning a greater share of the total vote: from an average of 11.8 per cent between 1982 and 1987 to an average of 16.6 per cent between 1996 and 1999.[35] It is possible that at least some of Sinn Féin's success within the nationalist bloc is a result of the party becoming more moderate rather than voters becoming more radical. However, as Sinn Féin remains clearly a radical nationalist party, its rise in popularity is difficult to reconcile with the view that identities are softening.

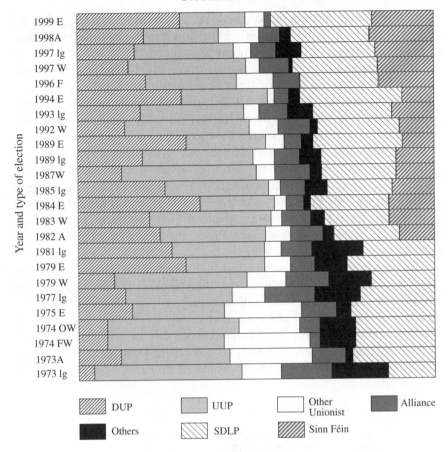

FIG. 14.1. Northern Ireland elections since 1973.
Key: E=European election, A=Assembly election, lg=local government election, W=Westminster election, F=February, O=October

Source: Nicholas Whyte, http://www.explorers.whyte.com

Within the unionist bloc, it is more difficult to measure electoral shifts between radical and moderate factions. This is because continuous fragmentation within unionism over the past thirty years has made it harder to compare party fortunes over time. It is also because there has been little to choose between the two leading unionist parties, the Democratic Unionist Party (DUP) and the Ulster Unionist Party (UUP), for much of this period, with both being equally intransigent. A gap between the two has only been apparent since the Good Friday Agreement of 1998, which was accepted, by the UUP, and rejected by the DUP. One consequence of the UUP's new 'moderation' is that its share of the UUP–DUP vote has gone down in the two elections that have been held since the Agreement was signed.[36]

If European integration was transforming Northern Ireland's politics, as Taylor has argued, one would reasonably expect this to register during election campaigns for the European Parliament. However, European elections in Northern Ireland are traditionally fought over the same constitutional issues as elections to Westminster, local government, and the Northern Ireland Assembly. The 1999 European election campaign, to take the latest case, was fought almost exclusively over the merits and demerits of the Good Friday Agreement rather than European issues. As the *Irish News* put it crudely during the campaign, 'The European election [has] nothing to do with Europe . . . [it is] about how many Prods and how many Fenians there are in the north' (11 May 1999).[37]

As Figure 14.2 indicates, the middle 'Europeanist' ground does not do any better in European elections than in other types of election in Northern Ireland. In fact, it does much worse. Whereas Alliance received 6.5 per cent of the vote in elections to the Northern Ireland Forum in 1996 and Northern Ireland Assembly in 1998, its share collapsed in the European election of 1999 to 2.1 per cent. This poor showing can be explained simply. Many of those who are prepared to

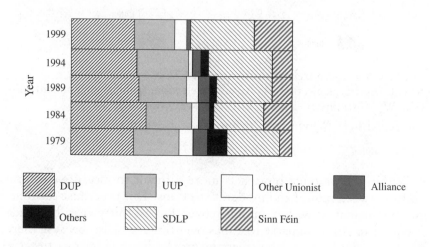

FIG. 14.2. Elections to the European Parliament

Source: Nicholas Whyte, http://www.explorers.whyte.com (following Whyte, I have included Bernardette Devlin-McAliskey's vote in 1979 as a vote for Sinn Féin).

vote for the middle ground in local government or Assembly elections, where they have some prospect of winning seats, choose to vote for nationalist or unionist parties, or to abstain, during European elections where, because of the size of the vote quota needed (169,703 in 1999), there is no prospect of electing a middle-ground candidate.

To the extent that Northern Ireland's people and politicians think about Europe at all, the tendency is for them to see it through a nationalist or unionist rather than a post-nationalist lenses. Nationalists, particularly the SDLP and its supporters,[38] endorse European integration largely for instrumental reasons, just as nationalists do in Scotland, the Basque Country, and Catalonia. For them, European integration has the advantage of eroding British sovereignty over Northern Ireland and reducing the importance of the border with the Irish Republic. It is seen, as discussed earlier, as having the potential to weaken the identity of unionists. European involvement is also welcomed because it internationalizes the conflict in a way that is generally helpful to the nationalist position. This explains why opinion surveys show nationalist voters as far more Europhile than their unionist counterparts,[39] and why nationalist politicians in the early 1990s called for the EU to be given a direct role in the internal government of Northern Ireland.[40]

Unionists are significantly more reluctant to embrace Europe, because it threatens British sovereignty and because European politicians are more sympathetic to Irish nationalism than to unionism. This reluctance is recorded in survey data (see note 39) and in the actions of unionist politicians. A strong majority of unionist MPs voted against the UK's accession to the EEC in the 1971 free vote at Westminster, and they have since allied themselves with the Euro-sceptic wing of the British Conservative Party.[41] While unionist MPs played, ironically, a crucial role in passing the Maastricht Treaty at Westminster in 1994, it was not because of latent pro-European sympathies, but rather because they knew a government defeat on this issue would mean an election, which was likely to result in a new and less sympathetic Labour government, and in the loss of their pivotal position in the British Parliament elected in 1992. Both the DUP and UUP remain Euro-sceptic.[42] Despite this, pragmatic considerations have allowed unionist politicians to participate in some European initiatives, such as sitting on cross-community partnership bodies established as part of the EU's Peace and Reconciliation programme, and to co-operate with the nationalist MEP John Hume in Brussels.[43] The MEP Ian Paisley's position on constitutional issues is ample proof that this pragmatic co-operation is not, as some would have it, evidence of weakening unionism.

The standard response of post-nationalists to the evidence presented by electoral data and party positions is that this detracts from evidence of post-national activity outside conventional politics. They claim that the preoccupation of political parties with constitutional issues has alienated significant numbers of people, who have instead channelled their energies into non-governmental organizations in what is called 'civil society'.[44] It is here, in organizations like the EU-sponsored partnership programmes, the Corrymeela Centre and All Children Together, that evidence for the transcendence of national identities is to be found.[45]

One problem with this argument is that it is not clear that Northern Ireland's people are 'alienated' from participation in conventional politics. If electoral turnout is used as a way of measuring alienation, Northern Ireland's electorate appears less alienated than Great Britain's. Turnout in local government and European elections in Northern Ireland is consistently much higher than in the rest of the United Kingdom, despite the fact that Northern Ireland's local governments have fewer powers than Great Britain's, and that Northern Ireland has more elections.[46] Turnout in elections to the Northern Ireland Forum in 1996 (64.7 per cent) and Assembly in 1998 (68.6 per cent) was higher than in the 1999 elections to the Scottish Parliament (59 per cent) and Welsh Assembly (45 per cent). Only in elections to the Westminster Parliament is turnout lower in Northern Ireland (67.4 per cent in 1997 and 69.8 per cent in 1992) than in Great Britain (71.4 and 77.9 per cent respectively).[47] Some of the variance here can be explained by the fact that elections to Westminster, unlike other elections in Northern Ireland, take place under the SMP electoral system. Given the absence of swing voters in Northern Ireland, SMP makes results fairly predictable, which can dampen enthusiasm for voting. Nor is there clear evidence that Northern Ireland's electorate has become less participatory over time: while there has been some drop-off in local government turnout over the past quarter-century, participation in European, Westminster, and Assembly or Forum elections has remained reasonably constant.[48]

Even if we focus on civil society, as post-nationalists suggest, it is not clear that it is above the ethno-national fray. The two most popular mass organizations, the Orange Order and Gaelic Athletic Association, are partisan unionist and nationalist respectively. Shane O'Neill observes that even Northern Ireland's politically active feminists, and activists from its gay and lesbian communities, seek to be recognized as one or other of the two national communities, with most of them 'freely [acknowledging] the political primacy of the national struggle'.[49] Many of the organizations in civil society that are committed to peace and conflict resolution understand that this will require the accommodation rather than the transcendence of nationalism and unionism. As Feargal Cochrane, the author of the most comprehensive study of these organizations, has pointed out, 'While some [peace and conflict resolution organizations] are working to erode the traditional political identities represented by unionism and nationalism, just as many (if not more) are committed to accommodating these alternative identities and establishing mechanisms that will allow them to coexist peacefully.'[50]

Those who believe that national identities are being eroded in Northern Ireland might well argue that the achievement of the Good Friday Agreement supports their claims. After all, both sides took major steps back in the Agreement from traditional positions on exclusive (British or Irish) state sovereignty, and the Agreement was endorsed in a referendum by an overwhelming majority of the electorate (71 per cent). Nationalists and republicans accepted there could not be a united Ireland without the consent of a majority in Northern Ireland. The unionists who endorsed the Agreement accepted a government in Northern Ireland in which nationalists are represented proportionately, a North–South Ministerial Council, and a number of all-Ireland 'implementation bodies' to administer various areas of public policy.[51]

It is more sensible, however, to see the Agreement as a *compromise* between rival national communities who grasped an opportunity for peace than as evidence of transformed or weakened identities. Nationalists embraced it overwhelmingly, even though it involved compromises on traditional demands, because it represented a significant advance from a unionist status quo. It also did not foreclose the achievement of a united Ireland, at least in the mid- to long-term. Indeed, in the weeks and months after the Agreement both the Irish Taoiseach, Bertie Ahern, and the leader of Sinn Féin, Gerry Adams, claimed there would be a united Ireland in their lifetime.[52]

Around half of the unionist community rejected the agreement outright, both in the referendum of May 1998, and in the elections to the new Northern Ireland Assembly, held in June 1998,[53] largely because they shared Ahern and Adams's analysis.[54] The unionist politicians who accepted the Agreement did so in the face of considerable pressure from the British and Irish governments.[55] London and Dublin had laid out the framework for what a settlement should contain in early 1995 and made it clear to unionists, particularly after Labour won office with a massive majority in May 1997, that the alternative to agreement was not the largely unionist status quo of direct rule from London, but the deepening of Anglo-Irish co-operation over Northern Ireland and the implementation of a range of reforms, including a reformed police and a new equality agenda. Unionists were offered the choice of participating in these reforms, or alienating the British public and watching them being implemented anyway. By itself, however, this pressure was insufficient, particularly to ensure grass-roots unionist support. There was also enough balance in the Agreement— including the removal of the Irish Republic's irredentist claim to Northern Ireland, a provision that Northern Ireland could only become part of a united Ireland if a majority of its people consented, and the creation of new British–Irish institutions—to allow pro-Agreement unionist politicians to market it as securing and even strengthening the Union.[56]

Continuing national polarization in Northern Ireland helps to explain why the Agreement has not yet been consolidated.[57] It also makes clear, however, why the Agreement which treats both ethno-national communities in an even-handed manner, is an appropriate way forward. Rather than entrenching divisions, as some post-nationalists suggest, the Agreement's institutions offer the possibility of nationalists and unionists co-operating with each other and building the trust that will allow them to transcend their differences in the longer term. Presumably this is why, as Cochrane points out, many of the conflict resolution organizations that want to see nationalism and unionism transcended support the agreement.[58]

Globalization and Difference Management

What, then, about the argument that globalization, while not reducing differences, facilitates their management? One version of this argument is that it has become more difficult for governments to repress minorities, and less likely that they will want to do so. This is said to be a result of several related phenomena: the international spread of democratic and human rights norms in the context of the war against Hitler, the decolonization of Asia and Africa, and the American civil rights campaign; advances in communications technology and a proliferation of intergovernmental and non-governmental agencies that together facilitate the global exposure of human rights transgressions; and the demonstration effect, again carried globally, of minorities struggling for rights.

One should be very sceptical of the universal application of such arguments, as the evidence from Rwanda, Iraq, and the Kurdish region of Turkey suggests. However, a good case can be made that Northern Ireland's nationalist minority has benefited from these developments. While the spread of human rights norms helped to unleash a minority revolt in the late 1960s, it also produced a raft of reforms from the British government. London suspended the exclusionary Stormont regime in 1972 and argued that future governments in Northern Ireland would have to be power-sharing in nature. It also introduced a number of positive changes, including the disbanding of the B Specials, the creation of an independent police authority, and the establishment of an impartial agency charged with the allocation of public housing.[59]

Britain has since relied on often counter-productive emergency legislation, and its security forces have been involved in a number of excesses.[60] However, it is also clear that it has been restrained by its own commitments under an emerging international human rights regime, and by external pressures from non-governmental organizations, external governments, and multi-government organizations. Criticism in the late 1970s by Amnesty International, as well as by the government's own Bennett Committee, led to new controls on police interrogation procedures.[61] The adoption by a number of United States states of the MacBride principles, which tied United States investment in Northern Ireland to a range of anti-discrimination and affirmative-action measures, 'provided the main impetus', in the view of one commentator, for the robust measures contained in Britain's Fair Employment Act (1989).[62] Apart from this, the UK government has been brought before the European Commission of Human Rights and the European Court of Human Rights on several occasions for its treatment of detainees and prisoners,[63] and has been criticized by a number of agencies, including the European Parliament, the United States Congress, the United Nations, Amnesty International, and British–Irish Human Rights Watch, for, among other matters, its handling of the 1981 hunger strikes, its use of plastic bullets, and the composition and practices of the Royal Ulster Constabulary.[64] As governments are normally reluctant to acknowledge the impact of external bodies on their decision-making, it is difficult to point to specific reforms resulting from these interventions. However, it is reasonable to argue that, at the very least, they contributed to 'non-decisions' and prevented matters from getting further out of hand.[65] As one knowledgeable commentator has pointed out, Britain's adherence to the European Convention on Human Rights helped to rule out 'the adoption of many of the security measures pressed for by Unionists and the associated political strategy of trying to crush Republican paramilitaries by military means'.[66]

Another development in the domestic affairs of states that has benefited some minorities is the trend towards third-party intervention, not just to enforce human rights, but in the related field of ethnic conflict resolution. Such interventions have forced external agencies to look beyond the promotion of universal (individual) human rights to the design of macro-political arrangements and provisions for 'group' rights that will allow rival ethnic groups to coexist in peace and justice.[67] In Northern Ireland, external interventions have helped to establish more equitable political arrangements between nationalists and unionists, and a more balanced relationship between the British and Irish governments. In 1978 the European Council agreed to give Northern Ireland three seats in the European Parliament, significant over-representation, to help ensure there would be one nationalist MEP.[68] Pressure from the United States also played a crucial role in the Conservative government's decision in 1979 to drop its pro-unionist integrationist policy in favour of a more even-handed approach based on a power-sharing government in Northern Ireland.[69]

Since the late 1970s both the United States and the European Parliament have called consistently for the British government to co-operate with the Irish government towards a resolution of the Northern Ireland conflict. In 1977 President Carter took the unprecedented step of indicating that the internal politics of Northern Ireland was a legitimate concern of American foreign policy, and expressed support for a peaceful settlement involving the Irish government.[70] A report of the European Parliament on Northern Ireland published in 1984 emphasized the need for cross-border co-operation and for the British and Irish governments to work together in Northern Ireland in certain specified fields.[71] In the view of an opponent of these developments, the report and the growing consensus in European circles behind the need for Anglo-Irish co-operation helped persuade Margaret Thatcher to sign the Anglo-Irish Agreement in 1985.[72] She was also pushed in this direction by the Reagan Administration in the United States.[73] Each time Thatcher visited the United States before 1985, Northern Ireland was raised, often by President Reagan himself. Reagan continued a promise made by Carter to provide aid in the event of a settlement, and praised the Report of the *New Ireland Forum Report*, a document on the way forward, produced by Ireland's main constitutional nationalist parties. When the Anglo-Irish agreement was signed, it was quickly endorsed by the United States and the

European Parliament, as well as by member states of the EEC, Canada, Australia, New Zealand, and Japan. This was a response that both vindicated the British approach and made it difficult for future governments to change course. There has been similar international approval for subsequent Anglo-Irish initiatives, including the Joint Declaration for Peace in December 1993 and the Good Friday Agreement of April 1998.

The American interest in conflict resolution in Northern Ireland increased dramatically in the 1990s, particularly after the election of President Clinton in 1992.[74] Clinton sent a special envoy to Northern Ireland during the early stages of the peace process; put some of his senior advisers, including National Security Adviser Anthony Lake, to work on Northern Ireland affairs;[75] regularly invited Northern Ireland politicians to the White House; persuaded the former Senate Majority Leader George Mitchell to chair a crucial committee on the decommissioning of paramilitary weapons and then to preside over the multi-party negotiations that produced the Good Friday Agreement; visited Northern Ireland three times in five years; and intervened directly during crucial periods of the negotiations. This close attention bolstered the position of the Irish government in nego-tiations with Britain. It also helped increase republicans' confidence about the utility of political negotiations.[76] In particular, Clinton's decision in early 1994 to issue a visa to Sinn Féin leader Gerry Adams helped give Adams the standing he needed to bring hard-line republi-cans behind his peace strategy. Adams has claimed the visit to the United States brought forward the IRA ceasefire, which occurred in August 1994, by one year.[77]

Writing in the late 1980s, Adrian Guelke, Northern Ireland's fore-most expert on the conflict's international dimensions, wrote that the impact of outside forces and international norms had been largely neg-ative.[78] Guelke noted the prevailing international view that colonies should be independent, and that the conflict in Northern Ireland was a hangover from the colonial era. As a result, most outsiders favoured a united Ireland. This, according to Guelke, helped to explain the con-stitutional stalemate because it increased unionist insecurities whilst reducing nationalists' incentive to compromise. It also helped to explain the violence. It promoted a siege mentality among unionists that provided a justification for the actions of loyalist paramilitaries. By bolstering the IRA claim that it was engaged in a legitimate anti-colonial struggle against British imperialism, and by facilitating fund-raising activities among Irish Americans, it encouraged the IRA to fight on.

We can see now, with the benefit of hindsight, that this analysis was too pessimistic. Not only did external actors play a less direct role in the 1980s, when Guelke wrote, than they have done since, but their role over the last decade has been generally constructive. The United States not only bolstered Dublin's diplomatic position and helped to bring republicans into constitutional politics, it managed to do so in a way that kept, or even made, key unionist politicians interested in compromise. Senator Mitchell, who presided over the negotiations that produced the Good Friday Agreement, won praise as an honest broker from both sides. Clinton's visit to Northern Ireland in November 1995, in which he visited both Protestant and Catholic areas and was careful not to give offence to either side in his speeches, was widely seen as a well-executed exercise in impartiality.[79] Unionist and loyalist politicians, not just nationalists, were given unprecedented access to the White House, and took it up.[80] While Clinton's success in coaxing republicans is often noted, he simultaneously managed to bring unionists along, with David Trimble acknowledging that a reassuring phone call from Clinton on the day the Agreement was reached helped convince him to sign it.[81]

The Anglo-Irish co-operation that has prevented the Northern Ireland conflict from escalating into something far worse,[82] and that produced the Anglo-Irish Agreement and eventually the Good Friday Agreement, was not just, or even mainly, a result of direct pressure from the European Parliament and Washington. It was also linked to the European integration process in indirect ways. By developing precedents of sovereignty-pooling, this helped to make thinkable the sort of trans-state institutions that are needed to govern Northern Ireland, and that are included in the Good Friday Agreement. In addition, the many meetings of European leaders that took place after Britain and Ireland's joint entry into the EEC in 1973 gave the Irish and British prime ministers opportunities to meet in the background to discuss Northern Ireland. This allowed friendships to develop and, more importantly, prevented megaphone diplomacy—the tendency of the two governments to communicate with each other through the media, usually with negative effects on their relations. The fact that Ireland is a member of the EU, with representation on a number of important bodies and veto power on the Council of Ministers, has led Britain to take it more seriously than in the past. The result has been a productive balance in the relationship that has led Britain to take the concerns of nationalists more seriously. As *The Economist* put it recently, the 'shared membership of the European Union gives Britain and Ireland sufficiently comparable status to dissolve the mutual chippiness of the past'.[83] The British–Irish rapprochement led, in the months after the Agreement, to an address by Tony Blair to the Irish Parliament, making him the first British prime minister to have been awarded such an honour, and possibly the first who would have taken it up. Interestingly, Blair used the opportunity to call for a joint British–Irish body to defend their archipelago's interests in the EU. It should be noted, however, that this increased co-operation cannot be explained in crude economic terms, as a result of increased Anglo-Irish economic transactions within the EU. Rather the effect of EU membership for Ireland has been a radical reduction in its dependence on the United Kingdom.[84]

Finally, European integration has created a context in which the aspirations of nationalists' for meaningful recognition of their national identity through all-island political institutions can be reconciled with unionists' preparedness to accept such institutions providing they are functionally useful and do not threaten Northern Ireland's constitutional position as a part of the United Kingdom. At least some unionists were persuaded during the negotiations that led to the Good Friday Agreement that all-island *economic* co-operation made sense in the context of Ireland's position on the periphery of the EU, and given the British government's handling of the BSE fiasco.[85] Unionist intellectuals, including one of Trimble's leading advisers, helpfully pointed out that cross-border co-operation occurred throughout the EU without threatening state sovereignty, and was a small price to pay, a 'fig leaf' as it was called, to win nationalist approval for the principle of majority consent.[86] Another unionist intellectual, who was a member of the UUP negotiating team and one of Northern Ireland's leading experts on the EU, argued that the cross-border arrangements accepted under the agreement fell in general 'into the pattern of existing European models'. He presented a paper to this effect to his colleagues during the negotiations.[87] European integration was one of the factors that made 1998 different from 1920 and 1974, when similar North–South institutions had been proposed but had been rejected by unionists.[88] One way to appreciate the importance of European integration on this aspect of the Agreement is to look at it counterfactually: what if the UUP had been asked to accept cross-border institutions in a state system whose members practised autarky? In this scenario it would have been a great deal more difficult to sell the institutions to the unionist community as economically pragmatic rather than as the straightforward political concession to nationalists depicted by the Agreement's unionist opponents.

Conclusion

There is little evidence that globalization or European integration has contributed to supranational identities anywhere, except in some intellectual circles. There is some evidence, including in the contributions to this volume, that European integration has weakened 'conglomerate' identities, such as those in Britain and Switzerland, in favour of Scottish identities or nested Scottish–British and French Swiss–Swiss identities. In Northern Ireland, however, European integration has not strengthened loyalties to Europe, or contributed to multiple, overlapping, or nested identities. Instead, Northern Ireland remains divided between British and Irish nationalists, as it has been since before the Treaty of Rome. Indeed these divisions have become more polarized during three decades of European integration, which is hardly surprising given a simultaneous violent conflict in which over 3,200 people have been killed and many thousands seriously injured.

The resilience of Northern Ireland's divisions explains the need for the power-sharing and border-transcending institutions contained in the Good Friday Agreement. The Agreement is a compromise between nationalism and unionism, and an important part of its appeal is that it allows nationalists and unionists to believe, respectively, that it is a necessary step towards reconciliation in Ireland and securing the Union. It is not unthinkable that Northern Ireland's communities may develop overlapping identities in the future.[89] This is only likely, however, if the local context is changed from one of hostility to one of co-operation, and this will depend more on the success of the institutions in the Good Friday Agreement than on international economic integration.

While globalization has not diluted identities in Northern Ireland, it has contributed to conflict management. An emerging international rights regime has constrained those parts of the British state that favour coercion over kindness, although the constraints have not always been apparent. Changing norms on state sovereignty have unleashed a range of benign effects, including the positive use of the United States' diplomacy in Northern Ireland as well as increased co-operation between the British and Irish states.

It is impossible, however, to be precise about the effects of globalization, and these should not be exaggerated. It must be kept in mind that there were other pressures pushing in the same direction. A thirty-year nationalist insurgency indicated the counter-productive folly of infringing human rights or supporting a political status quo that was unacceptable to a (growing) nationalist minority. The Anglo-

Irish co-operation that produced the Anglo-Irish Agreement and ultimately the Good Friday Agreement may have been made easier as a result of sovereignty-pooling and intergovernmental co-operation within the EU, but it was also due to a long learning curve on the part of London that Northern Ireland was a site of conflicting sovereignty claims that could not be managed within the traditional state system.[90] Globalization complemented these factors.

NOTES

I would like to thank Margaret Moore and Brendan O'Leary for insightful comments on this chapter, and Patti Lenard for her invaluable research assistance. The Social Sciences and Humanities Research Council of Canada funded the research.

1. For a discussion of difference-eliminating and difference-managing methods of ethnic conflict regulation, see J. McGarry and B. O'Leary, 'Eliminating and Managing Differences', in A. Smith and J. Hutchinson (eds.), *Ethnicity* (Oxford: Oxford University Press, 1996) 333–41.
2. B. Anderson, *Imagined Communities: Reflections on the Origin and Spread of Nationalism* (London: Verso, 1983); E. Gellner, *Nations and Nationalism* (Ithaca, NY: Cornell University Press, 1983); E. Hobsbawm, *Nations and Nationalism since 1870: Programme, Myth, Reality* (Cambridge: Cambridge University Press, 1990).
3. Hobsbawm, *Nations and Nationalism*, 183.
4. J. Waldron, 'Minority Cultures and the Cosmopolitan Alternative', in W. Kymlicka (ed.), *The Rights of Minority Cultures* (Oxford: Oxford University Press, 1995); M. Castells, *The Power of Identity* (Oxford: Blackwell, 1997).
5. K. Deutsch, *Nationalism and Social Communication: An Inquiry into the Foundations of Nationality* (Cambridge, Mass.: MIT Press, 1966); K. Marx and F. Engels, *Manifesto of the Communist Party* (Moscow: Progress, 1977).
6. E. Haas, *The Uniting of Europe: The Role of Political, Social and Economic Forces* (Stanford, Calif.: Stanford University Press, 1958).
7. As the UN secretary-general Kofi Annan put it recently, an international norm against ethnic repression is emerging 'that will and must take precedence over concerns of state sovereignty' (*Globe and Mail*, 17 May 1999). For a balanced and realistic view of how human rights norms are increasing in importance, see the special feature in *The Economist*, 'The World is Watching', 5 Dec. 1998. *The Economist* argues that state sovereignty still has 'plenty of life left in it' and that 'for most purposes, states will continue to respect each other's sovereignty'. However, it also argues that the sovereignty doctrine is being revised, is no longer absolute, and is becoming increasingly conditional on how states treat their citizens.
8. A. D. Smith, *The Ethnic Origins of Nations* (Oxford: Blackwell, 1986).
9. See Ch. 2.
10. T. Lyne, 'Ireland, Northern Ireland and 1992: The Barriers to Technocratic Anti-Partitionism', *Public Administration*, 68/4 (1990), 417–33.
11. G. FitzGerald, *Towards a New Ireland* (London: Charles Knight, 1972), 111–12.

12. Ibid. 110–11. As John Hume told the SDLP annual conference in 1997, 'By the way, does anyone believe that our interests in Europe would be better protected by London than by Dublin? Could anyone imagine Dublin failing so spectacularly and for so long on a priority matter like BSE?' Hume argued before his party's annual conference in 1997 that Northern Ireland would have been granted an exemption from the EU ban on British beef had the British government asked for one from the European Commission. The government didn't ask, he argued, because of fears about the reaction of farmers in England, Scotland, and Wales, and despite the fact that agriculture is a much more important part of Northern Ireland's economy than it is of any part of Britain's (*Irish News*, 17 Nov. 1997).

13. 'It can scarcely be doubted that, in the event of a political solution being found to the Northern Ireland problem, which is by far the biggest single source of unrest and violence within the frontiers of the present community, that institution would be willing to contribute financially to the transitional arrangements towards such a settlement' (Fine Gael, *Ireland: Our Future Together* (Dublin: Fine Gael, 1979)). The 'political solution' that Fine Gael was recommending was a united (federal) Ireland.

14. J. Hume, 'A New Ireland in a New Europe', in D. Keogh and M. Haltzel (eds.), *Northern Ireland and the Politics of Reconciliation* (Cambridge: Cambridge University Press, 1993), 227. Hume told his 1997 party conference that 'Europe through the Single Market has created an economic space where we can grow together . . . In almost every sector—farming, business, tourism, energy—the main groupings and interests on both sides of the border are calling for a more integrating, harmonised and united approach to marketing, to planning, to taxation, to regulation' (*Irish Times*, 17 Nov. 1997).

15. J. Anderson and I. Shuttleworth, 'Currency of Co-operation', *Fortnight*, 3/12 (Dec. 1992), 18.

16. These nationalist arguments have some academic support. A Cambridge economist, Bob Rowthorn, argues that closer economic cooperation between Northern Ireland and the Irish Republic in the context of the EU will lead unionists to shift their loyalties from London to Dublin (B. Rowthorn, 'Foreword', in R. Munck, *The Irish Economy* (London: Pluto Press, 1993)). An Israeli political sociologist, Sammy Smooha, who has examined Northern Ireland from a comparative perspective, claims that the option of a united Ireland 'will be less and less resisted' by unionists 'as Ireland, a member of the prospering European Union, [comes to] enjoy economic growth, expands its welfare services and secularizes' (S. Smooha, 'The Tenability of Partition as a Mode of Conflict-Regulation: Comparing Ireland with Palestine—Land of Israel', in J. McGarry (ed.), *Northern Ireland and the Divided World* (Oxford: Oxford University Press, 2001)).

17. See A. Guelke, *Northern Ireland: The International Perspective* (Dublin: Gill & Macmillan, 1988).

18. Cadogan Group, *Northern Limits* (Belfast: Cadogan Group, 1992). D. Kennedy, 'The European Union and the Northern Ireland Question', in B. Barton and P. Roche (eds.), *The Northern Ireland Question: Perspectives and Policies* (Aldershot: Avebury, 1994), 186.

19. Queen's University Belfast inaugural lecture, 'Citizenship and the European Community', 14 May 1992, cited approvingly in R. Kearney, *Postnationalist Ireland* (London: Routledge, 1997), 84. E. Meehan, 'Citizens are Plural', *Fortnight*, 311 (Nov. 1992), 13–14. Perhaps it is not surprising that Meehan, a holder of a Jean Monnet Chair in European Social Policy at Queen's, believes that Europe is having a benign effect.

20. R. Taylor, 'Northern Ireland: Consociation or Social Transformation', in McGarry (ed.), *Northern Ireland and the Divided World*.
21. Ibid.
22. K. Boyle, 'Northern Ireland: Allegiances and Identities', in B. Crick (ed.), *National Identities: The Constitution of the United Kingdom* (Oxford: Blackwell, 1991), 69, 78. Boyle and his colleague Tom Hadden have since tempered their Euro-enthusiasm. See K. Boyle and T. Hadden, *Northern Ireland: The Choice* (Harmondsworth: Penguin, 1994).
23. R. Kearney and R. Wilson, 'Northern Ireland's Future as a European Region', in Kearney, *Postnationalist Ireland*, 79.
24. C. McCall, 'Postmodern Europe and the Resources of Communal identities in Northern Ireland', *European Journal of Political Research*, 33 (1998), 406.
25. Taylor, 'Northern Ireland', 2.
26. B. Dooley, *Black and Green: The Fight for Civil Rights in Northern Ireland and Black America* (London: Pluto Press, 1998).
27. Apparently the civil rights marchers were aware of the benefits of satellite television technology. One of their chants was 'the whole world is watching'. Cited in Guelke, *Northern Ireland*, 1.
28. '. . . contingent developments opened Westminister's ears and eyes. As in the USA, national and global television made the exercise of hegemonic control over a local minority embarrassingly visible' (B. O'Leary and J. McGarry, *The Politics of Antagonism: Understanding Northern Ireland* (Athlone: London, 1993, 1996), 172; also see Kennedy, 'The European Union', 178). Not all regimes, as anyone familiar with Afghanistan and Iraq will appreciate, are vulnerable to the spread of human rights and democratic norms. Contrary to traditional Irish republican thinking, it was probably fortunate for the nationalist minority that Westminster and not Stormont had sovereignty over Northern Ireland. The unionists, with vital interests at stakes as well as being profoundly antagonistic towards nationalists, were not prepared to relax control voluntarily. Their position was similar to that of whites in the Deep South of the United States who were unwilling to relax control of blacks until forced to by the US federal government.
29. The 1967 survey was conducted by Richard Rose, and those in 1978 and 1989 by Edward Moxon-Browne. The results of all three are given in E. Moxon-Browne, 'National Identity in Northern Ireland', in P. Stringer and G. Robinson (eds.), *Social Attitudes in Northern Ireland: The First Report* (Belfast: Blackstaff Press, 1991).
30. Ibid.
31. K. Trew, 'National Identity', in R. Breen, P. Devine, and L. Dowds (eds.), *Social Attitudes in Northern Ireland* (Belfast: Appletree Press, 1996), table 1.
32. I have relied for these figures on the data reported on Nicholas Whyte's webpage http://www.explorers.whyte.com. The elections covered were different in their nature: in the 1973–5 period they include one local government election, two to Northern Ireland regional bodies (the 1973 Assembly and the 1975 Convention), and two Westminster elections; in the 1996–9 period they include one local government election, one Westminster election, two elections to Northern Ireland regional bodies (the 1996 Forum and 1998 Assembly), and an election to the European Parliament. One could make an argument that the data, as presented, exaggerate the increase in support for nationalist and unionist parties, as they include an election in the earlier period, the local government election of 1973, in which 'others' did unusually well (16%), and one in the later period, the European election of 1999, in which they did unusually poorly (2%). Even if one takes away these two election results, however, the share of the vote won by nationalist and unionist parties still increased from an average of 85% in 1973–5 to 89.2% in

1996–9. One should remember that all I have to do to discredit the post-modernist argument is show that the share of the vote won by nationalist and unionist parties has not gone down over the last twenty-six years.

33. Paradoxically, Alliance has done slightly better in recent Westminster elections, which employ SMP, than in Northern Ireland elections, which use PR.

Another way to show the extent of national polarization in Northern Ireland is to examine transfers in those elections that are based on PR-STV. In the European election of 1999, of Ian Paisley's surplus of 22,969, 22,162 were transferred to the unionist candidate Jim Nicholson and 32 to the nationalist and republican candidate Mitchell McLaughlin. The latter figure can safely be attributed to mistakes or mental disorders.

34. These figures have been calculated from the electoral data provided by Whyte, http://www.explorers.whyte.com.

35. In the 1973 election to the Northern Ireland Assembly, nationalists won 24.1% of the vote. In seven elections between 1982 and 1989, the nationalist share of the vote rose to 32.5%, and in five elections between 1996 and 1999, it increased to 39.8%. To the uninformed observer, this data might suggest support for the Irish nationalist– modernist argument that unionists are converting to nationalism. The shift, however, can be explained by Sinn Féin's participation in electoral politics since 1982, an increase in turn-out among nationalist voters, and an increase in the nationalist share of the population. It is not because the scales have fallen from unionists' eyes, as nationalists might have hoped. See O'Leary and McGarry, *The Politics of Antagonism*, 192; B. O'Leary and G. Evans, 'Northern Ireland: La Fin de Siècle, The Twilight of the Second Protestant Ascendancy and Sinn Féin's Second Coming', *Parliamentary Affairs*, 50 (1997), 672–80.

36. There have been two elections since the Good Friday Agreement, to the Northern Ireland Assembly in June 1998 and the European Parliament in June 1999. In the Assembly election the UUP won 53.1% of the DUP–UUP vote compared to 56% in elections to the Northern Ireland forum in 1996. In the European Parliament election it won 39.2% of the DUP–UUP vote compared to 45.3% in the preceding European election in 1994.

37. The focus of European elections on constitutional issues is partly obscured by John Hume's 'post-nationalist Eurospeak'. Outsiders listening to Hume could come away with the impression that he wants European integration to dissolve both nationalism and unionism. However, insiders understand that it is the 'divisions' between nationalists and unionists that Hume wants to dissolve, and that he sees this dissolution as creating the basis for 'a new Ireland' within Europe. As one unionist insider writes, the basis of Hume's position 'is the territorial unit of the island of Ireland, and its objective is to secure some form of political unity for that territory, despite the fact that a clear majority in one of the two political units now existing on the island is resolutely opposed to any form of unity . . . it is a nationalist demand, not a post-nationalist one' (Kennedy, 'The European Union and the Northern Ireland Question', 185).

38. Traditionally, the SDLP has been more Europhile than Sinn Féin. The latter has been relatively hostile to Europe because it sees European integration as weakening the sovereignty of the Irish state. In recent years Sinn Féin has moved closer to the SDLP position on Europe.

39. A 1967 opinion poll in Northern Ireland found that Catholics were four to one in favour of joining the European Economic Community, while Protestants were marginally against. A 1992 Gallup poll found that Catholics were five to one of the opinion that EC membership of the European Union was advantageous, while Protestants believed so by two to one. Catholics were in favour of the Maastricht

Treaty by almost two to one, while Protestants were narrowly against. Data from Kennedy, 'The European Union and the Northern Ireland Question', 166–7. A survey conducted by Evans and O'Leary in 1996 asked nationalists and unionists if 'Governments from the European Union . . . should be involved in the forthcoming negotiations'. The survey recorded the surplus of 'yes' over 'no' respondents. The score for nationalists was –1. SDLP supporters were in favour, scoring 8, while Sinn Féin supporters scored –14. The Sinn Féin negative score reflects the view of some republicans that the EU has weakened Ireland's political sovereignty, and that it involves Ireland in a body in which the United Kingdom plays a dominant role. By contrast, the unionist response was –50. G. Evans and B. O'Leary, 'Frameworked Futures: Intransigence and Flexibility in the Northern Ireland Elections of May 30, 1996', *Irish Political Studies*, 12 (1997), 32.

40. During 1991–2 John Hume tabled proposals for the creation of an executive to govern Northern Ireland modelled on the European Commission. The proposed executive would have included three elected representatives from Northern Ireland and three appointees, one each from the British government, the Irish government, and the European Commission.

41. P. Hainsworth, 'Northern Ireland and the European Union', in A. Aughey and D. Morrow (eds.), *Northern Ireland Politics* (London: Longman, 1996), 131.

42. For a UUP perspective, see 'United Ireland "will lose under emu"', *Irish News*, 20 Nov. 1997. In the European election of June 1999 David Ervine of the small Progressive Unionist Party became the first unionist candidate to stand on a pro-Europe platform.

43. Northern Ireland's representatives in the European Parliament may cooperate on economic matters, but they also have used the EU on several occasions as a platform for their opposing political aspirations. See E. Moxon-Browne, 'The Impact of the European Community', in B. Hadfield (ed.), *Northern Ireland: Politics and the Constitution* (Buckingham: Open University Press, 1992), 50–1.

44. A. Pollock (ed.), *A Citizen's Inquiry: The Opsahl Report on Northern Ireland* (Dublin: Lilliput Press, 1993), 90. The Opsahl Commission's views are cited approvingly by Taylor, 'Northern Ireland'.

45. Taylor, 'Northern Ireland'.

46. In elections to the European Parliament in 1994 and 1999, the turnout in Northern Ireland was 49.4% and 57% respectively. In the United Kingdom the turnout was 36.4% and 24%. While turnout in local government elections in Northern Ireland in the 1990s ranged between 54.7% (1997) and 56.6% (1993), turnout in Britain ranged between 32.5% (Metropolitan Boroughs in 1992) and an unusually high 53.4% (Welsh districts in 1991). All Northern Ireland data are from http://www.explorers.whyte.com. Data for turnout in European elections in the UK are from http://www2.europarl.eu.int/election/ results/uk_taux.htm. Data for local government results in Britain are from C. Rallings and M. Thrasher (eds.), *Local Elections in Britain* (New York: Routledge, 1997), 53.

47. Data for turnout in Great Britain for Westminster elections are from D. Butler and D. Kavanagh, *The British General Election of 1997* (New York: St Martin's Press, 1997), and D. Butler and D. Kavanagh, *The British General Election of 1992* (New York: St Martin's Press, 1992).

48. See Whyte, http://www.explorers.whyte.com. The turnout data do not show any significant trend during the period under review (1973–99). The highest turnout for a local government election between 1973 and 1997 was in 1973 (68.1%). The highest turnout for a Northern Ireland regional election between 1973 and 1998 was in 1998 (68.6%).

49. S. O'Neill, 'Mutual Recognition and the Accommodation of National Diversity: Constitutional Justice in Northern Ireland', MS, Queen's University, Belfast, 1999, 6.

50. F. Cochrane, 'Unsung Heroes? The Role of Peace and Conflict Resolution Organizations in the Northern Ireland Conflict', in McGarry (ed.), *Northern Ireland and the Divided World.*

51. It was subsequently agreed that the six implementation bodies would deal with inland waterways, food safety, trade and business development, special EU programmes, the Irish and Ulster Scots languages, and aquaculture and marine matters.

52. For Ahern's comments, see *Irish Times*, 27 Nov. 1998. For Adams's, see *Irish Times*, 20 Apr. 1998.

53. Exit polls from the referendum on the agreement in May of 1998 showed that only a bare majority of unionists voted 'yes'. In the Assembly elections of June 1998, unionists supporting the accord won 23.9% of the vote and 30 seats while unionist rejectionists won 24.9% of the vote and 28 seats. One member of the 'yes' side has since voted with the 'no' camp on a number of important decisions, which means, effectively, that the two sides are level in the Assembly.

54. The DUP claim that, under the Agreement, 'the Union would be fatally weakened ... Unionists know that any deal so enthusiastically endorsed by the Dublin government and the SDLP is something which represents a dilution and diminution of the Union' (*Irish Times*, 16 Apr. 1998).

55. For more details on this argument, see J. McGarry, 'Political Settlements in Northern Ireland and South Africa', *Political Studies*, 40/5 (Dec. 1998), 865–70.

56. The *Irish Times* recounted a Trimble speech to the Northern Ireland Forum in the week after the Agreement was signed: 'Mr. Trimble said the Agreement was a disaster for Sinn Féin and the IRA, and that it strengthened the North's position within the UK. Trimble claimed the alternative was the Anglo-Irish Agreement, and that he had achieved the ending of the Republic's territorial claim and a recognition of the territorial integrity of the UK' (18 Apr. 1998).

57. Pro-Agreement unionists won only a 'wafer-thin majority' in their bloc in both the referendum of May 1998 and the Assembly elections of June 1998 (see n. 53). Subsequently, even pro-Agreement unionists refused to establish the Agreement's central institutions, the executive and North–South Ministerial Council, apparently because of the IRA's failure to decommission weapons. The institutions were not set up, and powers were not devolved to the Assembly, until December 1999, twenty months after the Agreement was signed. Even this success was temporary. The continuing failure to reach agreement on decommissioning resulted in the British government suspending the institutions on 11 February 2000, and they were not re-established until 30 May 2000.

58. Cochrane, 'Unsung Heroes?', 30.

59. See O'Leary and McGarry, *The Politics of Antagonism*, 173–4.

60. J. McGarry and B. O'Leary, *Policing Northern Ireland: Proposals for a New Start* (Belfast: Blackstaff, 1999), 35–9.

61. Amnesty International, *Report of an Amnesty International Mission to Northern Ireland* (London: Amnesty International, 1977); Bennett Report, *Report of the Committee of Inquiry into Police Interrogation Procedures in Northern Ireland*, Cmnd. 7397 (1977).

62. Guelke, *Northern Ireland*, 151. Also see O'Leary and McGarry, *The Politics of Antagonism*, 215.

63. For details, see Guelke, *Northern Ireland*, 165–8.

64. See O'Leary and McGarry, *The Politics of Antagonism*, 214; Moxon-Browne, 'The Impact of the European Community', 51.
65. A non-decision occurs when a government decides not to do something. In this case, the argument is that if Britain had not been scrutinized by these external agencies and/or did not care about its international reputation, it would have engaged in more radical repression of nationalists.
66. Guelke, *Northern Ireland*, 68.
67. It is this trend, sometimes referred to in the international relations literature as 'peace-making', that explains the paradox whereby the United States, which champions individual rights over group rights at home, is forced to champion group rights in addition to individual rights in places like northern Iraq, Bosnia, and Kosovo.
68. J. Ruane and J. Todd, *The Dynamics of Conflict in Northern Ireland: Power, Conflict and Emancipation* (Cambridge: Cambridge University Press, 1996), 281.
69. See Guelke, *Northern Ireland*, 141–2. The *volte-face* was a response to concerns that Carter's campaign to secure the Democratic Party's presidential nomination would increase his administration's vulnerability to Irish-American pressure. News of the change in policy was first announced by the British ambassador to the United States, Sir Nicholas Henderson.
70. O'Leary and McGarry, *The Politics of Antagonism*, 214. By the late 1990s, US intervention in the internal affairs of Northern Ireland had become 'humdrum', according to Niall O'Dowd. He was writing on the occasion of a visit to Belfast by the US First Lady, Hillary Clinton, when she called for the loyalist killers of Catholic lawyer Rosemary Nelson to be brought to justice. In O'Dowd's view, 'a few years back the notion of an American First Lady speaking out on any aspect of life in Northern Ireland would have been taboo' (*Ireland on Sunday*, 16 May 1999).
71. N. J. Haagerup, *Report Drawn up on behalf of the Political Affairs Committee on the Situation in Northern Ireland*, European Parliament Working Documents, doc. 1-1526/83 (Strasbourg: European Parliament, 1984): Kennedy, 'The European Union and the Northern Ireland Question', 179.
72. Kennedy, 'The European Union and the Northern Ireland Question', 179.
73. See A. Wilson, 'From the Beltway to Belfast: The Clinton Administration, Sinn Féin, and the Northern Ireland Peace Process', *New Hibernia Review*, 1/3 (1997), 23. According to Guelke, the US role was a 'significant factor' in the making of the Anglo-Irish Agreement (*Northern Ireland*, 147).
74. Two sources attribute the increased American interest in conflict resolution in Northern Ireland to, among other things, international investment flows and European integration. From this perspective, America's intervention was due to its economic interest in stability in Ireland, which is the location of considerable and increasing American investment, and an important American foothold in the integrating EU. See R. MacGinty, 'American Influences on the Northern Ireland Peace Process', *Journal of Conflict Studies*, 43 (1997), and Wilson 'From the Beltway to Belfast', 36–7.

   Among the many additional, and complementary, reasons given for America's increasing role are: Clinton's perception of the importance of Irish-American votes in crucial primaries (J. O'Grady, 'An Irish Policy Born in the USA', *Foreign Affairs*, 75 (May–June 1996), 3, 6); a decline in the importance of the Anglo-American relationship in the context of the post-cold war era (ibid.); successful lobbying by Irish American groups (A. Guelke, 'The United States, Irish Americans and the Northern Ireland Peace Process', *International Affairs*, 72/3 (1996), 521); the idea that US success in brokering a settlement in Northern

Ireland would enhance American credibility in other ethnic disputes (ibid. 536); Clinton's perception that the conflict was ripe for resolution and that he could play a useful role (Wilson, 'From the Beltway to Belfast', 25).

75. It has been said that Lake devoted about one-quarter of his time to Northern Ireland (MacGinty, 'American Influences', 41).

76. According to Wilson, 'the belief that Clinton might use his power to push Britain into a political formula for Northern Ireland favourable to republicans' was an important factor in republican thinking (Wilson, 'From the Beltway to Belfast', 32). A 1994 republican document on the peace strategy, *Totally Unarmed Strategy*, was explicit about the importance of the American role, noting that 'there is potentially a very powerful Irish-American lobby not in hock to any particular party in Britain or Ireland' and that 'Clinton is perhaps the first US President in decades to be influenced by such a lobby' (cited in MacGinty, 'American Influences', 34; also see Guelke, 'The United States, Irish Americans and the Northern Ireland Peace Process', 534).

77. The announcement of the ceasefire closely followed a visit to Belfast by an American delegation led by Congressman Bruce Morrison, a close friend of Clinton's. According to O'Grady, the minutes of the meeting in which the IRA voted for the ceasefire indicated that the decision was taken 'mainly because of the power of the Irish-American lobby' (O'Grady, 'An Irish Policy Born in the USA', 5). This conclusion, however, appears to be O'Grady's interpretation and not a quote from the minutes themselves. O'Grady, not suprisingly, does not give a source for the minutes.

78. Guelke, *Northern Ireland*.

79. According to unionist Roy Bradford, Clinton's visit 'significantly changed the feeling among unionists that the American agenda is exclusively nationalist'. A *Belfast Telegraph* poll showed that 73% of people in Northern Ireland thought the visit had been helpful. Both cited in MacGinty, 'American Influences', 39.

80. See A. Wilson, 'The Billy Boys Meet Slick Willy: The Ulster Unionists and the American Dimension to the Northern Ireland Peace Process, 1993–98', *Policy Studies Journal*, (Spring 1999).

81. Ibid. 22.

82. Northern Ireland is, in Frank Wright's term, an 'ethnic frontier', a site of contested sovereignty between two broader national communities, one Irish and one British. In such frontier zones the level of conflict is crucially affected by the actions of external powers close to the frontier region. As Wright explained, an unstable external environment contributed to ferocious and bloody conflicts in the Balkans, Cyprus, and Lebanon. He believed, in my view correctly, that Anglo-Irish cooperation was crucial to containing the Northern Ireland conflict. F. Wright, *Northern Ireland: A Comparative Analysis* (Dublin: Gill & Macmillan, 1987), 276–7, 282–3, 285.

83. 'Anglo-Irish Relations: Entente Cordiale', *The Economist*, 28 Nov. 1998. A commentator who is relatively hostile to the Anglo-Irish entente, Denis Kennedy, a former head of the EU Commission Office in Belfast, argues that the enhanced Anglo-Irish cooperation would have been almost impossible outside the EU: 'the experience of working together in the institutions of the Community, particularly at Council of Minister and senior diplomat and official level, was slowly transforming the relationship . . . The patron–client pattern was dissolved; in the new circumstances British ministers and diplomats could see their Irish counterparts as clever partners in Europe. Without this transformation it is almost impossible to see how Dublin–London relations could have been transformed as they were

between the mid-seventies and the mid-eighties' (Kennedy, 'The European Union and the Northern Ireland Question', 177).

84. Whereas the United Kingdom took about 75% of Ireland's exports in 1960, by 1997 this share had dropped to approximately 21.4%. Imports dropped from 50% to 30.9%. While Ireland's recent economic miracle is closely tied to foreign direct investment, this is mostly from the United States rather than from the United Kingdom.

85. See n. 12. The same thinking explains the cooperation between unionists and nationalists in cross-border 'partnership' bodies set up as part of the EU's Peace and Reconciliation Programme. Rather than suggesting a weakening of identities, as Taylor seems to believe, they imply only a willingness to cooperate. As James Anderson writes about cross-border cooperation, 'The nationally "neutral" EU context was felt by some to be a crucial factor in getting together groups which would otherwise have been hostile to cross-border cooperation' (J. Anderson, 'Integrating Europe, Integrating Ireland: The Socio-Economic Dynamics', in J. Anderson and J. Goodman (eds.), *Disagreeing Ireland: Contexts, Obstacles, Hopes* (London: Pluto Press, 1998), 81–2).

86. The adviser is Paul Bew. He and two of his colleagues, Henry Patterson and Paul Teague, argued in 1997 that 'the history of the EU suggests that despite all the integration that has taken place, member states remain stubbornly intact as political, economic and social units. The lesson for unionists is that economic cooperation does not necessarily mean that Northern Ireland's position within the UK or the Protestant identity will be compromised to any great extent' (*Northern Ireland: Between War and Peace* (London: Lawrence & Wishart, 1997), 196). Richard Kearney also noted that 'the process of European integration has the potential to make the "nationalist aspiration" less unpalatable to unionists. For it becomes possible, in this context, to present closer relations between north and south as pragmatically desirable in a single-market Europe without frontiers, where people, goods and capital move freely across former barriers' (*Postnationalist Ireland*, 86–7).

87. This intellectual was Anthony Alcock, professor of modern languages at the University of Ulster. The importance of European precedents for unionists can be gleaned through reading their literature. In a critique of the 1995 'Framework' documents, the Cadogan Group, a unionist intellectual think-tank, accepted proposed cross-border arrangements but rejected all-island institutions, in part because, while there were precedents for cross-border cooperation between regions in the EU, there were no precedents for part of one state cooperating with another state (*Northern Limits*, 27–8). Alcock pointed out, on the other hand, that there are EU precedents for such arrangements (A. Alcock, 'From Conflict to Agreement in Northern Ireland: Lessons from Europe', in McGarry (ed.), *Northern Ireland and the Divided World*).

88. See also J. Anderson and J. Goodman, 'Nationalisms and Transnationalisms: Failures and Emancipation', in Anderson and Goodman (eds.), *Disagreeing Ireland*, 12.

89. Some identities will be easier for unionists and nationalists to don than others. Just as David Laitin shows that Slavs in post-Soviet Kazakhstan found it easier to swap their 'Soviet' identity for one as 'Russian speakers' rather than as 'Kazakhs', one could envisage unionists and nationalists coalescing around a 'Northern Irish' identity rather than an Irish or British one. See D. Laitin, *Identity in Formation: The Russian-Speaking Populations in the Near Abroad* (Ithaca, NY: Cornell University Press, 1998).

90. B. O'Leary, 'The Conservative Stewardship of Northern Ireland, 1979–97: Sound-Bottomed Contradictions or Slow Learning?', *Political Studies*, 45 (1997),

663–76. The sovereignty-pooling which lies at the heart of Anglo-Irish cooperation, while partly linked to European integration, also had older roots: similar
North–South institutions were part of the Government of Ireland Act, 1920.

CHAPTER 15

Ethnic Relations, Nationalism, and Minority Nationalism in South-Eastern Europe

Mitja Žagar

Provoked by worldwide developments in the 1990s, especially the tragic events in the Balkans, ethnicity, nationalism, and ethnic conflict have attracted the attention of both scholarly and public opinion. Once again, the world has been astonished by the social and political force of ethnicity, a phenomenon that had largely been discounted since the era of decolonization. The chapter discusses the importance of ethnic relations and nationalism in multi-ethnic societies, focusing on selected countries in south-eastern Europe. After a review of the concepts of ethnicity and nationalism, it looks at contemporary questions in the Balkans. This yields some general findings about ethnic conflict and its management and shows the ways in which the international community should develop a strategy to promote democracy, human rights, and ethnic relations based on equality, tolerance, and cooperation, including the protection of national minorities.

Ethnicity, Nation-States, and Nationalism

The tragic developments in the Balkans in recent years have shown the destructive potential of ethnic conflict and reconfirmed the importance of the successful management of ethnically diverse societies. Although ethnic diversity represents only one dimension of social pluralism in modern societies, its social role and potency should not be underestimated. Optimistic predictions by scholars and ideologists that modernization and globalization would reduce the social impact and importance of ethnicity by creating new global identities, or even do away with them altogether, have proved unfounded. Contrary to widespread expectation, modern technologies, global communication, cooperation, and the increased mobility of people appear to have contributed to increasing ethnic and cultural diversity in modern societies. Even if one rejects primordialist conceptions of ethnicity, one has to acknowledge the substantial social potency and perseverance of ethnicity in modern societies. In most environments, especially under local circumstances, it still plays a central role in political socialization and self-identification. Ethnic identities often remain the strongest collective identities in plural societies and have shown themselves able, in specific circumstances, to override individual identities or other collective identities.[1] One factor contributing to this is the prevailing perception that existing states are, or should be, ethnically based 'nation-states'.

Although the classic definition of states as persons of international law does not make reference to an ethnic basis,[2] the modern international community is still predominantly a community of nation-states.[3] According to the conception of the nation-state developed in Europe, mostly in the nineteenth century, nation-states are ethnically homogeneous states of particular 'titular nations'. This traditional concept is a product of a specific historic development in Europe that started in the sixteenth century, intensified after the Peace of Westphalia (1648), and reached fruition mostly in the nineteenth and twentieth centuries. The formation of modern nation-states went hand in hand with the process of formation of modern European nations as specific ethnic communities. In this process states that were established as single-nation states of 'titular nations' acquired their ethnic identity.[4] This concept can be explained by a simple equation: state = nation = people.[5] The idea has persisted to the end of the twentieth century.

In reality, however, nation-states have never been ethnically homogeneous and a certain level of ethnic and cultural diversity has always existed. It has existed even in France, often cited as the typical example of a homogeneous single-nation state. When the French nation-state and French nation were created in the sixteenth and seventeenth centuries, regional ethnic identities were much stronger than the newly invented French identity. Official French policy, based on the unity of the French nation, has never managed to do away with specific local and regional cultures, languages, and identities, although some of them have almost disappeared. Furthermore, in recent decades, France—like many other countries—has experienced a revival of regional ethnic sentiment.[6] Developed transportation and increased population mobility, intensified global communication, and international cooperation and interdependence in the world are key factors contributing to this trend, and this can only become more important in the future.[7] Existing symmetrical constitutional and political systems built on the traditional concept of ethnically homogeneous nation-states do not correspond to this multi-ethnic reality of modern societies. Often they lack the necessary flexibility and do not reflect adequately the existing social diversity and asymmetries. Nevertheless, the traditional concept of nation-states has not been transformed substantially and there is little evidence that it will give way soon to a more adequate concept, such as that of the multi-ethnic state.[8]

Faced with this contradiction, states have sought to impose ethnic homogeneity through socialization and by creating a myth of ethnic unity. In practice, the titular nation has often sought to impose its own definition of ethnic and national homogeneity, and then use the state to build a nation around it. The state in this context becomes more than just a socially neutral way of organizing society, but an agency for building the society itself. With the existence of ethnic minorities defined out of existence and not recognized in state constitutions, it is not surprising to find regular outbreaks of dissatisfaction on the part of non-state ethnic groups. In the absence of a model of the multi-ethnic state, these groups are stimulated to seek their own ethnically based nation-state as the only way out.

Considering its historic role, potency, and social importance, it is striking how little of a scholarly nature was written on nationalism before the 1990s.[9] This situation changed after the resurgence of nationalism in the last two decades of the twentieth century with an ever increasing volume of work being published.[10] As nationalism has become one of the central topics in current scholarly debate, however, it is subject to varying interpretations. The abundance of definitions reflects the fact that the very term 'nationalism' can be used in different ways and might have different meanings. It can describe:[11]

- an accentuated individual and collective feeling of ethnic identity and belonging to an ethnic community, usually to a nation. This identity is usually exclusive and defined in a negative way against 'others' who are not members of this ethnic community or who are not recognized as such;
- strong ethnic sentiment and emotion, often exaggerated and directed against 'others';

- a political and social ideology and a specific type of political philosophy;
- a specific political and social principle, used also as a criterion for the recognition of belonging to and membership of a certain ethnic community;
- a specific, usually ethnically exclusive, policy of social movements, political parties, or nation-states;
- political or social movements;
- a political concept and strategy aimed at political mobilization of people who feel members of a certain ethnicity; and
- a doctrine of political legitimacy.[12]

What all these meanings have in common is the idea of homogeneity, monolithism, and natural or enforced ethnic unity. The main objective of nationalism is to promote and defend the 'national interest' as it is formulated by the nationalist movement, party, or government. National interests are supreme and worth any sacrifice, including death. Whoever questions this risks being branded a traitor and expelled. An individual's duty to the polity, which represents the nation, 'overrides all public obligations, and in extreme cases (such as wars) all other obligations of whatever kind'.[13] In this way, nationalism is the most demanding form of ethnic or group identification. Nationalism in this account goes hand in hand with the existence of modern nations and nation-states: 'Nationalism is primarily a political principle, which holds that the political and national unit should be congruent . . . Nationalist sentiment is the feeling of anger aroused by the violation of the principle, or the feeling of satisfaction aroused by its fulfillment. A nationalist movement is one actuated by a sentiment of this kind.'[14]

Like the myth of national homogeneity, nationalist movements themselves do not always emerge well from serious historical analyses. These show a rather different and heterogeneous picture of nationalist movements:

Nationalist movements have never been monolithic, but were always internally divided and competitive. It is only the historiography of nationalism that always attempts to impose an interpretative patina of concord, once success has been achieved. The historiography of Italian nationalism, for example, has regularly described the profound political divisions between leaders and movements during the struggle for independence, as if they were resolved by the achievement of a state and henceforth reduced to parliamentary differences. The monuments in the urban landscape of every European country remain as testimonies to the victors' unilateral consensual reinterpretation of the past.[15]

Nonetheless, the myth of homogeneity and national unity has become an important component of every national history as it is reinterpreted by the victors, who also control the official textbooks. People brought up and schooled in the myths of national unity and homogeneity are taught to fear any possible danger to stability, homogeneity, and unity within the nation-state. This form of nationalism presents clear con-tradictions with liberal democracy, based, as this is, on pluralism and limitations on the dominance of majorities.

Yet it is too simple to conclude that all nationalism is anti-democratic. This depends on the definition of nationalism used, as well as the view-point of the observer. Nationalism was considered a positive phenome-non in the period of the formation of nations and nation-states during the nineteenth century and at the beginning of the twentieth century. The same was true in the period of decolonization, when nationalism was one of the driving forces of this process. The importance of nationalist movements in the process of nation-building and nation-state-building was reflected in the fact that some of the leaders of those movements were and are still considered 'fathers of their nation'.[16]

Some authors differentiate among types of nationalism. Valery Tishkov, among others, differentiates between 'ethnic nationalism' (or ethno-nationalism) and 'civic nationalism'. The former is ethnically defined, demands ethnic unity and homogeneity, and is usually exclu-sivist in its nature. The latter refers to an individual's belonging to and identification with a certain, at least theoretically, ethnically neutral state. This bond is usually based on citizenship as a predominantly legal link between an individual and a state. In this context, 'ethnic nationalism' is understood as a negative phenomenon, whilst 'civic nationalism' is a positive one.[17] Yael Tamir recognizes the important historic role of nationalism in the formation of nations and nation-states and in the process of modernization and its impact on liberalism and modern political philosophy. Her positive concept of 'liberal nationalism' is motivated by her commitment to pursue a national vision while remaining faithful to a set of liberal beliefs. This form of liberal nationalism is compatible with the concept of democratic citi-zenship, as advocated by the Council of Europe. Tamir explains:

I have consequently refrained from taking a frequently offered piece of advice suggesting I renounce the concept of 'nationalism' in favour of a less emo-tionally loaded term, such as 'people' or the much discussed 'community.' Although resorting to a less controversial and less pejorative term might have made my position more acceptable, I thought I would be wrong to bypass the concept of nationalism. Liberals who give up this term and surrender it to the use of conservative political forces, or note the difference, to chauvinist and racist ideologies, alienated themselves from a whole set of values that are of immense importance to a great many people, including liberals.[18]

She is aware of certain inherent tensions between liberal and national values, but nevertheless suggests:

that the liberal tradition, with its respect for personal autonomy, reflection, and choice, and the national tradition, with its emphasis on belonging, loyalty, and solidarity, although generally seen as mutually exclusive, can accommodate one another. Liberals can acknowledge the importance of belonging, membership, and cultural affiliations, as well as the particular moral commitments that follow from them. Nationalists can appreciate the value of personal autonomy and individual rights and freedoms, as well as sustain a commitment for social justice both between and within nations.[19]

Nationalism in south-eastern Europe in the past decades, however, bears very little or no resemblance to these positive conceptions. Nationalism in the Balkans is traditional ethnic nationalism largely based on west European Christian traditions, especially on the nineteenth-century concept of the unification of nations and nation-states. As such, it is usually exclusivist and often hegemonic. In its pursuit of national unity and homogeneity it is hostile to 'others'. Its hegemonic nature is reflected in the call of nationalist movements for the unification of all members of a certain nation within the borders of its nation-state. If an ethnic nation-state already exists, nationalist movements try to use it for that goal. If a certain ethnic community does not have an independent state of its own, the establishment of such a nation-state is declared a central goal. In any case, nationalists and especially nationalist leaders see an independent single-nation state of their own as the only efficient instrument for the realization of their national interests.[20] Although nationalists, for different reasons, including their public appearance and requests of the international community, have often called for democratization, this has not been their primary interest and has been subordinated to their self-defined national interests. It was this logic that led to the escalation of social and ethnic conflicts that accompanied the dismantling of the former Yugoslav federation.[21]

While mainstream nationalism is focused on the state or the pursuit of one, the nationalities question has other dimensions. So some authors talk about 'nationalism of nations without states' (stateless nations), 'diaspora nationalism', 'regional nationalism', and 'minority nationalism' in multi-ethnic states.[22] The nature of minority nationalism depends, to a large extent, on the local or regional situation of the minority group. It usually focuses on the preservation of the minority and its ethnic, cultural, linguistic, and historic identity. For that reason it can be described as a defensive nationalism that, although still exclusivist, does not build on the hostility to 'others'—in this case persons belonging to the majority population. Such a form of minority nationalism might be expected especially in those environments where relatively small national minorities are granted and guaranteed substantial minority rights and protection.

The size and political organization of a national minority represent important factors in minority nationalism.[23] If a national minority represents a relatively large share of the local or regional population, we could expect proposals for territorial autonomy including federalization of the existing unitary state. If dissatisfaction reaches a certain level, and particularly if minorities feel endangered within the existing nation-state, demands for independence might also be expected. Following the principle of self-determination, minority nationalism and nationalism of stateless nations played an important role in the formation of new nation-states in post-First World War Europe and during the era of decolonization.[24] Minority nationalisms have come to the fore in the former Federal Republic of Yugoslavia, especially in Kosovo, in a particularly virulent manner. Here nationalism has sometimes taken a pathological form, resulting in widespread violence and 'ethnic cleansing'. Yet this was not, as often thought, the inevitable result of ancient primordial hatreds suddenly released. Rather it stemmed from the specific circumstances of regime transition, compounded by failures on the part of the international community. There are important lessons here on how ethnic and nationalist conflict should be managed and on the role to be played by the international community.

Europe and the Balkans

Until quite recently, the Balkans was a forgotten, backward, and troubled region of Europe to which the international community paid attention only when it impinged upon the strategic interests of the great powers. Not much was known about the history, culture, and situation of the region, which was often portrayed in negative stereotypes. Attention was paid only when something unexpected, tragic, or spectacular happened, but the region was soon forgotten again. This changed dramatically in the 1990s. When a war broke out in the territory of the former Yugoslavia, the region came to the centre of the attention of the international public and community. The intensity of the conflict and atrocities that accompanied it astonished the world. The international community started to search for viable solutions to the problems, but only with partial success.

The Balkan Peninsula has shared a turbulent history. It is a natural bridge between Asia and Europe and has been a crossroad of different religions, cultures, and civilizations from prehistoric times. Frequent migrations of peoples constantly changed the ethnic composition of the region. When 'new historic peoples' arrived, the old population moved to remote areas and often managed to preserve their language, culture, and identity. The division of the Roman empire in the fourth century AD established a borderline, which to a considerable extent still exists, in the territory of Bosnia-Herzegovina. After the schism of 1054 AD this border divided two Christian cultures: a Roman Catholic culture in the west and an Orthodox culture in the east. The invasion of the Ottoman Turks in the fourteenth and fifteenth centuries brought Islamic religion and culture to the region. Although Islam dominated Eastern culture for five centuries, it did not eliminate Orthodox Christianity. Tolerance within the Ottoman Empire enabled several specific ethnic and regional Islamic and Orthodox cultures to coexist. Nevertheless, occasional conflicts existed as in every plural environment. The border between the Roman Catholic area and the Islamic–Orthodox area stabilized along the current political borders of Bosnia-Herzegovina. Rebellions against Ottoman rule in the nineteenth century eroded the Ottoman Empire and permitted the creation of new Balkan states. The political map of the region changed after the First World War, during the Second World War and after it, and again in the 1990s.[25]

Despite its turbulent history, and contrary to general belief, severe ethnic conflicts were not a traditional characteristic of the region. Until the 1980s the former Yugoslavia was cited as a successful multinational state that had managed to establish good ethnic relations. Even its citizens did not perceive Yugoslavia as a divided society or a fractured state. It did not match the typical model of a divided or bicommunal society characterized by protracted conflicts between two distinct ethnic, linguistic, or religious communities. Ethnic relations in Yugoslavia seemed good despite substantial ethnic diversity; ethnic conflicts that escalated occasionally in some regions were resolved successfully in a peaceful way. The war in the 1990s, however, changed the situation.

Disaggregating the Balkans

There are some important lessons to be drawn from the recent experience of the Balkans—at both the national and international levels.[26] It is especially important that the international community examines its role in historical developments in the region in different epochs. Special attention should be paid to its impact on ethnic relations taking into account substantial differences between countries and the specific situation and circumstances in each country.

Although the Balkans has always been a multi-ethnic, multicultural, multilingual, and multi-religious area[27] and occasional ethnic conflicts have existed, the region also has a tradition of ethnic and religious tolerance. Unfortunately several traditional mechanisms for the resolution of conflicts, ironically considered pre-modern, have been abolished and destroyed in the process of modernization in the past 150 years. The failure to replace these with adequate new ones helps to explain the disaster of the 1990s in the territory of the former Yugoslavia. Nevertheless, even now the ethnic situation is not uniformly bad, and besides continued conflicts there are instances of successful accommodation. So it is dangerous to make generalizations or to consign the whole region to the same category.

All countries share the history of the region, but perceptions and interpretations of this common history and many historical events differ substantially from country to country. For example, Croatia, Bosnia-Herzegovina, Macedonia, and the Federal Republic of Yugoslavia shared certain common historical experiences during the existence of the former Yugoslavia. Yet these shared experiences are evaluated and interpreted differently and often result in very different consequences and reactions.[28] The wars that broke up Yugoslavia in the 1990s and their tragic consequences added more material for historical interpretation and memory. Especially dangerous from the perspective of ethnic relations in these multi-ethnic societies are so-called 'new' interpretations of history produced and often used in daily politics by nationalists that can provoke new conflicts and fuel the existing ones. These 'new' histories may become major obstacles for the peace and stability in the region and for the promotion and rehabilitation of multi-ethnic societies in these countries.

It is clear that one condition for the successful management of ethnic difference is democracy, and the development of a democratic citizenship. Such a conception of democracy must include recognition of the right of groups to their own existence. There also needs to be a culture of respect for minorities and a move away from the old nation-state model in which the titular nationality has a monopoly of power. Mechanisms are also needed to ensure minority representation in politics and administration.[29] These mechanisms and arrangements can be successful only if they are adjusted to the specific situation, circumstances, and needs of each country. Concerted efforts to implement these general guidelines will be required not only by the countries in the region, but also by the European and international community.

A lesson to be drawn from the Yugoslav experience, however, is that formal democracy is not enough and that, if not introduced in the right way, it can even exacerbate the problem. Democratization in the former Yugoslavia started in the 1980s and progressed at different speeds in different parts of the country. Many believed that the formal introduction of democracy and the multi-party political system in the late 1980s and early 1990s would transform the country into a democratic society. They did not take into account the existing differences between republics and the fact that there was no adequate social infrastructure for democracy in most parts of the country. Historical experiences in now developed democracies show that democratization usually takes a long time, often several generations. A functioning democracy requires a democratic political culture and a certain level of political socialization. In Yugoslavia there were few democratic political traditions, and most politicians were politically socialized in a totalitarian system. There was no tradition of support for competing political parties, with stable bases of support. People were unfamiliar with the political ideologies found in democratic polities. In these conditions the political leaders and parties sought a way to mobilize the people successfully, and ethnicity and nationalism became an obvious dividing line.

To prevent this from developing into conflict, there should have been power-sharing institutions in place, as well as laws to ensure ethnic equality and protection of minorities. The international community had a role to play here. However, the Yugoslav crisis showed the lack of adequate mechanisms at the international level to manage and resolve such crises. The lack of adequate coherent international strategy contributed substantially to the escalation of the Yugoslav crisis. Mixed signals and the constantly shifting policy of individual Western countries and the European Community contributed to the confusion. All actors in the crisis interpreted these mixed signals as support from the international community for their cause. The Yugoslav president, Ante Markovic, and the federal government believed that the international community would support their economic and political reforms leading to democratization of the country. The democratic opposition and reformist political leaders in the republics (especially in Slovenia and Croatia) believed that the international community would do everything to protect them. Unitarists, including Slobodan Milošević,[30] thought that the international community would support their policy including the use of force to preserve the existing political arrangements, territorial integrity, and unity of the country. Such misperceptions played a central role in deepening the crisis that led to conflict. Moreover, when the conflict began, the international community failed to intervene in Croatia and waited until several thousand people were killed and hundreds of thousands driven from their homes in Bosnia-Herzegovina. To a large extent, the same mistakes were repeated in Kosovo.

The earlier intervention takes place, the easier it is to prevent conflict. In retrospect, we can detect several signals and warnings of the impending chaos, all of which were ignored. They were: growing intolerance; political mobilization along ethnic lines; increasing nationalism in different nations and the presentation of nationalist programmes that argue for exclusion or domination; lack of communication and cooperation; an absence of common interests; and calls for increasing autonomy and independence. Preventive intervention and the implementation of a range of prescriptions, including an accelerated process of integration of Yugoslavia into the European Community, would have gone a long way towards preventing disaster.

Conclusion: The Role of Europe and the International Community

The international community was caught off guard in Yugoslavia. Its failure there underlines the urgent need for the development of effective international strategies and mechanisms that would prevent similar failures in future.

The first step is for the international community to ensure that there are no gains from the chauvinistic policies that ruptured Yugoslavia's multi-ethnic societies. An important part of this is the effective punishment of those who are responsible for ethnic cleansing and war crimes. It is essential that Europe, as an important actor in the international community, presses for the successful establishment of the International Criminal Court and for the successful functioning of the international tribunal for the former Yugoslavia.

More is required than punitive measures, however. The international community, and Europe as an integral part of it, should recognize that the inclusion of different troubled regions in international cooperation and economic integration is the most productive way to prevent the outbreak and escalation of ethnic conflict. Such an approach has already proved very successful in central and eastern Europe. Inclusion in the North Atlantic Treaty Organization, the process of the eastern enlargement of the European Union (EU), and, in some cases, even the promise of future inclusion in this process have helped to stimulate salutary economic and democratic political reforms throughout central and eastern Europe (see Chapter 16).[31] Similarly, the most effective strategy for the resolution of problems in the Balkans is the inclusion of this region in the wider European order, including the EU. Admittedly, it will be very difficult for many of the Balkan countries to meet the required criteria for accession to the EU, but all of them, with the exception of Serbia, are committed to becoming EU members and are keen to do what is required.[32] The difficulties of including south-eastern Europe, moreover, have to be weighed against the costs of excluding it, and the danger of continuing political instability in the region.

The enlargement of the EU to include south-eastern Europe, rather than just central and eastern Europe, will have a number of positive effects on inter-ethnic relations in the region. In the short term the inclusion of Balkan countries as candidate members will require them to meet the EU's political conditions for accession, which include high standards of democracy and respect for minority rights. Membership, by enabling faster social development and a better life for people, can offer a viable alternative to traditional exclusive and aggressive nationalist ideologies.

International integration, particularly within the context of the EU, will allow for international cooperation of subnational regions and decentralization within states. Together, these may well provide new frameworks for the regulation and management of ethnic relations and conflicts.[33] They might produce mechanisms that would address specific needs and interests of different communities and environments by providing new functional frameworks beyond the nation-state. Trans-border cooperation and democratic institutions within new trans-border regions can address the specific interests of people living in a certain territory in a way that would be impossible within the borders of the existing nation-states, while the broader European context can assist the realization of other common interests. This might also change the traditional perception of majorities and minorities. Within Europe even the largest nations are, in a way, minorities, so they could become more receptive to ethnic and cultural diversity, ideas of multiculturalism and interculturalism, and the need for protection of minorities.

In the longer term the construction of a common European identity, built on principles of multiculturalism and interculturalism, could become a powerful alternative to existing exclusionist nationalist concepts and politics. As a multi-layered identity based on diversity, the new European identity should ensure tolerance and coexistence of different identities that are often seen as competing. The Council of Europe and the EU could and should play key roles in building this common European identity. Awareness-raising campaigns aimed at the promotion of multicultural societies, tolerance and cooperation, multiculturalism–interculturalism, and the protection of minorities would be important elements of their strategy. These campaigns should increase awareness of the potential danger and destructive power of nationalism in multi-ethnic societies—especially in generating and escalating violent ethnic conflicts.

In the period before the various countries of south-eastern Europe are admitted into the EU, or offered candidate status, the EU should seek to stimulate cooperation in the region and promote the improvement of ethnic relations and protection of minorities in multi-ethnic societies as vital fields of cooperation based on existing international legal standards, especially the conventions of the Council of Europe and the Copenhagen standards on democracy. Help with economic reconstruction will also be essential. The EU initiative to conclude and develop the Stability Pact for South-Eastern Europe, signed at Cologne in June 1999, is a good start in this direction. It is aimed at strengthening the countries of south-eastern Europe in their efforts to foster peace, democracy, respect for human rights, and economic prosperity. However, its success will depend largely on the commitment, financial and otherwise, of the various donor states.

On a broader note, to prevent similar tragic developments in other parts of the world the international community should develop precise rules and procedures for intervention in ethnic trouble-spots. They will have to determine decision-making procedures and the role that countries and international organizations should play in these activities. This process should include also international public awareness-raising campaigns that would explain the potential danger of exclusivist nationalism, xenophobia, and expansionism to the international public and mobilize the necessary support for international intervention. Considering the possibility of similar conflicts in

Europe, such mechanisms should become also a central segment of European integration processes. They should include early-warning systems that would give the international community the necessary response time for the development and implementation of measures for the prevention, management, and resolution of crises.

Intervention should encompass not simply peace-making, that is, putting an end to conflict, but also peace-building, which requires economic reconstruction and the establishment of political institutions that can serve as channels for the expression of existing pluralism and interests. Instead of nation-states that generate conflict through the promotion of nationalism and exclusionist practices, there should be an emphasis on the building of states based on the principle of multiculturalism and inter-culturalism.

NOTES

1. R. Jenkins, *Rethinking Ethnicity: Arguments and Explorations* (London: Sage, 1997), 44–8; A. D. Smith, *The Ethnic Origins of Nations* (Oxford: Blackwell, 1986).
2. This generally accepted definition in Article 1 of the Montevideo Convention on Rights and Duties of States of 1933 reads: 'The State as a person of international law should possess the following qualifications: a) permanent population; b) defined territory; c) government; and d) capacity to enter into relations with other states.' See also J. G. Starke, *Introduction to International Law,* 10th ed. (London: Butterworth, 1989).
3. K. W. Deutsch, *Political Community at the International Level: Problems of Definition and Measurement* (New York: Archon Books, 1970).
4. C. A. Macartney, *National States and National Minorities* (London: Oxford University Press, 1934), 192–211; H. Seton-Watson, *Nations and States* (London: Methuen, 1977); Smith, *The Ethnic Origin of Nations.*
5. E. J. Hobsbawm, *Nations and Nationalism since 1789: Programme, Myth, Reality* (Cambridge: Cambridge University Press, 1990), 23.
6. P. Fougeyrollas, *Pour une France fédérale—vers l'unité européenne par la révolution régionale* (Paris: Médiations, Éditions Denoel, 1968). Intensified (international) migrations and the existing (substantial) immigrant population contribute to additional ethnic and cultural diversity in France in the 20th century that is likely to increase in the future.
7. G. Ambrosius and W. H. Hubbard, *A Social and Economic History of Twentieth-Century Europe,* trans. F. Tribe and W. H. Hubbard (Cambridge, Mass.: Harvard University Press, 1989), 28–42, 84–6.
8. A series of interesting articles that discuss the adequacy of the traditional concept and model of (single) nation-states in multi-ethnic societies was published in recent years also in the journal *Treatises and Documents* published by the Institute for Ethnic Studies. See B. Bučar, 'The Emergence of New States, Borders and Minorities', *Razpave in gradivo/Treatises and Documents,* 32 (1997), 15–29; H. Gärntner, 'State, Nation and Security in Central Europe: Democratic States

without Nations', *Razpave in gradivo/Treatises and Documents*, 32 (1997), 31–64; M. Žagar, 'Constitutions in Multi-Ethnic Reality', *Razpave in gradivo/Treatises and Documents*, 29–30 (1994–5), 143–64; M. Žagar, 'Rešitev, ki je postala problem: Nacionalne države in večetnična realnost' ('A Solution that Became a Problem: Nation-States and Multiethnic Reality'), *Razpave in gradivo/Treatises and Documents*, 32 (1997), 7–13.

9. B. Anderson, *Imagined Communities: Reflection on the Origin and Spread of Nationalism* (London: Verso, 1983); J. Armstrong, *Nations before Nationalism* (Chapel Hill: University of North Carolina Press, 1982); I. Banac, *The National Question in Yugoslavia: Origins, History, Politics* (Ithaca, NY: Cornell University Press, 1993); M. Banton, *Racial and Ethnic Competition* (Cambridge: Cambridge University Press, 1983); E. Gellner, *Nations and Nationalism* (Oxford: Blackwell, 1983); W. Connor, *The National Question in Marxist–Leninist Theory and Strategy* (Princeton: Princeton University Press, 1984); K. Deutsch, *Nationalism and Social Communication: An Inquiry into the Foundations of Nationality*, 2nd ed. (Cambridge, Mass.: MIT Press, 1966); Hobsbawm, *Nations and Nationalism since 1789*; M. Keating, *State and Regional Nationalism: Territorial Politics and the European State* (Brighton: Harvester Wheatsheaf, 1988); E. Kedourie, *Nationalism*, 4th, expanded edn. (Oxford: Blackwell, 1993); Smith, *The Ethnic Origin of Nations*; P. F. Sugar and I. J. Lederer (eds.), *Nationalism in Eastern Europe* (Seattle: University of Washington Press, 1969).

10. S. R. Bollerup and C. D. Christensen, *Nationalism in Eastern Europe: Causes and Consequences of the National Revivals and Conflicts in Late-Twentieth-Century Europe* (New York: St Martin's Press, 1997); G. Brunner, *Nationality Problems and Minority Conflicts in Eastern Europe: Strategies for Europe*, updated and rev. edn. (Gütersloh: Bartelsman Foundation Publishers, 1996); W. Connor, *Ethnocentrism: The Quest for Understanding* (Princeton: Princeton University Press, 1994); E. Gellner, *Encounters with Nationalism* (Oxford: Blackwell, 1994); E. Gellner, *Nationalism* (Oxford: Blackwell, 1994); L. Greenfeld, *Nationalism: Five Roads to Modernity* (Cambridge, Mass.: Harvard University Press, 1992); M. Guibernau and J. Rex (eds.), *The Ethnicity Reader: Nationalism, Multiculturalism and Migration* (Cambridge: Polity Press, 1997); J. Hutchinson and A. D. Smith (eds.), *Ethnicity* (Oxford: Oxford University Press, 1996); J. Hutchinson and A. D. Smith (eds.), *Nationalism* (Oxford: Oxford University Press, 1994); Jenkins, *Rethinking Ethnicity*; J. Kellas, *Politics of Nationalism and Ethnicity* (New York: St Martin's Press, 1991); T. Nairn, *Faces of Nationalism: Janus Revisited* (New York: Verso, 1997); A. D. Smith, *National Identity* (London: Penguin, 1991); A. D. Smith, *Nationalism and Modernism: A Critical Survey of Recent Theories of Nations and Nationalism* (New York: Routledge, 1998); Y. Tamir, *Liberal Nationalism* (Princeton: Princeton University Press, 1993); S. Woolf (ed.), *Nationalism in Europe, 1815 to the Present: A Reader* (New York: Routledge, 1996).

11. M. Žagar, 'A Contribution to an "Ethnic Glossary"', *Razpave in gradivo/Treatises and Documents*, 28 (1993), 163–5, 168–9.

12. M. Guibernau, 'Nations without States: Catalonia, a Case Study', in Guibernau and Rex (eds.), *The Ethnicity Reader*, 133.

13. Hobsbawm, *Nations and Nationalism since 1789*, 9.

14. Gellner, *Nations and Nationalism*, 1.

15. S. Woolf, 'Introduction', in Woolf (ed.), *Nationalism in Europe*, 31.

16. The term 'nation' in this context usually refers to both—a nation and a state. It describes the role of these leaders in the transformation of an ethnic community into a modern nation, and in the formation of a single-nation state of this 'titular nation'.

17. Žagar, 'A Contribution to an "Ethnic Glossary"', 164.
18. Tamir, *Liberal Nationalism*, 5.
19. Ibid. 6.
20. J. Hutchinson and A. D. Smith, 'Introduction', in Hutchinson and Smith (eds.), *Nationalism*, 5–13.
21. Since a sufficient number of recent and relevant titles on this topic exist in many languages, it will not be discussed in this contribution.
22. Gellner, *Nations and Nationalism*, 101–9; Guibernau, 'Nations without States', 133–54; M. Keating, 'Asymmetrical Government: Multinational States in an integrating Europe', *Publius—The Journal of Federalism*, 29/1 (Winter 1999), 71–86; M. Keating, 'Regional Devolution: The West European Experience', *Public Money and Management*, 16/4 (1996), 35–42; Keating, *State and Regional Nationalism*; W. Kymlicka and C. Straehle, 'Cosmopolitanism, Nation-States, and Minority Nationalism: A Critical Review of Recent Literature', *European Journal of Philosophy*, 7/1 (1999), 65–88; Macartney, *National States and National Minorities*; M. Watson (ed.), *Contemporary Minority Nationalism* (New York: Routledge, 1992).
23. M. Keating, 'Northern Ireland and the Basque Country', in J. McGarry (ed.), *Northern Ireland in Comparative Perspective* (Oxford: Oxford University Press, 2001); G. Smith, 'Russia, Multiculturalism and Federal Justice', *Europe–Asia Studies*, 50/8 (1998), 1393–1411.
24. See Macartney, *National States and National Minorities*, 179–211.
25. See Banac, *The National Question in Yugoslavia*; R. Crampton and B. Crampton, *Atlas of Eastern Europe in the Twentieth Century* (New York: Routledge, 1997); C. Jelavich and B. Jelavich, *The Establishment of the Balkan National States, 1804–1920*, vol. viii of *A History of East Central Europe* (Seattle: University of Washington Press, 1977); Sugar and Lederer (eds.), *Nationalism in Eastern Europe*. For alternative accounts, see I. Ninić, *Migrations in Balkan History* (Belgrade: Serbian Academy of Sciences and Arts, Institute for Balkan Studies, 1989); L. S. Stavrianos, *The Balkans since 1453* (New York: Rinehart, 1958); Y. Stoyanov, *The Hidden Tradition in Europe: The Secret History of Medieval Christian Heresy* (London: Penguin, 1994).
26. This section is based on the work of the Special Delegation of Council of Europe Advisers on Minorities, of which the author was a member in 1999, author's research, and field trips to the region.
27. See *World Directory of Minorities* (London: Minority Rights Group International, 1997), 155–8 (Greece), 196–201 and 256–8 (central and eastern Europe—general), 201–5 (Albania), 205–8 (Bosnia-Herzegovina), 209–13 (Bulgaria), 213–16 (Croatia), 233–6 (Macedonia), 240–4 (Romania), 250–8 (Federal Republic of Yugoslavia—Serbia and Montenegro), and 378–84 (Turkey).
28. Such as the resistance during the Second World War, ethnic policy at different historic stages of the former Yugoslavia, evolution of its constitutional system, social and economic crisis in the 1980s, handling of this crisis by the federal authorities and authorities in individual federal units, reforms and process of democratization that started in the 1980s, disintegration of the former Yugoslavia. All mentioned historic events and experiences, and their specific interpretations and evaluations continue to have an impact also on ethnic relations in individual countries.
29. See *Promotion of Multi-Ethnic Society and Democratic Citizenship: Report of the Special Delegation of Council of Europe Advisers*, Stability Pact for South Eastern Europe, Working Table I on Democratisation and Human Rights (Strasbourg: Council of Europe, 6 Mar. 2000).

30. The Serbian communist leader Slobodan Milošević advocated a strong and centralized federation based on the monopoly of power of the (recentralized) League of Communists of Yugoslavia, hoping that this would ensure his power.

31. M. Wohlfeld, 'Sicherheit', in Bartelsmann Stiftung Forschungsgruppe Europa (ed.), *Kosten, Nutzen und Chancen der Osterweiterung für die Europäische Union* (Gütersloh: Verlag Bertelsmann Stiftung, 1998). See also A. Mayhew, *Recreating Europe: The European Union's Policy towards Central and Eastern Europe* (Cambridge: Cambridge University Press, 1998), 185–8; C. P. Wood, 'European Political Cooperation: Lessons from the Gulf War and Yugoslavia', in A. W. Cafruny and G. Rosenthal (eds.), *The Maastricht Debates and Beyond* (Boulder, Colo.: Lynne Rienner, 1993).

32. See e.g. I. Brinar and M. Svetličič, 'Enlargement of the European Union: The Case of Slovenia', *Journal of European Public Policy*, 6/5 (Dec. 1999), 802–21.

33. See e.g. B. Bučar, 'International Cooperation of European Subnational Regions', *Journal of International Relations*, 2/1 (1995), 4–17.

CHAPTER 16

Nationalism in Transition: Nationalizing Impulses and International Counterweights in Latvia and Estonia

Julie Bernier

The reconfiguration of political space along national lines following the collapse of the Soviet Union, of Yugoslavia, and of Czechoslovakia provides a striking example of the enduring potency of the nationality principle in the contemporary world, and seems to prove Ernest Gellner right when he asserts that 'one need not expect the age of nationalism to come to an end'.[1] Indeed, one of the most recurrent patterns observable in post-secession states in eastern Europe is the tendency to imprint the state with the identity of its ethnic or cultural majority. In most of these new states independence has been understood as the political affirmation of ethno-cultural majorities, and this despite the multinational character of many of these states.[2] Independence has reinforced and institutionalized the self-understanding of ethno-cultural majorities as the legitimate owners of the state, and their perception of minorities as mere guests in their house.[3]

This self-understanding has contributed, in some cases, to a rather despotic use of the principle of majority rule and a perversion of the democratic ideal of a 'government of the people, by the people, for the people' into a government 'of one kind of people, by that kind of people, for that kind of people, at the expense of all others'.[4] It has also led to the adoption of various 'nationalizing' measures, the main aim of which is to actualize and incarnate the connection between the core nation and the state, and 'to promote the language, culture, demographic preponderance, economic flourishing, or political hegemony of the core ethnocultural nation'.[5] The scope of these nationalizing policies varies significantly among new states, but they all seek, to a certain extent, to provide a national framework and character for the polity.

Nationalizing efforts undertaken by new states include a broad range of policies. The most notable ones concern the adoption of an official language, national symbols, and various provisions regulating citizenship, education, media, and public-sector employment.[6] These nationalizing policies encountered relatively little resistance in states like Armenia, Lithuania, and Slovenia, where the level of homogeneity is high. However, in states with significant minorities such measures have rarely been met with indifference and have often provoked minorities into counter-mobilization.

This chapter looks at the effectiveness of international organizations in providing a counterweight to these nationalizing impulses. It focuses on the case of Latvia and Estonia, since these countries have adopted some of the most extensive nationalizing measures of all the new states in eastern Europe, and since they have been under particularly intense scrutiny by international organizations. The chapter is divided into two main sections. The first shows that the adoption of nationalizing measures in Latvia and Estonia is rooted in concerns about the identity, demography, and social mobility of the core group. It outlines the type of nationalizing strategies that have been adopted to reallocate power, status, and resources in favour of this group. The second section examines interventions in Latvia and Estonia by the Organization for Security and Cooperation in Europe (OSCE) High Commissioner on National Minorities, the Council of Europe, and the European Union (EU). It is argued that the combination of these pressures has contributed in an important way to a recent relaxation of the nationalizing policies that were adopted in the first years of independence.

Nationalization, Language, and Citizenship in Latvia and Estonia

Latvia and Estonia were forcibly annexed to the Soviet Union in 1940 as a result of the Molotov–Ribbentrop pact between the Soviet Union and Nazi Germany. This annexation had a tremendous social, political, and demographic impact on both countries since Soviet authorities undertook massive deportation campaigns—which triggered the exile of many members of the Latvian and Estonian local elites—and encouraged large-scale immigration of Russians to work in the industrial and administrative sectors. The first direct impact of these policies was a steady reduction of the native Latvian and Estonian share of the population in both republics during the fifty years following annexation. For instance, while in 1935 the ethnic Latvian share of the population in Latvia was 77 per cent, by 1989 their share of the population had dropped to 52 per cent.[7] In 1934 the ethnic Estonian share of Estonia's was 88 per cent, but by 1989 it had dropped to 61.5 per cent.[8]

Another consequence of the annexation and of Soviet policies was a decline in the representation of local Latvians and Estonians in the power structures of both republics, particularly in the government and party positions. Indeed, just two years before Latvia achieved independence, Latvians accounted for only 39.7 per cent of the 184,182 party members and candidates, while the Russian share was 43.1 per cent.[9] The native Estonian population was similarly under-represented in Estonia, although its position there slowly began to improve under Gorbachev.[10]

A third effect of Soviet policies was a decline in the use of the Latvian and Estonian language and an increased use of Russian as the language of government and inter-ethnic communication. Although the native populations resisted this linguistic Russification and managed to retain their native languages, fluency in Russian was a requirement for many jobs both in the private and in the public sectors. The result was a situation of asymmetrical bilingualism: a high level of bilingualism among the native population and a strong unilingualism among ethnic Russians.[11]

It is not surprising, then, that upon achieving their independence, Latvians and Estonians were preoccupied with their demographic weight, their under-representation in power structures, and the situation of their languages.[12] After independence the governments of Latvia and Estonia relied on both restrictive citizenship policies and strict language requirements to reverse a status quo they saw as rooted in an historical injustice. Both excluded ethnic Russians and favoured their respective native populations in the distribution of jobs, resources, and political power. After independence both adopted citizenship laws—in 1992 in Estonia and 1994 in Latvia—that effectively excluded the great majority of ethnic Russians from citizenship. Instead of adopting, like most other post-Soviet republics, a citizenship policy that granted automatic citizenship to all inhabitants at the time of independence, Latvia and Estonia opted for a much more restrictive approach. Automatic citizenship was granted only to those who were citizens of the republics prior to their forced annexation to the Soviet Union in 1940 and to their descendants. The fundamental rationale behind the citizenship laws, as Jeff Chinn and Lise Truex note, was that the citizenry of the states should be the same as would have been the case had the Soviet annexation not taken place.[13]

In 1991 approximately a third of Latvia's and Estonia's population did not qualify for automatic citizenship.[14] The only way for these post-1940 migrants and their children to acquire Latvian or Estonian citizenship was to undergo a lengthy process of naturalization in which language requirements were central.[15] Language requirements were a particularly serious obstacle for ethnic Russians, who were an overwhelming majority among post-1940 migrants and who were mostly unilingual Russian speakers. Given this, very few ethnic Russians were able to acquire citizenship through the naturalization process. In Latvia obstacles to naturalization were even greater since non-citizens had to wait until 1994, when the law on citizenship was finally adopted, before knowing exactly what conditions they would have to fulfil in order to acquire citizenship. The law adopted in 1994 established the so-called 'window system', which limited the number of non-citizens who could apply for citizenship each year, and established an order of priority between categories of non-citizens. For instance, those who were born in Latvia were eligible to apply before those who were born outside the country, and among those who were born in Latvia, priority was given to younger age groups.[16] The result of all these obstacles to the acquisition of citizenship in Latvia and Estonia was, as Brubaker has observed, that the citizenry of these states was considerably more homogeneous than the population.[17]

The low proportion of citizens among ethnic Russians in both countries also had major implications for their access to political, social, and economic benefits. At the political level their ability to participate in the decision-making process was extremely limited as in both republics citizenship was a requirement for being able to exercise the right to vote in national elections and for holding office.[18] In Latvia fluency in Latvian was also required before one could become a candidate for the *Saiema* (Latvian legislature) or contest municipal elections. The results of these measures on the political representation of ethnic Russians were rather striking. In both countries the ethnic Russian share of elected representatives is much lower than their share of the total population. In Latvia, ethnic Russians—approximately 33 per cent of the population—constituted about 6 per cent of the legislature after the elections in 1993 and 1995.[19] After the parliamentary elections of 1992 in Estonia, ethnic Russians—approximately 30 per cent of the population—did not occupy a single seat. After elections in

1995 only six of the 101 members of the Estonian Parliament were ethnic Russians.[20] Amendments to the Parliamentary and Local Elections
Law adopted by the Estonian Parliament in 1998 are not likely to
improve the representation of ethnic Russians since these amendments
'stipulate that candidates for parliament and for municipal and district
councils must know the Estonian language at a level sufficient to participate "in the assembly's work and [understand] the contents of legal
acts"'.[21]

Citizenship laws and language requirements in Latvia and Estonia
also had an important effect on the allocation of jobs. When the
Latvian government amended its 1989 law on language in 1992,
fluency in Latvian became a requirement for many jobs in the public
and private sectors. For instance, Article 4 of the 1992 law specified
that 'all employees in bodies of state power, that is, all institutions,
enterprises, and organizations belonging to the state, had to have a
command of and employ the state language, as well as other languages,
to the extent required by the person's professional duties'.[22] In 1997
competence in the Latvian language became a prerequisite for receiving unemployment and social security benefits.[23] Estonia also had
citizenship and language requirements for the public service. The
Estonian Law on Public Service that went into effect in 1993 stated
that public servants had to be proficient in Estonian before the end of
1995. The law was amended in 1995 to extend the delay for language
proficiency until 1 February 1997, but it specified that 'no non-
citizens were to be hired after 1 January 1996'.[24]

Finally, citizenship laws have worked to the disadvantage of ethnic
Russians in the distribution of resources. Since a large share of ethnic
Russians and other minorities in Latvia and Estonia were not citizens
in the first years of independence when a large proportion of land,
housing, and businesses were privatized, they were disadvantaged in
the distribution of privatization vouchers. In Latvia, for instance, the
1991 law on the privatization of the premises of small-scale businesses
and services excluded non-citizens from the privatization process.[25] A
recent study on the impact of the laws regulating the distribution and
restitution of property that were adopted by the Estonian government
in the first years of independence concluded that there was 'a prevailing tendency of discrimination against the Russians'.[26]

All these nationalizing measures have created significant tensions
between the core nation and minorities in Latvia and Estonia. This
tense situation has raised concerns in the international community.
Over the years pressures for liberalization, particularly with respect to
citizenship and language issues, have been intensified. The next section

examines interventions from the OSCE's High Commissioner on National Minorities, the Council of Europe, and the EU, and shows that the combination of these pressures has provided an important stimulus for a liberalization of policy in Latvia and Estonia.

The OSCE High Commissioner on National Minorities

The involvement of the OSCE's High Commissioner on National Minorities in Estonia and Latvia started in 1993, two years after their admission to the OSCE (then the CSCE). The High Commissioner started his involvement in a context of rising tensions between majorities—bare majorities in both cases—and minorities in the two countries, and of a persisting Russian military presence in the Baltics. This situation was potentially explosive and appeared an appropriate task for the High Commissioner given his mandate to act as 'an instrument of conflict prevention at the earliest possible stage' in a conflict involving national minority issues, and to provide early warning and take early action to prevent conflict escalation.[27]

Since citizenship and language issues constituted the most fertile ground for an escalation of inter-ethnic conflict in both Estonia and Latvia, the High Commissioner focused his attention on these issues. The High Commissioner made it clear, from the beginning of his involvement, that the path taken by both countries to secure the 'privileged position' of the core group over minorities not only ran against international norms, but also disrupted internal social cohesion and damaged the prospects for an improvement of the relations between the two states and Russia. His letter to the Minister of Foreign Affairs of Estonia on 6 April 1993 outlined the various problems associated with this path, and suggested that the integration of minorities would be a better way to secure the cohesion and security of Estonia than the path of exclusion:

your Government is in my view, at least in theory, confronted with two completely contradictory options regarding the non-Estonian population of your country. The first is to try to assure in various ways a privileged position for its Estonian population. Apart from the fact that such a policy would scarcely be compatible with the spirit, if not the letter, of various international obligations Estonia has accepted, such a policy would, in my view involve a considerable risk of increasing tensions with the non-Estonian population which, in turn, could lead to a destabilization of the country as a whole. In addition, it would have strongly negative effect on relations between Estonia and the Russian Federation. The alternative policy is to aim at the integration of the non-Estonian population by a deliberate policy of facilitating the chances of acquiring Estonian citizenship for those who express such a wish, and of assuring them full equality with Estonian citizens. In my view, such a policy would greatly reduce the danger of destabilization, because it would considerably enhance the chances of the non-Estonian population developing a sense of loyalty towards Estonia. Furthermore, such a policy would certainly not be incompatible with the wish of the Estonians to ensure and strengthen their political, cultural, and linguistic identity.[28]

Although worded differently, the essential message of the High Commissioner in his 6 April 1993 letter to the Minister for Foreign Affairs of Latvia was the same: seeking to exclude non-Latvians through strict citizenship and language requirements would be counter-productive in the end.[29]

In fact, the goal of the High Commissioner concerning citizenship and language issues in Estonia and Latvia was not only to convince both governments that they had an interest in making a more or less gradual shift from exclusion to integration, but also to suggest, through various concrete and specific recommendations, how this could be done while taking into account the concerns of the majority population in both countries. In other words, his recommendations were aimed at re-establishing a certain balance between the interests of majorities and the rights and interests of minorities.

The various recommendations of the High Commissioner on citizenship issues in Estonia and Latvia are revealing in this respect. He never suggested that the only solution for these countries was to adopt laws granting automatic citizenship to all non-citizens. Instead, he took into account the specific historical and political context of both countries and favoured an approach that would provide non-citizens with 'a clear prospect of acquiring citizenship provided that they make a real effort to integrate'[30] into the society in which they live. It is in the spirit of providing non-citizens with 'a clear prospect of acquiring citizenship' and 'to stimulate the process of integration'[31] that the High Commissioner has been so persistent in recommending, for instance, that the requirements for acquiring citizenship be kept to the basics, i.e. 'a simple conversational knowledge' of the official language and a 'knowledge of the basic facts' of the country's history or constitution.[32] Other obstacles to acquiring citizenship like naturalization fees, language training fees, income requirements, and residency requirements have been the subject of various recommendations by the High Commissioner.[33] The 'window system' established by the 1994 Law on Citizenship in Latvia was another very significant obstacle for acquiring citizenship since 'the right to apply for naturalization was spread over 7 years, beginning in 1996'. In this instance, the High Commissioner recommended straightforwardly 'the abolishment of the "window" system'.[34]

The High Commissioner's insistence that children born in Latvia or Estonia 'who would otherwise be stateless' should be granted citizenship was also in line with his efforts to convince the governments of both countries that the path of integration and respect for international laws can be perfectly compatible with the linguistic, cultural, and security concerns of Latvians and Estonians. Indeed, the High Commissioner argued that granting citizenship—not automatically, but unconditionally upon request from their parents—to these children would have the advantage of promoting integration and demonstrating compliance with internationally recognized human rights, without jeopardizing in any way the interests of Latvians or Estonians. In the case of Latvia, for instance, he maintained that:

The children to be naturalized in accordance with the Convention [on the Rights of the Child] are nearly all born in Latvia, and most of them have few if any memories of the Soviet past. They are apt to consider Latvia not as a foreign country, but as their country. The language programme of the Government of Latvia which will increase in importance in the coming years, will ensure that they will get an adequate training of the Latvian language in their schools. There is every reason to assume that by the time they reach adulthood they will be well integrated in Latvian society.[35]

As this passage shows, the position of the High Commissioner concerning citizenship—that it should be used as an instrument of inclusion, not of exclusion—was also applied to language matters. In fact, the High Commissioner repeatedly insisted, in his various recommendations to both governments, that language training for children and adults would not only facilitate the integration of minorities, it was a prerequisite for it.[36] He added that this was perfectly compatible with the aim of strengthening the place of the state language in both countries. The High Commissioner insisted that focusing on language training would, in the end, be more fruitful and less conflict-prone than adopting extensive language laws that limit the participation of minorities in the political, social, and economic life of the country. It was in this spirit that he strongly objected to the amendments to the Parliamentary and Local Elections Law and to the 1995 Language Law, before they were adopted by the Estonian Parliament in December 1998.[37] The High Commissioner has also taken a strong stance against the new Language Law approved by the Latvian Parliament on 8 July 1999. He maintained that some provisions of the

law—like the mandatory use of the state language in the private sector—were in violation of international standards and discriminatory,
and urged the Latvian president to return the law to Parliament for
reconsideration.[38] In a subsequent statement he reiterated that language training is a key factor in the strengthening of the state language
and that it was possible to elaborate a language law that would both
contribute to this aim and be respectful of international norms and
standards:

I strongly support the aim of strengthening the role of the state language in
Latvia. The international community should support the promotion of the
Latvian language through increased contributions to Latvian language training provided to non-Latvians. It is my firm conviction that a State Language
Law can be elaborated by the parliament which will enhance the position of
the Latvian language while at the same time being in conformity with international standards.[39]

The Council of Europe

The Council of Europe's pressures on Estonia and Latvia concerning
minority issues have also been significant, although they have not been
as systematic and sustained as those of the OSCE. The Council's various recommendations and actions have sought to stimulate the integration of the non-citizen population and to bring the domestic policy
of both countries into greater compliance with European and international standards of human rights and minority rights.

Citizenship issues have had a central place in the Council of
Europe's interventions in Estonia and Latvia. The case of Latvia is particularly revealing of the importance that the Council has given to citizenship issues since its intervention there began even before it became
a member of the organization. Latvia applied to join the Council of
Europe in September 1991. Two years after this a report commissioned
to evaluate the 'conformity of Latvia's legislation with general principles of the Council of Europe and the European Convention of
Human Rights' was issued. The report concluded that the absence
of a citizenship law setting out the conditions for the naturalization of
non-citizens was an 'outstanding problem' and that Latvia could not
become a member until such a law was adopted.[40] In the course of
1993 and 1994 various draft laws on citizenship were presented to the
Council of Europe, but each of them was criticized and declared
unsatisfactory by the Council of Europe's experts. They were considered either to be too vague and arbitrary or as unduly limiting the pace

of naturalization.[41] In July 1994 the Parliament of Latvia finally adopted a law on citizenship that was deemed more satisfactory by the Council of Europe, and it was decided that since Latvia had fulfilled a major pre-accession condition, the procedures for its accession to the Council of Europe could be reactivated.[42]

In 1995 Latvia was finally invited to join the Council of Europe. Upon joining, the Latvian government formally committed itself 'to continue its consultation and co-operation with the Council of Europe' in implementing the law on citizenship, to work to the elimination of 'arbitrary and unjustified discrimination between citizens and non-citizens'.[43] More generally, this meant that the Latvian government was expected to take steps to facilitate the integration of its non-citizen population into Latvian society. In 1997 the Committee on the Honouring of Obligations and Commitments by Member States—a committee established to provide 'stimulus and guidance for the consolidation of democracy' in states who became members after 1989—started its monitoring procedures to evaluate the extent to which Latvia had honoured its commitments since 1995. In June 1998 rapporteurs of the Council of Europe issued a progress report which stated that many obstacles to the integration of non-citizens remained. Obstacles like the window system of naturalization, the 'classification of many children born in Latvia since 21 August 1991 as non-citizens', and the extensive requirements of the history test for naturalization were identified as being among the most important areas of concern.[44]

Pressures on Estonia concerning citizenship legislation seem to have been less intense than in the case of Latvia, partly because Estonia already had a law on citizenship since 1992 and because its law on citizenship did not include as strict a naturalization timetable as that of Latvia. Nevertheless, the Council of Europe has kept a close eye on the evolution of the citizenship situation in Estonia, and has pressed the Estonian government to increase its efforts at integrating its non-citizens. The *Report on the Honouring of Obligations and Commitments by Estonia* issued in 1996 noted that although Estonia had 'made considerable progress towards the fulfillment of her obligations and commitments since she became a member state on 14 May 1993', the 'treatment of the "non-historic" Russian-speaking minority', particularly with respect to citizenship, was still an area of concern.[45] The report underlined that there remained many obstacles to the naturalization of non-citizens, and it warned the Estonian authorities that if it did not make more efforts at facilitating the process of naturalization, the social cohesion of the Estonian society could be seriously affected. Indeed, the report noted that:

One cannot but detect a certain reluctance on behalf of the Estonian authorities to naturalise members of the 'non-historic' Russian-speaking population. As understandable as this reaction is, due to the history especially of the Soviet occupation, this policy of making it difficult for a large portion of the population to obtain citizenship, taking continuous recourse instead to a system of temporary residence permits, risks alienating people principally integrated in and loyal to the Estonian State and society.[46]

In its efforts to speed up the integration of non-citizens in both Latvia and Estonia the Council of Europe has repeatedly raised concerns about obstacles to citizenship like the overly high requirements of language and history tests for citizenship purposes, and the absence of adequate resources with respect to language training. With regards to the language and history test, it has invited both Latvia and Estonia to work in collaboration with its experts to redefine the threshold level of the tests and to develop a standardized method for administering them.[47] The Council's 1996 *Report on the Honouring of Obligations and Commitments by Estonia* noted:

We are of the opinion that the Estonian authorities should make it a priority to ensure that all ethnic non-Estonians who are loyal to the Estonian State and society are given the opportunity to integrate into this State and society by learning the language. School education of Estonian as a foreign language needs to be improved, and language courses should be offered to applicants for citizenship free of charge or at a reduced rate in such regions as Narva and Scillamäe.[48]

Providing such incentives for minorities to learn the state language was seen by the Council of Europe as being more conducive to integration and more respectful of human and minority rights than the imposition of the state language through a comprehensive language law, like the draft law on language that was being considered by the Parliament of Latvia in 1998. In this case, the Council of Europe noted that there was nothing illegitimate in trying to promote the state language through a language law, provided that the law makes the necessary distinction between the public sphere and the private sphere. Indeed, the 1999 *Information Report on the Honouring of Obligations and Commitments by Latvia* outlined that:

Where the integration of the non-citizen population into Latvia society is concerned, it is perfectly understandable and legitimate that the Latvian authorities are trying to promote the national language and culture. Nevertheless, they should avoid measures, such as the imposition of the state language in the private sphere.[49]

The European Union

The pressures exercised by the EU on Estonia and Latvia regarding citizenship and language issues have been sustained and extensive, particularly in the years following their application for membership of the EU in 1995.[50] An important aspect of these pressures has to do with the so-called Copenhagen 'political criteria'. Following a decision made by the European Council in Copenhagen in 1993, Estonia and Latvia, like 'all candidate countries in Central and Eastern Europe' had to meet 'a number of "political criteria"', that is, they had to achieve 'stability of institutions guaranteeing democracy, the rule of law, human rights and respect for and protection of minorities'.[51] In the cases of Estonia and Latvia, particular attention was given to the effects of citizenship and language requirements on minorities in both countries.

When the European Commission delivered its 'Opinions' on Latvia's and Estonia's applications for membership of the EU in July 1997, it made it clear that both were required 'to take measures to accelerate naturalisation procedures to enable Russian-speaking non-citizens to become better integrated into' the society.[52] The Commission also insisted in both 'Opinions' that Estonia and Latvia 'must consider ways to make it easier for stateless children born' on their territory 'to become naturalised'.[53] Finally, in the case of Latvia, the Commission outlined that 'the system of age brackets [the window system], initially devised as a way of preventing the administration from being overwhelmed by a flood of applications, has had an inhibiting effect' and maintained that 'Given this "shortage" of applications for naturalisation, such a system no longer appears warranted.'[54]

Citizenship issues were also given a central place in the *1998 Accession Partnership* documents on Estonia and Latvia, where priority areas for each country's membership preparations are identified each year. In both documents 'measures to facilitate the naturalisation process to better integrate non-citizens including stateless children' were identified as short-term priorities in the preparation for accession.[55]

Issues related to language also drew the Commission's attention. For instance, in the *Accession Partnership 1998* documents on Estonia and Latvia, language training for Russian speakers was identified as a short-term priority.[56] In the *Accession Partnership 1999* documents the necessity for better language training was reaffirmed as a short-term priority since it was deemed that Estonia and Latvia had only partially met the expectations identified in 1998.[57] The *1999 Regular Report from the Commission on Latvia's Progress towards Accession* and the *1999 Regular Report from the Commission on Estonia's Progress towards Accession* reiterated that language training remains a 'key instrument' for the integration of ethnic minorities in Estonia and Latvia.[58]

EU pressures on Estonia and Latvia have been particularly intense with respect to language laws. Pressure was applied before and after the adoption of a new language law by the Latvian Parliament on 8 July 1999, on the basis that the law failed to conform to international standards. In fact, both the European external affairs commissioner and the head of the EU mission in Riga warned Latvia 'that it would jeopardize its case for admission to the EU by adopting a "discriminatory" law'.[59] After its adoption by the Latvian Parliament, the EU, together with other international organizations, urged the Latvian president to send the law back to Parliament for reconsideration.[60]

The EU has also expressed deep concerns over the adoption of amendments to the 1995 Estonian State Language Law by the *Riigikogu*—the Estonian Parliament—in December 1998. The *Accession Partnership 1999* document identifies the necessity for Estonia to 'align the language legislation with international standards and the Europe Agreement' as a short-term priority.[61] At a conference on 'Estonia and the EU' held in Tallinn on 5 November 1999 Finish president Martti Ahtisaari, who then held the rotating presidency of the EU, reaffirmed the importance of Estonia aligning its language law with international and EU standards.[62]

International Pressures and Stimulus for Domestic Liberalization

Recent developments in Estonia and Latvia suggest that the combination of pressures identified in the previous section have had an impact on the domestic policy of these countries. As Estonia and Latvia are either members of, or wish to become members of, an increasing number of international organizations, pressures on these countries to harmonize their domestic policy with European and international standards have been multiplied. The following changes with respect to citizenship and linguistic policies seem revealing in this respect.

In 1998 both Estonia and Latvia took significant steps to liberalize their citizenship policies. In October 1998 important amendments to the Latvian Citizenship Law were approved in a referendum held at the same time as the parliamentary elections.[63] The most important amendments provided for the abolishment of the window system and for the granting of citizenship to stateless children born in Latvia after 21 August 1991, upon request from their parents but without further conditions with respect to language of knowledge history . Following the referendum, the OSCE, the Council of Europe, and the EU, who had all pressed for these changes, stated their satisfaction with the outcome. The OSCE's High Commissioner on National Minorities expressed his 'pleasure' with the decision and declared that the approved amendments were in line with his recommendations and 'a big stimulus for the process of integration in Latvia'.[64] A delegation of observers from the Council of Europe's Parliamentary Assembly issued a statement declaring that the outcomes of the referendum would favour the integration of non-citizens, and 'pave the way for the country's admission to European institutions'.[65] Finally, the EU issued a statement describing the referendum decision as 'farsighted' and 'consistent with the principles and aims of the European Union'.[66]

On 8 December 1998 the Estonian Parliament took similar steps to ease the acquisition of citizenship for children born in Estonia.[67] This decision was also welcomed, particularly by the OSCE and the EU, whose previous interventions in favour of the amendments had encountered significant resistance from some members of parliament.[68]

Other positive results have also been forthcoming. In accordance with many of the recommendations made by the OSCE, the Council of Europe, and the EU, various changes have been made to language and history tests in both countries, and naturalization fees have been reduced for certain categories of the population. In Latvia the history test has been made easier by reducing the number of questions (from 310 in 1996 to ninety-three now). Naturalization fees have been reduced for several groups of non-citizens, and it is estimated that only half of the candidates for citizenship now pay full naturalization fees.[69] The government of Estonia has also made its language and civic knowledge test easier in recent years, and abolished the written language test requirement for those applicants born before 1 January 1930.[70] Language training seems to have been intensified, with the support of the EU Phare Programme and of the United Nations Development Programme.[71]

The results of international pressure in the realm of language legislation have been more mixed thus far. It is reasonably clear that the strong protests issued by the OSCE and the EU were crucial in the recent decision by the president of Latvia not to promulgate the

Language Law adopted by the Latvian Parliament in July 1999. This resulted in the adoption of a revised version of the Language Law—this time compatible with international and European standards—in December 1999.[72] However, it seems that entreaties to the president of Estonia not to promulgate the amendments to the Parliamentary and Local Elections Law and to the 1995 Language Law, adopted by Estonia's Parliament in December 1998, have been less successful. It remains to be seen whether the current pressures, particularly from the EU, will yield results.[73] A recent remark from Toomas Hendrik Ilves, the Minister of Foreign Affairs of Estonia, appears to indicate that change may be on the way. In a speech on 'Euro-integration' delivered to members of the Riigikogu on 19 January 2000, Ilves referred to the EU's *1999 Accession Partnership* document on Estonia, which states that Estonia must 'align its language legislation with international standards and with the Europe Agreement', and argued that changes to the language legislation are 'among those initial tasks to be fulfilled during the year 2000' if Estonia is to keep its position in the competition over EU accession.[74]

Conclusion

In the first years following independence ethnic Estonians and Latvians sought to use their newly regained sovereignty to promote their identity and interests. Both states adopted various nationalizing measures—understood in Brubaker's sense—i.e. measures 'to promote the language, culture, demographic preponderance, economic flourishing, or political hegemony of the core ethnocultural nation'.[75] In the two cases, nationalizing efforts were focused mainly on citizenship and language policies. These policies were aimed at correcting past injustices, but they have also contributed to the exclusion of minorities from access to power and resources, and have been a prominent source of inter-ethnic tension.

In recent years, however, international pressure on Estonia and Latvia to liberalize their citizenship and language policies has been intensified. The OSCE's High Commissioner on National Minorities, the Council of Europe, and the EU have each in their own way sought to persuade both countries to bring their policies into line with European and international standards. The combination of these interventions has provided an important stimulus for recent change in Estonia and Latvia, and may also act as a deterrent for the adoption of new exclusionary policies in the future.

Of course, not all new democracies have been under such intense scrutiny from international organizations. The interest of international organizations in human and minority rights has been unevenly distributed across emerging democracies and has focused mostly on members and prospective members. This has left many cases of majority–minority conflicts relatively free from interference. Moreover, international organizations seem to have had a tendency to put smaller and more vulnerable countries under closer scrutiny and greater pressure than large and powerful ones. This should be a cause for concern. As Paul Globe recently noted, these double standards may generate 'a backlash among some of the supervised countries against such monitoring from the international community, a backlash some populist politicians have been quick to exploit'.[76] Given this, a failure to create a greater sense of fairness could fuel nationalist passions instead of tempering them.

NOTES

I wish to thank John McGarry, Michael Keating, and Marcel Filion for their helpful comments and suggestions.

1. E. Gellner, *Nations and Nationalism* (London: Blackwell, 1983), 121.
2. As Pal Kolsto notes for the Soviet Union: 'Almost everywhere the titular nationality has placed itself implicitly or explicitly at the center of the state-building project and awarded itself certain prerogatives as a result' ('Nation-Building in the Former USSR', *Journal of Democracy*, 17/1 (1996), 119–20).
3. As Donald Horowitz points out: 'Short of eliminating ethnic diversity in the physical sense, exclusionary groups seek to impose a homogenous identity on the state and to compel acknowledgment of their preeminence. It is as if a part claimed to be the whole. Members of other groups are relegated to the status of "guests"— a term frequently heard—with the implication that rules of the "household" are to be laid down by the "host"' (D. Horowitz, *Ethnic Groups in Conflict* (Los Angeles: University of California Press, 1985), 199; see also R. Brubaker, *Nationalism Reframed: Nationhood and the National Question in the New Europe* (Cambridge: Cambridge University Press, 1996), 46).
4. R. Hayden, 'The 1995 Agreements on Bosnia and Herzegovina and the Dayton Constitution: The Political Utility of a Constitutional Illusion', *Eastern European Constitutional Review*, 4/4 (Fall 1995), 64.
5. Brubaker, *Nationalism Reframed*, 9. Nationalizing in this context does not mean the process by which some states take control of property that was previously owned by the private sector. Rather, it refers to policies that are designed to promote the identity, and reflect the interests, of the state's dominant national group. The term was coined by Brubaker. For him, nationalizing states 'are states that are conceived by their dominant elites as nation-states, as the states of and for particular ethnocultural nations, yet as "incomplete" or "unrealized" nation-states, as insufficiently "national" in a variety of senses. To remedy this defect, and to

compensate for perceived past discrimination, nationalizing elites urge and under-take action to promote the language, culture, demographic preponderance, eco-nomic flourishing, or political hegemony of the core ethnocultural nation'. See also ibid. 63, 83–4, and 103.

6. See ibid. 106; J. Linz and A. Stepan, 'Toward Consolidated Democracies', in T. Inogushi, E. Newman, and J. Keane. (eds.), *The Changing Nature of Democracy* (New York: United Nations University Press, 1998), 58.

7. See N. Muiznieks, 'Latvia: Restoring a State, Rebuilding a Nation', in I. Bremmer and R. Taras (eds.), *New States, New Politics: Building the Post-Soviet Nations* (Cambridge: Cambridge University Press, 1997), 379. Moreover, in 1991 ethnic Russians made up a third of Latvia's population (2.6 million) ('Them and Us', *The Economist*, 17 August 1996, 67).

8. T. U. Raun, 'Estonia: Independence Redefined', in I. Bremmer and R. Taras (eds.), *New States, New Politics: Building the Post-Soviet Nations*, 405. In 1991, ethnic Russians made up a third of Estonia's population (1.5m), See 'Them and Us', *Economist*, 67.

9. Muiznieks, 'Latvia: Restoring a State, Rebuilding a Nation', 379. In fact, Muiznieks notes: 'as Russian cadres dominated politics in Moscow, Russians and Russian Latvians assumed most of the key posts in the local Latvian power structure'.

10. As Raun notes, 'although native Estonian communists did rise in the ranks of the party in the post-Stalinist era, they never attained decisive leadership positions until the Gorbachev era' (Raun, 'Estonia: Independence Redefined', 410). Raun also notes that 'over a period of nearly four decades the post of first secretary of the Communist Party of Estonia was held by two Russian Estonians . . . Moreover, the perceived foreignness of the CPE was heightened by the strong non-Estonian (mainly Russian) presence in its ranks, ranging in the post-Stalin era from 56 per cent in 1953 to a low of 48 per cent in the 1970s.'

11. For instance, in 1989, 68.7% of ethnic Latvians were fluent in Russian while only 22.3% of ethnic Russians had a knowledge of the Latvian language (Muiznieks, 'Latvia: Restoring a State, Rebuilding a Nation', 380). In Estonia an even smaller proportion of Russians, 14%, claimed to be fluent in the Estonian language. See P. Kolsto and B. Tsilevich, 'Patterns of Nation Building and Political Integration in a Bifurcated Postcommunist State: Ethnic Aspects of Parliamentary Elections in Latvia', *East European Politics and Societies*, 11/2 (Spring 1997), 385.

12. Of course, these issues were also important before independence, but native pop-ulations had limited power to act upon them. See D. Laitin, 'Revival and Assimilation in Estonia', *Post-Soviet Affairs*, 12/1 (1996), 31.

13. J. Chinn and L. A. Truex, 'The Question of Citizenship in the Baltics', *Journal of Democracy*, 17/1 (1996), 135.

14. This amounted to about 700,000 persons in Latvia (N. Muiznieks, 'Latvia: Restoring a State, Rebuilding a Nation', 392). About 64% of all non-citizens in Latvia in 1993 were ethnic Russians. In Estonia this amounted to about 500,000 persons. See *Minorities and Majorities in Estonia: Problems of Integration at the Threshold of the EU*, ECMI Report no. 2 (Flensburg: European Centre for Minority Issues, Mar. 1999), 7.

15. According to the 1992 Estonian Law on Citizenship, non-citizens had to fulfil the following requirements for naturalization: two years of residency counting from Mar. 1990, plus a waiting period of one more year; taking a loyalty oath; and demonstrating a command of Estonian (Raun, 'Estonia: Independence Redefined', 417). The 1995 Estonian Law on Citizenship extended the residency requirement to five years, plus a one-year waiting period, and added a require-ment regarding knowledge of the Estonian constitution and of the Law on

Citizenship. See *Estonia Country Report on Human Rights Practices for 1999* (Washington, DC: US Department of State, 25 Feb. 2000), sect. 3. According to the 1994 Law on Citizenship in Latvia, non-citizens had to fulfil the following main requirements: five years of residency counting from May 1990; demonstrating a familiarity with the history and constitution of Latvia; taking a loyalty oath; and demonstrating a command of Latvian.

16. See R. Zaagman, *Conflict Prevention in the Baltic States: The OSCE High Commissioner on National Minorities in Estonia, Latvia and Lithuania*, ECMI Monograph no. 1 (Flensburg: European Centre for Minority Issues, Apr. 1999), 42, and United Nations Development Program, *Latvia Human Development Report 1997* (Riga: UNDP, 1997), 53.

17. Brubaker, *Nationalism Reframed*, 104. See also Kolsto and Tsilevich, 'Patterns of Nation Building', 369–70.

18. In Latvia citizenship was required to vote and to be a candidate both in local and in national elections. In Estonia citizenship was required to vote at the national level, but not at the local level. However, citizenship is required at both levels for holding office. See Chinn and Truex, 'The Question of Citizenship in the Baltics', 136.

19. See A. Antane and B. Tsilevich, 'Nation-Building and Ethnic Integration in Latvia', in P. Kolsto (ed.), *Nation-Building and Ethnic Integration in Post-Soviet Societies: An Investigation of Latvia and Kazakstan* (Boulder, Colo.: Westview Press, 1999), 101.

20. See Kolsto and Tsilevich, 'Patterns of Nation Building', 383.

21. See *Jamestown Foundation Monitor*, 5/1 (4 Jan. 1999) at http://www.jamestown.org/pubs/view/mon_005_001_000.htm. See also Zaagman, *Conflict Prevention in the Baltic States*, 47.

22. See Antane and Tsilevich, 'Nation-Building and Ethnic Integration in Latvia', 112. See also Muiznieks, 'Latvia: Restoring a State, Rebuilding a Nation', 393. It should also be noted that, in addition to citizenship and language requirements, 'informal processes are at work that reduce the percentage of non-Latvians in the state apparatuses far below their 20 per cent share of the citizenry. The emergence of many new state institutions, services, and representative bodies has created a considerable number of new jobs in the state bureaucracy. Practically all of these have been occupied by ethnic Latvians. A survey conducted in the spring of 1993 revealed a 91.7 per cent share among employees in the Latvian state apparatus and a 1.7 per cent Russian share. In 1994, of 152 judges, 9 were Russians' (Kolsto and Tsilevich, 'Patterns of Nation Building', 371–2).

23. See *Latvia Country Report on Human Rights Practices for 1997* (Washington, DC: US Department of State, 30 Jan. 1998), sect. 5; this was amended in 1998. Proof of knowledge of the Latvian language is no longer a requirement for obtaining unemployment benefits. See *The Russian Minority in the Baltic States and the Enlargement of the EU*, Briefing Paper no. 42, PE 168.307 (Brussels: European Parliament, 1999), 11.

24. See *Estonia Country Report on Human Rights Practices for 1999*, sect. 5.

25. See *Latvia Human Development Report 1997*, 57.

26. E. A. Andersen, 'The Legal Status of Russians in Estonian Privatisation Legislation: 1989–1995', *Europe–Asia Studies*, 49/2 (1997).

27. See *Mandate of the CSCE High Commissioner on National Minorities* (1992), ch. II, provisions 2 and 3, in Zaagman, *Conflict Prevention in the Baltic States*. For the context of the High Commissioner's first interventions in the Baltics, see ibid. 25.

28. Letter of the High Commissioner on National Minorities to Trivimi Velliste, Minister for Foreign Affairs of the Republic of Estonia, 6 Apr. 1993.

29. Letter of the High Commissioner on National Minorities to Georgs Andrejevs,

Minister for Foreign Affairs of the Republic of Latvia, 6 Apr. 1993. The same message is reiterated in his comments on the 1993 draft law on citizenship in a letter sent to the minister of foreign affairs of Latvia on 10 Dec. 1993.

30. See the High Commissioner's letter to Georgs Andrejevs, 10 Dec. 1993. He specified that, in the case of Latvia, this would mean that 'non-Latvians, with the exception of those who constitute a clear threat to the vital interest of Latvia, will obtain the right to become Latvian citizens if they express such a wish, provided that they accept certain conditions. They would have to show their interest in becoming integrated into Latvian society by: 1) acquiring a basic knowledge of the Latvian language which will be tested in the course of the naturalization process according to standardized procedures; 2) acquiring a knowledge of the basic principles of the Latvian Constitution which will also be tested during the naturalization process according to standardized procedures; and 3) swearing an oath of loyalty to the Republic of Latvia.,

31. See Letter of the High Commissioner on National Minorities to Valdis Birkavs, Minister for Foreign Affairs of the Republic of Latvia, 14 Mar. 1996.

32. For the High Commissioner's recommendations on language requirements, see: letters of 6 Apr. 1993, 14 Mar. 1996, 23 May 1997, for Latvia; letters of 6 Apr. 1993, 1 July 1993, 11 Dec. 1995, for Estonia. For his recommendations on history and constitution tests, see: letters of 14 Mar. 1996 and 23 May 1997, for Latvia; letter of 11 Dec. 1995 for Estonia.

33. See e.g. Letters of the High Commissioner on National Minorities to the Minister of Foreign Affairs of Latvia of 14 Mar. 1996 and of 23 May 1997. See also his letter to the Minister of Foreign Affairs of Estonia of 6 Apr. 1993.

34. Letter of the High Commissioner on National Minorities to Valdis Birkavs, Minister for Foreign Affairs of the Republic of Latvia, 28 Oct. 1996. For his critique of the quota system of naturalization included in the draft law on citizenship adopted in first reading by the *Saiema* on 25 Nov. 1993, see the Letter of the High Commissioner on National Minorities to Georgs Andrejevs, Minister for Foreign Affairs of the Republic of Latvia, 10 Dec. 1993.

35. Letter of the High Commissioner on National Minorities to Valdis Birkavs, Minister for Foreign Affairs of the Republic of Latvia, 23 May 1997. For recommendations on children and citizenship, see also the High Commissioner's letters to the Minister for Foreign Affairs of Latvia on 6 Apr. 1993 and 10 Dec. 1993; for Estonia, see his letters to the Minister for Foreign Affairs of the Republic of Estonia on 6 Apr. 1993 and July 1993.

36. See e.g. Letters of the High Commissioner on National Minorities to the Minister for Foreign Affairs of Estonia on 6 Apr. 1993, 9 Mar. 1994, 28 Oct. 1996. See also his letters to the Minister for Foreign Affairs of Latvia on 6 Apr. 1993, 10 Dec. 1994, 23 May 1997.

37. The High Commissioner argued that 'the language proficiency requirement constituted discrimination and violated the European Convention on the Protection of Human Rights'. See *Jamestown Foundation Monitor*, 5/1 (4 Jan. 1999). See also Zaagman, *Conflict Prevention in the Baltic States*, 47.

38. See K. Cengel, 'Latvia: President Sends Language Law back to Parliament', *RFE/RL*, 15 July 1999. See also *Jamestown Foundation Monitor*, 5/134 (13 July 1999), at http://www.jamestown.org/pubs/view/mon_005_134_000.htm.

39. High Commissioner on National Minorities, *Press Release*, 15 July 1999.

40. See European Commission, Opinion no. 183 (1995), on the application by Latvia for membership of the Council of Europe, at http://stars.coe.fr/ta/ta95/eopi183. htm; and the *Report on the Application by Latvia for Membership of the Council of Europe*, doc. 7169, 6 Oct. 1994.

41. See the *Report on the Application by Latvia for Membership of the Council of Europe*, 8–9.

42. Ibid. 11.

43. See European Commission, Opinion no. 183 (1995), on the application by Latvia for membership of the Council of Europe. The Latvian government also committed itself to consult the Council of Europe 'in drawing up a law on the rights and status of "non-citizens"', to 'sign the European Convention on Human Rights at the moment of accession', and to sign and ratify various European conventions, protocols, and charters, within a reasonable amount of time.

44. See *Addendum I to the Progress Report of the Bureau of the Assembly*, doc. 8136, 9 June 1998, at http://stars.coe.fr/doc/doc98/edoc813adi.htm.

45. *Report on the Honouring of Obligations and Commitments by Estonia*, doc. 7715, 20 Dec. 1996, 1, at http://stars.coe.fr/doc/doc98/edoc7715.htm.

46. Ibid. 6.

47. See ibid. 8, and *Information Report on the Honouring of Obligations and Commitments by Latvia*, doc. 8426, 24 May 1999, 10, at http://stars.coe/fr/doc/doc99/edoc8426.htm.

48. *Report on the Honouring of Obligations and Commitments by Estonia*, 8.

49. *Information Report on the Honouring of Obligations and Commitments by Latvia*, 1.

50. Latvia presented its application for EU membership on 13 Oct. 1995. Estonia presented its application on 24 Nov. 1995.

51. See sect. B.1 ('Criteria for Membership') of European Commission, *Opinion on Estonia's Application for Membership of the European Union* (15 July 1997), at http://europa.eu.int/comm/enlargement/estonia/op_07_97/b1.htm; and of European Commission, *Opinion on Latvia's Application for Membership of the European Union* (15 July 1997), at http://europa.eu.int/comm/enlargement/latvia/op_08_97/61.htm.

52. See sect. 1.3 ('General Evaluation' of the political criteria) of the European Commission's *Opinion on Estonia's Application* and of the European Commission's *Opinion on Latvia's Application*.

53. See sect. 1.2 of both *Opinions*.

54. See sect. 1.2 of the *Opinion on Latvia's Application*.

55. See *Estonia: Accession Partnership 1998*, sect. 4.1, at http://europa.eu.int/comm/enlargement/estonia/ac_part_03_98/index.htm, and *Latvia: Accession Partnership 1998*, at http://europa.eu.int/comm/enlargement/lativa/ac_part_03_98/index.htm.

56. See *Estonia: Accession Partnership 1998*, sect. 4.1, and *Lativa: Accession Partnership 1998*.

57. See *Estonia: Accession Partnership 1999*, 4, at http://europa.eu.int/comm/enlargement/dwn/ap_02_00/en/ap_est_99.pdf, which states that Estonia is expected to 'implement concrete measures for the integration of non-citizens including language training and provide necessary financial support'; and *Latvia: Accession Partnership 1999*, 4, at http://europa.eu.int/comm/enlargement/dwm/ap_02_00/en/ap_lv_99.pdf, where Latvia is expected to take 'further concrete measures' in the same direction.

58. *1999 Regular Report from the Commission on Estonia's Progression towards Accession*, 14, and *1999 Regular Report from the Commission on Latvia's Progression towards Accession*, 17.

59. See *Jamestown Foundation Monitor*, 5/134 (13 July 1999). The *Latvia: Accession Partnership 1999* document also outlined (p. 4) the necessity for Latvia to 'align the Language Law with international standards and the Europe Agreement' as a 'short-term priority'.

60. See *Jamestown Foundation Monitor*, 5/134 (13 July 1999). See also Cengel, 'Latvia: President Sends Language Law back to Parliament'.
61. *Estonia: Accession Partnership 1999*, 4. See also *1999 Regular Report from the Commission on Estonia's Progression towards Accession*, 16, where the Commission argue that the Language Law, as amended in 1998, 'constitutes a step backwards and should be amended'.
62. *RFE/RL Newsline*, 8 Nov. 1999.
63. The amendments were approved by 53% of voters. See *Jamestown Foundation Monitor*, 4/182 (5 Oct. 1998), at http://www.jamestown.org/pubs/view/mon_004_182_000.htm.
64. See 'National Minorities Issues in the OSCE Area', Address by the High Commissioner on National Minorities to the Seminar on the Organization for Security and Cooperation in Europe, Oslo, 22 Oct. 1998. In the same address, the High Commission jumped on the opportunity to pressure the Estonian Parliament to make similar amendments regarding the children of stateless parents.
65. Council of Europe, *Press Release*, 5 Oct. 1998.
66. Quoted in Zaagman, *Conflict Prevention in the Baltic States*, 42.
67. The amendments passed by the *Riigikogu* provided that 'a stateless child born in Estonia after 1992 will be granted citizenship upon application by its parents if it is under the age of fifteen and if its parents are stateless and have legally resided in Estonia for at least five years prior to the moment the application is made' (ibid. 43).
68. See Zaagman, 43.
69. See *1999 Regular Report from the Commission on Latvia's Progression towards Accession*, 16.
70. For the simplification of language and civic tests, see *1998 Regular Report from the Commission on Estonia's Progression towards Accession*, 12. For the language written test exemption, see Rob Zaagman, *Conflict Prevention in the Baltic States*, 40.
71. See *1999 Regular Report from the Commission on Latvia's Progression towards Accession*, 7, and *1999 Regular Report from the Commission on Estonia's Progression towards Accession*, 7.
72. For indications that international pressures had a significant role in the president's decision, see *Jamestown Foundation Monitor*, 5/138 (19 July 1999), at http://www.jamestown.org/pubs/view/mon_005_138_000.htm, and Cengel, 'Latvia: President Sends Language Law back to Parliament'. For evidence that the Dec. 1999 version of the language law received a positive evaluation from international organizations, see e.g. *Jamestown Foundation Monitor*, 5/231 (14 Dec. 1999), and High Commissioner for National Minorities at http://www.jamestown.org/pubs/view/mon_005_231_000.htm, and *Press Release*, 9 Dec. 1999.
73. See *RFE/RL Newsline*, 8 Nov. 1999, and a joint press release of the Association Council between the EU and Estonia on 14 Feb. 2000, UE-EE 804/00 (Presse 43).
74. Remarks by Toomas Hendrik Ilves, Minister of Foreign Affairs of Estonia, at a discussion devoted to Euro-integration matters in the Riigikogu on 19 Jan. 2000. See the text at http://www.vm.ee/eng/pressreleases/speeches/2000/THI-Riigikoguing.htm.
75. Brubaker, *Nationalism Reframed*, 9.
76. P. Globe, 'OSCE: Countries Supervised and Not', *RFE/RL Weekday Magazine*, 20 July 1999.

INDEX